John Philip Kemble

John Philip Kemble

The Actor in His Theatre

BY

HERSCHEL BAKER

GREENWOOD PRESS, PUBLISHERS
NEW YORK

Copyright © 1942
by the President and Fellows of Harvard College

Reprinted by permission
of Harvard University Press

First Greenwood Reprinting 1969

Library of Congress Catalogue Card Number 76-90701

SBN 8371-2279-1

PRINTED IN UNITED STATES OF AMERICA

For
MY MOTHER

PREFACE

IT IS a pleasure to acknowledge my obligation to those who have been of service to me during the preparation of this book. First of all, Mr. Hyder Rollins has, over a period of years, been both my friend and teacher, and his unfailing kindness no less than his admirable scholarship has made my task much easier. He has watched this study at various stages of its development, and I can only hope it shows the result of his instruction, his criticism, and his generous interest. With the assistance of a Dexter Scholarship granted by the President and Fellows of Harvard College I was enabled to conduct my research abroad. The publication of this book was made possible by a liberal grant from the Research Council of the University of Texas, and to that body I wish to acknowledge my great indebtedness. Part of the material in the Prologue has appeared, in another form, in the twenty-first volume of the *Texas Studies in English*.

I can mention only a few of those disinterested spectators who graciously let themselves be made my accomplices. Mr. Gale Noyes, of Brown University, first suggested, in an idle moment, the subject of this investigation; at this late date, however, he may not care to own the soft impeachment. Mrs. Lillian A. Hall, formerly of the Harvard Theatre Collection, was a constant solace to me through her wide theatrical lore. Mr. Giles Dawson, of the Folger Shakespeare Library, proved to be extremely useful, as did the attendants of the manuscript collections of the British and South Kensington Museums. Mr. Robert Metzdorf very kindly put some interesting material at my disposal, and Messrs. R. A. Law and Theodore Hornberger, of the University of Texas,

acted as experienced mentors in preparing this volume fo
the press. Mr. Dumas Malone, of the Harvard Universit
Press, has been at all times an obliging ally and confederate
And I should not fail to give a nostalgic mention to th
faithful band of my former colleagues who amiably submittec
to the devious readings and discussions I inflicted upon them

My last and greatest obligation can be only suggested: ir
the multiple capacities of amanuensis, scribe, best friend and
severest critic, and general factotum my wife has labored with
zeal and devotion. The book is hers as much as mine.

H. B.

The University of Texas
15 January, 1942

CONTENTS

PROLOGUE 3

I. ENTER JOHN KEMBLE 19

II. THE STROLLER'S PROGRESS 95

III. MR. KEMBLE OF DRURY LANE 78

IV. OF A CRESCENT NOTE 39

V. DREST IN A LITTLE BRIEF AUTHORITY . . . 121

VI. A MAN OF PARTS 137

VII. SHAKESPEARE REDIVIVUS 154

VIII. A MANAGER'S WOES 167

IX. NOT SINGLE SPIES, BUT IN BATTALIONS . . . 190

X. THE SAVANT 211

XI. THE SCENE CHANGES 226

XII. THOU LAST OF ALL THE ROMANS 249

XIII. PASTURES NEW 270

XIV. BRITONS BE FIRM 295

XV. DÉNOUEMENT 316

XVI. EXEUNT OMNES 336

NOTES 351

BIBLIOGRAPHY 387

INDEX 395

John Philip Kemble

Prologue

> The mighty monarch, in theatric sack,
> Carries his whole regalia at his back;
> His royal consort heads the female band,
> And leads the heir apparent in her hand.
>
> CHARLES CHURCHILL

D R. SAMUEL JOHNSON, LL.D., who spoke so sagely on such a number of things, has distinguished a kind of biography beginning with a man's pedigree and ending with his funeral. And though venerable when the Doctor singled it out for scorn, the type is still a handy one. Even if Henry Fielding, whom the Great Cham so despised, likened the ferreting out of a genealogy to the exploration of the head-waters of the Nile, most biographers, before and since, have bowed deferentially in the direction of their subject's progenitors. We shall be no exception.

In spite of the calculating ferocity of Burleigh and Walsingham, those worthies who tried to stamp out all traces of Bloody Mary's Catholicism in order to make their own sovereign secure on her throne, bands of the faithful still gathered to observe the mass and turn their hearts towards Rome. In the western Midlands, at the opening of the sixteenth century, there flourished a stubborn family of such recalcitrants. Their name was Kemble. Herefordshire seems to have been the original home of the tribe, although later Kembles liked to think the family sprung from a certain George Kemble, of the county of Wilts, honored by William Camden (Clarencieux King-at-Arms for Elizabeth) with a coat of arms. The recusant Kembles were of humbler stock, and their principal occupation appears to have been getting their names in official records as a result of their notorious adherence to Catholicism. In 1605 the Bishop of Hereford reported with a certain vexation that "Mr. George Kemble of Londgrove hath with him one Stamp, a Jesuit Priest," and in a list reminiscent of the vindictive Mikado's he catalogues William, Walter, and Jane Kemble as recusants. So prolific and so intransigent were these early Kembles that in the latter half of the seventeenth century in the parish of Welsh Newton alone there were some twenty-three of them under surveillance for their obstinate faith. When these determined folk roamed abroad they took their religion with them: in 1609, in London, "Johannes Kemble [et] Anna uxor eius" were indicted for recusancy on the testimony of an informer named Bingham, and seventeen years later one Charles Kemble was found guilty of the same charge in the Old Bailey.[1]

Like all English Catholics who wanted university training, the Kembles were forced to go abroad, to Douay in France. Thither in 1624 went the most celebrated of all the seventeenth-century Kembles. John had been born at Rhydycar Farm, St. Weonard's parish, Herefordshire, in 1599, and, according to the yellowed pages of Douay records, he was twenty-six when he returned to his native heath from the English College in the Low Countries. There he "ad ordines minores promotus est," and as a priest dedicated to good works he spent his long and for the most part unchronicled life ministering to his charges. His death was more spectacular, and earned him his epithet Venerable John Kemble: in the excitement and political chicanery of the Popish Plot the old man, then in his eightieth year, was arrested for conspiracy by a certain Captain Scudamore of Kentchurch. Haled to London and there subjected to various indignities, he was presently compelled to return on foot to Hereford, where he was at last hanged. The bald account of a contemporary newspaper gives the details: "By letters from Hereford, we have advice that upon *Fryday* the Twenty-second Instant one *John Kemble*, a *Popish Priest*, Condemned the last Lent Assizes, was hanged, and afterwards beheaded there." The mutilated remains were claimed by a nephew, Captain George Kemble, and were buried in the churchyard at Welsh Newton, where an old tombstone still bears the legend: "I.K. / Dyed the 22th / of August Anno Do. / 1679." [2] Captain George himself was a man of some renown. He had fought valiantly for his king during the war, distinguishing himself at Worcester. But even before then, as early as 1630, he had become the proprietor of Pembridge Castle, near Monmouth — an estate he was compelled to surrender to his Parliamentary victors. Almost two centuries later, when John Philip Kemble, neatly tossing off his port, informed Sir Walter Scott that his family had been "ruined" for their royalist sympathies during the Rebellion, he was doubtless referring to the doughty captain who, although he lost his lands, retained his honor, proudly claiming and decently burying the criminal remains of his martyred kinsman. Pride and a certain native dignity were to be the not inconspicuous attributes of later and more celebrated Kembles.[3]

The family continued numerous in the Welsh Marshes throughout the early eighteenth century. We learn of various Kembles as substantial citizens. Daniel, for example, was one of the twenty-four "principal burgesses" of Tewkesbury in 1702, and when he died he bequeathed the "rents and profits" of some land to be "laid out in bread" for the poor as well as setting aside a hundred pounds worth of stock (South Sea, alas) for the indigent. Another Kemble, this one named Thomas, had an impressive coat of arms emblazoned on a monument in the Tewkesbury Abbey. Likewise, in the Cirencester church, under a flat stone bearing the arms "on a bend ermine three leopards heads caboshed" lie several worthy Kembles — Thomas (who died in 1710), Anne (died 1733), and William (died 1745).[4]

Finally, on May 1, 1721,* a Kemble was born who was destined to sire John Philip and Sarah (Siddons), thereby elevating to histrionic splendor a tribe consisting hitherto of small landholders and burgers. Roger Kemble's father (himself a Roger), who was admitted as a freeman of Hereford in 1713 as "a barber and periwig maker," had lived in London and subsequently in the forest of Dean in Gloucester, where he died about 1757. But before that melancholy event he married one Eleanor, daughter of Thomas Ford of Hereford, and begat upon her no less than nine children. Of these, only the seventh concerns us. Roger's parents certainly represented a minor and less affluent branch of the family than the Daniel and Thomas of emblazoned arms and charitable legacies, but they were decent folk, sending their son to a "very respectable" seminary near Hereford. Here the boy learned a little — he was a favorite of his master's — and enough of the genteel arts to make him very unhappy when he was presently apprenticed to "some ordinary calling." His trade was probably barbering, like his father's: a brother of Roger's who followed that ancient calling took occasion to be very rude once to starving young Thomas Holcroft, and John Philip himself while drunk indiscreetly told some companions that a near relation of his had been a barber. Although we hear vaguely of Roger's being a "hair-dresser" in Kent and elsewhere, it is certain that he very shortly tired of such a prosaic life. He had already asked his father's permission to follow the stage, and had received an emphatic denial for his pains. The old gentleman may have felt about the theatre as

---

* Thus wrote John Kemble in his journal for March 1, 1800. He goes on to say that since his father persisted in using the Old Style Calendar this was celebrated as his birthday, although "he is not really 78 till the twelfth of March" (British Museum Ad. MSS 31,972–31,975).

did Samuel Richardson: that although in the "gay Trappings" of the trade "a Man may represent a gentleman, yet
never can [he] be farther from that character." With an
astonishing show of virtue the youth "determined not to
violate his filial duty, or trespass upon the obedience which
he owed to his master," resigning himself to his period of
servitude.[5]

Whatever the changes and chances of Roger's early life —
and the record is extremely spotty — he gains interest for us
when he finally became a stroller — the first actor (so far as
we know) in a family that was to adorn the English stage for
more than a century. For Roger, strolling itself, if we may
believe Lee Lewes' *Memoirs*, was not much more glamorous
than barbering had been. He starved, as strollers must, and
finally found himself, in 1752, at Canterbury, where he fell
in with a troop headed by one Smith. Very quickly forming
"a very tender connection" with Fanny Furnival, a local
actress of some renown, Roger gained the lady's hand in
marriage. Poor Fanny, who had been "struck with Roger's
nose and athletic make," immediately addressed herself to
the task of making an actor of her new husband. But after
seven weeks' intensive coaching in the role of Serjeant Kite
(in Farquhar's *Recruiting Officer*), the erstwhile barber failed
so egregiously in the part that the irate Smith drove the
newly-weds from him in wrath.[6]

Strollers, however, generally were "at liberty," and Roger
was unconcerned. Presently he noticed in a London paper an
advertisement of John Ward, who managed a troop in Birmingham and was seeking "capital performers." The Kembles
set out posthaste to join Ward, but at Coventry, "being
grievously afflicted with what the French call the *maladie du
poche*," they almost succumbed to the blandishments of a
certain Quelch, who wanted them for his own troop. But
having pledged themselves to Ward, the two "jogged on" to

Birmingham. There the "celebrated" Fanny was unequivocally rejected, and Roger was kept only on probation. Poor Fanny took her own way back to Coventry and immediately made a great stir in Quelch's company. But two or three weeks later, when Roger came down to Coventry to see his wife, he found her with a brash young Irishman and a great crowd of male admirers at an inn. Fanny's muscular gallant set upon poor Roger fiercely, and the lady denounced her husband as a "cowardly caitiff," denying ever having been married to him. Roger, seeing valor in discretion, fled from Fanny's enraged retinue, and straightway returned to Ward in Birmingham. There he "laid close siege to the adamantine heart of Miss Sally [sic] Ward," his manager's daughter, and in 1753 he married her.[7]

Lewes' story is highly problematical, of course. Roger was almost certainly not married to Fanny, however intimate his connection with her might have been. If there had been such a colorful amorous episode in his past, Sarah Ward must have overlooked it, for on June 6, 1753, she eloped with him to Cirencester. There parish records still exhibit the signatures "Roger Kemble of Hereford & Sarah Ward of Gloucester." Sarah, an energetic and determined girl whose marriage was characteristic of her, had been the "main prop" of her father's troop in the "comic province," and her elopement left her parents in no amiable mood.[8]

Ward, however, was not a man to make an issue of the elopement: his whole career had been an essay in complacency. According to Ann Kemble Hatton,* one of Roger and

---

* This curious woman, who wasted her life away in scribbling and in unfortunate marriages, was living in 1830 as a derelict at Swansea. She had been the disgrace and despair of her family, and was bitterly resentful of her relatives' good fortune. I am drawing (for the first time) on a sketch of her family which she seems to have made for John Payne Collier. The original is in the Folger Library at Washington.

Sarah's daughters, the Kembles "had reasons for believing" John Ward to be "the offspring of a man of high Rank by a distant relation of his own, who did not outlive the infancy of her child." The boy was raised "liberally," being at length placed in the army with a commission. Ward was sent to Cork and there married a milliner who "without any ex-·traordinary talent for the profession, had imbibed a stormy desire to quit her humble occupation, and figure a heroine on the Stage." By his marriage Ward lost his father's assistance; he was forced to sell his commission and assume "the management of an itinerant company of comedians," of which he shortly became "the grand attraction and support." After this, his career was checkered. He appeared once on the London boards in Elijah Fenton's *Miriamne* (February 22, 1723), a play which Fielding thought was "horrible stuff," although the veteran Macklin told John Philip Kemble that his grandfather "was a great actor, he could make much out of little." The Wards were presently in Ireland again, acting (in 1731) in Dublin under Elrington, from whom they soon "revolted" to open a booth in Fownes Court. There Madame Violante had recently been pleasing the town with a young actress named Peg Woffington. The Wards themselves produced a daughter in Clonmel on September 2, 1735.[9]

And so fame passed them by. With their three children (there were two boys in addition to Sarah) the Wards returned to England sometime in the 'forties, transferring their strolling to the Midlands. John Ward almost gets into history when, on September 9, 1746, he plays a benefit of *Othello* at the town-hall in Stratford, the proceeds of which were given to restore the monument of Shakespeare in the church there. Presently, of course, — again Ann Hatton is reminiscing — Sarah was marriageable and was being wooed by a Quaker, her parents "harshly" pressing the suit on her. But the high-

spirited girl flatly refused, and indeed gave "secret encouragement" to Roger Kemble, then new in her father's troop.
Previously there had been a "young nobleman who loved her
'not wisely but unhappily too well' for though a rare instance
it is said, and believed in Warwickshire that he died for the
love of Sarah Ward." [10]

When Sarah had the temerity to marry Roger secretly, the
Wards enjoyed a proper "tempest of rage this dereliction of
duty on the part of their daughter, a girl not yet sixteen,
raised in their hearts — a hurricane not at all appeased by
the conviction, that Roger Kemble's person was his only
recommendation, it was obvious to them he had no talent
for the Stage his education had been circumscribed, he had
a good plain understanding but no genius." In spite of Ann
Hatton's grammar and punctuation — as well as exaggeration,
no doubt — it is easy to reconstruct the story. Roger Kemble
was handsome and charming — his wife thought him the
"only *gentleman* Falstaff" she had ever seen — and found it
easy as well as expedient to marry his manager's daughter.
Of course, the truants were soon back in Ward's company —
the wrath had subsided — and before long the old people
retired to Leominster in Herefordshire, after a hectic life,
living peacefully enough on an annuity from their son-in-law
for the use of their theatrical properties and wardrobes. In
the fullness of time they died and were buried at Leominster
under a stone with a properly pious inscription:

> Here waiting for the Savior's great Assize,
> And hoping thro' his merits there to rise
> In glorious mode, in this dark closet lies [*sic*]
> John Ward, Gent.
> who died Oct. 30, 1773, aged 69.
> Also Sarah his wife, who died Jan. 30, 1786,
> aged 75 years." [11]

Things at first were hard for the bride and groom. Even when their first child was born, two years later in Wales, Ann Hatton tells us, they were so poor that Roger was his wife's only attendant. And thus was the divine Siddons brought forth. Other children followed with comfortable eighteenth-century regularity: John Philip was born in 1757, and additional Kembles made their appearance at stated intervals for the next ten years until (with the birth of Jane, in 1777) an even dozen was attained. Ann records the names of the eight who reached maturity: Sarah ("born at Denbigh not Brecon"), John Philip ("designed for a Priest"), Stephen, Francis, Elizabeth, Ann, Charles, and Jane. Roger was a Catholic, of course, and Sarah a Protestant, and an incipient religious schism threatened until it was agreed to rear the sons in their father's faith, the girls in their mother's.[12]

The Kembles were all handsome people, and it was not by accident that John Philip and Mrs. Siddons came by their good looks. Thomas Campbell, who knew the elder Kembles in their old age, remembered them as "tall and comely personages," and Roger with all the grace and suavity of a gentleman of the old school. Boaden stoutly declared he had never known a man of "greater ease nor higher polish" than the aged Roger, and Charles Young, who had seen Mrs. Kemble act Lady Macbeth in a barn, thought Mrs. Siddons "immeasurably inferior to her mother in that part." But for all their native charms, the Kembles found life hard. If we may believe Ann, they "encountered all the hardships and privations arising from a numerous family and very slender means." Strolling up and down England for a quarter of a century, they pursued their slightly disreputable calling with a certain dignity. Their sons were given as much education as seemed feasible (John even went to a university); their daughters were decently married.[13]

Strolling, however, was not by the nature of things a very

lucrative calling. For one thing, the social opprobrium attached to it was enormous. One writer of rather settled convictions declared that most strollers "were got under Hedges, born in Barns, and brought up in Houses of Correction: Nor should they ever dare to shew their Faces in any Place but a wooden Booth." Even Thomas Holcroft, who once belonged to the profession, had nothing but contempt for the average manager of such a troop — an ignorant rogue who at the thought of his "own sagacity and importance" swelled "like an alderman saying grace after meat." The organization of such companies was admirably simple, deriving from the Elizabethan system of 'sharing.' That grand old man of the eighteenth-century theatre, Charles Macklin, has described it succinctly:

One man generally finds cloaths and Scenes, for which he has four shares of the profits. Every performer is a sharer, The Number of performers about sixteen or eighteen. The person who provides the Cloaths and Scenes is deemed the Master of the Company, who makes all contracts for rents, etc. and is responsible for all expenses and contingencies of every kind, incidental to the undertaking.

Of course, there were many complaints of rapacious managers, who seized all the profits by drawing shares for each of their numerous families. At best, the receipts of such troops were usually meager. We hear of one stroller who during a whole month did not make "above twelve shillings," and Charles Lamb's adored Fanny Kelley in her more affluent days recalled with petulance playing to no more than "two pounds seventeen shillings' worth of unappreciative people." [14]

The customary mode of transportation was by foot, some managers having a cart to carry their 'scenes,' such as they were. Anything with a roof could serve as a theatre, but a barn was the frequent habitat of the poorer troops. George

such renowned companies as Tate Wilkinson's in Yorkshire and Mrs. Baker's in Kent (these managers built up a well-paying clientele in a regular circuit, and in some cases even owned their theatres), he established a respectable place for his company in the Midlands. Thomas Holcroft acted with Roger for a time, and thought that the troop "was more respectable than many other companies of strolling players; but it was not in so flourishing a condition as to place the manager beyond the reach of the immediate smiles or frowns of fortune." Roger's peregrinations were wide, and his circuit apparently not fixed, although he seems always to have stayed fairly close to the counties (Gloucestershire and Herefordshire) around the mouth of the Severn. He may have been the manager of the theatre at Kington, in Herefordshire, around 1758, and later he managed a theatre at Tewkesbury in opposition to a company headed by Messrs. Robinson and Thornton. Usually, however, he was on the march, playing short engagements in hired buildings. Stocking the troop with his own numerous progeny was a politic and economic gesture, for it saved him the hiring of other actors. For instance, at Wolverhampton, on March 8, 1769, he announced in his playbill "with humble submission," that he would present a "Concert of Vocal and Instrumental Music," consisting of extracts from *Love in a Village*, the principal roles to be filled by himself, Mr. Henry Siddons (Sarah Kemble's future husband), Fanny Kemble, Sarah Kemble, and Mrs. Kemble. Roger must have had an altercation with some vigilant constable who had forbidden the performance, for he resorted to the old theatrical evasion of taking in no money at the door: no tickets would be available at the Town Hall, it is announced, but Mr. Latham, at the Swan, would deliver admissions "gratis to his Friends and Acquaintances." To which innocuous statement is added: "N.B. Mr. Latham has a Quantity of Tooth Powder (from

London) which he intends selling in Papers, at 2s. 1s. or 6d.
each. The same Powders may likewise be had at Mr. Smart's
and Mr. Smith's Printing-Offices, and at the Talbot in King-
Street." [17]
And so Roger Kemble managed his company through the
'sixties and 'seventies. A precarious and vagrant existence it
must have been, but on the whole a successful one. For a
while the Kembles seem to have made their home — or perhaps to have had their winter quarters — at Brecknock, in
Wales (Sarah was born there), but it is unlikely they remained any place very long. One remembers that nine of
their twelve children were born in different towns. Bills are
extant for a long stay at Worcester, in the winter of 1772–
1773, and as late as 1781 the elderly couple was heading a
company at Bedford and Newport Pagnell, in Buckingham-
shire, the latter a hamlet which Mrs. Siddons passed through
in the days of her glory and found to be a "poking little
village." [18]
In marked contrast to the hardships of most eighteenth-
century strollers, Roger and his troop enjoyed — at least for a
period — almost continued prosperity. Among the treasures
of the Harvard Theatre Collection is a professional journal
kept by the manager from 1766 until 1768, and the careful
records in Roger's florid handwriting reveal the activities of
a company considerably more affluent than most of its contemporaries. For one thing, we learn that the troop was fairly
large, including besides the manager himself (who appears
to have been the 'heavy' man), a certain Crump (in whose
own company young John Philip Kemble subsequently acted
after his wrathful father had expelled him for leaving the
English College at Douay), Henry Siddons, and six women
(among them Roger's wife, the mother of a famous acting
line).
The journal keeps us well informed of Roger's move-

ments, repertory, and income. At Coventry, in 1766, the company averaged fifteen or twenty pounds a night all during the autumn, and as the expenses appear to have been no more than ten shillings a performance the profits for the troop to share must have been gratifyingly large. Shakespeare was the backbone of the repertory, but such stock pieces as *The Orphan, George Barnwell, The Mourning Bride, Theodosius, Jane Shore, Cato,* and *The Beggars' Opera* were frequently acted. At Worcester, where the company went next, a total of sixty-five performances carried the players through to the early summer — another unusually long engagement for strollers — but the receipts scarcely ever came to more than ten pounds a night. The summer was spent in barnstorming: two weeks at Droitwych, which netted only fifteen pounds "shar'd excessive of our Expences"; then back to Worcester for three performances; then two more days again at Droitwych (which elicited Roger's cryptic "Cleard our Expences"); and finally two or three weeks at Bromsgrove before moving on to an extraordinarily profitable winter engagement at Bath.

By this time, however, the troop had been enlarged, and in his account of the "Situation of the Compy." Roger listed fifteen men and nine women. Of course, as the winter wore on there were changes. Mr. Gaudry departed "Clandestinly" on April 4, and Collins stole away on April 30, "being his Second Disappearance." But for all this, the Bath season was a continued triumph. Opening on September 26 to a house of forty pounds, the troop gave some ninety-four performances before it closed on June 4, 1768. Princess Amelia was taking the waters in Bath, and was pleased to command a performance of *The Devil to Pay* — an event balanced by compulsory closing of the theatre when the Duke of York died in September. The wretch Gaudry "decampt," as we have seen, and was followed by several of his colleagues: "May 31 Mr.

Wayte went off. June 1 Mr. Baker & June 3 Mr. Hartley all
3 Clandestinly which with Gaudry & Collins makes 5 this
Season." But in spite of these minor vexations the winter
was a good one. The repertory was extensive, the houses were
worth on an average of forty pounds a night (some performances brought as much as eighty pounds), and the gentry of
Bath were more suitable patrons than many rustic audiences
Roger had encountered.

On this happy note we may well leave the elder Kembles.
Roger's journal stops abruptly on June 4, 1768, with the close
of the Bath season, and his movements after that, for the
next twenty years, are shrouded in the same obscurity that
envelops most of his contemporary strollers. It is unlikely
that he ever attained so high a peak of popularity again,
although he must have maintained his comfortable position.
Perhaps it was not wholly fortuitous that two of the greatest
actors of English theatrical history sprang from Roger's troop,
which, though never so famous as Wilkinson's or Mrs. Baker's,
was far from being one of the wretched, ephemeral bands
that trudged from one barn to another, happy to make a few
shillings a night. After what must have been a busy if uneven
professional life, the aging Kembles withdrew to London to
bask in the glory of their children. Roger was present at
Mrs. Siddons' great triumph at Drury Lane on October 10,
1782, and at dinner later was so filled with parental bliss that
he threw back his silver hair and "gave way to tears of happiness." He and Sarah disposed of their scenes and properties,
and sought "a quiet asylum in London for the remainder of
their lives." Fanny Kemble, as the toast of London fifty years
later, recalls her grandmother as an "energetic, brave woman,
who, in the humblest sphere of life and most difficult circumstances, together with her husband fought manfully a hard
battle with poverty." It is pleasant to think that the old
couple could find security at last. Roger was tempted for the

last time to the boards when he appeared on August 26, 1788, at the Haymarket in *The Miller of Mansfield* for the benefit of his daughter-in-law, Mrs. Stephen Kemble, and acquitted himself well enough. Presently he and his wife, pining for a more bucolic environment, moved to a quiet cottage in Kentish Town, whence they made frequent trips to the city — among other things, for dinners at John's elegant establishment. Sir Thomas Lawrence, John Kemble's great friend, painted the portrait of the old man that shows all the aquiline dignity of the Kemble profile. Roger was impressive even in decay.* Thomas Holcroft spent an evening with the old people, and apart from Mrs. Kemble's rheumatism found them "cheerful and conversable," and happy to recall their old strolling days. In 1792, oddly enough, old Roger was granted a gentleman's coat of arms, a happy consummation for a lowly 'comedian.' And so the old people waited for the end, full of years and happy in their famous children. Roger at last died, at the age of eighty-one, in 1802 — "the death of the righteous," breathed Mrs. Siddons piously. His wife, at seventy-one, followed him four years later.[19]

* The portrait now hangs in the Deanery at Hereford, having been taken there when one of Fanny Kemble Butler's daughters married the Dean James Wentworth Leigh.

CHAPTER I

Enter John Kemble

Life, as Cowley seems to say, ought to resemble a well-ordered poem; of which one rule generally received is, that the exordium should be simple, and should promise little.

SAMUEL JOHNSON

TODAY a traveler approaching Prescot from smoky, sprawling Liverpool, only eight miles away by rail, is not apt to think that in the days of Edward III the little town was of sufficient importance to be granted a royal charter for a fair and market. Nor does he recall, perhaps, that once it was enough of a postal center to cause letters to be addressed "Liverpool, near Prescot." Being whisked over the flat coastal dunes along the mouth of the Mersey, he does not reflect on the great rambling mansion of the earls of Derby just north of Prescot — the moated grange built when the houses of York and Lancaster were making a shambles of all England.

What Roger Kemble thought as he plodded into the sleepy village in the winter of 1757, perhaps driving before him an aged horse which bore a few skimpy 'scenes' and costumes, must be left to conjecture. But we may imagine that his thoughts were of Sarah, leading a child of two and even then big with another. Little Sarah — destined to be the Immortal Siddons — had been born in Wales under conditions which, if we may credit her vindictive sister Ann, were something less than ideal. Roger and his wife had been enacting for the rustics of Brecknock the antics of Falstaff and Mrs. Ford when the lady, feeling her time was come upon her, was conveyed to her lodgings in the very buck-basket the gullible Falstaff had lately concealed himself in.[1]

The pinching economic determinism that had driven the young Kembles along the lanes of western England to a remote hamlet in Lancashire — where, on February 1, John Philip made his first entrance on the sorry stage of a stroller's life — is fairly clear. Roger, with admirable consistency, never let the impending arrival of a child interfere with his professional pursuits; consequently, most of his numerous progeny (twelve in all) boasted different birthplaces.[2]

The first-born son, we may assume, was trundled about England with his father's troop, growing up to know the precarious and volatile existence that attended all strollers. Mrs. Kemble, when not actively engaged in bearing children, spent most of her time helping her lord and master make a living, and Roger, like Wilkins Micawber, did not allow himself to be submerged in solicitous parenthood. Little John made his way the best he might, picking up scraps of *Cato* while his father bullied his actors and ranted before the country gentry. Roger, for all his indigent strolling ways, permitted himself to indulge in a certain *noblesse oblige*, and took comfort in observing that "he was come of a good house, though decayed." That, perhaps, is why little John was early placed in "a day school of Worcester" to learn his letters. But his schooling, for the nonce at least, was not oppressive: the canny Roger did not scruple to put his son upon the boards from time to time.[3]

The indiscriminate crowd of mercers, tanners, countrymen come to market day, and perhaps even a squire or so, was not, in all likelihood, moved at the sight of young Kemble as the Duke of York in Havard's *Charles the First*, that February day almost two hundred years ago, in Worcester. The King's Head had obligingly provided an improvised stage, and Roger had bustled about distributing bills which foretold that the characters would be "dressed in ancient habits, according to the fashion of those times." In spite of the herculean efforts of the whole tribe — both the parents, the young son, and two daughters had taken part in the play (today almost as completely forgotten as its author) — the evening's receipts came to only £11 13s. And there was an increase of only a pound when Roger repeated the offering five days later, perhaps in the pious hope that as a family spectacle if not as high tragedy the piece should do better.[4]

But such was strolling, and the Kembles, like the indefatigable Crummles, never despaired. Still at Worcester in the spring — John could have attended school with fair regularity — Roger arranged a "Concert of Musick," between the acts of which, he promised, "will be presented, *gratis*, a celebrated Comedy, call'd The Tempest; or the Inchanted Island." Not only Shakespeare, but his desecrating rewriters, Dryden and D'Avenant, would have been surprised, if not alarmed, to see the entire Kemble delegation troop forth (perhaps with little John as Stephano) "with all the Scenery, Machinery, Musick, Monsters, and other Decorations proper to the piece, entirely new." And the evening was to close with a grand tableau involving Neptune, "Poetick God of the Ocean," with Amphitrite in a chariot drawn by "Seahorses, accompanied with Mermaids, Tritons, etc." [5]

Happily, such excursions into spectacular theatrics were not frequent for young Kemble. Roger, knowing the bitter fruits of an actor's life, had expressly forbidden any of his children to follow the stage as a career. (It is interesting to note that most of them, with filial piety, disobeyed his commands, to their own great profit and their contemporaries' delight.) John, at any rate, was presently snatched from the pitfalls of a strolling troop, and was settled at a "Roman Catholic seminary of Sedgeley Park, in Staffordshire." The boy, according to his sister, was "designed for a Priest," and Roger had his heart set on that goal for his son. The manager, though an actor himself, shared fatherly old Samuel Richardson's belief that the company a player had to keep tended "little to the Improvement of your mind, or Amendment of your purse." The stay at Sedgeley Park has left few records, although a note in one of the college books is indicative of Roger's provision for his eldest son:

John and [sic] Philip Kemble came Nov. 3, 1767, and brought 4 suits of clothes, 12 shirts, 12 pairs of stockings, 6 pairs of shoes, 4 hats, 2 "Daily Companions," a Half Manual, knives, forks, spoons, "Aesop's Fables," combs, 1 brush, 8 handkerchiefs, 8 nightcaps. "Jack abiit," July 28, 1771.

The outfit was lavish, but times were good and Roger, as we have seen, was flourishing at Bath and elsewhere. The five years in the seminary must have equipped young Kemble with enough Latin and Greek for a university, for in 1771 we find him safely across the Channel at Douay.[6]

The choice was not a hard one. Roger was a good Catholic, and the English universities were out of the question, on both economic and religious grounds. The college at Douay had since Elizabethan times been the most accessible and best-known training-ground for English Catholics. Also, was not the Venerable John Kemble, who had suffered for his faith under Charles II and had subsequently become a Herefordshire legend, an alumnus? Roger, strong in his faith and in his pride of family ("though decayed"), straightway dispatched his first-born off to France, there to become a priest of Mother Church.[7]

What young John Philip felt about all this we do not know. At any rate, he submitted to the rigorous ecclesiastical training which the Catholic Church prescribes for its clergy, and seems to have achieved a certain measure of success in his studies. He of course learned French, in which language he ever afterwards professed a fair fluency; he read reams of Patristic Latin; and he even made "considerable progress" in Greek. There were Latin declamations to be rendered, there were school prizes to be won, and there was even a certain amount of pleasurable companionship to be enjoyed. The "writings of Stagyrite" impressed the boy, who was serious enough to exult in Butler's *Lives of the Saints*. Douay even encouraged young Kemble's flair for histrionics. So well known he became as an orator that "the whole body of fellows and professors constantly crowded the hall" whenever he was to speak: the tempo and formality of his characteristic declamation must have been particularly appropriate for his pious subject-matter. We may well believe that he became a "universal favorite" by one spectacular feat: when a master, angered at his class, demanded "vicarious atonement" by one of its member's memorizing two books of Homer, Kemble, with almost incredible magnanimity, volunteered, and presently he was able to repeat fifteen hundred lines with accuracy and *élan*. "The gallantry of the act," as one early biographer points out drily, "could not but endear him to his class, and acquire for him the esteem and strong attention of the masters." But Douay was not always so grim. Students were allowed to enact properly weighty plays, and Kemble took a leading part in the production of *Cato* and *Julius Caesar*.[8]

But already he felt immortal longings; an actor's blood was in his veins. One account, probably scurrilous, has it that half way through his studies John returned briefly to England to see his family. Roger was pleased as an alderman with his son's progress, and sent him back with his blessings. But falling in with a troop of strollers, the apostate forswore the Church and joined the company. An account generically related introduces sweet romance and has the boy entrapped by a conniving strumpet of an actress, whose troop he joined without further ado. The story is patently vilifying, and be-

much persuasion, had consented to contribute a guinea), but John was given to understand that thenceforth he was cast forth from the parental hearth and fireside. And so, at eighteen, a handsome youth, tall, Roman nosed, bearing the inherent dignity and *gravitas* so characteristic of all Roger's brood, young John Kemble set out to conquer the world.[11]

It was a life of vagabondage and privation that he chose, but he really knew no other. Hard though it was in the first years — and we, retracing his career from a distance of almost two centuries know it to have been cruelly hard — it was to lead him from the miseries of a barn-theatre to the manager-ship of both Drury Lane and Covent Garden, and make him finally the noblest Roman of them all.

First, of course, John had to find some sort of post in a strolling company. Retracing his steps to Gloucestershire, he sought out the troop of Chamberlain and Crump, of whom the latter had once trod the boards for Roger. It was not a good company — in fact, it was notoriously bad — but Kemble knew the managers and clutched at any chance to survive the winter. Then too, there was a precedent: when Sarah and her new husband, Henry Siddons, were fleeing from Roger's wrath the year before, they had found refuge with the two unsavory managers — one of whom was "blunt, morose, brutish" and the other "sly and cunning." As luck would have it, the almost destitute boy fell in with another alumnus of his father's troop, one Tom Shatford, who was himself on his way to Wolverhampton to join Chamberlain and Crump. John's Latin and Shatford's ingenuity made the long road easier:

On Christmas Day they found themselves at an inn without a penny in their pockets. They composed two letters, one in Latin to a parson, the other in English to a lawyer — charitable persons, we may presume, and known as such — in which they stated their destitute circumstances and solicited assistance. The appeal was responded to, and with the funds thus obtained the journey was completed.[12]

John was given a job, perhaps for old time's sake, and on the eighth of January, 1776, when across the Atlantic a group of obstinate colonials were misconducting themselves, a great career was launched in England. Sleepy little Wolverhampton perhaps enjoyed the ranting heroics in Nat Lee's *Theodosius*, blithely unaware of the historicity of the occasion.* Young boys were always running off to be actors in the eighteenth century. One remembers Parson Primrose's dismay at discovering his son strutting forth in *The Fair Penitent*. Kemble was quite likely no better, and very probably considerably worse, than most green young potential Garricks of the day. The company he was in was decidedly unpleasant, although he played leading roles. Perhaps to relieve the tedium, perhaps to forget his unhappy plight, John took to drink. We hear of his "unaccountable negligence" or of his "excessive indolence, and a propensity for ale-house tippling." His career, happily, was at its nadir, and the obscure period is perhaps best left in obscurity. It was a wandering, sordid life that he led, memorable only because he presently abandoned it, unlike hundreds of his nameless contemporaries who lived and died strollers.[13]

A mass of anecdotes, apocryphal and purposely defamatory, survive from these early days. Some of them Kemble himself, secure in his London glory, related afterwards with "great good humour," but most of them are the fanciful scandal of the great manager's detractors. Once, for example, the boy was penniless and threatened with eviction by his landlady:

* Boaden (I, 9) names Wolverhampton as the scene of the debut, and he probably had the information from Kemble himself. Other accounts place it at Cheltenham (Hannam-Clark, p. 75) and at "a small village near Cheltenham" (*Life*, p. 4). Thomas Holcroft (*Theatrical Record*, I [1805]. 284) accepts Wolverhampton.

In the room exactly under that occupied by Mr. Kemble the good woman's *cara sposa* lay ill, and as the apothecary was one day quitting the house, he left directions that the patient should be kept *quiet*: Kemble overhearing the injunction, instantly conceived the idea of converting the prescription of Esculapius to his own advantage. This he did by spinning a top, under the pretence of exercise being necessary to his health, with incessant noise and velocity, continuing this troublesome motion till his hostess was glad to purchase peace on any terms; a bargain was therefore struck, and Mr. Kemble took his departure exempt from all charges.

The legend became popular, and found a graphic representation during the hectic days of the O. P. riots, which marked the height of Kemble's unpopularity with London audiences. From the febrile excitement of the fall of 1809 has survived a hideously colored print of Kemble, unkempt and unshaven, furiously spinning a huge top with a whip, while a horrified landlady stands by in futile remonstrance, the caption reading "The Strolrs Pross pte 3. Black Jack commenced Stroller, and not being able to pay his rent in Staffordshire annoyed his dying Land [*sic*] in such a *Cruel* manner with a Savage Top which he borrowed that the people were glad to get rid of him without Payment." [14]

On another occasion the improvident youth was unable to settle a bill of fifteen pence with his laundress to get back a shirt which he needed badly (it being his only one) to play Ventidius in *All for Love*. The obdurate lady positively refused him the shirt until he paid her, "which, in the nature of things, amounted to an impossibility with our hero." At length he was "actually reduced to the necessity of shifting an odd ruffle from one wrist to the other, alternately, during the performance, concealing the naked one in his cloak, so as to prevent the audience from noticing the *mal-apropos* deficiency." [15]

Such an exigency of costuming was not uncommon for

strollers. We learn of one provincial Bajazet who wore a "tallow-chandler's Frock, for an Under-Dress, ty'd round with a Serjeant's Sash; and, over it, a blue Stuff Nightgown, which was design'd to pass for a Robe." The whole, ornamented with "white Paper, spotted with Ink," served as ermine. Even Kemble, years later, when in his cups could remember some very diverting strollers' costumes. Goldsmith's loquacious actor described a performance of *Romeo* in which the "same coat that served Romeo, turned with the blue lining outwards, served for his friend Mercutio; a large piece of crape sufficed at once for Juliet's petticoat and pall." Such wiles and stratagems were necessary for strollers.[16]

Young Kemble probably continued with Chamberlain and Crump all the winter of 1776, leaving it in the summer "after much mental and pecuniary suffering." Perhaps the troop was disbanded; at any rate, it disappears from our chronicle. Had it not been for Kemble's brief interlude with it, posterity would doubtless have let it rest in the total oblivion that envelops so many similar organizations of the eighteenth century.[17]

Still in his teens, then, and with a bit of acting experience behind him, John Kemble set forth again on the restless and parlous life of a stroller without employment. Of the next year we know even less, if possible, than of his first engagement with Chamberlain and Crump. His poverty must have been acute. Once, legend has it, the penniless boy received a dinner invitation from the celebrated Bishop Warburton of Gloucester, only to get tipsy at the good man's table and be gravely reprimanded for his loose ways. And one Craddock, at Leicester, befriended and encouraged the boy when "almost every body hissed" his performance.* But he was often

* Parson Este, an intimate friend of Kemble's, was responsible for the story (*Cabinet*, III [1808], 290–291) of Bishop Warburton and Craddock. Many years later, one day in May, 1797, Kemble happened to call on

hungry, and still oftener penniless, imploring, as one rhetorical contemporary puts it "in vain for one penny-worth of
bread and cheese, to appease the cravings of hunger — for one
pint of smallbeer, to slake his burning thirst." Sometimes,
however, there were kindly Craddocks to notice him, as when
a gruff Yorkshireman encouraged the lad even though he was
"ill-dressed for the character [of Lovell in *The Clandestine
Marriage*], with antiquated finery, unsuitable to a merchant's
clerk, and with black unpowdered hair." [18]

Presently he fell in with a stroller who went by the name of
Carleton — really John Boles Watson, who had perhaps played
under Roger's aegis, and who was one day to achieve a
certain fame as the manager of the Cheltenham theatre. The
two penniless youths, bowing to necessity, made their living
as they could, the stately Kemble sometimes delivering a
grave moral lecture which was followed by a few tricks of
legerdemain from the antic Carleton. On one occasion the
sleight-of-hand artist was discovered wooing the village carpenter's wife with a "gallantry not quite consistent with the
sentiments of Morality" that Kemble was "endeavouring to
inculcate," and the two entertainers, fleeing the wrath of the
carpenter, were compelled to "decamp with precipitation."
Again, seizing time by the forelock, they made of Kemble a
Methodist preacher who passed Carleton off as his clerk. This
nefarious scheme was put into practice at Tewkesbury, and
with considerable success. "A numerous congregation" was
assembled in a meadow (where those professing the enthusiastic new religion were wont to gather), and Kemble preached

his friend Isaac Reed, the distinguished theatrical historian and bibliophile. Reed, according to his own version of the affair (in a note-book
of Reed's in the British Museum Ad. MS 25,391) mentioned these
prevalent legends and asked if they were true. "He told me," observes
Reed, "that he had performed at Leicester & Gloucester & had been very
kindly noticed by one Craddock but as to the Anecdote of the Bishop
of Gloucestr [sic] there was no truth in it whatever."

with such persuasion that a "large collection was got," the "clerk" receiving the donations in a nutmeg grater which he preserved at Cheltenham "with scrupulous care" for the rest of his life.* Carleton (or Watson), unlike Kemble, had no scruples, in later life, in relating tenderly that they had "starved together," often being in such straits that they were "glad to get into a turnip-field, and make a meal of its produce uncooked." [19]

But the two ingenious strollers presently separated, and Kemble made his way alone. Once, hiding his only coat in the loft above the barn in which he was acting, he was dismayed to discover that a "mischievous elf" had climbed up and cut one of its sleeves off. But "summoning his philosophy to his aid, he assumed that look of *sang froid*, of which he is eminently capable, and, with one sleeved, and one sleeveless arm, he coolly walked through the town." When asked by a member of the troop why he did not wear another coat, he blandly replied, "Another, whose would it be? *I* have no other." [20]

But the worst was yet to come. In a single day, young John Kemble reached at once the lowest depth to which he was reduced as a stroller and the beginning of his rising fortune which was to culminate in his London glory. He had purchased, at Gloucester, a suit, and immediately, without going through the formality of paying for it, had left town. At Worcester the truant was arrested at the behest of the irate

---

* Lee Lewes (I, 97–98) has a similar anecdote (which he claims to have had from Watson himself), though placed in York. According to this version, Watson conceived the whole scheme. After the sermon he stood "at the door, and being gouty and upon crutches, with a most impressive *œillade* from the whites of his eyes only, and a dexterous conveyance of half a crown into the plate out of his own pocket, he caused a very spirited collection."

The episode found a place in Dinah Maria Mulock's *John Halifax, Gentleman* (chap. V).

tailor whom he had wronged, and was straightway clapped in jail. From this ignominious place he wrote his sister, Sarah Siddons, at the time acting for Younger's troop in Liverpool. That benevolent lady, then an actress of some standing and renown in the provinces (though her truimph in London was still five years off) came to her brother's rescue. She paid off the tailor, who was demanding his pound of flesh, and took her bedraggled kinsman back with her to Liverpool. There she introduced him to her manager, "a man who seemed born to administer to the wants and distresses of his fellow-creatures; — whose heart felt for, and whose hand was ever open to relieve, their miseries." Younger, a manager of some reputation, had been the first to exploit the talents of the celebrated Miss Farren and had already welcomed the rising Siddons to his company. He made a place for young Kemble, and by June, 1777, we find the boy beginning "to rise gradually in respectability and estimation." [21]

Sir Thomas Overbury, that Jacobean worthy who gave rise to one of the most infamous murder mysteries of all time, was the subject of a play — now happily forgotten — which enlisted Kemble's aid in late June. He played opposite his sister, and was heartily glad, we may suppose, to have a fairly respectable berth after two years of such desperate strolling. Perhaps during the spring — he seems to have been fetched from the Worcester jail late in the winter — he acted with Younger's troop on its regular circuit, but with the summer he was appearing with fair regularity before the Liverpoolers, although in secondary roles. Mrs. Siddons was a star; her brother was countenanced by Younger for purposes of policy, for leading ladies, then as now, were temperamental creatures and not unmixed blessings. Autumn found the troop in Manchester, where Sarah, not yet 'divine,' had the temerity to play Hamlet (an audacity she never attempted in London). The occasion was significant, for it marks Kemble's first recorded appearance in a play he was to make his particular province under happier skies.[22]

But with the winter came a new interest. The Henry Siddons, on January 18, 1778, had asked their colleagues, Mr. and Mrs. Henry Inchbald, in for a cup of tea. Kemble, of course, was present, and was there smitten by the vivacious Elizabeth Inchbald, twenty years her husband's junior and a woman of great parts. Soon the lady and her young protégé were getting on famously. Inchbald was a pedestrian actor and scene painter for whom his mettlesome wife felt no absorbing tenderness. Presently the proverbial triangle was established. With the advent of spring, the lady became "remarkably unsettled," confiding to her journal (which she later took the precaution to destroy) that she had "almost daily differences with Mr. Inchbald; and visits as constantly from Mr. Kemble." When summer came, there was nothing to do, Henry Siddons, always an officious fool, having quarreled with Younger over a matter of costumes, but for the twin ménages to leave the company together. The two women and young Kemble made an impressive exit in a post chaise — until very late in life Kemble was "an indifferent horseman" — and the husbands followed on horseback. Birmingham was the first stop after Manchester, and their stay there, perhaps in Mattock's troop, was very jolly and cozy. A communal establishment was set up: the Siddons acted with wide acclaim to the burgers of Birmingham, the puttering Inchbald dabbled away at his painting, and Elizabeth (a true bluestocking) undertook to instruct her new affinity in the arts and sciences proper to a gentleman. In a few weeks this pleasant life was disrupted in favor of one even more idyllic. Accompanied by two gentlemen named Lawe and Jefferson — actors, we may assume, and perfect gentlemen — the whole group, on March 24, retired to a "country lodging" on Russel Moor for a bucolic interlude. There a *ménage à sept* afforded infinite delight. Mr. Inchbald, a very foolish fond old man, was more engrossed than ever in his painting, while his wife found constant solace and delight in her reading and studying with Kemble. The group was incredibly amiable. "In the afternoon they all walk out, and in the evening play cards, and sometimes get more infantine in their sports: these clever people go out upon the moor to play at 'blindman's buff' and 'puss in the corner.' " [23]

From this charming rustic scene the Siddons had soon to depart, having secured an engagement with the much sought-after Tate Wilkinson, in Yorkshire. They left in April, but Kemble stayed on at Russel Moor with the Inchbalds — probably for the good and sufficient reason that he had no other place to go. But time did not drag: as he employed himself in reading a history of England, Elizabeth made "notes of the important facts as he proceeded." The tragic muse descended, and the composition of a sad and bloody play called *Belisarius* occupied much of the youth's time. When these intellectual pursuits cloyed, Mrs. Inchbald told her journal, the two amused themselves with "wax, dirt, thread, wire — any thing, in a word, that fancy could apply to the purposes of exercise and amusement." The Inchbalds were Catholic, and Kemble, always strong in the faith, joined in their devotions. When they could not go to Sunday mass, they read, eruditely enough, the service in French. Kemble, "designed for a priest," had the humility to forego the Latin version, which struck Mrs. Inchbald as a very handsome gesture: "He neither wished nor affected to be wiser or better than his companions."

But all good things must end. Though her stay with Wilkinson had been a phenomenal success, Mrs. Siddons at Whitsuntide hied back to Younger, with whom time and distance had healed all wounds. The happy group at Russel Moor met the triumphant Siddons at Manchester in the middle of May, and making their way to Birmingham, the friends parted — the Inchbalds for London and Canterbury in search of better fortune and the Siddons and Kemble back to Liverpool. During their six months of intimacy, John appears to have abstained rigorously from amorous dalliance. But in the absence of definite evidence, the world (as Boswell remarked of Richard Savage's parentage) must vibrate in a state of uncertainty as to what was the truth. It is doing no disservice to Mrs. Inchbald to observe that any advances, proper or otherwise, on the boy's part would probably have been welcomed by her. Their parting, at least, must have been without tears or recrimination, however much of a wrench it was: Kemble lost a trusted confidante and mentor, the lady an engaging companion. And Elizabeth, as we shall see, comforted herself with the reflection that it was never too late to hope. The whole affinity puzzled John — sober and decorous youth that he was becoming — and he parted from Mrs. Inchbald at Birmingham with no cosmic upheavals.

> Their last parting was pathetic,
> As partings often are, or ought to be.[24]

Accompanying his more affluent relatives to Warwick, with its fine old castle and its Shakespearian associations, Kemble went on with them to Wolverhampton, and thence back to Liverpool, where all was far from well. Younger made a practice of presenting at each performance at least a few actors who had appeared on the London boards. It was all very well to observe this pleasing whim in deference to the local gentry so long as the manager could hire such brilliant novices as Miss Farren and Mrs. Siddons. But for the summer season of 1778 Younger determined to put forward a company composed only of provincial favorites, a practice followed by Wilkinson in Yorkshire with conspicuous success. The crotchety Liverpool public got wind of the scheme, and set about living up to its reputation of being "prejudiced and tenacious." As a minatory gesture of independence the local bully boys threatened the manager with "all manner of pains and penalties" if he persisted in his wily enterprise — a warning that deterred him not at all. Kemble, in a letter to Mrs. Inchbald, movingly describes the "dreadful" result of Younger's temerity:

Before opening the Play, Mr. Younger advanced before the curtain, if possible to prevent any riot with which he had been threatened for assuming to bring any company to Liverpool who had not played before the King.

The audience hissed and howled poor Younger off the stage, whereupon the pompous Henry Siddons came forward "bearing a board large enough to secure his person, inscribed with Mr. Younger's petition to be heard. The rogues would hear nothing and Siddons may thank his wooden protector that his bones are whole." Finally, Mrs. Siddons and a Mrs. Knieveton made their vain appeals for clemency, the effect of which was rather marred by Mrs. Knieveton's falling down "in convulsions on the boards." At this point the audience gave itself over to the business of the evening. In accordance with an honored tradition of theatrical riots, this would consist of wrecking the playhouse, which whimsical pastime was forthwith undertaken with a will. The frolicsome Liverpool playgoers "extinguished all the Lights round the house, then jumped upon the Stage, brushed every lamp out with their hats, took back their money, left the theatre, and determined themselves to repeat this till they had another company." The next day the actors found every wall in the city covered with "verse and prose expressive of the contempt" the Younger troop was held in, and the harassed manager had to admit defeat.[25]

Kemble himself was tremendously depressed. He had finished *Belisarius* and hopefully dispatched it to Harris, the manager of Covent Garden, only to be told curtly that it would not do. "My health," he writes to Elizabeth in a mood of black despair,

declines every day. I have neither spirits, in which I never abounded, nor genius, of which inclination perhaps wholly supplied the place, to attempt any thing for my improvement in polite letters. You know me, I believe, well enough to feel for me when I say, that with all my ambition I am afraid I shall live and die a common fellow.

And now the ungrateful Liverpoolers had added to his injuries. With one accord the children of Roger Kemble resolved to shake the dust of the city from their feet as soon as possible. Mrs. Siddons roundly declared her intention of never playing in the odious place again, and her brother gave the bumptious Liverpoolers to understand that they were all like Captain Driver in *Oroonoko* — a play which had been banned from the local stage because it reflected unfavorably on the gentry of the city whose fortunes had been made in the slave trade.[26]

All hope was not gone, however. John revived his flagging spirits sufficiently to apply, on June 21, to Tate Wilkinson, the greatest of all provincial managers, for an engagement:

Sir,

If I thought our late Tumults here were unknown to you, I would describe them, but I believe I may be assured you have heard the whole Adventure, and spare myself the hateful office, of being the Historian of my own Disgrace —

Mr. Younger has sent out an Address to the Public in which he informs them, Mrs. Berry, Miss Younger, Mr. Lee Lewes, and Mr. Dodd [all established London players] have been applied to, and their Answers daily expected — He has promised not to offend them again, and now I believe they will suffer us, *Strollers*, to proceed, by way of keeping their Scenes and Benches in some tolerable good Humour —

But think not I will long their Triumph see,
None want the means, when the Soul dares be free —

I now, Sir, shall be happy, as I am determined not to be an Image for Scorn to point its Insults at, to know I can have the Honour of a Situation with you, as respectable as my former Application told you I aspired to — I have subjoined a Catalogue of what I have play'd, with a Star to those Characters I like most in the Plays — A full account of how far you can oblige me, as soon as possible will be esteemed a very great Favour by

> Your most obedient Servt —
> J: KEMBLE

It is a proud and seemly letter, and it raises interesting points. The affixed "Catalogue" is an impressive list of some one hundred and twenty-two roles, in almost as many plays, sixty-four of them tragic and fifty-eight comic. Shakespeare is liberally represented with about twenty pieces, while Rowe, Otway, Banks, Southerne, Phillips, Moore, Lillo, and a host of minor eighteenth-century playwrights fill up the tragic roster. Surprisingly enough, the comic range is almost as wide, with most of the names belonging to the Restoration and early eighteenth century. Now, either John Kemble was indulging, for the purposes at hand, in a prodigious lie, or he had had far more acting experience than we are able to account for from our meager records. The Younger engagement — his only one of any importance — cannot be discovered to have consisted of more than a half dozen performances a season, and it is unlikely that his earlier strolling embraced so wide a repertory as he lists. This was the second application to Wilkinson, perhaps inspired by Mrs. Siddons' great success with that manager, but the unknown young actor was firm in stipulating a "respectable" status in the company. An eminently characteristic note is appended to the "Catalogue" of roles:

N.B. I shall be glad if you will place a mark to those characters you intend for me, if we agree, either by an Additional Star, or double Cross thus # and if there are any Characters not expressed which you would wish me to play insert them in this Catalogue

which you will oblige me by inclosing in your Answer — By a
little Punctuality at first great Misunderstandings are prevented
— I speak this feelingly — and hope you will excuse the Freedom
I take in my Directions to you — It is not, I assure you, want of
Respect — it proceeds from my Desire to be long [*quaere*: belong?]
with you — —

Jovial Tate was moved enough to hire the boy, although
perhaps not for a month or so. Kemble was still in Liverpool
at the end of July, when he and Younger sent *Belisarius*, on
the twenty-seventh, up to London for licensing (apparently
in view of a production of the piece). But his propitious star
was rising. The event was favorable, and when the fall came,
he joined Wilkinson's troop.[27]

pany of the eighteenth century. His troop's circuit had once included York, Hull, Leeds, Wakefield, Doncaster, Ponte-fract, and occasionally Edinburgh, but later its scope was narrowed principally to York, Hull, and Leeds. In that sec-tion of England Tate's was a name to be conjured with. He was the manager "of whom every actor was talking," and a valuable person to know. A man of property and position, with extensive professional connections in London, he was during the 'eighties probably the most influential provincial manager in the country and one "of the most well-known characters which the dramatic world" of the late eighteenth century produced. "A mighty favorite in Yorkshire," his com-pany was "numerous and respectable," and to be included in its roster was in itself a mark of theatrical distinction.[1]

Tate was an opportunist: when he could make an honest shilling, he did. The troop had already played a stint at Wakefield that fall of 1778, but in October the manager thought perhaps one more week of theatre-going could be squeezed out of the gentry there. On the third night the novice appeared. Since the play was a stock piece — Far-quhar's *Recruiting Officer* — and the house was bad (only £12, records Tate lugubriously), what better time could young Kemble have to make his debut? But the occasion is unsung. How the boy did we do not know, for the manager was so disgruntled at the meager houses, he was glad to pack up and "get off if possible with safety with bag and baggage." Hull, however, was always a well-paying city, and there, on October 30, John Kemble made his first important appearance with the company — in *Macbeth*, no less. A few nights later, to show his versatility, he acted Archer in *The Beaux' Strata-gem*, and with uncommon success. Tate, jovial as always, rejoiced in his protégé's success: "He, from soon getting well connected at Hull, and from his merits rising daily as to reputation, aided by strong imagination, and a *nerved* understanding, it may easily be supposed soon gained popularity and attention, on and off the stage." Tate's syntax frequently passes all comprehension, but it is clear that Kemble was getting on well. His appearances were apparently not frequent, but each was a success. Even so soon, the boy had the knack of distinction, of arousing comment in his own proudly defiant way. For instance, he insisted on playing Lord Aimworth, as Wilkinson wonderingly relates, without songs — and the performance "was not the worse for that omission." But there were palliating circumstances: Kemble undertook the role "not from whim or choice, but to assist a brother actor on a benefit night." [2]

The winter at Hull must have been a happy one. To play in a good company, to act in a handsome theatre, to sleep in the same bed every night, to mix with such of the gentry as hankered after actors — all this meant success for John Kemble. His plays were the kind he liked: *Jane Shore*, *Venice Preserved*, and *The School for Scandal* (already pirated and enormously popular in the provinces). But his duties at the theatre were not too pressing, and he had time to polish up his Muse's first fruit. During the halcyon spring of '78 (only a few months before but how long ago it all seemed now), when he and Mrs. Inchbald were playing Ferdinand and Perdita to each other, the fledgling actor had been engaged in literary composition. And literary composition in its most virulent form, for he had seen fit to write a tragedy. Having finished it and dispatched it to Harris, at Covent Garden, he suffered a killing blow to have it returned unopened. But hope was not lost. The obliging Younger had submitted it to the Lord Chamberlain for licensing during the summer and had presumably produced it, though with no fanfare. In Hull, at long last, it was properly brought forward: either because of Kemble's popularity in the town or because of his own incorrigible soft heart, Tate decided to play the good angel. After all, had not Etherege had his Dorimant remark that " 'Tis not likely a man should be fond of seeing a damned old play when there is a new one acted?" The *première* of *Belisarius* was all the more touching because by this time the Inchbalds had returned to the north and were themselves acting with Wilkinson. Elizabeth had watched and nourished the composition of the piece, and it was inevitable she should play in it. In fact, it was to her that fell the signal honor of speaking the epilogue. The evening of December 29, 1778, was a gala one in Hull: in addition to Kemble's mighty line, the audience was entertained with the antics of a troop of acrobats and singers from Sadler's Wells, no doubt imported by Tate with great hopes of bowling over the Yorkshire rustics. The more gymnastic part of the evening's program was to conclude "with an Assembly of Pil'd Figures, Geometrically supported, (which has been the Admiration of all the European Courts,) call'd The Living Pyramid." Wilkinson's bills bore the blunt warning, in boldfaced type, that "nothing under full Price" could be accepted for this dazzling array of talent — a new tragedy by the popular Mr. Kemble and a spectacular exhibition by the vaudeville actors from London.[3]

However sadly true Burke's dictum that nothing is "more dull than telling the plot of a play," we must pause to examine *Belisarius; or, Injur'd Innocence.* The manuscript — for reasons soon to be apparent, the play was never printed — bears, as is proper for the work of a young classicist, the celebrated tag from Horace, *Heu! Fortune, quis est crudelior in nos te Deus?* and informs us that unity of time is not violated, the action covering precisely "24 Hours." The locale is Constantinople, just before the triumphant return of Belisarius, fresh from a three-year campaign against the Goths, and the plot is concerned chiefly with the amorous misfortunes of Lucretia, the general's daughter. Naturally, she is as beautiful as she is chaste. Flaminius, a manifest villain and the evil adviser of the weakling emperor Justinian, tries to force his attentions on the lady, not knowing she has been married these three years to Marcus, her father's trusted protégé in the long wars. The plot creaks forward (to the tune of numerous Shakespearian echoes) with attempted rape and dastardly plotting; the vehicle is blank verse of the most stilted eighteenth-century variety. Poor Belisarius himself, after a magnificent entry into the city, learns that his second wife, Offeirah, has become Flaminius' mistress and is strenuously urging that rogue to seize the throne. Talk not of love, the Byzantine Lady Macbeth tells her husband, properly amorous after his long absence:

> Talk not of Love, let Fame employ thy Thoughts!
> Say thou hast undergone unheard of Hardships.
> The Winter's Cold, and Summer's parching Sun —
> Say thou has [sic] pluck'd bright Honour from the Sea
> Of reeking Blood, that purpled all the Plain,
> As from thy Arm Destruction lanc'd flew round
> Clapping her iron Wings, while Side by Side
> Dismay and Slaughter mark'd her haggard Road —
> Love I despise and all its silly softness —
> I love thy Story, and adore thy Greatness.
> On with thy Triumph — and all the State attends
> To see thee enter — Bear your Banners high,
> And from your golden throats ye trumpets tell
> A God, a God is come to bless the land.*

* The unique MS, the one sent by Younger for licensing, is now in the Larpent Collection at the Huntington Library in San Marino, California. John Larpent (1741–1824) was appointed inspector of plays in November, 1778, by the Lord Chamberlain, then the Marquis of Hertford. He carefully preserved all the MSS submitted to him, and in addition secured almost all the MSS submitted after the Licensing Act of 1737. His collection of about 2,500 plays, mostly in manuscript, was sold by his widow in 1825 to John Payne Collier and his friend Amyot for £180. Twenty-eight years later Collier tried to dispose of it to the British Museum for the price he had paid; when his offer was refused

When Flaminius, in a scene execrably motivated, convinces Marcus that Lucretia has been unfaithful to him, the gullible husband rants, in an approved fashion, that

'Tis a vile World — phaugh — Shame — fie, fie — 'tis rank,
'Tis foul.

Marcus upbraids Lucretia in a scene strongly reminiscent of *Othello*, and, suggesting rather forcibly that she kill herself, leaves his innocent wife in a highly nervous state.[4]

The last two acts are melancholy chaos. Offeirah and Flaminius imprison and blind Belisarius and raise an insurrection against Justinian. The degraded general, as credulous as his son-in-law, tries to kill Lucretia for her infidelity to Marcus, but is treated with loving compassion in a scene that is a flagrant imitation of the close of *Lear*. Presently Marcus, reconciled to his wife, quells the revolt, thereby affording Offeirah opportunity for a shattering curtain speech before her suicide, much in the strain of Dryden's formidable Nourmahal:

See how the golden Stars in Fits expire!
Hark, how the ploughshare of Destruction grinds
Against the starting Hinges of the Globe!
Oh! save me, hide me — ha! — the Serpents hiss,
They wind about me, now they point their Tongues,
And grin Revenge.

In the last scene, Belisarius, who lies a-dying in prison, leaves the troubled state to the ministrations of Marcus, and the bloody tragedy comes to a faltering close. A bantering epilogue, spoken by Mrs. Inchbald in the character of Lucretia,

---

he sold the collection to the Earl of Ellesmere, though probably with the loss of some of the more interesting items. It came into the possession of Mr. Huntington when he secured the Bridgewater House library in February, 1917. The collection has recently been admirably catalogued by Dougald Macmillan. Cf. *The Huntington Library Bulletin*, No. I (May, 1931), 49–51.

reviews the plot to prove that the heroine was "a doting, doleful, humdrum pretty Creature" — a conclusion to which the reader heartily assents.

Apparently the audience at Hull did not take kindly to this eighty-four page tragedy. Even the country-folk could probably see that it was a monstrous amalgamation of Shakespeare and Edward Young. Though a 'regular' dramatic piece fulfilling all the requirements of neo-classical criticism, it is intolerably dull and pompous. Like the story told Philautus by Euphues, "the beginning I have forgotten, the middle I understand not, and the end hangeth not together." The Shakespearian echoes — from *Coriolanus*, *Cymbeline*, *Othello*, and *Lear* — naturally partake of none of the excellence of the original, and the rest is unrelieved rant. Years later, poor old Tate, trying to be complimentary to his celebrated alumnus, recorded that *Belisarius* was received "with candor, credit, and applause" — which for the voluble manager was damning with faint praise. Kemble, who must have played Marcus, could take comfort of a wry sort: "It is better to have written a damn'd play than no play at all, — it snatches a man from obscurity, and being particular, *as this world goes*, is a very great thing." A London critic of later days, Thomas Gilliland, found much to praise in Kemble's acting and little in his writing: "a man may be an excellent Tragedian, and but an indifferent writer of Tragedies." *Belisarius*, after all, does not alter Wilkinson's opinion that from the Restoration until the end of the eighteenth century Colley Cibber was the only actor who was "a sterling capital writer of plays." [5]

Young Kemble's tragedy, however unreadable today, was played by the frugal Tate as long as it could make any profit. At one performance, in Doncaster, some supernumeraries were needed, and when Lord Percy (later to be the Duke of Northumberland) was asked to furnish some soldiers of his regiment to serve as spear-bearers he graciously consented.

This was the beginning of a long friendship, and only one of several great favors the nobleman was to do the actor. Another friend was made: Mrs. Susanna Dobson, translator of the Abbé de Sade's *Mémoires pour la Vie de François Pétrarque*, felt strongly attracted to the young author, cultivating him as a kindred spirit. Perhaps Kemble was, in a small way, like Robert Southey when introduced to Hannah More and her four sisters: "brim full of literature, and one of the most elegant and intellectual young men they had ever seen." At any rate, our budding dramatist paid homage to his provincial bluestocking by composing "something in the poetical way in praise of her and the river Mersey." We may perhaps congratulate ourselves that no trace of this poem remains. An alternate title, ascribed by a contemporary wag, was "The Palace of Misery," a subject "on which an itinerant comedian might naturally be expected to be fluent." Generally, however, *Belisarius* simply added to the innumerable still-born tragedies that clutter up the stage-history of the eighteenth century. Presently Tate closed his engagement at Hull, on January 11, 1779, choosing for the occasion not the new piece but *The School for Scandal*. Young Kemble, more successful as an actor than a dramatist, stole the role of Joseph Surface from one Cummins, who before his rival's advent had been the company's leading man. And when the troop moved on, *Belisarius*, virtually abandoned, slipped into the obscurity which has since been its portion.[6]

In York, the next stop, all was not well in Tate's company. For one thing, Cummins was permitted to play to his old audiences for the first week or so, and Kemble was kept in reserve until late in the month when Ambrose Philips' *Distressed Mother* was put forward. At rehearsal, the lid was off — chiefly because the young lead was trying to assert his artistic prerogatives: Kemble insisted on making his entrance thus and so, only to have the rest of the company combat him fiercely.

However, the boy triumphed, or in Tate's words "preserved his situation, more from a shew of superiority and knowledge, I believe, than as to any real opinion being material." His next play did not receive more than casual courtesy from the honest Yorkshiremen, and before long the reason was obvious: Mr. Cummins was offering considerable competition. Kemble had the humiliation of being told one night from the galleries that "he cudna shoot oot laik Coomens": all York was strongly objecting to have a new actor supersede its favorite. Cummins, who once played a tragic role so boisterously a young lady in the audience "dropt down dead instantaneously in the box," was one of the old school of actors who bellowed their lines with such "a Dissonancy of Voice" as to convey to Mrs. Charlotte Charke the "strong Idea of a Cat in Labour." He was the sort of player who would appeal to Tom Jones' friend Partridge: "The King for my money," exclaims that enthusiastic critic; "he speaks all his words distinctly, half aloud again as the other. — Anybody may see he is an actor." Kemble, even in his salad days a restrained and decorous declaimer, found Cummins' competition hard to combat, and at York he did not enjoy the success he had at Hull. In later years he found occasion to complain of "continued neglect, while men of stronger lungs, and more boisterous action, were honoured with attention and applause." [7]

As the season wore on the young actor's star rose. *Belisarius* was revived for his benefit, and did fairly well. A certain Cornelius Swan, the dramatic arbiter of York, took kindly to the new actor, and his approbation was a great fillip. He had, the year before, joined the throng of Mrs. Siddons' admirers, and to her brother he transferred his allegiance. His patronage did much to establish Kemble's reputation, even though Cornelius himself had been accused by the unregenerate of "being almost unacquainted with theatrical affairs." He it was who probably wrote a widely-read notice of Kemble for the *York Annual Register*, in which such epithets as "masterly" and "inimitable" were liberally bestowed on the new actor. The winter at York was on the whole an exciting one. Kemble enjoyed a certain success for his reading of passages from Sterne, Collins' odes, Shakespeare, and the Bible ("An Attic Evening Entertainment" he called the potpourri, no doubt in imitation of old Thomas Sheridan), and in addition he delivered a lecture, "of his own composition," on sacred and profane oratory which attracted to him several local lights who fancied themselves men of letters. Another stroke of luck was his cutting up and pasting together again Shakespeare's *Julius Caesar* and Massinger's *Roman Actor:* the resulting mélange so impressed Wilkinson that fifteen years later he could take an old man's pride in claiming credit for the abortion — or at least, in "soliciting" Kemble's attention to the project.

The spring saw Kemble come forward once again as an author, this time of a farce called *The Female Officer*. The summer before, while negotiating with Tate, he had written to Mrs. Inchbald of a piece composed "since I saw you" which had been played at Manchester by the Younger troop "with great applause." * Wilkinson, undeterred by the fate of *Beli-*

---

* The play had been licensed January 1, 1778 (cf. Larpent MS 14.S), but the actual date of the performance is uncertain. The problem here is difficult: if the licensing date is correct, *The Female Officer* must have been written before Kemble ever met Mrs. Inchbald (in the spring following). I fail to see how it could have been written "since I saw you," for the Inchbalds had gone to London late in May, and so far as is known, the Younger troop had not played in Manchester between then and the time the letter was written in June. It may be, of course, that in his remark to Mrs. Inchbald Kemble is referring to something other than the farce in question.

The little piece, negligible in itself, presents other difficulties. J. P. Collier, whose veracity one must doubt, claimed to have examined the MS while the Larpent Collection was in his possession. The synopsis of the play which he published (in *The New Monthly Magazine and Literary Journal*, XXXIV [1832], 179) bears no resemblance whatever *sarius*, undertook to produce it, and *The Female Officer* was accordingly performed on April 10, 1779. In later years Tate professed to remember nothing of the piece save its title, and one cannot wonder. It is a lively but trivial little one-act farce, generously interspersed with songs. Hapen and his wife Temronde, favorites respectively of the Califf of Bagdad and his consort, find themselves in financial straits as a result of extravagance. A project is devised for raising money: Hapen tells the Califf that Temronde is dead, and is immediately consoled with a bag of gold. Temronde plays the same trick in reporting her husband's death to Tobeide, the Califf's wife, and she also is given money. When the Califf and his lady compare notes — in a scene of adroit bickering and recrimination — they are properly mystified. The truth comes to light, of course, the favorites are quickly forgiven, and all ends happily. The interpolated songs, in the manner of Sheridan's *Duenna*, are gay and deft in a mediocre way.

> Why should a man become a slave
> To state, to business, or a wife?
> The spark'ling glass is all we have
> To soothe the various plagues of life.

The dialogue, for the most part, is stiff enough, although there are moments when it goes along neatly and well paced. The natives of York probably found most to wonder at in the ballet scene, danced by "female slaves and Boys, after the Persian manner." But *The Female Officer* can hardly be

---

to a MS of *The Female Officer* now in the Harvard Theatre Collection. The Larpent MS (14.S) shows no indication of having been Kemble's work. The usual note to the licenser is signed by Thomas Linley, Sheridan's father-in-law, with whom Kemble had no connection during his early life. The Harvard MS, bearing the title *The Project, or A new way to fill an Empty Purse A Ballad Farce*, though not in Kemble's unmistakable handwriting, has been commonly ascribed to him, and for our purposes we may consider it the genuine copy. The title of *The Female Officer* seems to have been Wilkinson's contribution.

called a memorable event: Tate retained "the smallest re-membrance" of it, and even ventures the observation that Kemble, "now with the affairs of state he has upon his minis-terial shoulders, retains little more recollection of its merits or demerits than myself." As a matter of fact, Kemble re-membered it well enough to produce it later at Drury Lane, displaying, one fears, undue regard for his own inconsequen-tial work.[8]

That theatrical olio, *The Roman Actor*, was not the aspir-ing young actor-author's only attempt during the York season. In the spring he arranged a new version of *The Comedy of Errors*, confusing "the house as well as the stage" by his "whimsicality" of making the two Dromios black. In addi-tion, he brought forth an adaptation of Massinger's *New Way to Pay Old Debts*, an undertaking in which he if not the public was vastly interested. Another piece, *The School for Scandal Scandalized*, has been attributed to Kemble by John Payne Collier, but the manuscript in the Larpent Collection ("entirely in Kemble's hand-writing," thought Collier) bears no indication of his authorship. A one-act farce designed to be witty, it bears a marked resemblance to Molière's *Critique de l'Ecole des Femmes*, and is largely taken up with the char-acters' discussion of Sheridan's comedy, then new and appar-ently the rage of even remote Yorkshire. A note from Wilkin-son to the licenser tells us that the play was "intended to be Perform'd at the York Theatre," and gives the date of March 3, 1779, but of the author's name there is no mention. It may or may not be Kemble's — certainly it is better than *The Project* — but there is no justification for ascribing it to him gratuitously.[9]

Rather more exciting than these literary efforts was a dis-graceful performance of the York public. John Kemble's most harrowing — and triumphant — experience during the engagement occurred in April, 1779. Tate had hired a Mrs.

Mason, a woman "certainly destitute of voice, variety, and powers," and the young leading man consented to assist her first appearance in *Zenobia*. When the time for the performance came, a "lady of family" who was "possessed of strong sense, and with that a most poignant turn of satire," took up her position in the stage-box with a party of "beaux," and they all showed their distaste for the new actress "by the strongest marks of contempt and ridicule." The high-spirited lady's prejudice even extended to Kemble, who was playing Teribajus. In the last act, when the two leads were "fully employed in the agonizing scenes of death," the obstreperous auditor's "pointed rudeness" got out of all bounds, whereupon Kemble stopped speaking and gravely explained to the clamoring audience that he "was ready to proceed with the play as soon as *that* lady had finished her conversation, which he perceived the going on with the Tragedy only interrupted." At this, pandemonium broke forth. The public hissed the lady in the stage-box, and she assembled the officers of the North Riding Militia (most of whom were "unluckily" in the theatre) to avenge her. These intrepid gentlemen immediately repaired to Wilkinson's quarters and demanded that the insolent young actor be brought before them. Tate warned them that his new star was no ruffian and would not submit to any "ungentlemanlike degradation," whereupon he led him in and "left him to be directed by a judgment much superior to my own." Kemble was "cool, deliberate, and determined," but after a lengthy conversation with the representatives of the military agreed to make an extenuating address from the stage; at this the entire delegation returned to the theatre. There, however, things had taken a new turn, for the pit had turned with some violence against the noisy lady ("a constant disturber"), and when Kemble came forward shouts of "No apology! no apology!" went up. None the less, the actor proceeded to make

he was talking to the wind. The boy had his way; the performance was a great success; and poor Cummins, making the best of a bad thing, presently regained his "serenity." The harassed manager was accustomed to such artistic flare-ups. During the same engagement a certain Oram resented the efforts of a Mr. Piele to change his benefit night, and gave way "to a brutal savage temper, which was with great difficulty tamed." Oram was a blustering knave, a drunkard with the manners of a low stroller, and at last Wilkinson was compelled to sack him "and make him an example *in terrorem* to others." Fortunately, the rejected Oram's roles were of such inconsequence that bumbling Mr. Inchbald could fill them.[11]

Following these minor adjustments, the season at Leeds jogged along peaceably enough. Kemble produced his Attic Evening's Entertainment again, this time augmented with readings of "St. Paul's Defence at the Tribunal of King Agrippa," poetry by the speaker himself, "Declamatory" selections from *Hamlet,* and "Pathetic" excerpts from Sterne, Collins, and John Philip Kemble. In addition to his heavy roles, Kemble was acting (apparently without much competition from Cummins) in afterpieces. One of them, *The Touchstone of Truth,* boasted a "Variety of Scenery, Machinery, Music, Decorations, &c.," all of which had been prepared with infinite care. But tragedy stalked close behind these revels. One bright June Sunday — "one of the finest days ever seen, . . . when every face was dressed in smiles" — Mr. and Mrs. Wilkinson invited Mr. and Mrs. Inchbald to take tea with them. But during dinner, with the duck still uncarved and the green peas steaming in their bowl, Tate received the news of Joseph Inchbald's sudden death. So upset was he by the news that he felt the necessity of fortifying himself with "two or three glasses of wine" before sallying forth to console the widow. Inchbald's death, sad to say, was not deeply mourned by anyone. The pretty and vivacious Elizabeth shed

no superfluous tears over him, and Kemble, years later, recalled him merely as "the greatest Sloven, and in many particulars of the nicest Delicacy, too, that could be imagined."
The erudite young actor was called upon for a Latin epitaph
to adorn the stone, and later the muse labored again, bringing
forth an "Epithalium" rather more laudatory than truthful:

> Vir recti semper tenax
> Sociis clarus, in pauperes benignus,
> Pater optimus, Maritus fidelis. . . .

The vein was worked out in an English "Ode" on the worthy
Inchbald; a few lines from its opening will suffice:

> Here let me pause — and pay that tear I owe:
> Silent it trickles down my cheek, and drops
> Upon the recent sod
> That lightly clasps his heart.[12]

But life had to go on, funeral or no funeral. The repentant
Oram was hastily recalled to take Inchbald's parts, while Tate
muttered of being "a false knight and forsworn" for his
leniency. Elizabeth observed a decorous period of mourning,
but on the twenty-first of June she let herself be persuaded to
act for Kemble's benefit, in *The Distressed Mother*. In point
of fact, the state of affairs was plain as a pike-staff, at least to
Tate. The two were obviously in love, and everyone expected a wedding — after a proper interval, of course. Kemble,
if we may believe his chief, "bowed at her shrine, and felt
her dazzling power"; unfortunately, we cannot be so certain
of the attachment. Kemble in after life never committed
himself on the subject, but the lady was very careful to record
that "he was never at any time her *lover*." At any rate, the
two of them were much together. When the Leeds season
closed, earlier than usual, on July 12, Tate and his wife went
to Bath to recuperate, but some of the actors, including

Kemble, acted independently in a little summer theatre at Pontefract, near Wakefield. The widow Inchbald came along too, nominally to look after her step-son George, who had recently been hired by Tate. Curiously enough, Kemble stayed in the same house, "and, as usual, passed with her all the time he could spare." It was for all the world like the old days on Russel Moor.[13]

The end of the summer was spent in frantic movement throughout Yorkshire. The quiet and rustic interlude at Pontefract was followed by another engagement at York during the races — always a profitable time for the players. Then came Wakefield, and presently Doncaster, before the regular fall season opened on October 19, in Hull. Kemble acted frequently and successfully, chiefly in the standard repertory, although *The School for Scandal Scandalized* on one occasion served as an afterpiece for his *Hamlet*. Meanwhile, the curiously tepid romance continued its course. Elizabeth was busily winding up her first novel, *A Simple Story* (whose hero, Dorriforth, bears a marked resemblance to Kemble), and when it was finished she proudly showed it to her swain. He, characteristically and unromantically, sat down and "wrote her, at full length, his opinion of the work." This did not precisely accelerate the progress of the love affair. During the fall, he had called on her much less frequently than before, though "he observed her conduct with a strong degree of interest." Indeed, when Elizabeth became rather too intimate with a certain Miss Wilberforce, Kemble "cautioned her against precipitate engagements of this kind" — just the kind of conduct we should expect from a man who asked his lady to write him because of the pleasure he received from "the good stile, lively Ideas, and polish'd manner of your Letters." When Tate, about Christmas time, set off to launch another troop at Edinburgh, he left the regular company under "the discretion and direction of my trusty commander Cummins." The experiment turned out badly, however: the American war and the lack of ready money considerably darkened the stay at York, and when Tate returned to his "Southern forces" about the first of April he found them "very dull and glum." [14]

Even during this depressing winter the comely Inchbald had continued her conquests. The comedian Suett, one day to be famous in London, was smitten by the widow's charms and straightway "entrusted his passion" to Kemble, perhaps thinking him versed in the wiles of the lady. Although the coolness between the erstwhile lovers had increased — during the fall he had absented himself from her "on principle" — Kemble did not hesitate to present Suett's plea, which was instantly rejected. This melancholy village wooing was of only passing interest to him, however, for bigger things were afoot; he was about to make his first trip to London.[15]

In the eighteenth century, there stood on the south side of Soho Square, just below where Sutton Street joins it, a red brick mansion called the Carlisle House. Built in 1669, it had been at one time in the possession of the Earl of Carlisle, but about 1757 a certain Mrs. Theresa Cornelys came to London from Germany and converted it into a place for balls, concerts, masquerades, and all sorts of public meetings. The lady was apparently determined to rival Ranelagh and Vauxhall, and from the first her establishment prospered. She advertised extensively, both in papers and by hand-bills, and before long people were flocking to the "assemblies" at Carlisle House. Horace Walpole, along with the rest of the *haute monde*, frequented the place, and Mrs. Cornelys has the honor of being mentioned in one of Horace's letters to Horace Mann. She had become, says the gossipy proprietor of Strawberry Hill,

the Heidegger of the age, and presided over our diversions. Her taste and invention in pleasures and decorations are singular. She took Carlisle House in Soho-square, enlarged it, and established assemblies and balls by subscription. At first they scandalized, but soon drew in both righteous and ungodly. She went on building, and made her house a fairy palace, for balls, concerts, and masquerades.

But by the early 'seventies, competition became keen, and the resourceful Mrs. Cornelys began to lose many clients to the newer Pantheon and Almack's. Carlisle House degenerated into hiring itself out for concerts by Count Boruwlaski, the Dwarf, and the "School of Elegance." By the time "Mr. Kemble of the Theatre Royal in York" debated there in 1780, its former splendors were but memories.[16]

The debate in which the young actor from the north took a part was apparently held early in April, and one suspects it was a meeting of what the eighteenth century colorfully called a spouting club. These organizations, exceedingly undiscriminating as to members, were designed to afford stage-struck young gentlemen a chance to speak and rant publicly. When Thomas Weston made his initial appearance before one, his fellow spouters applauded vociferously, "though they all agreed his acting was execrable, and his voice no ways adapted to the stage." Leigh Hunt, in his youth, joined "a club of young men, who associated for the purpose of cultivating public speaking," and even James Boaden frequented such gatherings — which, he explained as an old man, he still preferred to the "noisy company" that men like Thelwall and Cobbett gathered around them. It was a meeting of this sort, then, before which young John Kemble, on what was probably his first visit to London, debated the question, "Whether the representatives of the people ought to be answerable in a private capacity for what they may say in their official ones." His partner was one Guinnass, "a student of the Temple," but it was the youthful actor who impressed the audience. "Mr. Kemble in his exordium, informed the auditors, it was

his first essay, which accounted to them for his diffidence."
His points were cogent and well-made, and though he was
"modest calm argumentative," he needed to speak louder. He
and his partner gained "warm applause" for their efforts, and
of all the debaters they were "particularly admired and with
justice." How long Kemble stayed in London is unknown,
but he must have returned soon to York, for in May Tate
took his troop to Leeds and the young debater, fresh from his
London triumph, was along.[17]

Acting, after all, was merely Kemble's vocation; his avoca-
tion was what we may, for want of a better term, call literature. Throughout his life he was to cherish the idea of the
gentleman-scholar, who could turn off a lyric as well as a
play, a play as well as a critical essay. He himself, at one time
or another essayed them all, and if he did not succeed, at least
he tried. During his stay with Wilkinson, as we have seen,
his interests had been divided between acting and writing,
and during the summer of 1780, when he was bustling about
from Wakefield to Leeds to Edinburgh (where he was quite
a "novelty"), his consuming passion was the publication of
Fugitive Pieces — a volume that eclipsed even Attic Evenings,
Belisarius, and Latin epitaphs on the unlamented Inchbald.
Perhaps, like Holofernes, Kemble "would something effect
the letter; for it argues facility," although his efforts in that
direction make lugubrious reading for his biographer. His
volume of verses is among the slightest productions of an age
notorious for slight poetry, but, as Sir Edmund Gosse once
remarked of a painful duty, we must conquer our repugnance,
and allow our attention to rest upon it. For do we not have
Dr. Johnson's word for it that "if a man is to write *A Pane-
gyrick*, he may keep vice out sight; but if he professes to write
A Life, he must represent it as it was"?

In a pompous preface to his little book, the author excuses
the publication by observing that "when a man's writings

must unavoidably be delivered into the hands of the public,"
it is well to send them forth in a properly accredited form.
The youthful actor had been wooing his muse for some years:
the Inchbald epitaph was only one of a number of effusions
that were gathered under the title-page, *coacta prodire*. *Fugitive Pieces* consists of sixteen poems and forty-four pages in
an edition of only two hundred copies. Most of the pieces
are conventionally inferior amorous ditties, addressed to a
lady (Mrs. Inchbald?) whom the poet chooses to call Hebe.
An excerpt from the first poem will indicate clearly enough
John Kemble's versifying prowess:

> Soon *Cyntherea* reached the skies;
> Each God, that day was there —
> She rais'd to *Jove* her wat'ry eyes,
> And thus she prefer'd her pray'r:
> No more mankind invokes my pow'r,
> Nor ardent vows arise
> From doting bosoms, love's no more,
> My Cupid's influence dies.

The burden of the complaint is that Hebe has pre-empted the
affections of earth-bound creatures, leaving deific match-
makers unemployed. One of the poems, called simply "Hebe,"
is a pastoral replete with "lambkins," "fav'rite pipe," and
"Sylvan strain," while another ("Eclogue. Night. Despair.")
complains that "relentless Hebe" has rejected her Daphnis.
Dreary reading they make. Although the curious Kemble-
Inchbald courtship had, by 1780, just about run its feeble
course, the actor may have generated enough enthusiasm for
his lady to produce these pallid love-lyrics. We hear, from an
extremely unreliable source, that "a young lady of family and
fortune" — not the widow, of course — had become infatu-
ated with the boy, who, after a turbulent interview with her
brother, made his retreat in good order. William Hazlitt,
many years later, would have us believe that Kemble's early

poetry was addressed to Elizabeth. If true, the actor could say with Mirabell:

I did as much as many man could, with any reasonable conscience; I proceeded to the very last act of flattery with her, and was guilty of a song in her commendation.[18]

These poetic tokens of affections — if they were written for Mrs. Inchbald and not for the nebulous young lady of fame and fortune -- must have been composed before 1780, for by that time the widow's attention had been engaged by a certain Colonel Glover. The insipid lyrics are probably an accurate gauge of Kemble's passion. He was later to acknowledge that to her he owed more "obligation already than I shall ever be able to return," for she had befriended him when he was lonely and without prospects. Always in his London fame he "expressed the affection of a brother" for Mrs. Inchbald, whose kindness of heart no one has ever doubted, but as an old woman she freely admitted to Kemble when he facetiously asked her if she would have married him, "Dear heart! I'd have j-j-j-jumped at you!" To her he was always "the man for wisdom's various arts renown'd," and she was ever the champion and apologist for his style of acting. Their life in London, one as a great actor, the other as an esteemed playwright, was always cordial if not intimate, but Kemble was no doubt sincere when he told her, after his first success at Drury Lane, that "there is no Woman I more truly admire, nor any Man whose Abilities I more highly value." [19]

Reading through the rest of *Fugitive Pieces* one finds such pedantic trifles in Latin as "Ode ad Somnum" and the Inchbald epitaph, as well as prologues on such edifying themes as the mutual assistance of Commerce and Compassion and the causes of insanity. The total impression, however, is that John Kemble had, as Mr. Saintsbury once said of another poetaster, a certain Occlevian power of counting on his fingers. The poems may have done him credit with the good people of York, but, adds one critic quickly, "not with the muses." Kemble, it is gratifying to record, was very soon painfully aware of his literary transgression, and he immediately — some say "the very day after their publication" — destroyed all the copies he could lay his hands on. As a matter of fact, the meager edition was by no means exhausted as late as 1803, when Kemble, "with much tranquillity," bought the remainder and cheerfully burned them. As late as 1817, a friend in Edinburgh got hold of a few copies of *Fugitive Pieces* and charitably presented them to the author. Kemble's letter of thanks for this kindness — which, by the way, was by no means inconsiderable, as the books were by that time a collector's item — is engagingly frank:

I did, indeed, put that nonsense to the press; but let me give [?] myself the credit with you to say, that I ran, the very morning I saw it in print, to suppress it, and unfortunately was too late to prevent the sale of those few copies which I so earnestly wish to send to the flames after all the rest of them.

It is to be regretted that Kemble's remorse did not occur sooner, in time to prevent the publication entirely. Today the few remaining copies of *Fugitive Pieces* bring a very high price as bibliographical rarities, but the only literary interest the volume possesses lies in showing relentlessly how sadly a man of genius may err. His own opinion of the work, written to Mrs. Inchbald only four years after it was published, is perhaps as good as any:

Alas! my poetical Days, I believe, are gone by — in my best Pretensions I was but an indifferent Rhymer — nor in my vainest Moments ever thought anything I did fit to be call'd Poetry.[20]

Kemble's last year with Wilkinson was uneventful. York and Hull and York again and Leeds — so the season passed

away. There were good nights and bad nights: the engagement at Hull was as calm as the rolling Humber, but a brief
stop in Sheffield was financially disastrous — "a disgraceful
enterprise," grumbles Tate. Edinburgh in the summer of '81
was eminently satisfactory; one can fairly see the jovial manager beaming his approval: "For the whole representation, I
think I can aver, take the plays together, they were never so
thoroughly well played at Edinburgh as at that time." For
one thing, Kemble appeared in a pretentious new role, Sir
Giles Overreach in *A New Way to Pay Old Debts*. The care
with which he approached every important assignment is well
and early illustrated in a letter to Mrs. Inchbald, who had
seen a London production of the play:

Madam, I take the liberty of writing to ask you a few questions
relative to the character of Sr: G: Over-reach — Mr: Wilkinson
obliges me to play it — Mr: Henderson's Performance is in every-
body's Mouth, and the People hereabouts are inclined to do me
the Honour of expecting I shall make a Figure in it — Perhaps
Mr: Hitchcock may have told you I am leaving my Yorkshire
Friends — 'tis true — and as I don't wish to lose in my very exit
the little Credit I may have gained in the long time I have
played before them, I would learn every mark of character in
the Body and Mind of this Villain that I may bring him off as
successfully as I possibly can — What Kind of Hat does Mr:
Henderson wear? What kind of Wig? — of Cravat? — of Ruffles?
— of Cloaths? — of Stockings, with or without embroidered Clocks?
— Square or ro[und]-toes Shoes? — I shall be uneasy if I have not
an [lacuna] Dress even to the shape of his Buckles and what
[lacuna] he wears on his Hands — Moroseness and Cruelty seem
to me the Ground-work of this monstrous Figure but I am at a
loss to know whether in copying it I should draw the lines that
express his Courtesy to Lord Lovell with an exaggerated or mere
natural Strength — Will you take the Pains to inform me in what
particular Points Mr: Henderson chiefly excelled, and in what
manner he executed them. . . .

I am desiring you to impose a very tedious Task on yourself —
If I knew how, I would apologize for the Unreasonableness of my

Requests — I can only say, and I say it with the untmost Sincerity,
if it ever be in my Power to serve and oblige you, the very high
Esteem I have for you will make the executing your Commands
the first Pleasure of my Life — I have the Honour [to assu]re you
that I shall always be your [*lacuna*] and Servant —

                              J. P. KEMBLE [21]

As Kemble told Mrs. Inchbald, his days with Tate were
numbered. He is writing her from Leeds, on June 26, and
has already determined to leave for Ireland. Hitchcock, who
had been a member of Wilkinson's company, went over to
Daly at Dublin in the summer of 1781 as "Sub-manager,
prompter, &c. *never to return*," Tate ominously explains,
and he took with him several promising actors from the Yorkshire troop, including the highly accomplished young author
of *Belisarius* and *Fugitive Pieces*. But Kemble stayed the
summer with his old manager. In Edinburgh, perhaps
through his admirable efforts as Sir Giles, his "rising and real
merit and genius" made him a public favorite, as Tate generously records, although the rest of the summer was too bustling
for artistry: the bedraggled troop finally plodded into its
home quarters at York, "truly wearied with fatigue, but not,
thank God, in want of provender after the hard duty from
Leeds to Sheffield, from Sheffield back again to Leeds, and
then from Leeds to Edinburgh, and from Edinburgh to Newcastle, and not a single play night omitted between Newcastle
and York, where we all safely arrived, myself truly harassed
and unfit for service; and here we played every night again." [22]

This theatrical hugger-mugger — the accepted training-
school for actors in the eighteenth century — Kemble was now
preparing to leave. His two years' stay with Tate had been
an unqualified success: he had come to him a raw stroller, and
he was leaving a cultivated and polished young gentleman-
actor. His acting, though more subtle, even-toned, and refined
than the Yorkshire audiences had been accustomed to, was

at least distinctive, and his literary efforts must have been sufficient to make for him a place in such intellectual circles as York boasted. Tate did not conceal the fact that he was glad to have such an elegant and accomplished young man in his company. But Hitchcock's blandishments were too alluring to be resisted. On August 31, 1781, John Kemble made his last appearance with the Yorkshire troop (as Jaffier in *Venice Preserved*), and then left his genial manager for the "douceurs from King Daly" in Ireland.[23]

When John Kemble came to Dublin in the fall of 1781, he was simply moving from one provincial company to another. Daly's troop, though called by a contemporary who must have been prejudiced "the best company out of London," was in point of fact a far-flung and insignificant group of players, remote from the theatrical center of England. In its roster were names later destined to become celebrated, but then unknown. Kemble was not wholly a stranger in a foreign land. Hitchcock, the assistant manager, he had known in Yorkshire, and when he arrived in Dublin he found a younger member of Roger's numerous brood, his brother Stephen, who was, however, soon to go to Yorkshire to act with Wilkinson. The other men in the troop were Daly, Lee Digges, John Bernard, and two gentlemen named O'Reilly and Kane. Among the women were Miss Younge, Mrs. Melmouth, Miss Bersanti, Mrs. Bernard, and the charming Miss Phillips. But above all, there was the entrancing Miss Frances. Already the charming girl who was one day to become the toast of London and the mistress of the Duke of Clarence (afterwards William IV, to whom she was to bear ten children) had broken all the hearts in Dublin. Mrs. Jordan — in those days she was known as Miss Frances — had completely bowled over all the young blades in Cork, and when Daly took the company to Waterford she captivated a Lieutenant Doynes. His small salary, fortunately for the English stage, prevented a marriage:

it would be a problem, pointed out Miss Frances' mother, "from what source they were to draw their support — with the probability too of a family." Unhappily, the treacherous Daly raped the girl, and she was forced to flee to save what honor she had left — and to bear his child. In light of her subsequent career Miss Frances' youthful revulsion at Daly's act is nothing short of miraculous. But we anticipate, for when Kemble joined the troop she, presumably still unsullied, was a member of it.[24]

Dublin theatres of the late eighteenth century were anything but resplendent. In 1782 the city supported three companies — Daly's in Smock Alley, Crawford's in Crow Street, and Truby and Watt's in Old Fishamble Street. "The ill Success they have," observed one newspaper, "can scarcely be called Subsistence." Kemble was obviously not impressed with conditions as he found them. Later he was to spurn "the ragamuffishness of the players, and the filthy meanness of everything behind the scenes (I don't know how I can say scenes, when there are none)" that characterized the Dublin theatre. But even as a fledgling, before his London fame had made him fastidious, he objected to the "idleness, drunkenness, and dirt" that he found in Smock Alley. However unpleasant his situation was, the agreement had been made. He was to receive five pounds a week from Daly, and a salary of that sort could compensate for almost any amount of personal discomfort.[25]

The new actor made his Dublin debut on November 2 as Hamlet, a pretentious beginning. Daly, probably for the sake of variety, next put him forward as Sir George Touchwood in Mrs. Cowley's *Belle's Stratagem*, a proceeding exceedingly ill advised, for in comedy the Dubliners found young Kemble sadly wanting. The manager hurriedly got up *Alexander the Great* to regain lost ground, for it was readily apparent that the expensive new leading man was turning out to be a bad

investment. "His negligent delivery and heaviness of deportment impeded his progress," and nothing could make the
"grave and heavy line" he employed for comedy popular.[26]

It was just about this time that Daly, through some singular
good fortune, happened to give a dinner party at which
Kemble was seated next to the celebrated Captain Jephson.
The Captain was a well-known Dublin character, generally
esteemed a man of parts. He had undertaken to adapt Horace
Walpole's *Castle of Otranto* to the theatre, for that worthy
considered Jephson "the only man capable of restoring and
improving our stage." *The Count of Narbonne*, as the piece
was called, was played in London on November 17, 1781, after
Walpole had spent three days "tending and nursing and waiting on Mr. Jephson's play." The lurid drama was a success,
and with obvious relief Horace wrote Henry Seymour Conway of its reception:

I have brought it into the world, was well delivered of it, it can
stand on its own legs — and I am going back to my own quiet
hill, never likely to have anything more to do with theatres.

Edmond Malone, a school-boy friend of Jephson's, had used
his influence to have Drury Lane produce the play, and even
contributed a wholly undistinguished epilogue to the piece.
In his younger days, Jephson had moved freely in the intellectual circles of London, and was even a friend of the great
Garrick's. An earlier play, *Braganza*, with prologue by
Arthur Murphy and epilogue by Horace Walpole, had been
produced at Drury Lane in 1775, and the Captain on one
occasion played *Macbeth* at Phoenix Park in Dublin. It was
only natural, then, that he fancied himself something of a
theatrical arbiter in the Irish capital. He was surprised, at
Daly's dinner party, to discover that the unpromising new
actor possessed all the requisites of a great tragedian, and
"above all" he marveled at his "classical knowledge." He

immediately envisaged John Kemble as Raymond in *The Count of Narbonne*, then in preparation at Smock Alley, and undertook to groom him for the part. A letter of Kemble's, hitherto unpublished, lets us know what the young actor thought of the opportunity of being sponsored by one of the most important literary and social leaders of the city:

I am truly happy to know by a Note from the elegant Author of the Count of Narbonne to Mrs. Montague that I may take the liberty to offer you my Respects — No Actor in the World stands more in need of Improvement than I do — I am eager to receive your Instructions, and wait with Impatience to know what Time to-morrow I shall have the Honour to wait upon you —

As a matter of fact, the Captain's patronage was a godsend for John Kemble, and proved to be the turning-point of his career in Dublin. Jephson hired "a drill-serjeant and a foreign dancing-master" as tutors for his new protégé. Under their instruction the boy (who had been thought accomplished by Wilkinson) "was enabled to hold up his head and get rid of his lounging gait." For the important matter of voice-production, however, solicitous Captain Jephson trusted no one but himself. After all, "these things he understood perhaps better than any other person then living, Garrick excepted." The result was most gratifying. When *The Count of Narbonne* was produced, Kemble made a tremendous hit. "No trace of his former manner" marred the performance, and the "impression he made was unexampled." Jephson's play became the talk of the town. "Extremely profitable" for Daly, it was presented "thirty nights in the course of the season," and John Kemble woke up to find himself the most popular actor in Dublin. The critics and criticasters of the city "were boisterous in their approbation of this Adonis of the buskin, and the play-going beings of this fluctuating capital were on tiptoe at the mention of the great Kemble!" [27]

Once *The Count of Narbonne* had succeeded, the season

went swimmingly for Kemble. Jephson, benevolent if something of an officious fool, tutored his new find for *Macbeth*, which venerable piece was followed by a succession of moderate triumphs. The handsome young Englishman — already the chief impression he gave was one of invulnerable dignity and elevation — and Miss Frances together formed the chief attractions of Daly's troop. That winter in Dublin was a busy one for Kemble, both in tragedy and in comedy. Two years later, when he made his London debut, he had acted thirty-two leading tragic roles, as well as many comic ones.* The latter, one critic took occasion to remark, were "much below the attention of such a performer." [28]

Kemble's popularity in Dublin for the next two years continued great. One writer, whose veracity one feels inclined to question, accounts for this on religious grounds:

The Romish communion carried their affection for him [Kemble, who was, of course, a Catholic] to such height in Dublin, that the titular archbishop, and others of their clergy, gave a publick dinner when he was about to depart, to which the principal merchants and others were invited, and the day was crowned with the utmost festivity.

When we learn that he "was particularly run after by the students, and they uniformly supported him on his benefit nights," we are surprised by such an unflattering critique as this:

His tones are least of all adapted to the expression of extreme tenderness, or violent grief; though sometimes they have reached both successfully; but oftener the former passion raises them into

* The list is of interest: Hamlet, Earl of Essex, Earl of Warwick, Iago, King Charles, Osman, Richard III, Leon, Alexander, Shylock, Orestes, Edward the Black Prince, Bajazet, Philaster, Beverley, the Roman Actor, Othello, Mark Antony, Horatio, Romeo, Jaffier, Macbeth, Sir Giles Overreach, King John, Demetrius, Oroonoko, Achmet, Henry V, and the Count of Narbonne; cf. *The Gentleman's Magazine*, LIII (1783), 310.

a sort of whine, and the latter sinks them into a smothered and inaudible murmur.

Kemble's voice, as we shall have abundant proof of later, was always one of his greatest handicaps. In the eighteenth century, when an actor's excellence was considered in direct ratio to the volume of sound he produced, a naturally weak and studied delivery such as Kemble's was slow in being accepted.[29]

Kemble undoubtedly enjoyed a very successful season with Daly's troop. Though he did not continue his flights into blank verse tragedies and verse, he did win the town by his acting. Jephson's aid and interest were largely responsible for his popularity among the *cognoscenti* in the boxes, and the pit was apparently enthusiastic in its reception of his declamation of the ranting heroes. Declamation, after all, was a form of studied rant — a technique completely mastered by John Kemble and through his influence made predominant until the advent of a romantic genius whose performances, said Coleridge, were like reading Shakespeare by flashes of lightning. But in 1782 Edmund Kean and his school of acting were the least of the worries on the mind of the grave young Englishman in Smock Alley.

Curiously enough, the chief worry seems to have been a hot-headed gentleman named Richard Daly. After the affable, complacent Tate Wilkinson, the Irish manager must have come as a surprise to Kemble. Daly was a man of great talent, but he was a rounder and an unscrupulous entrepreneur. As it happened, he met his mate in his new star. When Kemble played Sir George Touchwood in Mrs. Cowley's *Belle's Stratagem* to Daly's Doricourt, the manager

thought that Mr. Kemble did not display sufficient *spirit* in his part, and told him so behind the scenes, and that he must exert himself more and take pattern from him. This imperious conduct did not suit our hero's temper at all; he warmly resented it, immediately changed his dress, and told Mr. Daly he might get some one else to finish the part, nor would he resume it till the manager had asked his pardon.

This was high-handed conduct, and with a man like Daly also dangerous. The proprietor of Smock Alley "had fought sixteen duels in the space of two years: three with swords and thirteen with pistols; yet, with so little skill, or so much good fortune, that not a wound worth mentioning occurred in the course of the whole." It must have been a great wonder to the company that he did not call out his insolent new player on the spot, for there was nothing he relished more than a passage at arms. Such an event was a field-day for the exhibitionist manager. Once, when he had challenged Jonah Barrington, his attire on the field of honor was miraculous:

he wore a pea-green coat; a large tucker with a diamond brooch stuck in it; a three-cocked hat with a gold button-loop and tassels; and silk stockings; and a couteau-de-chasse hung gracefully dangling from his thigh.

There was bad blood between him and Kemble from the beginning. In addition to contesting Daly's managerial prerogative in instructing him for his roles, Kemble before very long made it known he expected an increase in salary. After the success of *The Count of Narbonne,* which had been largely a personal triumph for the new actor, he could expect a raise, but Daly muttered surily that "the Roscius of Smock Alley cost him above forty pounds a month in squibs and crackers, about his inimitable, superlative, and most wonderful performances." There may have been an open altercation over the matter. At least John Taylor has it that there was a duel between the manager and his star, although he gives no particulars. Whatever the complications, Kemble won the point. When he came to Drury Lane he was receiving ten pounds a week in Smock Alley, "which, in respect to mere emolument," pointed out one money-wise journalist, "is better than Twelve Pounds in London." [30]

But all of life in Dublin was not so unpleasant. One night when he was playing *All for Love*, Kemble noticed an "old gentleman leaning over the upper boxes, with a listening trumpet in his ear." Vainly trying to suppress the "risible emotion" which the sight for some reason excited in him, Kemble "burst into loud and reiterated shouts of laughter, and it was some time before he could resume himself." Such laxity of stage presence was probably not out of the ordinary at Smock Alley, but one cannot imagine an older and more punctilious Kemble tolerating it at Drury Lane. When Daly took his company down to Cork and Limerick in the summer of 1782, his new star seems not to have taken his professional duties very seriously. At Limerick, where he was to play *Richard III*, the Richmond became ill, and Kemble was compelled to have as a rival on Bosworth field the only available substitute, a dwarf four feet tall. The leading man had unfortunately omitted attending the morning rehearsal, being "busy looking at the gaol, and the different places in the town," and he had heard nothing of the emergency. When he arrived at the theatre he found the stage manager unhappily explaining that the new Richmond could not fence. But Kemble was unmoved. "How will you die, Sir — how will you die, Mr. Kemble — how will you die, pray?" "My dear Mr. Fulham, don't make yourself unhappy; we shall manage very well, I dare say, when it comes to the fight why — I'll *poke* at him, he'll *poke* at me, I'll fall, and the curtain will drop." But that night such crude stage craft was too much for even a Limerick audience to accept complacently: "*Richard* died amid peals of laughter." [31]

Trooping it in Ireland in 1782 was not like playing Tate Wilkinson's well-established circuit. The traveling was hard and the audiences none too enlightened, but the company

made something of a lark out of the expedition. The lovely
Miss Phillips and her father traveled in a chaise, while John
and Stephen Kemble and Digges used a "light wagon." Some
of the more active males in the troop rode horseback, and
served as couriers to the procession, "riding on in advance to
order meals and prepare beds." On the way from Limerick
to Cork, in a little town called Butterfelt, Bernard and Bowles
(who was the comedian of the troop) were shown through an
old abbey by a "superannuated Sacristan" named Michael
O'Galloghan. The churchyard of the establishment contained
a pile of whitened bones, relics of a battle fought centuries
before. They had been blessed by the priest, and, as Bernard
explains, it "was thought a sacred influence consisted in their
safe preservation." But Bowles was not awed by the ecclesiastical formality, and he stole one of the skulls, for, as he told
his companions that night at dinner, it would come in handy
for Yorick. "At this, John Kemble increased the longitude of
his countenance an inch, and laying down his knife and fork,
exclaimed — 'Really — Mr. Bowles — if you go on in this manner — it will be — dangerous to travel with you — I appeal
to — the company — if such conduct — is not — ' But Stephen
[Kemble] and Digges were roaring with laughter," and the
pious objections of the leading man were overruled. Bowles
was allowed to keep his booty.[32]

All our anecdotes of Kemble do not show him such a complete formalist. During the summer tour John Bernard's
wife became ill, and the actor's resources were "greatly strait-
ened." Stephen Kemble, "my most intimate friend," as
Bernard tells us, knew of his plight, but he was quite unable
to help him. He did tell John Kemble about it, however, and
Bernard was surprised that the young actor "one morning,
at breakfast," paid him a visit. Asking after Mrs. Bernard
"with a face and accent sufficiently full of sadness," he requested a favor — to be made Bernard's banker until things

got better. " 'Here's money to buy pins — marriage is change-able'; with which words he gave my hand a squeeze, and left his purse containing five guineas in it. He then took up his hat and strode out of the room, with the same slow and solemn step that he entered it." This kindness, Bernard relates with obvious sincerity many years later, he could never forget.[33]

Almost inevitably, young love made its appearance in the Daly troop. The handsome daughter of Peregrine Phillips, "a girl of about sixteen, very beautiful, and very clever," began receiving marked attentions from the leading man. Kemble was a friend of her father's, and the young people were naturally thrown much together. "As they were neither of them blind or insensible," explains the lady's biographer, "it was impossible for them to meet without admiring each other for personal and professional attractions." Before long the company recognized that there was a "growing attach-ment" between the two young people.[34]

Kemble's devotion was shortly put to a severe test. He was a member of an organization called the Dublin Volunteer Corps, and when the corps held a drill in Limerick during Daly's engagement there, the young actor "was exempted from his dramatic to attend to his military duties." A dinner party was held by the amateur soldiers, and, as is the way with dinner parties, the company became mellow as the evening wore on. The gentleman sitting next to Kemble, happily for Miss Phillips' honor, nudged his companion and told him slyly that "there was rare joke going on at the Theatre." Upon further inquiry the young swain was told that Lord Clanwilliam, assisted by a troop of his cavalry officers, had "laid a plan to carry off Miss Phillips after the performance." Completely sobered by this information, Kemble unobtru-sively took his leave and hastened to protect his lady from the rapacious military. When he arrived at the theatre he found the evil Lord Clanwilliam sauntering about; at this he decided to act. "With the utmost decision but indifference," the actor took his stand by Miss Phillips' dressing room, and when she came off stage warned her — in a loud voice — of "the most unmanly and disgraceful plot." At this the lady "clasped her hands" and the crowd backstage "stared in confusion." While Miss Phillips retired to her room (where she "burst into a flood of tears") Kemble staunchly stood guard at her door with his unsheathed regimental sword in his hand. The frustrated officers, seeing their noisome scheme foiled, sneaked away, and the intrepid young actor escorted Miss Phillips to her home in safety. Michael Kelly, who loved to squeeze a story dry, adds an interesting finale. According to him, one of the drunken officers (Yelverton by name) lost control of himself as Kemble was triumphantly conducting his lady through the line of disgruntled kidnapers. Drawing his saber, he swung viciously at the actor's head and would, in all probability, have killed him had not the blow been seen and deflected (how, we are not told) by a dresser, Judy Cameron.

Kemble saw the whole transaction; and without the smallest alteration in look or manner, or being in the slightest degree moved, he turned to his preserver, Judy, and said, "Well done, Euphrasia!" * 35

For his gallantry and courage in this affair Kemble became "the general theme of conversation." More than ever, reports of a "particular attachment" — and even immediate marriage — were heard. But as in the case of Mrs. Inchbald, the romance came to nothing. After his triumphant London debut, even, Miss Phillips could not become ardent over John Kemble. She "expressed herself warmly" in praising his histrionic gifts, "and professed a sincere friendship for him in his private character, which she always represented as very

---

* The "Well done, Euphrasia" is a famous line in Arthur Murphy's *Grecian Daughter* (V, iii), uttered when Euphrasia strikes down the tyrant Dionysius in the nick of time to save her aged father Evadner.

amiable; but she never appeared to have a more *tender* partiality for him." As a matter of fact, she bluntly told a friend of hers that *"love* is quite out of the question" as far as Kemble was concerned. The actor's loss was by no means irreparable. Before going on the stage, Miss Phillips had been "on the point of being married to a gentleman who had acquired a large fortune in India," and a bit later "marriage was certainly on foot" between her and a certain Mr. Loftus in Ireland, but both these prospects had fallen through. After she became Mrs. Crouch, and acquired fame for her singing of opera in London, the lady settled down for the rest of her life to being the mistress of Michael Kelly. There we might leave her.[36]

It is unfortunate that no trace of Kemble's engagement with Daly remains save a string of anecdotes. But playbills of the period are not to be found. The winter of 1782–1783 found the troop back at Smock Alley after the summer excursion to Cork and Limerick. Of Kemble's roles, however, we have no knowledge. In October of that year, on the night of the tenth, Mrs. Siddons made her thrilling and memorable success at Drury Lane in *Isabella*, and within a month of that triumph (which only Garrick's debut as Richard in 1741 can equal) the London managers had sent emissaries to Dublin to look over her young brother. He may have been promised for Drury Lane at that time, though it is doubtful. During the winter he played at Smock Alley, and the tedium of the provincial capital was for the most part unrelieved. True, Mrs. Inchbald, signed by Daly to act in his company, arrived on November 9. Apparently the lady, still hopeful, resumed operations on Kemble, but with no success. "Whatever he felt," gingerly explains Boaden, "he appears to have cautiously abstained from any thing by which it could be supposed he stood pledged to any connection nearer than friendship." But Mrs. Inchbald was a woman not easily deterred:

She reads his books; writes to him; has notes, sometimes beautiful, at others *strange*. When he calls she either welcomes or refuses him admittance: he yields to her humour for the time, but returns, and is again in favour; and thus the matter stood until she quitted Dublin.

Such coquetry, no doubt, was more amusing than perplexing to Kemble.[37]

As it happened, however, Mrs. Inchbald was not to be with the Smock Alley troop very long. Her acting was tolerable — "a pretty but not clever woman, with an impediment in her speech, which stage-fright always took away," recalls John Bernard — but she had the misfortune to attract the lecherous Daly. This gentleman, obviously a man of impetuous action, had driven the desirable Miss Frances from his troop when she revealed his conduct towards her. And now his fatal gaze was fixed on the charming widow. As was his wont, Daly lost no time in making his position clear. When the lady indignantly spurned his advances, he immediately called for her benefit and discharged her. Kemble himself, on May 23, 1783, brought "her heavy guineas for the payment," and two days later she left Ireland. Kemble, however, was soon to follow, and he may have already by that time had a definite contract with Drury Lane.[38]

In the summer, Mrs. Siddons, flushed with her overwhelming success in London, came as a guest star to Smock Alley. Her impressions of the Irish capital, unflattering to a degree, she was later to make public. But for the time she was content to be wined and dined by the cream of Dublin society. Her arrival had been prepared for by a banquet that Jephson gave. Kemble was there, of course, and he had the pleasure of seeing Lord Inchiquin toast the glorious Siddons while flourishing her miniature in a ring. By this time, however, John Kemble, at the threshold of his London career, had become something of a celebrity himself. He was the intimate of the Inchiquins and the Gardiners (Mountjoy) in Dublin, and "all those who aimed at mental distinction" were eager to have him as a guest in their houses. He had become friendly with the powerful Lord O'Neil and his handsome wife, the former Henrietta Boyle, who had known and sponsored Mrs. Siddons in her days of poverty at Cheltenham. By the time his celebrated sister arrived, Kemble had already begun his life-long practice of cultivating important and socially prominent people.[39]

After two years with Daly and the "filthy meanness" of Smock Alley, John Kemble was ready to move on to Drury Lane. His progress had been rapid, and he had reason to congratulate himself. Some provincial actors spent long and poverty-stricken lives trying to get to London. Kemble, once his unsavory apprenticeship of strolling was passed, had advanced easily and rapidly from the respectability of Younger's troop to the affluence of Wilkinson's. The Daly engagement he may have considered a promotion. At least he was eminently successful in each company he graced, and with a powerful sister using her influence for him at Drury Lane, his prospects were bright indeed.

CHAPTER III

Mr. Kemble of Drury Lane

> A young fellow should be ambitious to shine in everything; and, of the two always rather overdo than underdo.
>
> LORD CHESTERFIELD

THE APPROACH to London was not without alarums and excursions. Mrs. Siddons must have been at work: hers was a persuasive charm, and we may be certain Drury Lane had been appraised of the merits of her younger brother. At any rate, the emissaries of both Drury Lane and Covent Garden raced to Dublin with a contract for the rapidly rising Kemble, for Harris, of the rival house, had sent his messenger as soon as he heard Drury Lane was after him. And so, after some confusion, the future leader of the English stage turned his steps to London. It was August, 1783. At Liverpool, on his way from Ireland, Kemble had written Elizabeth Inchbald, by this time settled in the metropolis, about living quarters. It had been agreed that he should occupy her rooms during her absence from London during the fall; "I shall be lord of your Tenement in about a fortnight — I understand moreover, that I am to enter it just as it is — you won't surely be so cruel as to be aiding or consenting to the removal of any Part of the Furniture." And by the middle of the month John Kemble was ensconced at No. 2, Leicester Court, Castle Street, Leicester Fields — very young, very diligent, and very ambitious.[1]

Mrs. Siddons' presence made things easier, of course. She,

with sisterly devotion, had "prepared her friends" to welcome the stranger, and the important journals were properly informed of his arrival. The publicity, incidentally, had been very competently handled. The influential *Gentleman's Magazine*, the spring before, had carried a lavish puff from Dublin and paved the way: "few of his profession have been more universally the topic of discourse, and subject of admiration, than Mr. Kemble." After his arrival in London, the querulous began to suspect that the actor himself was the author of the more laudatory notices in the press. Such was most likely the case, for the venality of the newspapers, complained one observer, was so "obvious to every person who knows any thing about the stage and its *appendages*" that most thinking people ignored journalistic fillips. The critical profession was followed either by knaves who could be bought for a good dinner or by pretentious fools who, as Dr. Johnson had complained, "grow important and formidable at very small expense." Until the advent of Leigh Hunt and Hazlitt, much later, most criticism was either servile or bludgeoning: William Gifford, for example, was accused by Southey of regarding authors as Isaac Walton did the worm. But even twenty years after Kemble's debut the righteous could complain that "Most, if not all, of the London Journalists, are *bribed* by the Managers of Covent Garden and Drury Lane Theatres." [2]

John Kemble appeared on the theatrical scene when both the stage and the drama had attained a conspicuously low point. The great Garrick was dead, and only Henderson, a second-stringer at best, was left to carry on the remarkable style so brilliantly launched in the middle of the century. Covent Garden was in the control of Harris, a person with no imagination but a keen head for business, and Drury Lane had just entered on that long period of decadence which was to be synonymous with the gross mismanagement of Sheridan

— the *Wunderkind* who half a dozen years before had produced his string of dazzlingly successful comedies. The licensing act of 1737, fostered by Walpole and nobly opposed by Chesterfield, had effectually prevented the rise of any theatres apart from the two great patent houses (although, through special favor Foote had been holding forth at the Haymarket). Physically the playhouses were inadequate for any except the most antiquated stagecraft. If in good Queen Bess' glorious reign Thomas Heywood could call the theatres "an ornament to the City," a citizen under George III could speak of them only with shame. Indeed, a French traveler to England the year of Kemble's debut at Drury Lane found that "celebrated Slaughter-House of Dramatick Poetry" a poor thing:

The boxes are flimsy, the decoration poor, and the ensemble has neither the gravity nor the dignity that befits a public edifice. The seating is not very different from that in our little boulevard theatres: a pit with benches, three tiers of boxes at the sides, and three galleries at the back. As for the tone, that of our fair booths is infinitely more decent. People sing, whistle, howl, drink, eat oranges and throw down the peel, without, by the way, any intention of insulting the person who gets it in the face. And nobody objects.[3]

The drama itself, as everyone knows, was for the most part pompous imitation of French neo-classicism or inconsequential comedy. The sparkling works of Sheridan only make their contemporary pieces all the drearier by contrast. Intelligent people largely shunned the theatres. Anna Seward, that memorable bluestocking, was "in general, sick of modern comedies," and young Robert Southey, a few years later, was so disgusted by Young's *Revenge* that even after a decade of abstinence had softened the memory he wrote Landor that "I verily believe I shall never set foot in a theatre again." "Take a Coquette," suggested one wag, "a Beau, a Lover, a Valet, a miserly Father, and mix them well. . . . Let the

Coquette use her Lover like a dog for some time, then marry him unaccountably to his great wonder and astonishment, then put in a Song and a Dance, and you have a complete Comedy." The eighteenth century had produced a distressingly long list of pretentious inanities that passed for tragedies — plays, as Lamb wittily remarked, in which "two persons talk themselves into a fit of fury, and then in a surprising manner talk themselves out of it again." Tragedy was sanguinary; as Thomas Rymer long before complained, "on our Stage are more Murders than on all the Theatres in *Europe*." Intrigue chiefly passed for comedy, and "huddling too much matter together" was the stock in trade of Mrs. Cowley and Frederick Reynolds. The "rapid" school of comedies, sneered one critic, "are below criticism. Farce and O'Keefe have seized upon the stage." Horace Walpole, one feels, was right when he croaked that the "measure of our dullness is full." Sheridan maintained the comic line from Goldsmith, but tragedy was consigned to the elephantine hand of writers like Robert Jephson and Richard Cumberland. England, feeling the disastrous effects of George III's first twenty years, was losing wars abroad and sinking into the doldrums at home. A few years later the mordant wits of *The Anti-Jacobin* could write with a certain justice that when one views

> Our stage, verse, pamphlets, politics, and news,
> He loathes the world, — or, with reflection sad,
> Concludes it irrevocably mad;
> Of taste, of learning, morals, all bereft,
> No hope, no prospect to redeem it left.[4]

This, then, was the London of the late eighteenth century in which John Kemble set out to make his reputation. In many ways it was a scintillating capital; in others it was a sink of corruption. The estimable George III was forty-five, and his first determined efforts to emasculate Parliament had been foiled. The result, however, was almost chaos: the American war was lost; Wilkes was ending his days in the opulence of a Lord Mayor's robes after his earlier vicissitudes; and there was springing up a race of brilliant new politicians — Lord North's disastrous regime ended with the emergence of such celebrities as Charles James Fox (in politics since 1770, when he was twenty), Edmund Burke (in his mid-fifties entering into the climax of his career), William Wilberforce (a boy of twenty-one), Richard Brinsley Sheridan (turned politician from playwriting), and the great William Pitt the Younger (who had become Prime Minister at twenty-four). Though socially the London of Pitt and Channing and Erskine fairly glittered, it was none the less a city of frightened, reactionary men. The golden day of classicism was past, and the first fresh triumphs of the romantics were in the future. For two decades the shadow of a revolutionary France was to direct England's illiberal politics. For three decades John Philip Kemble was to be the guiding influence in its theatre.

In those halcyon days of the Prince of Wales' hectic courtship of Mrs. Fitzherbert — when providing for the mistresses of the Royal Family was no inconsiderable factor in domestic policy — "the actor and not the dramatist ruled the theatre." It was an age of execrable playwrights but lavish playhouses — of a deplorable national drama but ostentatious production. If, as Bernard Shaw has declared, English drama has been the disgrace of literature since Fielding's day, certainly the close of the eighteenth century must be called the nadir of the disgrace. Conditions were bad indeed, barks Macaulay, when Hayley (who stumbled into playwriting) could be thought a great poet. The eighteenth century perhaps rendered an ill account to drama because, as has been suggested by Mr. Cross, the form failed to express realistically and philosophically what the new novel could: playwrights were unable to reconstruct life "in accord with the prevailing view," but novelists, employing a technique more minute and more analytical,

pleased the age. By Kemble's time, oratory had almost replaced acting: Burke and Sheridan, rolling forth their eloquence in Parliament, represented to their contemporaries
most perfectly what Oliver Elton has called the "graver passions" of the day. Rhetoric supplanted passion; declamation
crowded out the realistic ebb and flow of Garrick's art. Although the memory of Garrick was still green, John Kemble
determined to be the great man's successor. He may have
realized, as did Hazlitt and anyone else who took the trouble
to think about the matter, that the age was essentially not
dramatic, but he was fired with the ambition to dominate it,
and to impose his own acting standards upon it. His success
constitutes his major triumph.[5]

It was a brilliant audience assembled in Old Drury that
night of September 30, 1783 — probably the most important
night in John Kemble's life. Here was the one-time stroller,
the son of a stroller, acting in London at five guineas a week
and appearing before the exacting metropolitan audience in
the most taxing role in English drama. The whole world
was there to see his *Hamlet*, and for the most part the whole
world was pleased. For one thing, the cast assigned to the
novice was a good one: Bensley as the Ghost, Farren as
Horatio, Baddely as Polonius, Barrymore as Laertes, Mrs.
Hopkins (Kemble's future mother-in-law) as the Queen, and
Miss Field as Ophelia. But all eyes were upon Kemble. Peregrine Phillips, his friend since the Smock Alley days with
Daly, was transported in his enthusiasm, as would be natural,
but less partisan critics were also impressed. Thomas Davies,
once bookseller in whose back-room had occurred the memorable first meeting between Dr. Johnson and Boswell, roundly
declared he had never seen an audience more moved or more
grateful to an actor; the *European Magazine* predicted a great
future for the neophyte; the influential *Morning Chronicle*
congratulated the public on getting another gifted member

of the Siddons family — "a valuable acquisition to the theatre." And so it went, apart from a few captious critics. John Taylor found Kemble's style pedantic (as indeed it was, and was to remain), and Richard Twining thought "he died ill," although otherwise superior. Generally, however, the evening was a success: here was a young man who knew what he was about, an actor and not a ranter, a man of "superior learning" who would teach the public more Shakespeare than "all the commentators that ever stained paper." Although we must be chary in accepting the playbill's announcement that *Hamlet* would be given "as originally written by Shakespeare," we may be sure Kemble's innovations were conspicuous in that age of editorial caprice. The business of trailing the sword, instead of pointing it at the ghost, was heartily applauded, even if the device of using two miniature cases in the bedchamber scene came off badly. Moreover, Hamlet's instructions to the players were omitted "upon the modest principle, that he must first be admitted a master in the faculty, before he presumed to censure the faults of others." But the consensus was favorable: finished throughout, judged one critic, and the best acting since Garrick's days said another. Especially notable — and this is a criticism we will seldom encounter again — was Kemble's adroit change of pace: one observer was "absolutely electrified" by the transition from a gallant lover to an anguished avenger.[6]

Before the week was out, all London knew about Kemble and either passionately approved or just as passionately disapproved of him. The sensation the debut made, recalls John Adolphus many years later, was a "great" one. Those who remembered Garrick were severe (as well they might be), pointing out defects in posture and voice and immobility. But Kemble's style was to be unvarying. Where Garrick's brand of romantic realism — if we may borrow the term — employed a natural ease and almost conversational agility,

Kemble's static, declamatory style made for a certain statuesque nobility. As Lamb was to remark, he took a stance and orated. His was the style of Siddons, by and large — a style of long, sweeping lines and detached, almost impersonal grandeur. It was a histrionic counterpart of what Sir Joshua Reynolds demanded in painting: a marmoreal loftiness and zealous avoidance of the minute, the particular, the personal. "He neither walks the stage, nor turns his head, nor moves his limbs with ease," complained one critic, and John Taylor was so repelled by the "stiff, conceited, and unnatural" technique that he wrote a series of flat epigrams on the subject. But the dissenting voices were to die down, and Kemble's style was to be *the* style of London for three decades. A great career was launched.[7]

The hurly-burly of his debut safely behind him, John Kemble settled down to becoming a fashionable young man of the theatre. Five years of hard work were ahead of him before he was to become manager of Drury Lane in 1788, or before he was to assume the semi-public character which he bore with such *éclat* after he was a recognized figure in high society. At the moment, however, he was a nervous but elated novice, secure in the knowledge that his debut had pleased the town, yet apprehensive of making his way against the powerful rivalry of Henderson at the other house. For that matter, his Drury Lane competitors were formidable. King, anything but a great actor, had a large following and the clutch of seniority on the choicest tragic roles, while Smith was a universal favorite in the lighter parts. As has been often pointed out, John Kemble's appearance in London was timed with singular good fortune. Competent comedians — Palmer, Bensley, Parsons — were numerous, but in tragedy there was really no dominating figure. Once the new actor established any sort of following, he could step almost uncontested into the best heavy roles. When Kemble arrived in

London, John Henderson, if anyone, was the only possible
successor to Garrick. His reputation was large, and it would
have been larger had he lived longer. Perhaps the most
fortunate event of Kemble's career was Henderson's early
death in 1785 — just about the time the younger actor was
ready to assume a position of importance on the stage. Samuel
Rogers, who knew everyone, remembered Henderson as "a
truly great actor," and the judgment is borne out by many
contemporaries. Kemble himself considered his colleague's
Shylock the "greatest effort" that he ever witnessed on the
stage, and his Falstaff (a celebrated interpretation) struck
Thomas Davies as a "master-piece." Richard Cumberland's
remarks, one feels, are not exaggerated:

He was an actor of uncommon power, and a man of the brightest
intellect, formed to be the delight of society, and few indeed are
those men of distinguished talents, who have been more prematurely lost to the world, or more lastingly regretted.

After his fame was secure and invulnerable, Kemble mentioned as "one of his misfortunes" the fact that "he had never
had the advantage of improving by any performer better than
himself, except Mr. Henderson." [8]

The chief business at hand, then, was for the fledgling to
act as much and as impressively as possible. His *Hamlet* was
one of the most popular attractions of the season. The *Morning Herald* observed that Henderson had played the part
"above forty times in London, and Kemble seems going on
for as many." As a matter of fact, he did do the play twelve
times his first season. The town, once the novelty of the
debut was over, agreed that "the success was complete," and
the detailed criticisms of the performance showed that his
innovations were "at least entitled to notice." Mrs. Siddons'
triumph of the year before was ratified the following season,
and Drury Lane was in a fair way of being swamped by the
Kembles. In addition to Sarah and John, Elizabeth was acting

for the theatre, though not with the success of her older
brother and sister. The *New Spectator* was pleased to observe
that when the three of them attended the theatre, they "decently seated themselves in the pit, and behaved in such a
manner as ought to make their professional friends blush for
those impudent and fantastic airs by which they usually are
distinguished in the green boxes." But there was some murmuring at the Misses Kembles' being allotted choice roles, as
they "are universally allowed to be very incompetent to the
sustaining of any of those characters, when there are several
ladies in the same company, by whom they would be supported, at least with decency." The scurrilous John Williams
thought the matter worthy of his heavy-handed satire a bit
later:

> With Kembles on Kembles they've chok'd Drury Lane;
> The family rubbish have seiz'd public bounty,
> And Kings, Queens and Heroes pour forth from each county:
> The barns are unpeopled — their half-famish'd sons
> Waste the regions of taste like th' irruption of Huns.

But by and large the sons and daughters of Roger Kemble
were prospering in London. Mrs. Siddons played so frequently during the season that she often fainted away at the
close of her performances, and to see her one had, like the
Swan of Lichfield, to struggle "through the terrible, fierce,
maddening crowd into the pit." [9]

John Kemble, however, was not compelled to undergo such
strenuous popularity at the moment. On October 20 he made
a fresh attack on the town by appearing in *Edward the Black
Prince*. The impression he made is fairly well reflected by the
critic of the *Morning Herald*:

Edward the Black Prince was very unequally sustained by Mr.
Kemble; in the impassioned scenes he was nervous, and dignified;
but in those less interesting, offensively emphatic, and monotonous. The character, sufficiently wretched in itself, stands in

need of no additional aquatics, to *drivelize* it into contempt, and therefore we trust Mr. Kemble will be less lavish of his tremulous tears in future.

Another paper, however, suggested that the new actor might lend the play "a grace by his performance, that may possibly keep it before the public longer, than it otherwise would continue." Such proved to be the case, for the piece was played eight times before the year was out.[10]

A more important occasion was the new star's appearance in that time-honored favorite, *Richard III* (in Cibber's version, of course), on November 6. In a strongly derogatory critique the *Morning Chronicle* expressed surprise that Kemble "should conceive the character so very differently from the manner in which it has hitherto been read." The haughty king showed a "coldness and degradation" that ill befitted "the serious art, the swelling pride" of the role. What the critic objects to, of course, is the studied absence of rant; Richard for almost two centuries had been a loud-shouting, vigorous part, played for all it was worth, and the restraint and subtlety that the new actor brought to the role was too novel to be immediately acceptable. The eclectic, studious nature of Kemble's technique — which in these days he was consciously developing — is ridiculed by an epigram which was going the rounds:

> Thou soul of Betterton, thou voice of Booth,
> Graceful in all, in nothing uncouth;
> Thou eye of Garrick, with the form of Barry,
> Sure Nature's choicest bounties thou dost carry!
> What crouds on crouds attend thee every night,
> To see thee stalk and stare, or dance and fight!
> Talk not of Quin, let Garrick be forgot;
> For great John Kemble's all — that they were not.

When *A New Way to Pay Old Debts* brought the new actor forward in another noisy stock part a week later, the dissatisfaction was general. His Richard is inferior to Smith's, complained the *European Magazine*, "and his Sir Giles Overreach is by no means the performance we expected. Henderson is excellent throughout in this arduous character, but Mr. Kemble, his best friends must subscribe to the assertion, is not." [11]

An event of the season, however, after these rather unfortunate early efforts, was the first appearance of the great Siddons and her brother together. *The Gamester*, that highly moral piece, was given by royal command, and the choice of play "was happily without offence to any other performers." It had been unacted for four years, and Smith, with admirable judgment, scorned the role of Beverley. Siddons, of course, was superb as the abused wife; in the last scene she and her brother were "accompanied with as many tears as ever were shed in a theatre on one evening." Kemble, it was generally agreed, was improving. His Beverley, "was more equal than any of his performances hitherto, though he had not quite divested himself of the peculiarity of his tones, and the studied art of expression." But one critic, evidently a die-hard, still objected to acting that exhibited study or care or preparation. To his way of thinking, Kemble was "too fond of pointing out niceties; he discovered the *actor*, and by this means cancelled the pity he had excited for the unfortunate Gamester." There were those, however, who spoke admiringly of his "masterly powers" and "critical judgment of the meaning of each sentence," and Thomas Davies gravely congratulated the public "on the prospect of much rational entertainment" from the new school of acting.[12]

The success of the Kembles was marred by only one thing. Their disreputable sister Ann, who was currently known as Mrs. Curtis, was doing her best to be completely objectionable. When Mrs. Siddons and Kemble (perhaps a little callously, though we do not know the circumstances) turned deaf ears to her demands for money, she resolved to bring upon them all the unfavorable publicity she could. With this purpose, she ostentatiously swallowed poison in Westminster Abbey, and advertised for work in the papers, explaining that she was "the youngest sister of Mess. Kemble and Mrs. Siddons, whom she has repeatedly solicited for relief, which they have flatly refused her; it therefore becomes necessary to solicit, in her behalf, the benevolent generosity of that Public who have so liberally supported them." Later the enterprising Mrs. Curtis gave public lectures on "Women"— which, the advertisements explained, were "perfectly chaste and delicate and extremely interesting." Such publicity, of course, was unsavory for the ambitious members of the family. The *European Magazine* expressed its dubiety at reports of Kemble's "exquisite feelings" and generosity, especially "while his unfortunate sister is compelled, through dire necessity, to cleanse the Augean stables in Pall Mall, by delivering lectures on chastity, and other delicate subjects, for a trifling reward." The publication of a volume of verse, *Poems on Miscellaneous Subjects: By Ann Curtis, sister of Mrs. Siddons*, occurred during Kemble's first winter in London. Mrs. Curtis later described the poems as childish: "I say childish because I was not then more than eighteen and those poems were written when I was some years younger." Dedicated to the Duchess of Devonshire, the little volume named an impressive list of subscribers, and it may have made a little money for its unhappy author. Typical of the contents is a piece called "To a Friend, who Bade Me Hope!"

> Think'st thou, that Hope's delusive pow'r
> Can aught of joy impart,
> To calm the tumults of my mind,
> Or ease a breaking heart? [13]

When Mr. Curtis was proved a bigamist, Ann married a gentleman named Hatton. The couple went to America, but

by 1800 were back in England, keeping a hotel at Swansea.
The last thirty years of her life Mrs. Hatton devoted to writing very bad novels under the name "Anne of Swansea" and
dunning her affluent relatives for funds. She never associated
with Kemble or Mrs. Siddons, although they both gave her
an annuity. "It is a tale that has unhappily been too frequently told," she once wrote in a letter, "that the rich and
prosperous members of a family, have combined to neglect
and calumniate the less fortunate — of this truth myself and
Mrs. Mason [another impoverished sister of whom almost
nothing is known] are living instances. . . . From the age of
fifteen to the time of their death, I have had cause to complain
of oppression, and hardness of heart, yet let the ashes of Mrs.
Siddons and John Kemble rest." Ann's scurrilous memoirs
of her family we have already examined — she must have been
an embittered and vindictive woman. That her more affluent
relatives did undertake to support their disreputable sister is
shown by an interesting letter that John Kemble once wrote
her:

Dear Anne [*sic*],
   This line will not reach you till three or four days later than
it ought: but I have waited for a frank, which I know I should
be able to procure to-day, in order to save you the expense of a
package which from this place to Swansea must be very considerable. I am, dear Ann, yours truly, —
                           J. P. KEMBLE

June 18th 1813.
Baron's Court.
Newtown Stewart.
Tyrone.
      Ireland.

Ann's comment on the back of the sheet is revealing: "much
more considerate than usual it would have been been [*sic*]
better had the 13 pounds been thirty of which God knows I
am much in want." Poor old Roger Kemble had no illusions

about his daughter Ann. When he died in 1802, he left her an annuity of £20 to be paid by John, but not under any circumstances "without a Receipt from under the said Ann Hatton's own hand." [14]

But we anticipate. The winter of 1783–84 continued to be an exciting one for the Kembles. John was making headway against the formidable opposition of Henderson at Covent Garden, although the stately, leisurely pace of his acting did not burst into popularity as did the nervous, colorful style of Kean a generation later. Presently he moved to new quarters at 25 Henrietta Street — Mrs. Inchbald had returned to claim her lodgings — and there the scholar of Douay and the *littérateur* of York wrote such letters as this one:

I have been hunting about an Hour for the 2nd. vol. of Ovid, and cannot light upon it high or low — What can be become of it I can't imagine, I had it in my Hand a day or two ago.
I send my Compts: to Mrs. Whitfield, and return her Lord and Master his two Books — They told me Randolph was a poet — God help — Some Men are strangely fortunate — I have read his works twice over, and for the life of me I have not been able to make out his Title to any thing more on Parnassus, than a very small Plot, and that at its Foot, thickly sprinkled with a few gay, but common flowers, and for the most part overrun with Weeds and Brambles —

Scholarship was not wholly abandoned. Kemble's work in progress was a translation of Ovid's epistle from Oenone to Paris, an ambitious effort which never quite pleased him. From Liverpool, the following summer, he complained to Mrs. Inchbald that it would never do: "I have labour'd and labour'd so long in vain at it, that it is now thrown aside from an absolute Conscience of wasting so much time to no manner of Purpose." Eventually, with true Elizabethan gentility, he did circulate the manuscript amongst his literary friends, who found much to marvel at. We, however, cannot deplore its loss. Meanwhile, of course, the theatrical season was progressing. Just before Christmas Kemble was "very finely" coached by old Tom Sheridan, the perennial orator, for *King John*, and shortly afterwards he challenged the veteran Macklin (who had virtually retired) by playing Shylock. For the most part, he had the incalculable aid of his sister. She appeared with him in his benefit, *The Countess of Salisbury*, a play which had been nothing with Smith but was a success with the newcomer. When the brother and sister appeared in *Tancred and Sigismunda*, late in April, they were so effective "as to leave few, if any dry eyes in the house." But before the end of the season three new plays were in store for Kemble: *Cato*, Addison's hoary stock piece: *Love Makes a Man*, in which he played opposite Mrs. Brereton, who was presently to be Mrs. John Kemble; and Dryden's *Amphytryon*, which came off badly.[15]

All in all, the season had been a success for Kemble. His was not the fate of so many promising actors imported from the provinces: a few nervous appearances, and then a disgraceful retirement to less exacting audiences. He, of course, was powerfully supported by his sister, now become a personage of importance, but in addition he had a certain tenacity and ambition that overleaped obstacles. He was willing to let the critics come around to his style of acting, and did not bow to their standards. Although his press had been generally favorable — this was long before those hectic days when he would be referred to as "anonymous liar" and "a midnight assassin" — he was quick to resent unfavorable criticism. As an unfortunate and ill-considered manifesto of artistic independence, a letter of his to the *Morning Chronicle* is worth resurrecting from the yellowed pages where it first shocked and amused the town:

Sir,
I beg leave to distinguish what you would dignify with the

character of criticism in the Morning Chronicle. — Some of your remarks, whence gathered I do not now enquire, are good, and liberal — some are nonsensical, and studiously abusive — the former deserve my actor's attention; the latter ought to rouze every actor's resentment. — Under the exact notion of a gentleman's despising the slander of a bully, yet thinking it necessary to cane him for his impudence —

> — Keep your secret — and reform with a good grace. —
> J. P. KEMBLE

Happily for the young hot-head, this Johnsonian epistle got a tempered and coldly perfunctory rejoinder from Woodfall, the editor. Such impudence and audacity might well have been the undoing of less gifted men; Kemble, chastening his spirit, bowed his neck to the journalists, although he never concealed his contempt for the tribe.[16]

The first wearing year was now past. Wilkinson's alumnus had made his way in the city, appearing fifty-five times in thirteen roles — by no means an ordinary beginning for a novice from the hinterlands. With the summer came a return to the provinces, of course. The triumphant Siddons was off for Edinburgh and Ireland, but her brothers, John and Stephen, were willing to act in less pretentious surroundings. Curiously enough, it was back to Liverpool, which he had left in wrath six years before as an unknown stroller, that John made his way. Younger was still the manager there, and for all the star's London success he would not be talked into extravagant wages. John Kemble was "to study, rehearse, and perform" in all "plays, operas, farces, and pantomimes" that should be allotted him — and all for the munificent salary of ten shillings a night plus one benefit from which Younger was to get thirty-five pounds. There would come a day, though, when Kemble would bargain in scores of pounds, not in shillings. For the moment, he no doubt thought himself a most fortunate young actor.[17]

CHAPTER IV

Of a Crescent Note

Gott giebt die Nüsse, aber er bricht sie nicht auf.
GOETHE

MRS. SIDDONS, even two years after the febrile excitement of her debut, continued the rage of London. Anna Seward, always proper, admitted that to see the great Sarah one had to forget one's dignity. "Most people," she told Dr. Whalley, "quitted their coaches, we amongst the rest, and struggled for admission through columns of fine people, fierce and violent as the canaille when the Siddons plays." Forty years later, a fat old woman, Sarah liked to think of those golden days and of "the awe she felt, and the power of the excitement given to her by the sight of Burke, Fox, Sheridan, and Sir Joshua Reynolds in the pit." Her younger brother, generally acknowledged a capable enough fellow — he had all of Siddons' declamatory dignity without her fire — attracted no such enthusiastic following. For one thing, the very popular Smith had returned to Drury Lane and by his seniority had snatched some of the choicest roles to himself; for another, Henderson was still in his heyday at Covent Garden. For John Kemble the glitter and the fame were to come later, but already, with his salary doubled to ten guineas a week, he was looked upon by many as the tragedian of the morrow — even as the manager of Drury Lane. The actor himself, intensely ambitious, was nothing loath: he realized his sister's prestige "powerfully contributed" to his progress and made the most of her support; he made every effort to establish himself socially, attracting friends, it was suggested by some of the querulous, because he fed the sycophants well. Some of his followers, it was rumored, paid court to him by comparing him favorably with the great Garrick; indeed, one old gentleman confided to the new star that at his best Garrick had looked like nothing so much as a little butler. Kemble had to take what comfort he could from such observations, for his newspaper notices fell off conspicuously: when the critics did speak of him, it was almost always to proffer pontifical advice about the suitability of 'natural' acting.[1]

The season advanced slowly enough for John Kemble. When he came forward for the first time as Hamlet, on September 21, most critics took up the familiar cry. "He discovered *study* in every phrase," complained one of them, "in every verse, but certainly sacrificed the enthusiasm of the part." His reading of the line, "Did not *you* speak to it?" occasioned a prodigious spilling of ink, all to no purpose. When Henry Fielding came upon Shakespeare refereeing a dispute between Betterton and Booth in Elysium — the point at issue being a similar matter of accentuation — he was delighted to hear the poet exclaim in desperation, "Faith gentlemen, it is so long since I wrote the line, I have forgot my meaning. This I know, could I have dreamt so much nonsense would have been talked, and written about it, I would have blotted it out of my works." But in certain quarters Kemble's innovations were still fiercely opposed:

> If *singularity* was Briton's choice,
> In Kemble then must ev'ry heart rejoice.[2]

The initial appearance of Mrs. Siddons and Kemble together was almost disastrous. In Ireland, the summer before, the actress had become involved in a most unsavory scandal, growing out of her refusal (so her enemies said) to act in a benefit for disabled actors. Much publicity had been given the incident, and when the great lady walked on the London boards for the first time that season (in *The Gamester*) the uproarious audience hooted her off. Her attempted explanation was futile; she could not be heard. Now John Kemble was not a man to cower before an audience. Already he had won his spurs in subduing a Yorkshire clique. In a fine rage, he came forward to his sister's aid, bowed coldly to the pit, and led Mrs. Siddons off with all the dignity in the world. Presently, when the house was calmer she was allowed to make her explanation and the play went on: the Kembles won the field.[3]

Riotous audiences were not the only vexation of the new season. There were rivals to be overcome. During the fall of 1784 two young gentlemen — Holman at Covent Garden and Pope at Drury Lane — enjoyed the patronage of the town and effectively threatened John Kemble's popularity. The one cut a dashing figure as Romeo and the other was handsome enough to be an attractive lead. The Kemble dynasty followed the careers of such rivals with attention. In fact, the entire family attended one of Holman's performances, and from a front box "paid a liberal testimony of approbation." But Kemble's fears, if he had any, were vain. Holman, after a brief day of glory, presently dropped out of favor, and Pope settled back into the inconspicuous place he was to hold for the next forty years. Both of them merely added to the many now forgotten actors who occupied inglorious posts during the transitional period from the romantic realism of Garrick to the grand formalism of the Kembles. For the time being, however, the new school was far from secure. A string of apathetic performances — *Tancred and Sigismunda*, *A New Way to Pay Old Debts*, *Cato*, and Cumberland's new *Carmelite* — did nothing to increase Kemble's prestige. How could he play opposite his sister, marveled one critic, and not be carried away? "He had 'a muse of fire!' before him; —

why did he not kindle at her inspiration!" The complaint
was a common one.

Why will Mr. Kemble restrain himself, by critical *refinements*?
Why will he not give the passions fuller scope? He is beyond
compare the most graceful actor upon the stage; but he must get
rid of his *reserve*, and assume greater animation, before he can
be the best. We must, however, acknowledge that he comes forth
with new advantages, whenever he appears.[4]

The muse was about to descend again. When Kemble had
his alteration of Massinger's *Maid of Honour* produced (January 27), the response was not particularly gratifying. The
revision, of course, was in the interests of delicacy, and the
most critics could praise was to comment on the "extreme
labour" of the undertaking. Scenes from *The Maid's Tragedy*
which were interpolated in the last act did not seem very
congruous, and the whole play creaked. In point of fact, it
was given a bad production. Although Kemble acted "extremely well" as Adorni, Mrs. Siddons completely botched
the epilogue; the costumes and sets were characterized chiefly
by "too much *frugality*," and even the callous London audiences found reason to object to the mixture of a Roman toga
with Turkish slippers and sable-colored stockings. When
Kemble acted in *Othello*, however, his success was great. Even
the Royal Family (dullards though they were they loved the
theatre) were vastly moved by the performance, and accorded
the young man the honor of coming to Buckingham Palace
with his sister to read for the court. The occasion did not
come off with great *éclat*, despite the trappings of royalty.
Mrs. Siddons, who was in what was then referred to as an
interesting condition, found the strain very wearing, and was
in imminent danger of swooning away — because she was not
permitted to sit in the presence of the king and queen. Happily, the reading ended at a crucial point, and the royal personages left the apartment so the ailing actress could sink in

exhaustion on a chair. It was not until the Lord Chamberlain gave his express permission, Kemble told Sir Francis Bourgeois, that the actors dared look to Mrs. Siddons' comfort.[5]

The season ended on a more cheerful note. Kemble finally succeeded in wresting *Macbeth* from King, who had played it all year. For his benefit, it was performed, as the playbill announced, with Matthew Locke's music — in other words, Drury Lane was still using, in 1785, the Restoration monstrosity that had so pleased the town a century before. But the house was a huge and fashionable one, the applause was flattering, and a seal of approval was set upon Kemble's second season. True, it had not been so brilliant as the first. He had played in only nine plays, most of them produced to show off his noble sister. *The Maid of Honour* failed to please, and his role in *The Carmelite* was minor. None the less, he had survived the inevitable slackening of interest after his novelty had worn off, and he looked to the future confidently. He was definitely "of a crescent note." [6]

The summer's touring was in Ireland, where Kemble acted once more for his old manager, Daly. Hard feelings flared up again, this time erupting into an open altercation. Daly had the temerity to put off his star's benefit, and Kemble, "somewhat inebriated," came behind the scenes to demand an explanation:

Mr. D. was proceeding to make a circumstantial apology, but was interrupted by Mr. K. who desired superciliously that he may not be imposed on by any *monkeyish tricks*. An explanation was demanded, which Mr. K. refused: the parties immediately adjourned to Ryan's Tavern, where the decision of the quarrel was, at the desire of Mr. K. adjourned until next morning, to be finally determined at Luttrelstown; there the Sheriff with his *posse* intervened. Mr. D. escaped, but Mr. K. remained in the carriage until he was taken, brought to town, and bound over. At length, through the mediation of friends, matters were made up by Mr. K's making the necessary concessions.[7]

The tide of Kemble's rising fortunes assuredly set in during the fall of 1785. Henderson, a serious rival and an extremely popular actor, died just on the threshold of his career, while Smith, at Drury Lane, was about to retire to the obscurity he so richly merited. Those who had held high hopes for such younger men as Pope and Holman were disappointed. John Kemble, reinforced by two London seasons and his mighty sister's influence, had a virtually clear field for becoming "the acknowledged first male tragedian of the age." The press, for instance, changed its tone almost overnight. So adulatory were some of the critiques in the *Morning Chronicle* that certain narrow-souled persons suggested they were written by Kemble himself — an "absurd" insinuation which the paper indignantly denied. On all sides were Kemble's admirers: young ladies, previously of a blameless life, were moved to poetry at the sight of the stately young Hamlet; certain critics, misguided by their zeal, even suggested that Kemble might make an eminent comedian; and "Anthony Pasquin," the "vain, vulgar, insolent, and overbearing" John Ambrose Williams whose writings reached a new depth of scurrility, was compelled to acknowledge Kemble peerless since Henderson's untimely death:

> In this dearth of desert few his claims will examine:
> Thus rats become dainties where God sends a famine.[8]

The repertory that season was for the most part unchanged, the only difference being that where before Kemble acted one or two nights a week, he was now acting five or six — and in the best roles, too. Othello, Jaffier, Hamlet, Tancred, Philotas, Beverley — all charmed the town. As Tancred, decided one critic, he was "not much inferior" to his sister, and in Otway's masterpiece, another reported, Drury Lane with Siddons and Kemble was truly the home of the muses. The *Morning Post*, which had seen little to admire in Kemble from the start, at last had to admit his excellence, but it could not forbear a parting thrust:

A flexibility of opinion, an attention to modulation of voice, a volubility of utterance, and an easy pliability of deportment, rather than statuary precision, would soon give him a pre-eminence equal to his own opinion and ambition.

But it was just these desiderata, oddly enough, that Garrick's successor was to banish from the English stage for a genera-tion.[9]

For the most part the season continued to be a triumph for the new tragedian. With good plays and bad plays he pleased the town and the critics. His old patron Jephson had in 1775 labored and brought forth a first tragedy, *Braganza*, in the revival of which Kemble was "affecting, dignified, and im-pressive"; in fact, the critic tried in vain to find a single flaw in the performance. His polished and gentlemanly acting, it was suggested, was a natural result of his consorting with the best company socially — an observation significant of what passed for criticism at the end of the eighteenth century. In Shakespeare — *Hamlet, Macbeth, Cymbeline*, and *King John*, all produced within a week (November 17–22) — Kemble was an unquestioned success. The press comments were a cre-scendo of praise, so much so, in fact, that the *Morning Chronicle* felt moved to inject a warning note: why should trumpeting Kemble's merits involve an attack on his rivals? "What has Mr. Smith done that he is to be made the victim and sacrificed at Kemble's shrine?" But the rage was on; the Kemble star was rising, and there were few dissenters. Even the tepid receptions that his own work, *The Project*, and *The Romp* got could not dampen his popularity. Dr. Delap's mournful tragedy, *The Captives*, ran only three nights, and then, "like the spirit of Ossian which pervaded it, was gathered to its fathers." The production as a whole was slovenly, Kemble wearing the only Scottish costume Drury Lane was willing to provide. It was thought that when the piece was published, the irate author would pay his respects to the way his play had been treated, but Kemble, writing to Edmond Malone, laughed off the complaints: "I see the doctor publishes the play this week. If his reverence should be severe, the best thing we can hope is, that all who read the preface may read the play." [10]

The indefatigable Kemble managed to find time, while acting almost every night, to try his hand at literature again. In 1785 Thomas Whatley had published an essay he wrote in 1770, *Remarks on Some of the Characters of Shakespeare.* Whatley set out to prove, by examining the characters of Macbeth and Richard, that the Scotch usurper was essentially cowardly. The significance of his little book lies in its critical approach, which emphasized Shakespeare's "distinction and preservation of *Character.*" The two unscrupulous men, so similar in external circumstances, "agree in nothing but their fortunes."

Both are so divers, both imposters; both attain the throne by the same means, by treason and murder; and both lose it too in the same manner, in battle against the person claiming it as lawful heir. Perfidy, violence and tyranny are common to both.

Shakespeare's distinction lies in ascribing "opposite principles and motives to the same designs and actions, and various effects to the operation of the same events upon different tempers." Whatley's work is interesting and readable, and for its time remarkably psychological in method. Written before (though published after) William Richardson's *Philosophical Analysis and Illustration of Some of Shakespeare's Remarkable Characters* (1774) and Maurice Morgann's *Essay on the Dramatic Character of Sir John Falstaff* (1777), it is the first book in English "to concern itself with the psychological analysis of Shakespearian characters." [11]

The book created no great stir when it was published in

1785, but Kemble, disagreeing with its premises, seized the opportunity to make his formal entrance into the polite literary set of London by refuting it. The actor, a great admirer of *Macbeth*, undertook to prove that soldier's courage by a minute examination of his actions — the method pursued by Whatley to gain precisely opposite ends. *Macbeth Reconsidered; an Essay: Intended as an Answer to Part of the Remarks on Some of the Characters of Shakespeare*, an unpretentious pamphlet of thirty-six pages dedicated to Edmond Malone, appeared in 1786. One rejoices to find no personalities or recriminations; the tone throughout is one of well-mannered disputation, and Whatley's work is gracefully spoken of as one "so usefully intended, and so elegantly perform'd." Kemble simply tries to show that there was no distinction between Macbeth and Richard "in the quality of personal courage." Questioning Whatley's justification in calling Richard's courage "intrepedity" and Macbeth's "no more than resolution," he examines with some care the latter's character before his encounter with the witches, his conduct towards Banquo and Macduff, and his bravery in violent action. His arguments are cogent and eloquent, and his psychological insight on the whole remarkable. Both men, Kemble maintains with conviction, are motivated by ambition; their difference lies between Richard's deceitful cruelty and Macbeth's hypocrisy. "Richard's character," he concludes, "is simple, Macbeth's mix'd. Richard is only intrepid, Macbeth intrepid, and feeling." [12]

Kemble's little book served effectively enough to mark his acceptance into the literary aristocracy of London. Dedicated to Malone, and written as it was by the leading young tragedian of the town, it commanded an audience fit though few. Far from one of the seminal works of the barren period — it was, after all, an age of scholars, of Malone, Steevens, Porson, and Burney — Kemble's essay stood as proof that an actor could be a scholar and a gentleman — that he could toss off a polished bit of prose as readily as he could win the pit by stomping about the stage in Tamerlane's turban. Through his long career it was to be pointed to by his apologists as a token of his literary accomplishment. The little book, badly treated by some of the more surly reviewers, was a useful gesture in the direction of *belles-lettres*, even though the merciless Hazlitt, years later, contemptuously termed it nothing but "literary foppery." The great critic, with his unfailing acumen, one fears, gave it a true title.[13]

The new season, 1786–1787, was a repetition of Kemble's triumphant third winter with Drury Lane. Wildly applauded on his first appearance, he stalked through the winter with his ineffable gravity and solemnity — the ideal tragedian in the opinion of most of his contemporaries. The event of the year, once Kemble had sailed like a Spanish galleon through all his old stock pieces, was one of those fabulous hits not explicable by tracing cause and effect. On October 24, as an afterpiece to *The Winter's Tale*, General Burgoyne — considerably more effective as a playwright than as George III's commander in America — brought forth his adaptation of Sedaine's *Richard Coeur de Lion*. It took the town by storm. Long before had Colley Cibber, wise in the ways of the theatre, explained that the public preferred trivial operatic spectacle to serious drama because "many more People there are, that can see and hear, than think and judge." There were many persons, like Sir John Brute, who "wou'd not give a Fig for a Song that is not full of Sin and Impudence," while others, in language regrettably less colorful, objected to opera on commercial, chauvinistic, and aesthetic grounds. Pope, in his well-known prologue to Addison's *Cato*, complained tersely that

> Our scene percariously subsists too long
> On *French* translation and *Italian* song.

The author himself of that celebrated tragedy, a notable and eloquent opponent of the foreign genre, held it as axiomatic "that nothing is capable of being well set to music, that is not nonsense," and his stout collaborator, Dick Steele, unceremoniously bade all Italians of "Emasculating Voice" to hie them home again: "Shall *British* Freedom thus become the Prey?" Caustic young Horace Walpole, on his grand tour, thought the music of French opera "resembles a gooseberry tart as much as it does harmony." Poor Charles Lamb, an avowed obscurantist in matters musical, suffered most:

I have sat through an Italian Opera, till, for sheer pain, and inexplicable anguish, I have rushed out into the noisiest places of the crowded streets to solace myself with sounds, which I was not obliged to follow.

But in 1786 Continental opera was as popular as ever, in spite of the lugubrious and ill-tempered croakings of intellectuals for a century. In Olympian disgust did Walpole the fastidious write Lady Ossory of a performance by the enormously popular Vestris:

the audience fell into convulsions of applause: the men thundered; the ladies, forgetting their delicacy and weakness, clapped with such vehemence that seventeen broke their arms, sixty-nine sprained their wrists, and three cried bravo! bravissimo! so rashly that they have not been able to utter so much as *no* since, any more than both Houses of Parliament.

But London loved the opera. *Timour the Tartar,* one of the favorites, although written (in the words of Lewes, its author) "as a *vehicle* for the horses" made thousands of pounds. And John Braham, a sweet singer of melodious song who was one day to be immortalized by Thackeray, was commonly understood to make some £14,000 a year.[14]

The town, true to tradition, completely succumbed to the facile ease and spectacle of Burgoyne's opera. Let the singing singers, it cried in the words of Henry Carey,

let the singing singers,
With vocal voices, most vociferous,
In sweet vociferation, outvociferize
Ev'n sound itself.

Michael Kelly had seen the French original, with Sedaine's text set to Grétry's ingratiating music, in Paris, and found it "charming." In London, both theatres raced to bring the new piece forward first, and Covent Garden's version, by MacNally, preceded General Burgoyne's by a week. Happily, it "produced no effect at all." When the Drury Lane version appeared, on October 24, it boasted the stellar cast of Kemble, Suett, Mrs. Crouch (the Miss Phillips of Smock Alley), Miss De Camp (later Mrs. Charles Kemble and the mother of Fanny), and the vivacious Mrs. Jordan. Mr. Edward Dent. when he came to trace the development of English opera, did not except *Richard Coeur de Lion* in calling his work "the record of three centuries of failure." But his criteria were artistic, not commercial. The 1786 production at Drury Lane was an unqualified success for the treasury. Probably it was crude enough musically; we hear derisive accounts of the theatre's "thrummers of wire and scrapers of cat-gut," and whatever the merits of the other performers, Kemble in the title-role was a conspicuous vocal failure. Michael Kelly, "astonished" at his inability to sing, was told that the tragedian had assumed the part "to serve the proprietors" since "there was no singer in the theatre capable of representing it." No one, decided one critic, could "call Mr. Kemble a warbler":

a shaker he may be; for his responsive morsel was uttered, as if it had been a severe frosty morning, and the teeth had chattered in his head.

But if Kemble's singing was unfortunate, lamely apologizes the faithful Boaden, "the spectators enjoyed the sight of his noble figure, pacing his melancholy exercise within the walls

of his prison." One newspaper, studiously omitting any reference to his vocalism, reported that the tragedian "personates
the royal dignity, with a mixture of force, spirit, and tenderness, that evinces great powers of performance." Kemble's
incapacity for singing became, before the end of his career,
almost proverbial, and one of the most ubiquitous anecdotes
concerning him had to do with the sadly harassed Mr. Shaw,
who conducted the music for *Richard Coeur de Lion*. Fanny
Kemble's version of the story is as good as any:

Mr. Shaw was painfully endeavouring to teach my uncle, who
was entirely without musical ear, and whose all but insuperable
difficulty consisted in repeating a few bars of the melody supposed to be sung under his prison window by the faithful minstrel
Blondel. "Mr. Kemble, Mr. Kemble, you are murdering the time,
sir!" cried the exasperated musician; to which my uncle replied,
"Very well, sir, and you are forever beating it."

But for all Kemble's bad singing, *Richard Coeur de Lion*
continued to be the hit of the winter. After fifteen nights it
could still draw a "very full" house, and for many seasons
(long after Kemble had gratefully resigned his role to Michael
Kelly) it was a highly popular attraction.[15]

The tinsel and shallow spectacle of the opera, in point of
fact, drew larger houses than some more respectable offerings.
When Dodsley's really excellent (but now quite forgotten)
Cleone had been first produced, in 1758, Samuel Johnson
related spitefully Garrick's remark that the two Warton
brothers, in town for the occasion, were "starved for want of
company to keep them warm" at the playhouse. In reality,
the piece had done well, selling over two thousand copies.
But when it was revived for Siddons (and Kemble, to a lesser
degree), in 1786, it failed dismally — for the simple reason,
suggested one critic of discrimination, that "the refined feelings of the present times affect to revolt at Tragedies where
insipidity does not prevail." Kemble, with youthful abandon

and indiscretion, was having a fling at comedy. Mrs. Cowley, she of the Della Cruscan inner circle, had turned Mrs. Behn's spirited *Lucky Changes* into *A School for Gray-beards,* in which the erstwhile tragedian was moderately successful as Don Henry. This was followed by Valentine in Congreve's brilliant *Love for Love* (a production in which Mrs. Jordan, who had achieved a dazzling success of her own in London, played Miss Prue), and by Holcroft's *Seduction,* itself a remarkably provocative work among the sterile intrigue pieces of the day.[16]

There was little to disturb Kemble's monotonous triumph. One night (it was February 2), Kemble notes on a playbill, a fire broke out in Brydges Street near the theatre, and the audience very unceremoniously left the theatre in the middle of the fourth act of *Rule a Wife and Have a Wife.* As a matter of fact, the roof above their heads had been ignited, but the fire was quickly suppressed. It was thought best, for matters of policy, not to have a play the next evening, although on the following Monday the king himself, to show his confidence, graciously commanded a performance. When Mrs. Hester Thrale Piozzi returned to London after two and a half years of gaiety on the Continent with her new husband — Dr. Johnson was now in his grave and missed the disgraceful spectacle — all the town was excited. Unfortunately, however, the lady did not choose Drury Lane for her first public appearance. Instead, as she entered a box at the Haymarket her "flashing little figure with her fiery auburn wig, her carmine cheeks, her satin, her spangles, her flirting fan, her perky graces and her careless audacity, made a very considerable impression." With the spring came Jephson's eagerly awaited new tragedy, *Julia,* and Kemble was naturally chosen for the lead. The benevolent Malone nursed Jephson through the writing of the piece, suggesting changes and even contributing a prologue which was spoken by the young tragedian.

Although the dreary play was a *succès d'estime,* the public did not take to it kindly. Poor Kemble worked so hard in preparing the role of Mentevole that "a severe indisposition was the consequence, which procrastinated its future representations." The memory of the play's cool reception, explained Anna Seward when she was importuned to write a tragedy, simply froze "the Melpomenean ink in my standish." [17]

Kemble was steadily gaining an ever-increasing following, not only among the clerks and shop-assistants of the pit, but also among the intellectuals and society leaders who from their place in the boxes determined the tone of the theatre-going public. The arbiters of the profession had already come to look upon the great Siddons' brother as a gifted and enlightened actor, and a man who by his unusual literary and social attributes could take his place as Garrick's successor. The season of 1787–1788 merely ratified his position. Dramatically it was not of much moment: the hoary old stock pieces were paraded across the stage of Drury Lane with all the stately and declamatory gravity in Kemble's power. There were still those recalcitrants who hankered after the ease and facile charm of Garrick's style, but they were a minority. Did Garrick, asked one exasperated apologist for the new order, lay down "specific rules for acting, to deviate the least from which must be esteemed the grossest self-conceit in the actor, and an unpardonable offence against the Drama?" Pope's remark on the acting profession in the early part of the century was still applicable: "In Betterton's days the older sort of people talked of Harte's being his superior, just as we do of Betterton's being superior to those now." Although Drury Lane itself, through Sheridan's Olympian negligence and King's pedestrian management, showed the "greatest feebleness," Kemble's personal career continued triumphant. At thirty he was unquestionably the ablest English tragedian

— much as some people were reluctant to admit that fact.[18] There had been, it appears, no successor to Mrs. Inchbald of the Yorkshire days or to Miss Phillips of Smock Alley; for his first four years in London, the young actor's life had been completely absorbed in the theatre. In the fall of 1788, his reputation established and his future relatively secure, John Kemble set about looking for a wife in the same preoccupied way he undertook to assume a new character at Drury Lane — deliberately, rationally, and thoughtfully. His chief desiderata in a wife, relates Boaden complacently, were "quiet manners, steady principle, and gentle temper." The story all the town was whispering was not so prim, however. Rumor had it that the capricious young daughter of a "nobleman, once a minister of state" (no less a personage, indeed, than the estimable Lord North of unblessed memory), conceived "a lurking attachment in favour of our hero," and plans for marriage were made. But at this point his Lordship, outraged at the actor's presumption, called the swain on the carpet, flatly forbade the match, and brutally offered him four thousand pounds if he "would quiet his paternal apprehensions, by taking to himself a wife." The noble lord's only stipulation was that the substitute marriage take place within a fortnight "at the farthest." Kemble unhesitatingly agreed, and immediately made the match with a member of Drury Lane, the widow of Mr. Brereton. But when Kemble called for the four thousand pounds a week or so later, there was perfidy revealed. "His Lordship received him with great politeness, and congratulated him on his nuptials," but at the mention of the blood money he "rebutted in a strain of the most galling and severe irony." The nonplussed young actor was "asked what interest his Lordship could have in his domestic arrangements? On what plea he expected to be paid £4000 for marrying a pretty girl? — Was he in earnest, or was he acting?" And so the deal fell through. When Kemble, years later, saw this bit of scurrility in a pamphlet, he took great pains to note on the margin, "A Lie!" And such it probably was.[19]

By early December the papers were announcing that a marriage "will shortly be consummated between Mr. *Kemble* and Mrs. *Brereton*; the courtship, in respect to *time, place,* and *action,* was strictly according to Aristotle's Rules for a Drama, compact in every respect!" The wooing must have been graced by no superfluous preliminaries. Mrs. Brereton, who had been acting at Drury Lane with Kemble for several seasons, was the daughter of the Hopkins who had been prompter under Garrick; her first husband, an undistinguished actor, had in 1786 attempted suicide in Dublin (in a fit of unrequited passion, some said, for the glorious Siddons), after which he was confined, as poor Mary Lamb was to be, in the asylum at Hoxton, where the next year he died. One evening the comely widow came to her mother in great perplexity:

"My dear mother," she said, "I cannot guess what Mr. Kemble means: he passed me just now, going up to his dressing room, and chucking me under the chin said, 'Ha, Pop! I should not wonder if you were soon to hear something very much to your advantage.' What could he mean?"

The wordly-wise Mrs. Hopkins, obviously not quite so naive as her daughter, explained that marriage was in the offing; her advice was to accept Kemble the minute he proposed. On December 8 the Rev. Mr. Bale of St. Martin's performed the ceremony, which was later repeated by a Catholic priest for the benefit of the groom. Bannister, the comedian, gave the bride away, and the wedding party went to his quarters to wait until Kemble had finished his preparations for the dinner which had been planned. As the day passed, nothing was heard from the groom, and though messengers were sent searching for him, he was not to be found. All his servant knew was that "a bit of a mistress was coming home." Finally, the distressed ladies of the Hopkins family took potluck with the obliging Bannister, but the best he could provide was the "blade-bone of a baked shoulder of mutton." When the enraged Mrs. Hopkins took her daughter to her new husband's home that night he was still missing, and all the two could find to eat was "some cheese and red-herring from a chandler's shop." When Kemble at last appeared, very late, he made no explanation. "It seems he had been absorbed in a brown study, so as entirely to have lost all recollection of his marriage." John Kemble never condescended to contest the gossip that his public ascribed to him, and at least it entertained two generations of play-goers.[20]

Priscilla Kemble seems to have been a good wife. Boaden thought that "never certainly was an union formed with sounder judgment, as far as permanent happiness was likely to be the result of discretion in the choice." Mrs. Kemble managed her home at No. 13 Caroline Street, Bedford Square, with charm and tact. "There is economy," decided Thomas Lawrence, a frequent visitor there, "but it is well judged." Mrs. Kemble enjoyed being the wife of a great manager, and she enjoyed the social position that she and her husband came to occupy. They entertained a great deal, and they came to know in time most of the notables of the day as friends. Fanny Kemble, who never got on particularly well with the prim widow of her great uncle, thought she was "quick, keen, clever, and shrewd," with the appearance, at least, of a woman of the world.[21]

As an actress Mrs. Kemble was certainly no equal to her great sister-in-law. Her distinguishing characteristic on the stage, recorded one critic, was "delicacy." "Petite in figure, and in voice confined, she laid no claim to the pre-eminent distinctions of her profession." She acted rather infrequently after her marriage, but always with fair success. When she and Kemble, a week after the wedding, appeared at Drury Lane as Margaret and Sir Giles Overreach, the audience was jocularly appreciative. Near the end of the fourth act, Kemble, as Sir Giles, had to say,

> Is there aught else to be wish'd after these two
> That are already offer'd, — marriage first,
> And lawful pleasure after: — what would you more?

At this point the pit "burst into a tumult of laughter and applause," but Kemble, grave and decorous, did not "show the least consciousness of the rough thought which pervaded the theatre." Mrs. Kemble retired permanently from the theatre on the night of her benefit, May 23, 1796. The play, curiously enough, was the *mélange* of which Tate Wilkinson had been so proud years before in Yorkshire, *The Roman Actor*, and the audience was deeply affected when the manager led his wife off the stage after she had delivered, "very inarticulately, a short address, descriptive of her feelings on the occasion." [22]

During the fall before his marriage, Kemble prepared for Drury Lane an alteration of Fletcher's comedy, *The Pilgrim*. Though not one of his significant productions, the version he brought forward illustrates the methods he was to follow in preparing his great Shakespearian revivals later; for that reason it will repay us to examine it in some detail. As everyone knows, eighteenth-century managers almost never produced a play without more or less extensive revision. Fielding, satirizing Cibber's presumptuous treatment of Shakespeare, remarks that

it was a Maxim of mine, when I was at the Head of Theatrical Affairs, that no Play, tho' ever so good, would do without Alteration.

Especially did the Elizabethan and Restoration plays suffer from the ministrations of the reviser. For purposes of delicacy or regularity they were unscrupulously altered, sometimes almost beyond recognition. Horace Walpole's pet prejudice was against low-bred actors and their high-handed practices; when he wrote his *Mysterious Mother* he told George Montagu that he was eager to see it produced, except that he was unwilling to expose himself to the "impertinences of that jackanapes Garrick, who lets nothing appear but his own wretched stuff, or that of creatures still duller, who suffer him to alter their pieces as he pleases." But leading critics found Shakespeare altered out of all recognition and thought "the castrations and purgations praiseworthy," and Kemble, along with most of his contemporaries, believed the early plays "spoken upon our stages needed the most careful revision." Theophilus Cibber tells of an actor who found a play too long; he "gave it his Cat to play with: — What Puss claw'd off, the Actor left out; yet he generally found enough remain'd to satisfy the Audience." It is safe to say that not once during the eighteenth century was an early play acted precisely as the author wrote it; alteration was the first essential of a revival.[23]

The Pilgrim, Fletcher's cruelly brilliant comedy, had been acted at court in 1621, and seventy-nine years later an extensive alteration by Dryden's "good friend Mr. Vanbrook" was presented to the town. The production was chiefly notable for Dryden's prologue and epilogue, as well as the superb *Secular Masque* which was written, as the title-page of the first edition informs us, "just before his Death, being the last of his works." It was as Alinda that Mrs. Oldfield had her first important role, and the brash young Colley Cibber was accorded the unusual privilege of speaking Dryden's prologue and epilogue. Vanbrugh turned all Fletcher's verse into prose, and made some drastic cuts in the dialogue, but he was happily unconcerned about the verbal emasculation of the ribald text. After all, the righteous Jeremy Collier, who was by way of being an authority on things objectionable, decided that Beaumont and Fletcher's plays were not nearly so bad as some of the contemporary pieces: "the Oaths are not so full of Hell and Defiance, as in the Moderns." But for his alteration Kemble mercilessly "pruned away the indelicacies," leaving the play "pure enough in all conscience." [24]

When, on October 26, 1787, the town was presented a new version of *The Pilgrim* by the elegant Mr. Kemble, the piece it saw bore only generic resemblances to the original. The acting and production must have been fairly good, for the young tragedian himself played Pedro, Barrymore did Roderigo, Baddeley Antonio, and frisky Mrs. Jordan Juletta. But the piece on the stage was a far cry from the lusty, sprawling comedy of Fletcher's. In point of fact, what the audience saw was the old Vanbrugh alteration of 1700 divested of its obscenity and profanity. The sequence of scenes and progression of dialogue in the Restoration are closely matched in Kemble's version, but the delightful freedom of the language is naturally missing. Juletta's ribald chatter to her mistress in the first act is entirely out, and nothing but a pious circumlocution is left of

Abed, abed, D'ye hear? abed, Sir. She wou'd find him so rugged there, I'll warrant you: She'll find ways to soften him.

These alterations and omissions in the interests of purity are too numerous to enumerate separately, but a few characteristic ones might be cited. Vanbrugh's "Whoring and drinking" becomes "Wenching and drinking" in Kemble's bowdlerized version, and such an inoffensive line as "i'th name of Venus" is changed to "i'th name of wonder." When Vanbrugh, following Fletcher, has a girl spoken of as "a short Breakfast for a hot Appetite," Kemble simply omits the whole line.[25]

The young actor, perhaps with the immortal longings that

inspired *Fugitive Pieces* still working within him, tacked on scraps of verse to the Vanbrugh. At the close of the first act he assigns to Alinda an original soliloquy in blank-verse:

> Forgive me, duty, if I break thy laws!
> My father's harsh and bitter treatment
> Makes me renounce my home — home I have none
> Without the youth I love — Oh Pedro!
> Thro' ev'ry change of Fortune will I fly,
> Thro' all inclemencies of earth and sky,
> The sharpest trials of my fortunes prove,
> To follow, and reward my constant love.

Another poetic interpolation of Kemble's is a long, six-stanza song given to Juletta as she goes to seek her mistress in the forest; one almost thinks of W. S. Gilbert in reading such a bit as this:

> Some trim disguise,
> No doubt she tries,
>   I'll follow her example:
> Of faith, of skill,
> And wit at will,
>   I'll give 'em straight a sample.

Although Kemble omits a quatrain found in both Fletcher and Vanbrugh, he appends a closing tag to the third scene of the fifth act:

> The dangerous tempest of our woes blown o'er
> Safely we land upon love's peaceful shore;
> Unnumber'd blessings now attend thy youth,
> The sure reward of piety and truth.[26]

Kemble's divagations from Vanbrugh (who, more than Fletcher, may be considered his original) are almost all made with an eye for brevity and speed of action. This, as we shall see, was to be his salient principle as a reviser when he came to alter Shakespeare, and in such an early piece as *The Pilgrim* his method may be clearly seen. Vanbrugh is often wordy and static, and Kemble's excisions are obviously made to increase the pace of the action on the stage. A man of the theatre, his criterion for judging a scene was almost always to be, would it have tempo and momentum in actual performance? He would naturally omit such a scene as the long and tedious discussion by the domestics of Alinda's flight, and he would drastically truncate Alphonso's fulminations at the beginning of the first act. Parts of the rather perplexing mad house scenes are cut, such as the latter half of the sixth scene of act three — a practice to which one objects when one of Fletcher's best spots, the meeting between Pedro and Alinda is completely omitted, perhaps because of its questionable propriety. Curiously enough, however, Kemble retains one of Vanbrugh's coarse and most repellent additions — old Alphonso's vindictive remark about his daughter when he thinks he hears robbers coming through the forest: "That I had but the Strumpet here now, to find 'em a little Play while I may make my escape." It is obvious that in general Kemble's changes were motivated solely by his desire for tempo and brevity. That and his fastidious omission of indelicate lines really constitute his method in all his alterations.[27]

Following the production of *The Pilgrim*, which was no great success, the Drury Lane season rocked along comfortably enough. Kemble played frequently, continuing to please the town in such favorites as he had been acting for the past four years. On January 21, the night of Mrs. Siddons' benefit, Nahum Tate's hoary old version of *Lear*, "Not acted these Nine Years" according to the playbill, was resurrected. The great actress chose this piece, says Boaden, for the sole purpose of exhibiting her brother in the title-role. The performance was a triumph for Kemble. Later, after George III had relapsed into permanent insanity, the play was banned for years. But never again did Kemble attain the passion and terror of his early performance. Never again did the "grandeur" of his interpretation so nearly approach Michael Angelo.[28]

Mrs. Cowley's *Fate of Sparta*, a new play, had the advantage of being brought forward with both Kemble and Mrs. Siddons in the cast, but even so it was unsuccessful. In fact, one suspects sabotage when Boaden blandly observes that Kemble assumed the role of Cleombrotus "without being able to see in it what the fair writer intended should be there; and I think he never condescended to give the semblance of power where it strictly could not be found." He thought little enough of the short-lived tragedy to pen on the back of his playbill an epigram by William Parsons, one of Mrs. Cowley's Della Cruscan colleagues:

> Ingenious Cowley, when we view'd
> Of Sparta's Sons the lot severe,
> We caught the Spartan's Fortitude,
> And saw their Woes without a Tear.[29]

Shortly after his own benefit, *Jane Shore*, on March 13, Kemble took part in another dolorous contemporary piece — this time Bertie Greatheed's *Regent*. When the fashionable author's play was produced on March 28 the *haute monde* was out in full regalia at Drury Lane. Bertie, a precocious Della Cruscan and a great friend of Mrs. Siddons, was a well-known and inane young man in London society. He had "considerable genius — is dashing — self-sufficient, and utterly without taste." Even though the role of Manuel was designed especially for showing off Kemble — "in all probability" it was "fashioned by his advice" — the play failed to please the *cognoscenti*. Even Mrs. Piozzi's epilogue failed to please. The vicious William Gifford lashed out with his wonted ferocity:

The plot of it was childish, the conduct absurd, the language unintelligible, the thoughts false and confused, the metaphors incongruous, the general style groveling and base, and to sum up all in a word, the whole piece the most execrable abortion of stupidity that ever disgraced the stage.

Even the pallid Henry Siddons, fortunately less agitated than Gifford, decided that "the poetry seems to be all its merit." [30]

The season was drawing to a close. On April 30, following *Much Ado about Nothing* in which Kemble played Benedick for the first time, the audience had the privilege of hearing the young tragedian recite, "by particular Desire," his old declamation of the York days, Collins' "Ode to the Passions." The last important appearance that Kemble made was on the fifth of May, when he and his sister played in Dryden's *All for Love*, which they followed by both appearing in the boisterous afterpiece, *Catharine and Petruchio*. The performance drew such a crowd to Drury Lane that "Nine Rows of the Pit were added to the Boxes — so that there were but five Rows left for the Pit audiences. A circumstance never known before." So Kemble himself noted on the back of the playbill.[31]

Drury Lane closed late, on June 13, and Kemble undertook his regular summer tour to the hinterlands. In July, he wrote Malone from Ireland that "never was a town so empty as Dublin is now, since Marc Anthony was left alone in the market-place with the air which was uncivilly tempted also to forsake him." But theatrically things are good:

The *Count of Narbonne*, however, brought all the country round into the play-house, and will be acted to another crowded theatre, I dare say, again on Saturday. The ragamuffishness of the players, and the filthy meanness of everything behind the scenes (I don't know how I can say scenes, when there are none) of the *New Theatre Royal* surprises [sic] even me, who lived two years at Smock Alley, in which I thought was reasonably good idleness, drunkenness, and dirt.

Dublin had undergone physical improvement since the old

days; "the lights," reported the young actor in amazement, "are as regularly sustained by night as they are in London." His benefit came to the surprisingly large total of £140, and when he moved on to rejoin his old manager, Tate Wilkinson, in York, he proved to be "all in all — and all in every Part." But by the time he got to Leeds and Wakefield, he was too ill to act, and the latter part of the summer found him eager to return to London. Changes were afoot at Drury Lane, and Kemble probably knew that it was important for him to be on hand for any promotion that might come his way. The autumn would find him capping his brief London career by becoming manager of the theatre where Garrick had ruled the English stage for a quarter of a century. In five seasons, the almost unknown youth from the provinces had risen from obscurity to fame, and the season ahead would virtually inaugurate and ratify the Kemble dynasty that was to dominate the London stage until the rise of Edmund Kean.[32]

CHAPTER V

Drest In a Little Brief Authority

Bad Plays are best descry'd by showing good:
Sit silent then, that my pleas'd Soul may see
A judging Audience once, and worthy me.

JOHN DRYDEN

A BLACK PALL hung over the opening of the new season.
Sheridan, much more to be seen at Westminster Hall
than at Drury Lane, was too engrossed in politics to do more
than clean the theatre's treasury of all he could lay his hands
on; King, the popular actor-manager, felt too aged and care-
worn to subsist longer on Sheri's blandishments; financially
and artistically Drury Lane was in the most precarious condition it had been in since the 'forties, when Garrick had
stepped in to rehabilitate it. Even after the plays had begun,
both the public and the press sensed something was afoot:
rumors of upheavals were rife. Presently the lid blew off.
Poor old King, on October 8, several weeks after leaving the
theatre in disgust, made clear to all the world his intolerable
position at Drury Lane. "I have been called to account," he
explained bitterly in the press, "by Ladies and Gentlemen,
authors of various dramatic pieces, for breach of promise in
the non-performance of works which I never heard of —
arraigned for rejecting performers with whom I had no power
to treat — and censured for the very limited number of Pieces
produced, which it was not any part of my province to provide." The full extent of Sheridan's caprice and laxness was
made all too clear, and King's lamentation was from the

heart, hearty: He could not pass on new plays; he could neither hire nor discharge actors; indeed, he could not on his own authority, "command the cleaning of a coat, or adding, by way of decoration, a yard of copper lace: both of which, it must be allowed, were often much wanted." [1]

The upshot of the sorry business was that King incontinently threw up the management, and Drury Lane was left to the tender ministrations of the chief patentee, Richard Brinsley Sheridan. Inevitably conditions became indescribably bad, and the papers, with a great show of divine guidance, declared majestically that if something were not done, the result would be "injurious." Meanwhile the town buzzed with gossip: some had it that King would continue if his salary were raised, some that Wroughton was to succeed to the managership, and some that the brilliant young tragedian, John Philip Kemble, was to be the next victim of Sheri's inefficiency. Soon the die was cast, and on September 23, 1788, Kemble recorded in his journal what must have been proud words to him: "This day I undertook the Management of D. L. Theatre." Although the post was an ungrateful one, it carried distinction. In Kemble's hands, it was to carry more than it ever had before. In general the public was pleased. Naturally, it was hinted in certain quarters that Mrs. Siddons had not been without influence in her brother's promotion. One gentleman, with complete inaccuracy, prognosticated that because of Kemble's "placid and diffident nature" the new regime at Drury Lane would be "characterized by the benign and gentle virtues." In point of fact, there was not any appreciable change of policy immediately. Kemble produced his first play, *The Jealous Wife*, on September 25, to a house of £169 11s.,*

* A word about Kemble's journal: as soon as he became manager of Drury Lane, he made it his practice to record in his day-book the play and the receipts for each performance, together with such comments and personal matters as might occur to him. Covering twenty-seven

and for a week or so did little acting himself. Of course, the
gossip-mongers were abroad. Kemble was Sheri's dupe;
Kemble's position would be even more humiliating than
King's; Kemble had slyly maneuvered against King. "The
ambition, the spleen, and the rapacity" which have been
declared characteristic of all theatrical people, past and present, were not absent on this occasion. Presently King himself
came to the rescue of his successor, and effectually silenced
the jealous coterie yelping around Kemble's heels: "the
Gentleman who succeeds to my unenviable office, whatever
it may be called," had always been his friend and faithful
colleague. Not only had he not jockeyed King out of office;
he was not appointed to the managership until King had,
"most peremptorily, renounced my situation." And a few
days later, in the *Morning Post*, Kemble himself declared:
"No humiliation degrades my services to those who do me the
honour to employ me." Moreover — and this is a revelation
— the conditions of his contract, contrary to public opinion,
were "perfectly satisfactory to my own feelings, and entirely
adequate to the liberal encouragement of Poets, or Performers, and to the conduct of the whole business of the Theatre." [2]

However politic this may have been, it was scarcely true.
Although Kemble was commonly thought, as time went by,
to be "invested with absolute tragic sway" — Sir Walter Scott,
who should have known better, thought the "whole dramatic
business" was in his hands — he was, in point of fact, still
under Sheridan's thumb. Boaden, his intimate friend and
biographer, was positive that he could do nothing without

---

years of his professional life — the last entry is for June 6, 1815 — the
journal is an invaluable commentary and source-book for dramatic
affairs of the period. It is now in four octavo volumes in the British
Museum (Ad. MSS 31,972–31,975). I have used it extensively in tracing Kemble's managerial career, and the citations which will follow
represent a hitherto unexploited body of facts.

Sheri's express permission, and as we shall have occasion to
see, many was the time poor Kemble, groaning in the spirit,
was compelled to produce and even act in plays which his
master had brought forward. Although he became a great
man and a power in things theatrical, for the next fourteen
years, until in desperation he left Sheridan forever, Kemble
was to be subjected to the financial irresponsibility and exasperating carelessness of the autocratic, domineering patentee.
One might almost say, as Leigh Hunt did of Byron's connection with Old Drury, that "he got nothing by it but petty
vexations and a good deal of scandal." [3]

But in the first glow of satisfaction at his new post, Kemble
must have been happy. His company was strong: Suett,
Bannister, Parsons, Palmer, Aickin, Barrymore led the men
and Siddons, Crouch, Farren, Pope, Jordan were the admired
and beloved (often the latter) of all London. His salary was
good, for almost sixty pounds a week (when it was paid)
represented solid comfort for old Roger's son. The bustling
new manager soon made his presence felt around Drury Lane.
Nothing was too insignificant to come to his attention; he
was determined to strike a valiant blow, in so far as he was
able, for the restoration of great drama, carefully and authen-
tically produced. "It is a *literal* and *positive* fact," reported
one scandalized play-goer, "that not a *Lady's petticoat* is
trimmed without first consulting Mr. Kemble." He studied
and tried to improve the unspeakably trivial afterpieces, much
to John Taylor's surprise; he undertook to coach young
Michael Kelly in the role of Macheath; he argued with actors
about acting as well as salary; he troubled himself to show a
neophyte how to walk across the stage properly; he even
organized theatrical drill-squads behind the scenes. All this
was mightily upsetting for the old hands at Drury Lane. Before Kemble's day, precision and discipline in the conduct of
the theatre were unknown: the miserable managers all took

their cue from the patentee. Rehearsals were negligible: during one, a few years before, "Lewes interrupted the performance to show one of the actors a paragraph in the newspapers — Mrs. Mattocks requested the Prompter to take good care of her, as she was very imperfect — and Miss Younge did not attend at all." The youthful new manager, however, was by way of being a martinet. Because he insisted on such essentials as promptness at rehearsals he gained a reputation for "uncommon asperity." Although his actors feared and respected him, they muttered behind his back at his "proud and imperious" manner. Kemble's friends were among the titled and the wealthy, never among his own profession. Indeed, he despised actors. Years later, when he was watching a performance of the Comédie Française backstage with the great Talma, Kemble was impressed to see one minor player carefully rehearsing a five-word speech, and when he returned to England he complained bitterly to Sir Walter Scott that there was none of this zealous artistry on the London stage: if a man does not have a leading part, he remarked, he does not take the trouble to play either carefully or well. As a young manager, he must have taken malicious delight in inaugurating one of his most conspicuous reforms: on his printed programs he billed his actors not according to their reputation or notoriety — in varying size of type — but to the rank of the role they played. In the fullness of time, Kemble the manager was to become almost synonymous with Kemble the actor. But to us, he has a larger claim to fame in the former role.[4]

After 1788 Kemble entered into the most active and enthusiastic period of his life. Young in years — he was only thirty-one — and comparatively naive in the devious ways of theatrical management, he exhibited during the next few seasons a fresh, ingratiating approach to his duties that was to disappear as he grew more worldly-wise. Later, his fame was to be ossified and secure; at the moment it was tentative, and the town itself was divided in its opinion of Drury Lane's new leader. One party looked to Kemble as the apostle of "reviving sense," the other as a chauvinist who would sacrifice the stage to the rising house of Kemble. And although the opposition never died out entirely, Kemble's reputation and prestige grew yearly more and more. As his methods became known and his aims manifest, the London audience, both pit and boxes, realized that here at last was the successor to Garrick — that another great man of the theatre had risen. In his first season as manager he not only signified his independence but also gave a foretaste of his future policy: the classics were supreme. Drury Lane, he told Boaden, did not want new plays: "the treasures of our ancient authors" were in his opinion "inexhaustible." Of course, "shewy afterpieces and laughable farces might be necessary, but what could be expected now in the way of the regular drama, that previously had not been better done?" The first month of the new season brought seven Shakespearian pieces, all starring Kemble. For the first time since he had been in London, he had virtually an open field for the heavy tragic roles: "Gentleman" Smith, his old rival, had decided to withdraw while his retreat could still be orderly, and King had retired in high dudgeon after his quarrel with Sheridan. Kemble could romp at will through the previously jealously cherished leading roles. His *Love for Love* (October 11) received "abundant applause," and the town could expect many more such sterling classics, reported the *World* breathlessly: "*Julius Caesar, Romeo and Juliet, Coriolanus, Plain Dealer* — are to come." Although *Richard III* got mixed reactions on the acting, its production was notable: "the arrangements of the Play looked like good *Management* — the Banners with the red and white Roses, were well — the Dresses were superb." [5]

Most of the flattering notices of Kemble's regime had been in the *World* — a hectic sheet whose dramatic criticism was from the pen of a certain Parson Este. The public knew Este to be a man of violent and unthoughtful tastes, and discounted his remarks accordingly. But when, writing of Kemble's Macbeth, he trumpeted that art "can go no further," that Kemble *"is better than Garrick,"* that "the Band were incomparable," then the more temperate *Morning Post*, shaking its angry locks, injected a note of caution. Kemble's Macbeth, it felt "bound to affirm," was not only "far, far remote from the excellence which Mr. Garrick displayed in that character, but much below the exhibition of Mr. Smith." Este shook off the rebuke with ease. The curious man, who seems at one time actually to have been a clergyman, was accustomed to criticism. He had, at Kemble's advent on the London scene, been a rhapsodic puffer of Henderson, and as such drubbed the new pretender unmercifully. But when Kemble assumed the lead in his profession, no one was more obsequious in his flattery than Este, and the actor, be it said, was singularly gullible in swallowing it. Other journalists had nothing but defamation for the parson: "an illiberal newspaper dealer in puzzling periods, and awkward and unmeaning attempts at wit and poignancy," declared the *Post* of his staccato, extravagant, and aposiopetic journalese. The *World*, whence issued a stream of encomia for Kemble, had been established by Major Edward Topham and Este after the parson had left the *Public Advertiser*. Before long the new sheet was carrying, in addition to absurdly laudatory notices of Kemble, poetical effusions by Robert Merry, Hannah Cowley, and other Della Cruscans. John Taylor has it that Kemble, who by this time was an intimate friend of Este, had sunk three hundred pounds in the paper — which may explain the sort of panegyric he was receiving. The press began making malodorous remarks about Kemble's "bigoted eenth-century conception of reality, we shall discover, was something quite remote from the devastating naturalism of the twentieth-century *Tobacco Road*. Kemble's approach to theatrical realism was charged with the contemporary enthusiasm for the antique, and it is curious to note that his famous realistic revivals were all of plays of a past conveniently remote. That he produced *Coriolanus* with some care to the sets and costumes is interesting; if he had pursued the same method for one of Holcroft's comedies he would have been a really significant precursor of Tom Robertson. Boaden — the admirable Boaden — dwells on his master's originality: the processions showed unmistakable evidence of Kemble research into the "picturesque." And although the money spent on the production would have "defrayed the demands during a whole season of any former management" the production was a success. Kemble played Cromwell, that he might have more time to supervise the preparations, but Mrs. Siddons, we learn from her brother's journal, was "supremely pathetick" as the Queen. The press was unanimous in its approval: Este was in ecstasy at the "classic propriety and attention to stage *minutiae*"; the *Post* marveled primly at the "considerable splendor" of the settings; the *Times* was gracious, but objected to the amount of chalk on the wigs. *Henry VIII* was a fillip to Kemble's career, and the public, awed by Siddons as much as the scenery, paid very handsomely for twelve performances.[8]

Kemble's life during his first year as director of Drury Lane, however, was not entirely taken up with such rewarding labors as the *Henry VIII* revival. He encountered, in addition to the inevitable hostility from certain gentlemen of the press, rather decided opposition from members of his own company. We have noticed his strict disciplinarian methods already; before the season was far advanced they had caused open revolt among the more temperamental ladies of the theatre. Mrs. Goodall, an actress who fancied herself Mrs. Jordan's rival as a comedienne, had been engaged from the Bath theatre, and after her successful debut as Rosalind (on October 22) she considered herself one of the privileged characters of the company. Kemble, as manager, had cast her for the role of Lady Anne in *Richard III*, a part she flatly refused to play. When she was fined five guineas for insubordination, she carried her grievances to the press, and the case became a *cause célèbre*. Although the *Morning Post* attacked Kemble vigorously for his "caprice" and dictatorial treatment of Mrs. Goodall, he fined her another five guineas on November 17 for refusing the role a second time, declaring "his determination of persisting to do so every time he appears in *Richard*, till she submits." At this point Mrs. Goodall's husband stepped into the fray by writing a defense of his wife; she had, according to him, been engaged solely for comedy, and her professional dignity was hurt when Kemble insolently suggested if the fines "aggrieved her, she had better withdraw herself from the theatre." The *Morning Post*, continuing to play up the story for all it was worth, reported on November 24 that if Kemble, as the rumor went, had discharged Mrs. Goodall for "refusing" demands beyond her contract, "we wish the aggressor in better hands than a London audience." Two days later, however, the uxorious Mr. Goodall reported that all difficulties had been removed "in every respect to my satisfaction," and the *Morning Post* blandly expressed its satisfaction at Kemble's "acceding to the demands of *Mr. Goodall* on the part of his wife." [9]

At this Kemble dropped his managerial reserve, stating his position in a strongly-worded letter to the paper that had made so much capital of the controversy. There had not been, he indignantly informed the public, the slightest "sacrifice of the laws and customs" of the theatre in the interests of the Goodalls. The manager's prerogative to allot any role to any actor is invulnerable, said the zealous young director, and the offending actress' fine "was levyed justly." Kemble denied having discharged Mrs. Goodall, but he admitted that he agreed with the lady's irate husband when he threatened her leaving the theatre that if she could not submit to "the Laws of the Community she was a member of, I thought it would be better she *should* leave at once." This, added the manager, "was my opinion then, and it is my opinion still."

The public must see that my duty to them, to the Proprietors, and to my Fellow Performers, places me in a very arduous situation; I cannot hope always to please every body, but I can promise never to wrong any.

Now this, it must be admitted, is a very handsome statement of the case, and the public was unanimous in acquitting Kemble of perfidy or unfair discrimination in his treatment of Mrs. Goodall. The actress stayed on at Drury Lane, agreeing to submit herself to the management, and Kemble's first bout as a manager proved to be a decisive victory. "If there ever was a doubt to the disadvantage of the Drury-lane Management," crowed the *World*, "it is now no more." [10]

Once the Goodall fracas was safely past, however, other disputes rose to take its place. Mrs. Crouch — all tender memories of those idyllic days in Ireland obviously forgotten — was barbarously fined five guineas for refusing to appear when she and Kemble "had a desperate quarrel concerning her clothes," and it was thought in certain quarters that the lovely singer was a wronged woman. More cosmic was the altercation with Mrs. Jordan. She was an enormously popular actress, and as mistress successively to some of the most important men in London — the number of her children places her "among the rank of those who are termed prolific females" — merited considerable respect in the theatre. When the lady's brother was summarily ejected from behind the scenes of Drury Lane and the poor door-keeper who let him in was fined five shillings, the uproar was tremendous. "Veritas" wrote the *Morning Post* a letter praising such judicious action. According to him, Kemble had even requested the great Siddons to stop coming behind the scenes unnecessarily, "as he was resolved that it should not be said that he allowed a freedom to his family which he refused to that of others." Mrs. Jordan had to submit on this occasion, for her brother (not even a member of the company) was clearly in the wrong to dispute the manager's sway backstage. But revenge was sweet. Since 1785, she had been making only twelve pounds a week, and the thirty pounds a performance Mrs. Siddons received was galling; the comedienne chose this time to demand an increase in salary. "There is at present a difference between the Managers of Drury Lane and Mrs. Jordan," reported the *Morning Post*, "and the subject, we understand, is a demand of an increase of salary." Poor Kemble was sadly harassed. "Great Quarrel with Miss Farren about her Dress," he noted in his journal on December 17; "she acted at last, however, for I w'd not change the Play for her Humour." Five days later occurs another melancholy entry: "Mrs. Jordan again fancied herself ill. I spent above Two Hours in coaxing her to act — N.B. She was as well as ever she was in her life, and stayed when she had done her Part to see the whole Pantomime." And on January 1, when she was scheduled to play in *The Wonder*, "Mrs. Jordan pretends to be ill again." The press was beginning to murmur at the actress' caprice, however:

It is supposed that the lady takes advantage of her popularity *to be ill when she pleases,* and has refused to perform in a farce when Mrs. Siddons performs in a play, and for this modest reason, "that *she* will not fill the house and let Mrs. Siddons run away with the reputation of it."

Mrs. Jordan, in a speech from the stage one evening, took the public into her confidence and denied such base motives,

but behind the scenes she did not relent in her nagging of
Kemble. Like Mrs. Charlotte Charke, another woman of
temperament, she would take "a *French Leave*" of the manager without "the least Patience or Consideration," and even
so "was idle enough to conceive" that she "had done a very
meritorious thing." [11]

Finally, however, Kemble had to give in, and her salary
was increased from twelve to thirty pounds a week — which,
in point of fact, was no more than Mrs. Jordan was worth to
the theatre. The irate actress had gone to Sheridan himself,
reported one chronicler, flaunting before him a flattering
offer she had received from Covent Garden and airing her
"grievances respecting the Kemble coterie." At this, the
patentee promptly ordered the increase in salary. Battered
and disillusioned from these civil broils, Kemble noted in his
journal a most important precept:

Always keep well with the leading Performers, particularly with
the Women, though they should be even unreasonably troublesome. By humouring half a dozen you uncontrolably command
three score.

It must have been from such encounters as those of his first
strenuous year that Kemble came to possess "the singular
faculty of persuading a person contrary to what he knew to
be his own interest, and yet of doing it in such a manner as
to preclude opposition." [12]

What with sumptuous revivals and intermittent warfare
with his temperamental subordinates, Kemble's winter was a
full one. In January, we learn from his journal, he assumed
new duties: "This day [January 1, 1789] I agreed to take the
Liverpool Theatre with Mr. F. Aickin for seven years. Our
Rent is to be 350 Pounds p. ann. We are only to use the
Theatre six months of the twelve, and are to pay down twelve
hundred Pounds for the Purchase of Wardrobe &c. Felix
sit! — " Although the bid of Kemble and his partner (who

was a well-known actor both in London and the provinces) was lower than several of their rivals, it was accepted by the Liverpool proprietors because both gentlemen were so well established in the profession. Under their management there was a "certainty of an improving stage." Liverpool was a fairly good town for the theatre, even if Kemble himself had been badly treated there in his salad days. He went to open his new theatre with what was generally conceded to be a very indifferent address, and Aickin stayed on as the resident manager. The venture did not prosper, however. Aickin was cordially disliked, and apparently Kemble troubled himself about the matter no further. Presently — we cannot be sure just when — the two retreated, no doubt having lost heavily on their investment.[13]

The season at London, meanwhile, was fairly uneventful. When the Honorable Mr. St. John's *Mary Queen of Scots* — how many bad plays have been written about this unfortunate lady? — proved a failure in spite of the polite applause from the author's socially prominent friends, Kemble was held accountable. St. John had acted badly at rehearsal: although enraged at what seemed Kemble's delay and lack of interest, he found himself unable to stoop to calling out such a low-bred person. Kemble, as usual, rose to the occasion. "You are a man whom I can turn out, and therefore I desire you will leave this place immediately." And though St. John flung himself off in high dudgeon, he returned to apologize. But such incidents were becoming fairly common; such was the life of a manager. Meanwhile, he continued to act, chiefly in a string of inconsequential comedies. *The Careless Husband* was revived for the first time in twenty years, and to close the season Kemble produced his own alteration of Charles Johnson's *Country Lasses* (1743). His version, called *The Farm House*, proved popular enough. The young manager obviously had a feeling for the theatre and for those old pieces — however negligible — that would go well in revival. His new effort, aided by a plot strongly reminiscent of *The Peaux' Stratagem*, was full of bustle and action and surprisingly good dialogue; it was welcomed by the London audiences and went through numerous editions, both English and American. With it, Kemble virtually closed his professional activities for the year.[14]

Naturally, there had been certain drawbacks to that first season. Kemble confessed to his journal that he was sorry his "luck was to commence Manager this Year — The Theatre laboured under great Disadvantages from frequent Indispositions of the Performers, from the uncommon Severity of the Winter, from the Concern all People took in his Majesty's Indisposition and from their loyal Joy for his Recovery. Long may he live! God everlastingly bless him, and us under him! — " But for all these petty vexations, things had turned out well enough, and Kemble could congratulate himself on his novitiate. A strict disciplinarian, he had naturally antagonized many people, some of whom were embarrassingly vocal. For example, a certain "Senex," early in the season, had spoken his mind without reserve on such subjects as "hired applause scattered through the Pit" and newfangled ideas in acting. I adjure you, he concluded earnestly, "not to poison the very sources of our amusement (as from your situation you may easily do) by disseminating your imperfections and false taste amongst the rising candidates for public favour." John Kemble, of course, was oblivious to such talk. In spite of opposition — some of it formidable and well organized, as in the Goodall and Jordan affairs — he had serenely pursued his way, maddeningly indifferent to his detractors. He had the great gift of preserving an intolerable detachment in the face of the most violent criticism, and it was to serve him well in the years ahead. But for the moment, his hopes were centered on his rising star. He had run the theatre as it

CHAPTER VI

A Man of Parts

Let us have another tankard, for, ah, how charming
a tankard looks when full.

OLIVER GOLDSMITH

O^N THE comfortable assurance of one early biographer of
Kemble's that for a half dozen years following his debut
as a manager there were in his career no "incidents or events
calculated to excite interest," we may perhaps take a chapter's
recess from listing performances at Drury Lane, and turn to
the more interesting duty of examining his non-professional
life. As any who has glanced, however cursorily, at the
diaries and memoirs of the period knows, John Kemble cut a
formidable figure in the brilliant Whig society at the turn of
the eighteenth century. The son of Roger Kemble, stroller,
very shortly became a personage in London: he knew the
people worth knowing, he got drunk with some of the bluest
blood in England, he consorted freely with the nobility at
their town and country houses. By the time he was established professionally the old prejudice against actors which
was echoed so colorfully by the Great Cham had largely
ceased to exist. "Players, Sir!" snorted Dr. Johnson; "I look
on them as no better than creatures set upon tables and joint-
stools to make faces and produce laughter, like dancing dogs."
But for thirty years Garrick moved gracefully and easily
among the titled and the wealthy, pleasing all but the most
unregenerate snobs. Walpole, it is true, thought him an
impertinent jackanapes: *"sur un assez bon ton* for a player,"

he sniffed when he found Davy dining with the Duke of
Grafton and the Lord and Lady Rochford. But Sterne (who
after all had most of his life been an obscure clergyman)
gratefully acknowledged that Garrick's friendship had set the
seal on his social career. Why, the great man, he wrote,
breathless with adoration, "pays me all & more honour than
I could look for. I dined with him to-day, & he has promised numbers of great People to carry me to dine w^{th}.
'em." [1]

Garrick unquestionably had wrought valiantly for the
emancipation of his profession, and by the time John Kemble
(who fondly thought himself the heir apparent and then
successor) arrived on the London scene his path was easier.
The king, Fox, Pitt, Burke — all the notables of the period —
flocked to the theatre; Lady Holland maintained her box in
state, and the Prince of Wales himself did not scruple to be
known as a boon companion of the acting gentry. Indeed, his
brother, the Duke of Clarence (one day to be William IV)
found in Mrs. Jordan one of his amiable and constant mistresses. Although Kemble was never knighted — that honor
was to be reserved for Henry Irving half a century and more
after the Regent had been delighted by Kemble's polished
gravity — no other actor "of any age or country (Garrick excepted) lived upon such intimate and equal terms with the
great." There was "such a natural patent of gentility about
him," explained Lady Morgan, "that the highest nobility of
the land gave way to it." From the flamboyant Mrs. Hester
Thrale Piozzi — those "kind charming Kembles" exclaimed
that accomplished butterfly — to the Regent himself, all the
great and near great of London's literary and social set came
to look on John Kemble as a peer, acceptable in Holland
House as well as at the Prince's own board. His house at
89 Great Russell Street — "it was a good, comfortable, substantial house" as Fanny Kemble remembered it — echoed

with the urbane conversation of the town's notables for nearly three decades.[2]

Kemble did not intrude his profession on his friends. As time passed, it was tacitly understood that he was the *pontifex maximus* of the stage, but he was accepted into high society as a gentleman. To those indelicate persons who talked shop with him away from the theatre, asking his opinion of a certain role or a certain passage, he always retorted — rather coldly, one fancies — "You must come and see me do it." His almost hieratical position, of course, accorded well with his status in "the most polished circles in literature and fashion." And as Boaden pointed out, his "reputation as a man passed beyond the circle of his friendships, and became a sort of public property." Although Leigh Hunt — between whom and Kemble no love was ever lost — had to report that the tragedian moved in the "truly best circles," Kemble in his moments of modesty called himself only a player, nothing more, as Dr. Johnson viciously observed, than "a fellow who exhibits himself for a shilling." Even the formidable Doctor, however, had a good word to say for the rising Kemble dynasty. When Mrs. Siddons, in her early London glory, visited the sick, unhappy old man, he reported that she "left nothing behind her to be censured or despised," and her brother, Mrs. Thrale was dutifully told, "pleases me very well." [3]

Dr. Johnson was not the first to be captivated by the inherent charm and dignity of the Kembles. In the early 'eighties, new to London, John had begun cultivating people of importance. Francis Twiss took a "strong interest" in him, and Mrs. Tickell (Sheridan's sister-in-law) found him "quite a gentleman." One is not surprised to learn that as early as 1788 the Duchess of Devonshire was dining and jesting with him at Sheri's, or that presently he was sitting down to the Prince of Wales' hospitable table at Carlton House. If

Kemble had not gone on the stage, thought an Edinburgh friend of his, his native talent and ambition would have taken him high in any other sphere. John Taylor, that incorrigible *bon vivant*, decided that under happier skies the actor would have become a great politician: he had spirit, fortune, liberality, style — in short, he was to the manner born. His friends came to include all the great names of the period. The Regent himself, who for all his sins did cultivate people worth cultivating, was not beneath learning from John Kemble. As King George IV he was fond of reminiscing about the friendship: he liked the young actor much — "he was one of my earliest friends" — and they were often together. Once, as it happened, the Royal Personage offered him a pinch of snuff, and when Kemble modestly refused, he was pressed: "Take some, pray; you will *obleege* me." And although the actor accepted, it was not before he had corrected the royal pronunciation. Which daring anecdote, when told by His Majesty with great geniality, had an "astonishing effect" on his listeners. But by then John Kemble was dead, and George IV was presently to go to his grave unwept, and it was all very long ago.[4]

Kemble was a stylist, on and off the stage. Once while walking with Charles Bannister, he gracefully dropped a coin into a beggar's hat. "It is not often I do these things, Bannister," he remarked, "but when I do them, it is with dignity." This dignity — some called it pride, some superciliousness — often annoyed people. Kemble, once established, did not seek out or welcome new acquaintances, and his shield of "courteous taciturnity" struck terror into many lesser hearts. You need not trouble yourself so much about saying harsh things to people, he told Northcote; "others never think of them afterwards." But his actors feared him and kept their distance, and even his non-professional friends did not intrude themselves. When young Thomas Campbell was presented to the great man he expected "little notice" from a person "so proverbially proud and reserved," but he was accorded the most charming civility — for all the world like Hamlet greeting Horatio. Sharp-tongued Samuel Rogers thought he "could make a fortune buying Kemble at other people's valuation and selling him at his own," but then Rogers never cared for Kemble (or asked him to his house again) after the actor, while drunk, had been tactless enough to tell him that *The Pleasures of Memory* was "faint, & a little womanish." Kemble had an unfortunate capacity for enraging people by his intolerable superiority and detachment. Once when he came outrageously late to a breakfast he "drawled out" a set of perfunctory excuses and blandly informed his host that he had already breakfasted. This was too much: "I have no doubt you have, and upon a *poached curtain-rod*, if I may judge from your manner and appearance." The waggish Michael Kelly was one of the few who could joke with Kemble about his gravity and forbidding decorum. "Come, Kemble," he would say to the aloof spectre at a cheerful gathering, "open thy ponderous and marble jaws, and give us your opinion." Coleridge was another who would not let himself be awed, even though he had a sort of "nondescript reverence" for the "quaint creature." It is Coleridge, in fact, who tells the fine story about Kemble at a great dinner party. He was holding forth in his customary pontifical manner when a lackey announced his carriage. He nodded, and continued his discourse, even though the message was respectfully whispered to him several times. At last the servant took matters in his own hands, and made bold to say that Mrs. Kemble had the "rheumatise" and could not wait for him. " 'Add ism!' dropped John, in a parenthesis, and proceeded quietly in his harangue." [5]

At the Kembles' one could meet such notables as Edmond Malone, Sheridan, Lord Abercorn, the Earl of Guilford —

the company was usually large and varied. Perhaps one night Lord Derby would escort the lovely Miss Farren (one day to be his wife) to her manager's *soirée*; the next evening might find Lord Barrymore — a "great friend" of the actor's — at his Great Russell Street house. Old friends, of course, were always welcome. Once Mrs. Inchbald took Godwin and Mary Wollstonecraft there for dinner, and the alarmingly radical philosopher always remembered the evening with delight because most of the conversation was about love. Kemble did not have many intimates in his profession. Bannister's "good sense and taste" appealed to him, and Suett (an old friend of the York days) was "very intimate" with his chief. The two frequently rode horseback together, even though Kemble did deplore the unsavory acquaintances Suett had among "the lower performers." Michael Kelly, if we may believe that genial wind-bag, lived for many years "in habits of the strictest intimacy" with the great man, being drawn to him by his "intellectual endowments" and the scope of his learning. As if Kelly were concerned with "intellectual endowments." Sheridan and Kemble, of course, were thrown much together, even if they were not David and Jonathan. The man of genius thought Kemble a dull dog of great industry; the actor looked upon his superior as an untrustworthy, unscrupulous time-server. True, Sheri admitted, Kemble was excellent in his way, but very "limited in his genius" — a Jesuit "in everything but *ability*." Many were the drinking bouts they had together, some of them amiable, some violent. On one occasion, Kemble, "who waxed majestic as he grew mellower," was so agitated by Sheri's taunts that he threw a decanter — the handiest weapon — at him. All was made well, however, and by the time the evening was over the two left "in perfect amity together." [6]

John Taylor, who knew the whole world, of course knew Kemble. For many years, he reminisced, he regularly dropped in on him each Sunday morning; when the two would meet during the week, Kemble would always enjoin Taylor to "remember the hebdomadal." Usually Kemble would be found in his study, deep in some play or theatrical document. "Sometimes he was cold, negligent, and less courteous than at others, and then feeling disgusted, I resolved to forbear my visit the next week, but the pleasure I always found in his company overcame my temporary spleen." Taylor, if we may trust the gossipy Farington, was not the affable martyr and faithful friend he himself would have us think. To his intimates he was accustomed to speak of Kemble "as not being a man of quick parts" and as a *"manufactured Actor"* — pronouncements quite unlike those absurdly laudatory poetical compliments he paid the actor. And Kemble, who never knew the perfidy, assured Taylor he "only wished He merited such a description" as he had given him in *The Stage*.[7]

There were, however, those great and good friends who were always loyal to Kemble. One of them was Walter Scott, whose capacity for friendship was not the least of his many gifts. Scott first met the actor at Lord Abercorn's villa near Stanmore, and for many years the two men, each so eminent in his own province and so dissimilar, were intimate. Their correspondence, especially in their later years, was spirited, and when Kemble was in Scotland he was frequently a guest under Scott's baronial roof. In those days Edinburgh was truly the Athens of the north: there Kemble mingled as freely with the brilliant Tories as he did with the more brilliant Whigs in London. John Ballantyne's place on the Firth of Forth, near Trinity, was a favorite rendezvous for visiting celebrities, and of course Kemble was well known there. Lord Abercorn's country house at Bentley Priory, "the resort of the most distinguished part of the fashionable world," welcomed Kemble as a frequent guest. Perhaps it was in the elegant company there that Scott delighted to hear Kemble and Mrs. Siddons unconsciously turn their casual conversation into blank verse, as when Mrs. Siddons imperiously told a servant, "You've brought me water, boy, — I asked for beer." [8]

One of the closest of all Kemble's high-born friends was Francis North, the fourth Earl of Guilford. This gentleman, a rather insipid aristocrat, among his other amiable foibles had a devotion to the theatre, and he was never so happy as when surrounded by a crowd of theatrical notables. Of course, Kemble was the high priest of the cult. The coterie was famous in its day — so much so, in fact, that His Majesty George III felt moved to voice his royal regret that a nobleman like North should see fit to squander his time "with Kemble, Jack Bannister, and such people." The Earl was a gay, irresponsible hedonist whose reputation among his peers was not of the best. "His *manière d'être*," complained Lord Glenbervie, "his prologues and epilogues, etc., the sort of society he lives in — young Colman, Kemble, etc., — give me the idea of the sort of person meant in the miscellanies of the seventeenth century when a prologue or copy of verses is described as written by a *person of honour*." Kemble, reported Sir Walter, lived in "close intimacy" with Francis North, and the lovely country home, Wroxton Abbey, was almost a second home to the actor weary of the bustle of the theatre. Often he and North, "witht. any other person present," would sit drinking "till 2 or 3 in the morng. and Kemble wd. continued to drink the whole time, till he was tipsy." Michael Kelly, another hanger-on in North's circle, recalled one gay house party at the Abbey when the Kembles and a "house full of visitors" staged an amateur performance of *The Mayor of Garratt*. Kemble, as stately as one might wish in a full wig, was the star of the evening. And at dinner afterwards, one of the guests, a courteous old gentleman from Banbury, remarked that although the impersonation was a good one, he had always thought Kemble's "powers lay more in the tragic than the comic line." Which observation brought more laughter than even the sight of John Kemble in a farce.[9]

Painters attracted John Kemble almost as much as noble lords. Thomas Lawrence, long before he acquired his later fame and wealth, was a friend of his, and as the two men grew old and celebrated together their intimacy increased. Unfortunately, Lawrence, one of the most devastating heartbreakers of the day, became engaged to Mrs. Siddons' daughter, Sarah — only to change his mind and ask for the hand of her sister, Maria. The odd request was granted, but Maria died before the wedding took place. On her deathbed, however, she exacted her sister's promise never to be Lawrence's wife. The unhappy Sarah (who seems pretty generally to have got the bad end of the bargain) promised, but she died soon afterwards herself. Although all intercourse between Lawrence and Mrs. Siddons was broken off by this melancholy imbroglio, Kemble continued his fast friend. And no friendship in history, observed John Taylor, "was more sincere and warm than that between the great painter and the great actor." Kemble was painted many times by Lawrence (even old Roger sat for a portrait), and after his death in Switzerland Priscilla wrote the president of the Royal Academy (as he was by that time) that "none stood higher" among those whom her husband loved. "He felt a pride in having a conviction that by your aid he should be remembered." [10]

Kemble's interest in painting and painters was lifelong. Even in his lean early days in London he seems to have subsidized, in a small way, some struggling artist, and he delighted in sending young Flaxman tickets for the theatre with a little note of congratulation "on the Figure he makes in the Exhibition." Later he became an intimate of Sir

Francis Bourgeois, and in the fulness of time he very tenderly attended that gentleman on his deathbed. Unhappily, there were occasional misunderstandings between them — as when Kemble, in his tactless way, quite readily confessed to Sir Francis that he considered Lawrence the first painter in the Kingdom. This, the offended artist testily replied, was a pronouncement which "He cd. not agree to." When Kemble called to placate him, Sir Francis very ostentatiously called to his servant, "that Kemble might hear him, that 'He was not at home.'" But when Thomas Holcroft dropped in on Bourgeois to see some of his portraits of Kemble, the artist spoke highly in praise of the actor's "sagacity, versatility or manner with different people, etc." At his death, Sir Francis left "a sum" to Kemble, as had Desenfans (who willed him a hundred pounds). Northcote, another of the many artists who painted Kemble, did not feel moved to distribute such *largesse* to his client. The harassed painter was trying to do a portrait of him as Richard III meeting the young princes, but Kemble, complained Northcote, made no effort whatever to get the proper expression. This was Kemble's way, consoled Boaden: "he never put himself to any exertion, except in his professional character." [11]

Boswell, in a characteristic letter describing with painful exactness a recent orgy of his, observed piously that "the drunken manners of this country are very bad." This melancholy truism is copiously illustrated by Kemble's own alcoholic career; no account of his progress through high society would be complete without a glance at his enormous reputation as a drinker. Englishmen, of course, have always drunk heavily, but John Kemble had the fortune — good or bad, as the case might be — to flourish in the most alcoholic era of British history. "More gout was manufactured," notes Sheridan's biographer ruefully, during the eighteenth century than at any other period of recorded time. And Kemble, from abundant indications, manufactured his share. Colley Cibber, wise in the foibles of nondescript actors, held it axiomatic that strong drink and good acting never went together. "The briskest loose liver or intemperate Man (though Morality were out of the question), can never arrive at the necessary Excellencies of a good or useful Actor." Kemble was a living refutation of this pronouncement. He drank early and he drank late, alone and in company, among the vegetable peddlers of Covent Garden or in the drawing-room of a duchess. But it was *de rigueur* in that age of prodigious drunkards — heroic in their endurance, herculean in their capacity — because, as a noble lord once put it, nobody ever "appeals to Kemble sober against Kemble tipsy — he is such an excellent fellow, and such a perfect gentleman." Even Sam Rogers, who could see no good in him, admitted that Kemble could be "very amusing" if he were drunk enough. Boaden, more delicately, suggested that liquor simply made him "utterly and mischievously ungovernable" — so much so, indeed, that he would even joke with his audiences.[12]

Because he drank with everyone, and because everyone wrote memoirs, Kemble's excesses have survived in a very diverting set of anecdotes. There is the one about his turning up at five one morning in a Covent Garden pub, "very much the worse for a late dinner party." In the subsequent argument with his partner in crime over the proper pronunciation of the word Coriolanus, his enthusiasm (even to breaking every glass in sight) amused everyone except mine host. Kemble's erudition in his drunkenness became proverbial. "When we have heard Kemble pour forth the treasures of his critical knowledge over a bottle," recollected Sir Walter, "we were irresistibly reminded of the author of Epicene giving law at the Mermaid or the Apollo." Returning home a bit the worse for Lord Abercorn's liquor one evening, Kemble was kept waiting for change at a toll-gate; the gate-keeper was surprised to be railed at, in the best Kemble manner, with "We seek no *change*; and, least of all, such *change* as he would bring us." Another time, he got very drunk at a dinner, and refused to leave with the other guests. "I see this is the last time I shall be invited to this house, so now, I will make the most of it." And he stayed until the next day, "the whole time lauding the classical drama, and attacking the *modern comedy*." [13]

Drinking bouts in those days were protracted undertakings. Lady Holland records quite casually in her journal a dinner party consisting of the Prince of Wales, Grey, the Duke of Norfolk, Lord Suffolk, Sheridan, and other celebrities: when the party began to break up at midnight, most of the gathering were only a "little gay," curiously enough, but before Sheri could take supper he first "lost his dinner." Michael Kelly tells of a session which included Kemble, the Earl of Guilford, the Marquis of Ormond, Sir Charles Bampfylde, Sir Francis Burdett, and several others. At five in the morning these stout-hearted gentlemen were reluctant to break up such a merry gathering so unseasonably. And another time, when Kemble and Colman were asked in for a few drinks by a gentlemen's club at Turnham Green (where the actor had a little summer place) the two guests sat drinking all night, long after their hosts had "gradually" withdrawn. Charles Incledon, the singer, was no mean drinker himself, and his greatest boast was that he could consume more Burgundy than the fabulous Kemble. For "eight whole hours" one night the two of them matched bottle for bottle without making any noticeable progress. Finally, Kemble suggested they resort to half-pint bumpers — a move which proved his undoing, for when he drained his first one, he fell under the table, and Incledon was left to crow in triumph, "Served up the governor, by —!" [14]

But John Kemble, like his contemporaries, did not confine

his heavy drinking to stag-parties. One time he appeared "half tipsy" at Lady Cork's when that great personage was presenting the beautiful Sydney Owenson to London society. Years after she became the wife of Sir Charles Morgan, the lovely Irish woman recalled that when the great actor was introduced to her he recognized her with a "kindly nod" and fixed on her a searching stare. At last, evidently impressed by the girl's coiffure, he reached over, "actually stuck his claws in my locks, and addressing me in the deepest sepulchral tones, asked — 'Little girl, where did you buy your wig?' " Kemble drunk, of course, was a very different person from Kemble sober. In his customary reserve he would sit for hours without condescending to speak a word, but once drunk he would leap from his chair, "swear he'll be a member of Parliament," and proceed to make an impassioned speech of the most "unintelligible nonsense." And having finished, sit down as pleased as punch. Generally his drunken maunderings took the form of self-praise. Nothing pleased him more, when drunk, than to point out his own merits. At one convivial gathering where he and Perry (of the *Morning Chronicle*) had a heated argument, he was presently driven to sniff, "A lion preys not on carcasses." As the quotation did not at the moment seem fitting to Perry, "serious hostilities" almost resulted. Happily the two champions were reconciled, however.[15]

One of the best anecdotes of Kemble drunk is John Taylor's. One night, returning late from an all-night party at Dr. Charles Burney's on the Hammersmith road, Kemble caught a ride to London on a fish-monger's wagon. He asked to be carried on to Billingsgate, and so well did he and the driver get on together that when they arrived at the fish market Kemble was unwilling to part with his new friend. A crowd gathered round to watch the antics of the famous man, who was recognized, and presently a certain Mr. Pearce,

"an eminent fish-monger," took Kemble in hand, offering to
show him the market. Kemble was charmed, and during the
whole tour of inspection kept the crowd vastly amused by his
"humorous sallies." When at last he thought it time to leave,
he requested, in addition to a coach, a turbot for Mrs. Kemble.
And as he drove off to the cheers of the assembled multitudes
he bowed with the greatest *éclat* to the right and then to the
left.[16]

Kemble's invitation to join the celebrated Beefsteak Club
signalized his ultimate acceptance as a *bon vivant* by the
drinking and roistering aristocracy of the town. The organization was venerable. As early as 1705 there was a club which,
according to William Chetwood, was composed of the "chief
Wits and great Men of the Nation." Dick Estcourt, to whose
conviviality Steele paid eloquent tribute, was the guiding
spirit of these early meetings, but it is not certain if they gave
rise to the Sublime Society of Beefsteaks which was founded
in 1735 by John Rich, then manager of Covent Garden. This
organization continued until 1867, and included among its
members many illustrious men: Hogarth, Theophilus Cibber,
Garrick, John Wilkes, George Colman, Samuel Johnson, the
Prince of Wales (later George IV), the Duke of Clarence, the
Duke of Sussex, and many more. The club was primarily an
eating organization, for many years meeting in Covent Garden
Theatre to grill steaks over the original grate furnished for
that purpose by John Rich. After the theatre burned in
1808 — when £1500 worth of fine wines belonging to the club
went up in flames along with Kemble's costumes and Händel's
scores — it moved its meetings to the Bedford Coffee House
and later (in 1830) to the Lyceum. Membership was restricted
to twenty-four chosen spirits, but the quota was raised to
twenty-five so that the Prince of Wales might be admitted.
The meetings were weekly, from November to June, on Sat-

urday, and the principal fare was steak and alcohol in various forms — porter, port, punch and whisky toddy.[17]

Members of the Sublime Society of Beefsteaks did not take up the weekly meetings with only the relatively pious pastime of eating. Most of the gentlemen were heavy drinkers, and sometimes the gatherings got even more heated than was to be expected. Once when Frederick Reynolds was a guest at such a session the political arguments became so violent that the resourceful visitor proposed a conciliatory toast "to prevent bloodshed." John Kemble, among such rioters, slipped frequently into temptation. He had often "sworn to forbear the juice of the grape beyond a pint," but when the company was merry and the wine good he could not keep to his resolution. He and the Duke of Norfolk, a colleague and cup-fellow in the club, were drawn together because of their extraordinary capacities — a point of mutual admiration. The Duke, at the close of a long night's drinking, would "become immoveable in his chair, as if deprived of all muscular animation." And then a solemn ceremony would occur: he would ring thrice, at which "four domestics" came pacing in with a litter swung from belts. This they would place under him and thus, "with a gentle swinging motion," bear him thence. "Upon these occasions, the Duke would say nothing; but the whole thing was managed with great system, and in perfect silence." [18]

Although Kemble drank much and often, he was always singularly high-minded and virtuous (save for one unfortunate lapse, the De Camp episode). Loose conversation, he told Mrs. Inchbald (of all people), is pardonable, "but nasty Conversation is always inexcusable — The former certainly offers very pleasing and alluring Ideas — the latter, in stead of soliciting the Imagination, presents it nothing but what is the Property of a fine Mind to turn from with Disgust and loathing." Disgust and loathing, however, had nothing to do with hard drinking. Even the virtuous Scott admitted that Kemble "was the only man who ever seduced him into very deep potations in his middle life," and he was not the only one of his willing victims. On one occasion Kemble burst into Dick Peake's house "half-cocked," claiming he had an engagement there with Sheridan. Peake (the treasurer of Drury Lane) asked him to take tea with him and his family, but Kemble demanded wine instead, on the pretext that he had "not had time to take my usual quantity today." The ladies discreetly retired, and Peake, Kemble, and William Dunn got " 'mortal drunk,' and all three fell fast asleep." But presently Kemble began his wonted boasting, talking long and vehemently about his peculiar excellencies and attacking his rivals. So the night wore away, and when the three roisterers awoke about eight the next morning, Kemble muttered something about Sheri never keeping his appointments. "Slapping his hat on his head," he stalked away.[19]

Kemble, like many a man before and since, often got belligerent after a few drinks. One night, following a lively party at Dr. Burney's, young Pryse Gordon offered to see the great man to his home. Just as the two revelers reached Covent Garden Kemble became suddenly pugnacious. "Staggering back a step or two, [he] said, 'who the d——l are you? I can walk without your assistance — do you imagine Sir, that I am drunk? I know nothing about you, Sir, but I will fight you on the spot, to show you I am as sober as you are.' " Poor Gordon's good offices as a guide were angrily spurned, and when he went on, alone, he left Kemble in the middle of the market haranguing a large crowd and challenging anyone in his hearing to step out like a man and fight.[20]

And so the anecdotes pile up — Kemble berating an audience while tipsy, Kemble undertaking to thrash two burly servants, Kemble drinking noble lords under their own tables. It is with a certain regret one learns of his reformation during the last years of his life. The ungodly will deplore the influence of Mrs. Priscilla Kemble on her husband, for she it was who brought the pressure to bear. John Taylor, with evident displeasure, tells of dining with them one night "not long before he quitted the stage." For old times' sake the guest called for his host to drink a glass of wine with him, only to be reminded very primly from the other end of the table that "Mr. Kemble does not drink wine." Such abstinence, Taylor was certain, "probably injured his health." By 1811, afflictions — headaches, asthma, and gout — had got so trying that he resolved to hear the chimes at midnight no longer. Lawrence was not impressed, however. Kemble had often quit before, "but when tempted has again drank wine." But as his life drew to a close, Kemble did succeed in reforming himself. His habits, indeed, became conspicuously "domestic." [21]

Relatively early in his career, John Kemble was accepted as the leader of his profession. As such, his social status was impregnable. His coldness, his polished ease among the highborn, his withering scorn of theatrical inferiors, his taste and capacity for liquor — all are as much a part of the glittering social tapestry of the day as Sam Roger's breakfasts and the Prince of Wales' troubles with Caroline. Kemble was a public figure, the intimate of the great and the gifted in almost every department of late eighteenth-century England. The fact that he carried over his aloofness and cold dignity into private life naturally made enemies for him. But his friends were numerous and loyal, and throughout a long and brilliant career he maintained with conspicuous ease the esteem of the most colorful people in a period of colorful personalities.

CHAPTER VII

Shakespeare Redivivus

[At a performance of Dryden's version of *The Tempest*:] All that afforded me any entertainment was looking at Mr. Thrale, who turned up his nose with an expression of contempt at the beginning of the performance, and never suffered it to return to its usual place till it was ended.

FANNY BURNEY

JOHN KEMBLE had learned many things in his first season of managing Drury Lane. He had learned that actresses would not hesitate to disrupt the whole schedule of a theatre simply because — like Miss Farren when she had refused to play in *The Careless Husband* — they did not like the costumes assigned them. He had learned to run a theatre even when he himself was "confined to my Bed for something like Gout in my Knee" and half the stars of the company were either disgruntled or ill. He had learned how to manipulate the huge Drury Lane troop of some ninety members to the best advantage against the other house — as when "Mrs. Siddons was so kind as to play in the Farce to give us Power against Covt. Garden, where Miss Walker appeared this day in Sigismunda." He had learned to be patient with Sheridan's maddening inefficiency. He had learned to bear himself calmly and to pursue his own methods in the face of virulent criticism.[1]

The season of 1788–1789 was of chief importance to Kemble, however, in settling once and for all his artistic aims and policies. For the rest of his career he was to pursue his calling along the lines laid down during the first season he managed Drury Lane. He was manifestly to cast his lot on the side of a formal, classical, tragic repertory in preference to gratifying the poor taste of the town with light comedies and spectacles. Boaden puts the matter quite bluntly, for a wonder: Kemble "saw that the elder dramatists alone afforded him sufficient scope, and he was too excellent a critic not to feel the palpable deficiency of the writers for the modern stage." It was this principle that guided him in establishing the Drury Lane repertory. In his official capacity, Kemble read each season between seventy-five and a hundred manuscripts submitted hopefully to Drury Lane for acting, and it was seldom that he voluntarily — without Sheridan's coercion — chose any of them for production. If a manager receives a manuscript from an unknown author, advises a certain satirical pamphlet directed at Kemble, he should "send it back, or throw it amongst your lumber; but be sure do not read it." The implication is a bit unfair, for Drury Lane's conscientious young manager read countless dull plays with admirable fortitude, even if he did refuse most of them. He was a severe critic, but a frank one, as a highly characteristic note to Prince Hoare shows:

My dear Hoare,

You have written a volume, very well I confess, where two words would have done your Business — If you have a Tragedy send it to me, — If I can act it, I will — If I can't, I shall tell you so frankly — and so no more from yours truly.

J. P. KEMBLE [2]

Disappointed authors, languishing for a kindly nod from hard-hearted managers, were numerous. The poor playwright, as one sympathetic person put it, is compelled

to dance Attendance for two or three Years together; they [the managers] refer him to one, then to another, so to a third, till

they have run the whole round with him, and then dismiss him
with an, *It won't do*; when they have already plunder'd it of all
that was either new or well express'd, to dress up their own
Collections.

A manager, explained one critic, should be "thoroughly acquainted with the doctrines of dramatic poems, in order to
be able to speak to the purpose with such gentlemen as offer
him pieces for representation, and to support his opinion
either in favour of, or against them." Kemble frankly preferred acting Shakespeare to anything else. He could not take
comfort, reading through stacks of negligible comedies, in
Dorlent's reflection that bad playwrights had to "follow their
copy, the age," and he ruthlessly rejected most of the pieces
submitted to him.[3]

It is interesting to read Kemble's comments on the plays
produced under his direction during his first season as manager of Drury Lane. The empty, inane spectacle of Garrick's
celebrated *Jubilee* did not impress him; it "is very expensive,
very troublesome," he found. "I shall not repeat this experiment." *False Appearances*, though a fairly successful comedy,
merited nothing but his scorn. "It is a poor thing, as most of
the French Comedies are." Audience reaction meant less
than nothing to the classically-minded young idealist. Cumberland's *Impostors* was also "a poor thing; but received no
mark of Disapprobation from the Audience." Such an expensive production as the troublesome St. John's *Mary Queen of
Scots* failed to impress its unsympathetic director: "Mrs.
Siddons was dressed with extreme Propriety and Effect. All
the witty leaders of the Opposition and all the Beauties of
the Party supported this Play, from Regard for the Author,
but John Bull will never think it a good one." The change
of tone in speaking of the rather unsuccessful revival of
Coriolanus is striking. "This Play was very splendidly ornamented — Mrs. Siddons was prodigiously admired, and it was

said that I never acted better. The whole Play was greatly applauded." Such comments pretty plainly show what was in store for London audiences — traditional heavy tragedy, produced according to John Kemble's ideas of propriety and accuracy. That he could so influence popular taste as to make it coincide with his own was not his least notable achievement.[4]

Kemble's second season as Drury Lane's manager was handicapped from the start. The incomparable Siddons, vexed with a great deal of nagging journalistic criticism and with Sheridan's protean subterfuges for paying her salary, stalked like an avenging goddess from the boards, vowing to return no more. Her loss to her brother's tragic repertory was of course incalculable, but he set to work with a will to produce worthy drama. *Henry V* was the big revival of the fall, and like *Henry VIII* the year before it was another studiously prepared exhibition piece. The text was cut to tatters — or, in Boaden's more kindly words, Kemble meditated on what "could be cut out in the representation to the habits of the audience, or a little favouring the powers of his actors." As he had treated Fletcher's *Pilgrim* (whose emendations we have examined in some detail), so he treated Shakespeare. There were always certain enlightened persons, of course, who considered such free handling of Shakespeare barbarous. The national poet, jeered Fielding, "is already good enough for people of taste," but he "must be alter'd to the palates of those who have none." And Hazlitt, one is happy to find, thought current treatments of Shakespeare "a disgrace to the English stage." But these were voices crying in the wilderness. Although all of George III's subjects did not share their monarch's enlightenment — "Is there not here sad stuff? — What? — what?" he inquired concerning Shakespeare — they did not care to take the Bard neat, without a chaser. To play *Othello* unexpurgated, explained one righteous critic, would commit "such a

violence on the modesty and decency of the house as is altogether intolerable." And Kemble himself considered Colley
Cibber's almost unrecognizable version of *Richard III* "admirable." It remained for foreigners like Ludwig Tieck to
marvel at the castrated Shakespeare Englishmen hankered
after.[5]

Mr. Harold Child, in a penetrating essay, has observed that
Kemble saw the Shakespearian corpus "as rather flabby material upon which a form *must* be imposed. He wanted, as we
should say now, to 'stylize' it — it having no particular style
of its own." This, I think, is the key to understanding
Kemble's very free omissions, rearrangements, bowdlerizings,
and even verbal alterations of a poet whom he professed to
adore. 'Poet' is probably the wrong word here. For Kemble's
purposes, Shakespeare was first and last a playwright — a
very gifted but still rather crude playwright whose works
had to be rigorously reworked for presentation on the sacred
boards of Drury Lane. His alterations, "more or less material,
as modern manners might happen to require," were all made
with an eye to that *leitmotif* of the eighteenth century, 'regularity.' The action must be swift, compressed, and cogent;
the diction must be free from any taint of obscenity. Kemble
consistently tried to work Shakespeare into a "form which
the educated people of his time would admit to be shapely
and polite and 'classical.' " There are, remarked Sneer, two
houses preserved in the midst of a "luxurious and dissipated
age" where at least "the conversation was always moral . . .
if not entertaining," and Dangle ruefully confessed this to be
true.

Now, egad, I think the worst alteration is in the nicety of the
audience. — No double entendre, no smart innuendo admitted;
even Vanbrugh and Congreve obliged to undergo a bungling
reformation.[6]

For all his heavy declamation and his own leisurely paced
style of acting, Kemble had a real feeling for the theatre. His

love of processions and costume and elaborate setting was more than a personal taste; it was a gesture of deference to the spectacle-loving audiences of the late eighteenth century. He visualized a play as he read it, translating the words into stage-effect and action. A play, he said frankly,

a play is written on some event, for the purpose of being acted; and plays are so inseparable from the notion of action, that, in reading them, our Reflection, necessarily bodying forth the carriage which it conceives the various characters would sustain on the stage, becomes its own theatre, and gratifies itself with an ideal representation of the piece.

Kemble was peculiarly at liberty in making his alterations. In addition to his really excellent feeling for the theatre, he was oppressed by no remorse in shuffling Shakespeare about to suit his own convenience. "A critical eye," he blandly told a fellow-member of the Beefsteak Club, could easily discern that all Shakespeare's historical plays except *Richard III* and *Henry VIII* — "which were unquestionably and exclusively his own" — showed marks of careless writing and extensive collaboration. *King John*, for example, was obviously a "patch-work of this kind," largely the effort of another writer. A person of such easy scruples would not hesitate, of course, in cutting out "very judiciously, every word offensive to Ophelia's delicacy." [7]

It is curious to think that Kemble's contemporaries accepted him as the high-priest of Shakespeare. He became, naturally, the official voice of the national poet — the arbiter, *par excellence*, of Shakespeare on the stage. His conception and interpretation of the plays were imposed on an entire generation of play-goers — play-goers comfortably oblivious, for the most part, of well-established texts and authenticated readings. No man, praised one critic,

no man has studied Shakspeare more critically — none more happily conceives him. Proud as this country must be of Shakspeare, it is justly proud of him who embodies all his finest images, and supplies, by the most delicate touches of art and taste, those various meanings he has not in terms expressed. — While England venerates SHAKSPEARE, it must cherish KEMBLE.[8]

For the most part, posterity has not held such a flattering opinion of Kemble's labors in behalf of Shakespeare. Edward Fitzgerald quite baldly told Fanny Kemble that one would not profit greatly by studying the tragedian's alterations, "unless in seeing what pains your noble Uncle took with his Calling." But Mr. Odell, taking a long perspective of the matter, confesses that "it is with something like reverence that one approaches the name of John Kemble, certainly the first great 'producer' of Shakespeare on the English stage." One cannot, certainly, cavil at Kemble's attainments as a producer and exponent of Shakespeare; it is simply the questionable freedom he allowed himself that causes modern critics to think with Hazlitt that such representations were "barbarous." Indeed, Mr. Bernard Shaw believes that managers still follow the eighteenth-century tradition of mangling the original "by a process which no doubt presents itself to the adapter's mind as one of masterly amelioration, but which must necessarily be mainly one of debasement and mutilation whenever, as occasionally happens, the adapter is inferior to the author." Mr. Thomas Lounsbury, exposed to an unfortunately large number of eighteenth-century versions of the national poet, reluctantly admitted that some of Kemble's alterations appeared "even viler" than Garrick's *Hamlet*. When we remember that Kemble played *Lear* in a *mélange* of Nahum Tate and Thomson, and *Richard III* in Cibber's monstrous (if theatrically effective) redaction, we tend to agree in his harsh pronouncement.[9]

The *Henry V* revival, which has led us into such a long digression, was a great success in the early fall of 1789. Boaden, of course, was vastly impressed by Kemble's portrayal of the title role; not even his famed Coriolanus, he thought, "exceeded his 'royal Hal.' " There were, of course, those who murmured against such heavy tragic repertory. "The Managers [of Drury Lane]," complained one critic, "seem industrious to find out dramatic Poets, who are unacquainted with actual incidents and never delineate the People we live with." The charge, of course, could apply as well to some of the more unsuccessful modern tragedies that Kemble (reluctantly, one thinks) brought forward from time to time as well as to a historical play that had not been seen in London for twenty years. Another querulous observer pointed out that "little pains have been taken to secure the public applause" at Drury Lane. Mrs. Siddons, like Achilles, was sulking in her tent, and Mrs. Jordan, expecting her confinement, was sorely missed. "Mr. Kemble," the caustic writer went on, "seems to think that the exhibition of his own person, on all occasions, however ill adapted to display it to advantage, can alone afford an adequate compensation for the absence of superior performers." [10]

Although the season progressed comfortably enough with the standard repertory, Kemble himself was concentrating on revivals — always more and more revivals. *The Tempest* he tried to make "prodigiously attractive." After all, it had paid well ever since the Restoration redactors first bludgeoned it into an opera. Shadwell's version, according to John Downes, had so impressed the town with its "flying away" scenes and its elaborate machines "that not any succeeding Opera got more Money." Kemble, as it happened, went to Dryden's alteration, and virtually duplicated that gentleman's operatic *mélange*. Purcell's music was retained, and Linley warbled sweetly the additional airs provided by Arne. The plot, in Kemble's hands, becomes incredibly trashy. The ridiculous plot of Hippolyto and Dorinda provided the vulgar amorosity Shakespeare failed to give, and the poet's language is stripped to enough dialogue to articulate the action. Everywhere are songs: where the original was lacking in this commodity, the want has been supplied by such tuneful ditties as "Arise, ye terrors of the storm," tastefully rendered by a group of storm demons. Kemble had the good taste, at least, to omit Dryden's elaborate masque-like close with Neptune, Aeolus, and sea-nymphs; instead, Prospero's ineffably tender lines, "These our actors," are shifted to the very end of the play, following a "Quartetto and chorus" rendition of "Where the bee sucks, there suck I." [11]

The monstrosity pleased the town — after all, virtually the same piece had *been* pleasing the town for more than a century — and Kemble noted gleefully in his journal that the production "was recd. with great Applause — Miss Farren and Mr Moody acted inimitably — Mr Kelly and Mrs. Crouch considerably aided the success of the piece — and General Burgoyne's Epilogue gave a fine close to it." These ladies, by the by, who played Miranda and Dorinda, were garbed "in white ornamented with spotted furs; coral beads adorned their heads, necks and arms." [12]

The revival of Vanbrugh's *False Friend*, not in such spectacular bad taste, was a failure: remove the obscenity and you remove the wit, explained one judicious critic. Kemble himself was dissatisfied with the production: "I thought this Play wd. have been more diverting than it proved." And when, at the second (and last) performance the house came to only £136, the play was withdrawn. "I shall play this Comedy no more — Miss Farren does not like her Part, and acts abominably." After this, things seemed to go badly at Drury Lane. In November, William Hayley's *Marcella* was ignominiously dropped after a single performance — but with a reason. Harris, at Covent Garden, had been preparing ostentatiously to make the piece one of the season's chief offerings, and when the news got to Drury Lane Sheridan and Kemble combined resources to forestall their rival. A copy of the play was got —

perhaps pirated at rehearsal — and after the most meager preparation, given a ludicrously bad production. *Marcella* would, they hoped, be ruined for Harris (although, as it happened, he went ahead and produced it successfully). Of course, there was a roar of indignation from the opposition. Hayley, the harassed author, called on Kemble to demand an explanation, and got one of a sort. "My adventures in this business would furnish some good scenes for a comedy," he recollected in a more mellow mood; "but they concluded with a very full, candid, and flattering apology, which put me into perfect good humour with this great theatrical offender." Managers then as now lived largely by their wits in a highly competitive profession: Lady Holland was amused when Sheridan told her that "formerly" the two great theatres regularly sent their lackeys to hiss new plays at the other house.[13]

Kemble's hopeful string of Shakespearian revivals for the mid-winter proved fairly unexciting, sandwiched as they were among the innumerable performances of a prodigious hit, Cobb's *Haunted Tower*. The amazing popularity of this trivial spectacle, we may imagine, did little to console the ardent manager for the failure of *The Two Gentlemen of Verona*. The critics were beginning to mutter at Kemble's resurrecting pieces so "deservedly consigned to oblivion," and even he realized his error in this instance: "A very ineffectual Play, and I am sorry I ever took the Trouble to revive it. N.B. It was very ill acted into the Bargain. There was a fine Scene of a Wood in Act 5th."[14]

Four days after the unfortunate revival, Kemble had to leave London suddenly. The year before he had sent his youngest (and favorite) brother, Charles, to Douay for training in the English College which he himself attended twenty years before. Report of the boy's being seriously ill came to Kemble, and he immediately set off for France. But the expedition ended happily. Kemble "was sitting alone in his carriage, reading," when he saw another coach approaching. As the two passed, "he raised his eyes from the book, and exclaimed, 'Charles!' The meeting was quite theatrical." The reunion took place "a little on this Side of St. Omer," and as Charles was "far better" than Kemble had expected to find him, the two returned to England immediately. By the twenty-fifth of January, the actor was able to record that "today I reached London after my Travels!" [15]

Back at Drury Lane, however, things were going none too well. Mrs. Jordan, having borne her third child to her current lover, Richard Ford, had returned to the theatre demanding special privileges relating to what the papers gleefuly called the "conjunction copulative." Mrs. Siddons, of course, was not acting, and the exasperating Jordan was determined to have extraordinary billing, with her name set off in splendid isolation by the "conjunction copulative," thus:

And
The Romp by Mrs. Jordan.

Kemble unwillingly acceded to her demands, and underwent even more galling concessions by hiring her brother — the troublesome gentleman whom he had peremptorily ordered out from behind the scenes the year before — as a Sebastian to Mrs. Jordan's Viola. The lady's triumph, after the altercations of the previous season, must have been sweet.[16]

The early spring was enlivened by a popular revival of Mrs. Behn's merrily licentious comedy, *The Rover*. It is curious that Kemble, who so unblushingly emasculated Shakespeare in order not to offend the delicate virgins of his audiences, should have chosen such a suggestive play for alteration. So proper a critic as Mr. Montague Summers has commended the piece for "its verve, bustle and wit, utterly defiant of the modest Josephs and qualmy prudes who censured these lively scenes." The Divine Astrea, in point of fact, impressed even her contemporaries by her unladylike frankness. Pope commented wittily on how fairly she put all her characters to bed, and Sir Richard Steele, noticing the number of assignations in *The Rover* — "above once every Act" — thought it "not wholly unnatural; for, they say, the Men Authors draw themselves in their chief Characters, and the Women-Writers may be allowed the same Liberty." Mrs. Behn herself, in her prologue, had impudently implied that her play was "stuff'd with Wits, and with Debauches." In all her work the lady had, as has been recently said, but one theme, and that was sex.[17]

Kemble's version, as we might expect, retains only the skeletal outline of Mrs. Behn's lively comedy; all of Astrea's bustling bawdiness is omitted, and the result, naturally, does not represent an improvement on the delightful original. Some of the alterations are amusingly insignificant. "Youthful Itch" becomes "youthful longing," and "lovely Virgin's heart" is changed by the righteous Kemble into "lovely girl's heart." Mrs. Behn's bold "Pox on't" turns up as "Plague on't" in Kemble's version; "the Rogue is stark mad for a Wench" becomes transformed to "the fellow is certainly stark mad"; and even the stage direction, "Enter *Willmore* drunk" is purified into "Enter *Willmore*, a little drunk." Some of Kemble's alterations, of course, are more drastic. Mrs. Behn's open bawdiness is converted into romantic wooing, and some of the slower parts of the original are given decided impetus by Kemble's ruthless excisions. Although the sprightly Astrea might not have recognized her play — the title itself was changed to *Love in Many Masks* — it was, in Kemble's hands, still a humorous, well-paced comedy, even without the witty obscenity of the original dialogue. The town in general liked it mightily, although one critic suggested that the union of Kemble's "formal Pegasus" and Mrs.

Behn's "frolicsome muse" was for all the world like the off-spring of a cart-horse and a blood-mare. The young manager himself was delighted with the production, as well he might have been, for it served him faithfully for many years, both at Drury Lane and in the provinces. Young William Hazlitt, aged thirteen, was taken the following summer to Liverpool to see the great star from London in this very play, and he liked Kemble better on that occasion than he ever did again.[18]

At the close of the season Kemble's account was in good order. His successful revivals — *Henry V*, *The Tempest*, and *Love in Many Masks* — had been relatively inexpensive, and had offset the string of failures in the mid-winter. And also *The Haunted Tower* was not only paying its way but the rest of the repertory's as well. After his first year as manager, Kemble calculated the receipts as £29,644 7s. 6d., but after his second, the books showed a gross income for Drury Lane of £32,750 1s. Sheridan's new manager, his acting, and his revivals were obviously succeeding.[19]

CHAPTER VIII

A Manager's Woes

> Man never hath one day of entire peace from the things of the world, but either something troubles him, or nothing satisfies him, or his very fulness swells and makes him breathe short upon his bed.
>
> JEREMY TAYLOR

OLD DRURY was getting older; everywhere there was talk of its rebuilding, but, as was pointed out, like London Bridge it still stood. With the new season (1790–1791), however, Sheridan had made up his mind on a new theatre. The house which had been built by Wren and immortalized by Garrick opened its last round of performances with so trivial a thing as *The Haunted Tower*. London audiences, like the lackey in Shadwell, loved "Dramas, and Trumpets, and much ranting, roaring, hissing and fretting, and good store of noise in a Play." King, who had been nursing his grievances for two years, was back once more with the company; and John Palmer, after his unfortunate attempt at bucking patent houses with the Royalty Theatre, returned sheepishly to the fold. Kemble himself was quiescent during the early fall: he hauled out such former successes as *Henry V* and *The Tempest*, but he contented himself for the most part with such mellow stock-pieces as *Richard III* and *As You Like It*. The autumn was filled with vexation. For one thing, the Duke of Cumberland, brother to the King, died on September 18, and the Marquis of Salisbury, as Lord Chamberlain, immediately closed all the theatres until after the funeral. During the enforced idleness, however, the John Kembles enjoyed their social gadding. One night it would be a staid party at Sir Joshua Reynolds', in company with such decorous esthetes as the Misses Boswell, their brother, Malone, Jephson, and Dr. Blagdon. The next evening Kemble would spend with Malone, examining curious theatrical arcana until all hours. And then there came a two-day house-party "at Signor Piozzi's at Streatham" (shades of Dr. Johnson!). On this particular occasion, Kemble left the gay party there — the Greatheeds, Mrs. Siddons, Cecilia Thrale, "an ex. jesuit," and other socialites — to return to town for a dinner with Horne Tooke, Dr. Burney, Arthur Murphy, and Dr. Pearson. When the theatre opened again, however, it was to find things going none too well. During the first week in November, receipts averaged only £150 a night, a condition that seemed to the manager "not to be favourable to the Theatre." *The Rivals*, yet another remnant of the previous season, was dug up again with fair success. But Parsons was ill and Baddeley refused to act David — which bit of insubordination caused Kemble to note ominously in his journal, "I will not forget him." [1]

The *prime donne* of Drury Lane were being extraordinarily wilfull and capricious, in addition to everything else. On the fifteenth of September, for example, Miss Farren had announced that she positively would not appear in *The Heiress*. Kemble and Parson Este, his man Friday, immediately called on the obdurate lady, only to be told her salary must be raised from eighteen to twenty pounds a week. The poor manager, hardened to such incidents, assured her that Sheridan was out of town, and that he himself had no power to make such an advance, but he begged her not to "distress the Affairs of the Theatre by refusing to act the next night — After about two Hours Entreaty she consented to perform the ensuing Evening." Later, when Kemble broached the subject to Sheridan, he flatly refused to raise her salary, and the manager had the delicate task of relaying this information to Miss Farren. But she took the matter with surprising calm, only remarking that "if she could not have her wish she could not; that she was not a Person to squabble for a Pound or two a week, but that Mr. Sheridan would some time or other be sorry for his Refusal." [2]

Rather more serious was the periodic dispute with Mrs. Dorothy Jordan. Her salary had been ten pounds a night when she acted — which was three times a week when the theatre was open six evenings, twice when it was open less than six — in addition to one benefit at the usual charges. But the lady thought her popularity warranted better pay, and she demanded thirty pounds a week (whether she acted or not), two benefits (which she assured Kemble had been promised her by Sheridan), and the immediate engagement of her brother (at two pounds a week). "I agreed to engage her Brother," records Kemble rather wearily, "though I had no use for him." He also capitulated on the matter of the benefits, in view of Sheridan's promise, but he refused to provide Mrs. Jordan a salary when she did not act — which was often, as a result of her very frequent confinements. She did not insist on this last point, and Kemble left her in apparently good spirits. Later she wrote him requesting his written approbation of her brother's engagement, prompt payment of her salary, and guarantee of not being waited on by Mrs. Crouch's dresser. All unsuspecting, he sent her a note, readily agreeing on these points. And here the plot thickened. Armed with this written proof of the manager's concessions, Mrs. Jordan told Sheridan that Kemble had promised her *two* benefits. The patentee, naturally, was enraged at such presumption, and for a while things looked bad for the young manager. Kemble, when he learned of Mrs. Jordan's duplicity, was thoroughly frightened. If Sheridan, he reflected

later, "had not honoured me with his good opinion and Belief, I might have fallen into disgrace for ever." But as soon
as the manager and the patentee compared notes, the full
enormity of Mrs. Jordan's transgression came to light. "Finding I had defeated her Plot," Kemble explained,

and disappointed her Hopes, she boldly declared I had broke my
Word with her, and produced my Letter to prove to the World
that I had agreed to her Proposals; but she never ventured to show
the Copy of the Proposals themselves to which I had agreed; for
that very Copy would have proclaimed her Falsehood, and entirely justified me in the Eyes of every body — I am only surprised,
for she is capable of anything, that she did not forge a Note with
contents moulded to her own Purpose, and affirm it was that to
which I had subscribed. Under that Fraud I must have sunk. My
own Carelessness had put me in her Power, I confess, but Fortune,
who takes Care of Fools, does not forsake me — I was firm to my
Resolution, in spite of my Danger, which I really trembled at.

Such were theatrical politics in those parlous days.[3]

One of the most melancholy events in this melancholy
season was Kemble's assumption of the role of Charles Surface. He had been playing stock comic parts — Valentine,
Benedick, Orlando, Doricourt — for several seasons, but without conspicuous success. A natural tragedian, Kemble had
no aptitude whatever for comedy. No man, thought one
contemporary, was "less adapted physically or morally" for
the lighter roles, and "Anthony Pasquin" decided that he
overthrew the very "axioms of glee." Sheridan, however, was
"sufficiently lunatic" to let him attempt Charles Surface, and
the young manager set about preparing for the role with his
customary care. Taylor called one day to find him "sitting
in his great chair with his nightcap on," hard at work on the
play. When the jovial guest pointed out that Charles was a
"gay, free, spirited, convivial fellow," Kemble argued for his
fundamental seriousness on the grounds of his being a "gentleman." And so the grave, decorous Kemble — "merry as a

funeral, and as lively as an elephant" — disported himself as Sir Oliver Surface's heir to the malicious glee of the town. The performance came to assume legendary proportions for its complete lack of merit, although at the time it merely distressed the more sensitive theatre-goers. Kemble hoped against hope that it had succeeded, very primly thanking the audience (in his journal) "for the encouraging Applause they honoured me with." To his brother Charles, Kemble spoke freely. Thanking him for his kindly congratulations on the performance, he goes on to say:

I will study to deserve more: your knowledge of the style will induce you to believe me, when I say I was horribly frightened, and will persuade you to attribute some of my awkwardness of manner and defects of voice to my embarrassment. . . . I have much, very much, at stake on my success in this delightful comedy.

The cast was a good one — King as Sir Peter, Palmer as Joseph Surface, and Miss Farren as Lady Teazle — and Sheridan had the grace to tell the manager that he had "entirely executed his design." Other critics, however were not so kind. There had been those actors, like Garrick, who could be as great in Lear as in Abel Drugger — Sterne had marveled at such versatility — but Kemble was not among them. "His adoption of Charles [Surface]," explained one gentleman, "is undoubtedly his own choice; he, therefore, has no reason to complain of the Managers for endangering his reputation, by putting him in characters that are not appropriate to his abilities." The crowning indignity, perhaps, came when Kemble, having insulted a gentleman on the street one night while drunk, offered the next day to make any restitution that might be required. He was told — and it is greatly to his credit that he related the story on himself — that he would oblige all London very much by withdrawing from the role of Charles Surface.[4]

The spring was largely taken up with numberless performances of the new operatic spectacle — only the names are different. This year it was *The Siege of Belgrade,* and its interminable run was only briefly disturbed when Kemble persuaded his great sister to act once a week for him (at the handsome fee of £500). Once the opera settled into its long spring run, the manager hied himself to Bath in company with Thomas Linley. There the two London celebrities were much in evidence — at the theatre, at the Pump Room, and in society. One night it would be a dinner at "Mr. Simond's a Surgeon — his Wife is a great Naturalist — Shells, &c. — and talks learnedly," and the next an elegant gathering at Dr. Whalley's, the great and good friend of Mrs. Siddons. When Kemble did return to London for his benefit, it brought, he records gleefully in his journal, "the greatest House that ever was Known" — a gross of £412 6s. And although he was ill — because of "shining too brightly, and wasting the Oyl in the Lamp" at Bath, thought Mrs. Piozzi — he was presently back in society again. Of course, there was much dining out to wind up the spring social season. At Charles Andrews' one night, in such high company as the Duke of Leeds and Lord Dudley, "some of us staid till near eight in the Morning — Andrews wished us at the Devil." More decorous was the evening at Miss Farren's, where the aging Horace Walpole was told that young Kemble "shone in Othello." The theatre, it appears, was the least of its manager's concerns. One evening there was a near riot because part of the audience objected to the rain pouring in through the ventilators, but when Kemble "most elegantly exemplified" his managerial tact by coming forward and putting things to right, all went well again. Apart from that, and from falling off a ladder in his "Book-room" so that Barrymore had to substitute as Orlando for him, Kemble passed the close of the season without incident. Although the year had been a dull one artistically, the receipts continued to leap upwards: this season had brought £39,264 9s. to Drury Lane, or almost ten thousand pounds more than during his first year of management.[5]

The summer brought even further altercations with Mrs. Jordan. The Kembles happened to be in York during August, and as luck would have it, the temperamental actress was filling an engagement with Tate Wilkinson. Owing to a series of misunderstandings and the maddening apathy of the local audiences, Mrs. Jordan, true to form, broke her contract with poor old Tate, and declared she would never set foot on the York stage again. Wilkinson, late at night, went seeking Kemble, who was staying as a guest in the home of Mr. Wilson, the mayor, loitering in his old haunts before joining his brother Stephen's company at Newcastle. After much discussion, the great London celebrity agreed to act as a favor to Tate during the week of August 16 if Mrs. Jordan would go down and help Stephen during the assizes. But with the famed Kemble parsimony, he demanded thirty guineas instead of the thirty pounds promised Mrs. Jordan. Wilkinson — always in some such predicament — reluctantly met the terms of his old protégé, and the next day posted bills announcing the substitution.[6]

The following evening, however, when Kemble and his wife were dining with the Wilkinsons, the actor blandly announced to his host that "without any impeachment of their friendship, as he trusted, he was bound to tell him that he had reflected on the engagement he had made, which his understanding told him was a very foolish one, and that he would act on *shares* on the Tuesday [in *Othello*], or not at all; for unless he got 160 *l.* in the week, it was not worth his while to play there." Wilkinson, naturally, was outraged at such an imposition, and "the parties separated equally obstinate." Finally, about one o'clock the next day, to the relief of the whole town, Kemble agreed to stand by the original terms, and he acted *Othello* that night to a huge house. His conduct was unscrupulous, of course, but it was no more than a country manager might expect from a great London star. Poor provincial players resented fiercely the guest appearances of such celebrities "upon very exorbitant terms, to the certain ruin and discomfiture of the country actor, who has toiled for months in his vocation on a miserable stipend, and whose hopes were ultimately fixed on a benefit." It is pleasant to record, however, that Mrs. Jordan came out badly at Newcastle, and left the north of England with a profound distaste for its boorish and unappreciative audiences.[7]

Back in London, the fall season opened in the worst possible way — with a riot. The old theatre in Drury Lane was finally abandoned, preparatory to building a new one, and the company moved, "at enormous expence," to the Haymarket for the winter. In the advertisements, the manager was careful to point out this "great and unavoidable increase of expence," and even affixed an affidavit from the treasurer showing an £11,000 addition in operating costs for the new location — all serving as an excuse for the raise in prices of admission, the boxes to six shillings, the pit to three and six, and the gallery to two shillings. Oddly enough, there was no objection to these new rates. The *Morning Post* thought the public should "cheerfully accede" to them, and the *Public Advertiser* commended the management highly on its forthright explanation for the increase. "Such an alteration would, *prima facie*, have revolted the public mind; but on a fair consideration of its justice, it will be evident that the matter could not have proved otherwise."[8]

The riot came about otherwise. For one thing, the night of the opening, September 22, the doors were not opened at the hour announced, and when the "immense" crowd surged in, there was "hurry, bustle, and confusion" in seating it. Such turmoil "occasioned much disgust among the audience," which immediately began shouting for an explanation.

About *fifty* persons out of *four thousand*, which the house must
have contained, began to hiss and call for the Manager before
the commencement of the Prelude. — When the Curtain rose, the
efforts made to silence the disorder increased the clamour to such
a degree that little of the Dialogue could be heard.

Palmer and Parsons vainly tried to speak the prologue, and
finally Kemble himself, "very urgently called for," came
forward. He "stood the fire well," and when a paper listing
the grievances at such inconsiderable delay was handed him
from the pit, promised to remedy such bad management. At
length, the performance was allowed to continue. The prologue, a piece which proved to be highly popular, was *Poor
Old Drury*, and the much admired *Haunted Tower* followed it.[9]

The season quickly settled down to its dull mediocrity.
"All goes well," reported Mrs. Piozzi gratefully; the entrance
and exits were clearly marked, for which concession the public
was willing to pay the new prices. Although nothing of the
slightest consequence was acted for a month — *Poor Old Drury*
was the staple item — the house was making money. When
Kemble brought forth his annual string of Shakespearian
pieces in November, they were as enthusiastically received as
ever. Mrs. Jordan, as usual, was a trouble-maker, cutting so
many of her scheduled appearances that her public began to
tire of the lady's caprice, and on one occasion staged a near
riot. The papers took up the cry and roundly vilified her, and
not until she had publicly apologized from the stage and in-
serted a humble note in the press was she forgiven: "Nothing,"
she wailed, "can be more cruel and unfounded than the insinuation" that she feigned illness when she had no better reason for missing a performance. Kemble himself was having
difficulties, of a rather more intimate variety. The town was
amused to read one day in December that a certain gentleman
named Fisher had brought charges of assault against the actor

at King's Bench, Guildhall. It was the old story, of course: Kemble had been uproariously drunk. One night in November, it transpired, he had dined convivially with a gentleman in Covent Garden, and when the two emerged in a very mellow state they fell into an altercation with one of the numerous grocers that operated in the Piazza. Kemble was, as usual, truculently drunk, and when the conversation got so heated that he was given the lie by Fisher, he instantly knocked that worthy merchant down. In the *mêlée* that followed, all the combatants were bustled off to the "Watch-house" by the constabulary. Fisher, of course, had a good case, reinforced by his attorney who contented himself with stating the facts and demanding £20 damages. Mr. Erskine, Kemble's attorney, built the defense by dwelling on the actor's pre-eminence in his profession. The court was not impressed, however: Fisher got his twenty pounds, Kemble got a stiff rebuke from Lord Kenyon, the presiding judge, and the town got a laugh from its staid classicist engaging in such a plebeian brawl. Certain newspapers felt moved to advise Kemble "to besot his talents no more." [10]

Artaxerxes was the money-maker of the season, and when the public tired of its spectacle Kemble obligingly resurrected Garrick's *Cymon* to take its place. Garrick had had the good sense to admit that the play's "Plot, Wit, Humour, Language" were negligible, but it was flashy, and would serve. Kemble, always the perfectionist, took as much care in the preparation of these trifles as in his important revivals. On one occasion, working on a projected pantomime, he made elaborate sketches and plans for the *décorateur* to follow: "The banners, *Anglo-Saxon, Dane, Saxon Line restored,* and *Norman,* should be very large, and the words upon them in silver, as that will be seen better, I think, than gold: — these banners, Rollo, Plantagenet, York, Tudor, Stuart, and Brunswick, should be smaller; these banners I call specific: let all be of a very beautiful form, and very richly ornamented. . . . You will observe there are no arms borne in England before Richard I., and then I give every king his arms and motto on shields of shapes proper to the times." *Cymon*, elaborately got up, and adorned with such stars as Michael Kelly and Mrs. Crouch, took the town by storm — especially with the splendid pageant at the close, in which two knights jousted on live horses. Such was drama in 1794.[11]

Kemble's private troubles seemed to increase. When he forbade orders at the theatre, for the first time, some of the actors almost rioted — "but I quieted them." By the end of the week, all necks were bowed. "I heard no more objections," was Kemble's bland comment in his journal, "and now exercise the Right of admitting or forbidding orders peaceably. This comes of Revolution." There were always bad plays to produce at Sheridan's instigation. Miss Brand's *Huniades* failed dismally once, was withdrawn and reworked and produced again (as *Agamunda*), and finally was given over for good — even though too much money had been spent on new costumes and sets for it. "Miserable Play!" snorted the disgusted Kemble. Another brawl — every week brought a new one — occurred when "Tyrant" Aickin fancied himself insulted by Kemble at rehearsal. He straightway issued a challenge — he always had "the trick of calling for pistols upon any real or imaginary grievance" — and Kemble, almost as if to oblige him, for he could "easily have avoided" the encounter, readily accepted. That night the two of them acted together, and early the next morning, "in a field near Marybone," they met. Kemble, with his customary good breeding, suggested that since Aickin was the aggrieved he should fire first, but this was refused; and when "Tyrant" proposed they fire together, Kemble demurred because he had come out for Aickin's satisfaction. At "conduct so honourable," the aggressor became unnerved: three times he raised his pistol to take aim, and three times he dropped his arm again. Kemble, understandably exhausting his gallantry, asked "For God's sake" why did Aickin not shoot — whereupon he *did*, and missed. After Kemble had fired his gun in the air, both parties were "perfectly" satisfied, and returned to town in the greatest good spirits.[12]

The spring was enlivened by much social activity as well as dueling. In March there came a dinner invitation from the Prince of Wales. "I believe," observed the delighted recipient, "I should call it a Command." During Passion Week, when the theatres were closed, the Kembles rusticated with the Twisses at Calton, near Norwich, but they were back in town again for the innumerable dinner parties of the late spring. Sir Joshua was fond of having a few friends in, and Sheridan entertained lavishly — although he himself most frequently was delayed at the House of Commons until long after dinner. But nothing could be more characteristic of Sheri than to fill his house with people and fail to appear himself. The season finally wore itself out, rather unsuccessfully, as it happened, for receipts had fallen off almost seven thousand pounds from the year before. The move to the Haymarket had been costly and inconvenient, and during the early fall the house had to be shared with the Italian Opera troop. Although Kemble and his sister had stalked through their usual repertory in the spring, the year had not been brilliant artistically. Everyone was marking time until the opening of the new theatre — which was a-building.[13]

In the north, where he toured during the summer, Kemble met his customary acclaim. In Edinburgh, there was one youth — Tom Cooper, a friend of Godwin's — that was so impressed he instantly resolved to go on the stage. Kemble was his proverbial icy self, however. When the poor boy came, by appointment, to read for him, he learned that the great man had been compelled to go to Leith. And when he finally did get to act before Kemble, he was immediately called aside and told he would never do, being too impassioned. But Douglas (the part that Cooper was reading) was a man of very strong anger, he pointed out. "Certainly," sniffed Kemble, "but he was angry with good manners." Nothing could serve better as a clue to Kemble's own style than this. Cooper was kept on, however, on a "shaking foundation," until he completely muffled an important curtain-line at Newcastle. Then the axe fell, and fell speedily. Not for nothing was Kemble known as a terror to his actors.[14]

Kemble was, of course, back in London for the opening of the new season. An astute man of the theatre by now, he had weathered ten seasons at Drury Lane, and there was little he did not know about theatrical tactics. For example, when Covent Garden opened with raised prices and stirred up a riot, the wily Kemble had his house act out of sequence "to divide the Covt. Garden Rioters, if possible." And he was able to record that "the Riot was totally quell'd to-night." Some of the lessons taught him by hard experience in running Drury Lane were neatly set forth in his memorandum; quaint as they are, they are interesting in showing the minute attention Kemble gave to every department of the huge organization under his direction:

Always take Care to have a Singer of the Deepest Bass; no matter how he speaks; the Gallery loves a Rumble — The elder Mr. Banister [*sic*] no Actor — great Favourite.

Never let an old Actor of Merit want an Engagement on any Account — It is the true Interest of the Stage. Monopoly not to suffer the Publick that there is not Room enough for every body at the two Theatres.

Little Children have a very pleasing Effect in Pantomimes, Processions, &c.

Always keep well with the leading Performers, particularly with the Women, though they should be ever so unreasonably troublesome. By humouring half a dozen you uncontrolably command three score.

There are one hundred thirty-six Lights in the Front of Covent

Garden Theatre, and seventy-two in the Front of Drury-Lane Theatre.

Whenever there is Danger of a Riot, always act an Opera; for Musick drowns the noise of Opposition.[15]

These scraps of information were useful at the time, for the new Drury Lane playhouse was under construction, and already plans were being made for the company's triumphant return to its old location. Kemble, of course, was fascinated by the proceedings; on occasion, he passed the whole day watching the workmen, suggesting "various improvements," and he had even taken the trouble to be present when the first stone was laid. "There was," he remarked a bit dolefully, "hardly anybody there except Mr. Johnson the Machinist, who put some Coins under it." To his journal he again confided some of his ideas for the new theatre:

Grooves all of one Height — five Cuts in each Groove.
Three Green-rooms as near the Stage as may be.
Seats in the Pit an Inch higher than those in Opera-house.
There should be at least three Entrances into the Pit.
The Bottom of the Stage should not be circular but in a strait [sic] line.

It was Sheri's quixotic idea to put into the new stage a plank from the old one — which Garrick had so notably trod. Plans for the new theatre had called for £140,000, and Sheridan, with his customary insouciant charm, had talked three hundred people into buying debentures of £500 each. Somebody's scheme it was to incorporate shops into the new building (to provide more income, of course), but characteristically the plans went askew. Moreover, the architect exceeded the estimated costs. And to crown it all, £31,500 was suddenly called for — to secure Sheri's title to Drury Lane, of all things. After he had secured his impressive list of subscribers, he learned that there was no patent for Drury Lane — that highly necessary document having got through a curious mischance into the hands of Harris, the proprietor of Covent Garden. The subscribers, of course, refused to put any money into such a shaky establishment as a royal theatre without a patent, and poor Sheridan had to pay Harris heavily to get the charter back. Under such difficulties was the new Drury Lane being built.[16]

The season, meanwhile, was ambling along in a most uninteresting manner. Kemble, perhaps because of the confusion over the patent, was thoroughly disgusted with Sheridan and "greatly annoyed in his management." For the past season or so, opera had almost monopolized the activities of the theatre, and Kemble's cherished tragedies had assumed a very subsidiary position to such well-paying, though inane, spectacles as *The Haunted Tower* and *The Siege of Belgrade*. The "musical junto" — Kelly, Mrs. Crouch, and their colleagues — were great personal favorites of Sheridan's, and "constituted no inferior power to that of the manager." All in all, Kemble was "with the greatest difficulty induced to retain his situation," but he kept his patience and bided his time, no doubt hoping for better days when the elegant new Drury Lane should be opened under his direction. The fall season of 1792 was singularly dull until Mrs. Siddons put in her appearance just before Christmas. This, naturally, was the cue for a string of revivals of her best parts, and the mid-winter saw the two stately tragedians going through most of their celebrated roles. The production was elaborate, the costuming rich, the acting perfect in its way.[17]

The almost unbroken succession of high tragedies played in the grand style was interrupted by occasional disturbances. *Cymon*, so successful the season before, was produced again, live horses and all:

The procession is certainly the most splendid spectacle we ever witnessed; three beautiful white horses were introduced in the tournament; and considering it was their first appearance, performed extremely well: when the banner of France appeared, a universal hiss with the cry of Off, off was heard from every part of the house.

Such anti-Gallic demonstrations were called forth, of course, by the turn of events during the Terror in Paris. It was, in fact, this very night of the brave procession in *Cymon* that Kemble announced from the stage that out of deference for the martyred king of France the theatre would be closed the next night. Sheridan, out of town at the time, was "highly incensed" at his manager's presumption in taking matters in his own hands; it was, he indignantly told his subordinate, not his policy to introduce "politics into the theatre." [18]

For another thing, Mrs. Jordan was causing trouble again. In January, she wrote Sheridan that, although she was drawing a salary, her appearances at the theatre were far too few — a result, she implied, of Kemble's enmity towards her. I am, she complained, "totally at a loss to account for the conduct of the manager in any other way than his *continued disinclination* to let me appear in any new character whatever." Sheridan, eager to placate his star comedienne, took her part against Kemble, and a new piece by a Miss Culbertson, *Anna*, was suggested as a vehicle for the languishing Jordan. This, flatly announced Kemble, was "an outrageous insult to his authority," and he threatened to resign if concessions were made to the actress. "Disputes ran very high" over the production, but Mrs. Jordan, as usual, had her way, and the play was acted. It was a dismal failure, and when given out for a second performance "a considerable part of the crowded House strongly objected." Kemble, gratified at the result, declared that it was a "wretched play," and, he added contemptuously, "suffer'd only one Night." He was, he noted in his journal, "very averse" to Mrs. Jordan's acting it, "and a fine Quarrel we had about it." [19]

Except for performances of *All in the Wrong*, with King as Sir John Restless, Kemble as Beverley, and Mrs. Jordan as Lady Restless, and *The Fair Penitent*, with Kemble and Mrs. Siddons, the manager acted little more during the last of the season. It had been a good one for him, in spite of its slow start. The long string of tragedies, in which he and his sister had been kept so busy during the winter, was the most extensive acting he had done in several years. Apparently, London welcomed such plays as much as the musical spectacles of the previous seasons, for the 1792–1793 receipts reached the stupendous total of £51,659 6s. Kemble himself was becoming a relatively wealthy man from his acting. His salary for a hundred and ninety-one nights' performing was £541 3s. 6d.; he received £500 as manager; and there was another £200 in lieu of a benefit.[20]

For the early part of the 1793–1794 season Drury Lane offered no performances. The new playhouse was being completed during the winter. On March 12 there had been a prodigious concert of sacred music, but it was not until spring that the company began acting in its new home. April 21 was a gala night for the theatre-goers of London. An audience "the most numerous and elegant that we have ever witnessed in any place of public resort" thronged into the handsome new theatre to see Kemble and his sister act *Macbeth*. Had the ghost of Garrick frequented the old haunts between the Strand and Longacre Street, it would not have recognized the theatre. Almost twice as large, the new Drury Lane was equipped with such modern contrivances as an iron curtain and a water-tank for fire protection; the pit was flanked by eight boxes on either side, above which were two more rows of boxes and two galleries — to say nothing of the elegant new boxes on the sides of the stage. And everywhere were cut-glass chandeliers: the whole huge auditorium, marveled young Robert Southey, was lighted as if by the sun at noon.

The era of the massive theatre was launched, and the harmful effects on the drama would be hard to over-estimate. Spectacle and ranting, more than ever, would now take the place of Garrick's delicate and intimate finesse.[21]

"The public tell you they like small theatres," snorted Kemble; "Sir, they Lie; they like large theatres." Cibber, whose feeling for the theatre is always impressive, thought different about the new Haymarket that was opened in 1705; in that building, large for its day, "almost every proper Quality and Convenience of a good Theatre had been sacrificed or neglected to shew the Spectator a vast triumphal Piece of Architecture!" He should have seen Sheridan's new house. The stage itself required scenery thirty-four feet high and forty-two feet wide, "so that an entire suite of new scenes was essential on great occasions." Forward-looking persons even then realized that such monstrous theatres as the new Drury Lane boded ill for the drama: everything to be made broader, more obvious, more gross. Farce supplants comedy, mourned Southey, and tragedy becomes a thing of "processions, pageants, battles and explosions." But the larger the theatre, the more people could be crowded into it. Boaden was in raptures over the possibilities: the four tiers of boxes would hold 1828 persons, the pit, 800, the two-shilling gallery 675, and the shilling gallery 308, "making a grand total of 3611 persons, who, if they all paid, sent no less sum than 826 *l.* 6 *s.* into the treasury, for one night's amusement." After all, a theatre in which the dome itself was "positively at the height of fifty-six feet and a half from its floor" was worth crowing about.[22]

It was appropriate that *Macbeth*, which Kemble considered "the finest tragedy that has ever been written," should be chosen to open the new palace. The manager himself spoke the prologue written by Major-General Fitzpatrick, dedicating the theatre to the honor of Shakespeare — with some variety allowed:

> Some licence temper'd judgment will permit,
> To Congreve's, Wycherley's, or Vanbrugh's wit;
> Nor, for an ill-timed ribald jest, refuse
> A tear to Otway's, or to Southern's, Muse.

Miss Farren was assigned the honor of delivering Colman's epilogue, the burden of which was Drury Lane's invulnerability against fire, what with an iron curtain and a water-tank.[23]

For the opening, Kemble devised his own fresh version of *Macbeth*, drawing heavily on earlier alterations. "It is humbly hoped," he wrote, "that in this Edition of Macbeth the omission of two or three short passages, and the Introduction of a few Lines written by Mr. Garrick, will meet the same allowance with which the Publick has received Sir William Davenant's Additions to this sublime Tragedy." For the most part, D'Avenant's 1674 version is followed, and the "few Lines written by Mr. Garrick" cannot be said to constitute an improvement on Shakespeare's last speech for Macbeth:

> 'Tis done! the scene of life will quickly close.
> Ambition's vain delusive dreams are fled,
> And now I wake to darkness, guilt and horror;
> I cannot bear it! let me shake it off —
> It will not be; my soul is clogg'd with blood —
> I cannot rise! I dare not ask for mercy —
> It is too late, hell drags me down; I sink,
> I sink, — my soul is lost for ever! —
> Oh — Oh! —[24]

Kemble's production was elaborate. Capon, with "all the zeal of an antiquary," devised sets which were dazzling to audiences accustomed to seeing Macbeth, dressed in a British grenadier's uniform, stalk about on a stage adorned with ordinary flats. This romantic antiquarianism — it cannot truthfully be called realism — gave much opportunity for flashy costumes and processions, and it rather disgusted certain conservatives. "This is a decorative *era* (as that is the word) of the Stage," grumbled the *Oracle*, "and if the People pant after a procession, they may have it with more profit in Shakspere than about a Pantomime." 25

Kemble was insistent on improved costumes. They were to be "accurate, which was *not* expensive, and the materials were to be genuine, not imitative, which certainly *was* expensive, and heavily so." A German visitor who had seen Kemble and Mrs. Siddons act *Macbeth* three or four years before had seen room for improvements on this line:

There was too much that was not Shakespeare, too much bad taste and shabbiness in the costumes of the witches, and all in all too much claptrap.

But for the 1794 production, "the witches no longer wore mittens, plaited caps, laced aprons, and stomachers, ruffs, &c." Those creatures which had excited in no less a personage than Mrs. Montagu "a species of terror, that cannot be effected by the operation of human agency" were made much of by Kemble. Their weird costumes and tastefully interpolated songs were designed to impress the populace, and they did. "In justice to the Managers," decided one critic, "we must observe, that the Magnificence of the Dresses, the grandeur of the Processions, and the picturesque beauty of the Scenery, all correspond with that splendour and elegance, which so peculiarly belongs to this splendid Edifice." 26

The performance had, naturally, its misfortunes. For one thing, the audience was vastly perplexed by the absence of Banquo's ghost; Kemble indulged in the "strange and un-Shakspearian novelty of leaving the presence of Banquo's ghost to be signified solely by the agitation and horror of the actor," an innovation which he defended by making a distinction "between a *Ghost* and an *Apparition*":

Banquo, said He, is a *ghost*, & should be pictured only in words as an idea; on the contrary in Hamlet, the [father] of Hamlet is an apparition, which has a part to perform.

There was also a slight disturbance during the elaborately prepared incantation scene of the fourth act. Kemble, who thought "little Children have a very pleasing Effect in Panto-mimes, Processions, &c.," conceived the idea of having a troop of little boys scurry about the stage in elf-like abandon during the singing of "Black spirits and white." The youthful Edmund Kean happened to be one of the sprites, and in later years he took malicious pleasure in telling how he "tripped up his brother sprites so that they tumbled 'like a pack of cards,' greatly to the wrath of Black Jack Kemble." The manager was furious that his carefully planned scene should be ruined; he instantly dismissed "the whole tribe of phan-toms," and vented his anger on Kean with "thumps and reproaches." All in all, however, the evening went off ad-mirably. Some of the critics were a little disappointed in Kemble himself, who seemed so fatigued from his exertions in opening the new house he was not his usual impressive self. The *Oracle* liked the manager in the dagger soliloquy, the murder, and the battle; "all the rest was unworthy of him." Generally, however, the splendid new theatre and the spec-tacular production were a thumping success, and at the close of the evening, "the audience retired in admirable harmony, delighted and amazed." [27]

Kemble's regular string of tragedies paid well during the spring, as did the chauvinistic occasion piece, *The Glorious First of June*, which celebrated General Howe's recent victory over the French. But the overwhelming success of the spring was another musical spectacle — another specimen of "exotick and irrational entertainment, which has been always com-batted, and always has prevailed." Curiously enough, this one, *Lodoiska*, was Kemble's own production, contrived, as one unkindly critic had it, by "cutting, pasting, and putting together" materials from French sources. Based on an opera of Dejaure's (itself taken from a scurrilous novel by Louvet),

Lodoiska was one more in the interminable list of works which Cibber truculently called "Ginshops of the Stage, that intoxicate its Auditors and dishonour their Understanding." Produced on the ninth of June, Kemble's opera was a prodigious success, and like so many others was patronized "to the exclusion of the more important and regular Drama." [28]

Kemble seems to have taken some pains with the production, but as Steele's Indiana had long before observed, "in the main all the pleasure the best opera gives us, is but mere sensation." In almost all respects *Lodoiska* followed Dryden's definition of an opera by being "a poetical Tale or Fiction, represented by Vocal and Instrumental Musick, adorned with Scenes, Machines, and Dancing." The locale is Poland, where Count Floreski seeks his beloved Lodoiska in the castle of the wicked Baron Lodinski, the villain who holds the maiden captive because she spurned his advances. The wicked Baron, before the third act, captures Floreski and Lodoiska's unsuspecting father, and is on the point of putting them to a horrible death before the lady's eyes, but just at this point the castle is surprised by a band of Tartars. The leader of the horde, Kera Khan, turns out to be a friend of Floreski, and after the two of them successfully quell the Baron, the lovers are united.[29]

Of the numerous lyrics sprinkled through the piece, this one is typical:

> Sweet bird, that cheer'st the heavy hours
> Of winter's dreary reign,
> O, still exert thy tuneful pow'rs,
> And pour the vocal strain!

This low order of mediocrity is no worse than much of the dialogue, which is stilted to a degree. When Floreski is told by the Baron that he is to be executed before Lodoiska's very eyes, the hero rapturously exclaims:

Before her face! — Then I am blest indeed; I shall once more behold her. — Come, why dost thou pause? — Summon thy executioners, prepare the rack, and thou shalt see me spring to my glorious death, proud as impatient martyrs on their road to heaven.

The piece makes its halting way to the big scene, in which the Tartars storm the blazing castle. It was at this point that Mrs. Crouch, owing to a carpenter's "prematurely" taking away a support of the bridge on which she was standing, inadvertently fell screaming to the floor "with a violent crash." But Kelly, the dashing Floreski, with great agility and incredible presence of mind, caught her safely and to "loud and continued" applause carried her to the front of the stage.[30]

The London audiences doted on the burning castles and gallant battling in *Lodoiska*. It is rather to Kemble's credit that he, avowed classicist that he was, could stoop down and captivate the Philistines when he chose. Dryden's worldlywise precept may have been in his mind as he contrived for Kera Khan so melodiously to foil the nefarious schemes of Baron Lodinski:

I dare establish it for a rule of practice on the stage, that we are bound to please those whom we pretend to entertain.

To read, *Lodoiska* is pretty dull stuff, but with the charming Mrs. Crouch and the gallant Mr. Kelly singing the music of Cherubine, Kreutzer, and Andreozzi, it may have been, as John Genest grudgingly admitted, "a pretty good piece for the sort of thing." It completely monopolized the end of the season, and closed the theatre on July 7.[31]

CHAPTER IX

Not Single Spies, But in Battalions

> Pray that our enemies join not in a hot day; for, by
> the Lord, I take but two shirts out with me, and I
> mean not to sweat extraordinarily.
>
> SHAKESPEARE

SHERIDAN'S gaudy new playhouse wore out the spring with
infinite bombast circumstance in the form of a long string
of operas and farces — a "species of intellectual prostitution,"
sneered Hazlitt. Kemble's own *Lodoiska* headed the bill
almost every night, displaying, as one critic delicately put
it, no great efforts after "intellectual smartness." But such
fare paid well, and in Sheri's view that fact compensated for
artistic losses. After all, twenty-two thousand pounds was an
impressive gross, and though Shakespeare was to be desired,
the complaisant Garrick had pointed out long before that
the managers would "change the nobler scene" if heavy
tragedy did not pay:

> Quit poets, and set carpenters to work,
> Shew gaudy scenes, or mount the vaulting *Turk*.[1]

The autumn was different, however, and Kemble had his
inning with a long list of his own favorites such as *Henry V,
Douglas, Macbeth, Isabella* — pieces in which he and the
statuesque Siddons showed to great personal if not financial
advantage. And by and large, the discriminating were
pleased. For one thing, the actor's voice was better, and
there were those who welcomed their old favorite after seeing the classic roles "misrepresented" by juveniles. Errors

of judgment were made, of course; even Kemble was of the terse opinion that Thompson's version of *Emilia Galotti* was "nothing," and *All's Well* fared badly on its one night's run because the star was "too ill to do any thing." But *Measure for Measure*, a great personal triumph for Kemble, was "very much approv'd of by the Public." And in George Colman's *Mountaineers*, flimsy thing though it be, Kemble found one of his best roles: his Octavian made strong men gulp and impressionable young ladies commit their suppressed desires to bad poetry. But through it all Sheridan demanded his well-paying opera and spectacle, and *Alexander the Great* was the success of the winter: "the marshalling on a first night FOUR HUNDRED people, the discipling HORSE, the moving such ponderous SCENERY — all constitute a difficulty, that it is wonderful to find overcome." [2]

If cataloguing plays is dull, scandal is always interesting. We shall not partake of the righteous Boaden's reticence when he primly admits that "on some few, a very few points, in the exercise of, I hope, a sound discretion, I have ventured to baffle the search of the malignant." Miss De Camp, for one thing, was of surpassing beauty. A talented singer, she had made her name as Polly in *The Beggars' Opera*, that perennial favorite, and all the young blades of the town were prostrate before her. Her celebrated daughter, Fanny Kemble, recalls that her "figure was beautiful, and her face very handsome and strikingly expressive," while Leigh Hunt, sixty years later, could still feel himself stirred by the remembrance of her "fine dark eyes, and elevated features." The lady's beauty — her virtue cannot be questioned — was almost her undoing, for John Kemble, of all men, looked on her with lustful eyes. The result was more comic than tragic. He must have been drinking that night, and, as the whole town knew, Kemble when drunk was an elfish creature. His passion was not to be denied. The door of the lady's dressing room was flung open: "he would — she would not — he took hold — she screamed," and before he knew it the austere manager was surrounded by a crowd of pardonably curious people. Caught red-handed as he was, he rose to the occasion with his customary aplomb, and on January 27, 1795, his *amende honorable* appeared in the London papers:

I, John Philip Kemble, of the Theatre Royal Drury Lane, do adopt this method of publicly apologizing to Miss De Camp, for the very improper and unjustifiable behaviour I was lately guilty of towards her, which I do further declare her conduct and character had in no instance authorized; but, on the contrary, I do know and believe both to be irreproachable.

The lurid incident was the talk of the town. Mrs. Piozzi made bold to remark that Kemble's apology was like "that of a penitent Hackney Coachman under the threatened *Lash* of a sharp persecution," but most of the gentry looked upon the whole matter "more as a jest than as an enormity." [3]

Kemble was properly chastened. The day following his advertisement he made his private apologies to the outraged maiden:

As I have never been so fortunate as to find you at home, when I have Called at your house to Express my sincere regret for the disquiet I have been the occasion of to you I beg Leave to do it in this Letter; and, at the same time, to Assure you, that I shall always Endeavour, by the most respectful means, to Prove my high opinion of your exemplary Conduct, in every regulation of Life.*

Miss De Camp's behavior, it was generally conceded, was notable in its restraint: she "impressed the town greatly in favor of her discretion in private life." And presently the entire affair was forgotten. True, there was some hissing at

* This letter, here reprinted from a MS in the Harvard Theatre Collection, is not in Kemble's hand, but on the assumption that it is a copy, I see no reason to question its authenticity.

his first performance following the escapade, but it was drowned in the applause. As for the lady, she continued her duties at the theatre and in the fullness of time married John Kemble's favorite brother, Charles — not, it was darkly hinted in certain quarters, without opposition from the malignant head of the family.[4]

A month later, at all events, disgrace was swallowed up in one of the most permanent triumphs of Kemble's whole career — his Penruddock in Cumberland's *Wheel of Fortune*. He recognized the potentialities of the gloomy misanthrope when he first read the play, confiding to Michael Kelly that there was a role in it "that will do something for *me*; at least I feel that I can do something with *it*." The result is now history, and it is not a little to Kemble's credit that he could sustain for twenty years, on the strength of his own performance, a play so thoroughly bad. Fifty years later, an old habitué of the Garrick Club was given to reminiscing of the interpretation, recalling the general "gulping" sound, "mingled with sobbings and blowings of noses." Even Cumberland admitted that Kemble saved the play, and in no other role, decided Mrs. Inchbald, did Kemble "evince a more complete mastery of his art than in Penruddock."[5]

A more melancholy *première* was Madame D'Arblay's — the fabulous Fanny Burney's — *Edwy and Elgiva*, which survived a single night. In her youth Fanny had written the engaging *Evelina* (still one of the best first novels in the language), and had subsequently been the toast of the town, the pet of the bluestockings, and the prime favorite of no less a personage than Dr. Samuel Johnson, LL.D. Since those happy days, Fanny had chafed under the rigors of Queen Charlotte's court etiquette and had married one of the French *émigrés* that were swarming to England. What unhappy chance moved her to write a play remains obscure, but once written, it was submitted to Kemble's tender offices. As the great and good drinking companion of Fanny's brother, the celebrated classical scholar, the Rev. Charles Burney, Kemble had the grace to accept it, though with private qualms. Its reading in the green room coincided with the birth of Fanny's son, and on its performance it proved a dismal failure — or, in the manager's own typical understatement, "it was not approv'd of." The audience laughed through most of it, and shouted Kemble down when he came forward to announce a second presentation. The journalists were vicious, and poor Fanny, in great distress, had the candor to admit that "a thousand things" needed revision. The fault, however, was not entirely hers:

The performers, too, were cruelly imperfect, and made blunders I blush to have pass for mine, — added to what belong to me. The most important character after the hero and heroine had but two lines of his part by heart! He made all the rest at random, and such nonsense as put all the other actors out as much as himself; so that a more wretched performance, except Mrs. Siddons, Mr. Kemble, and Mr. Bensley, could not be exhibited in a barn.

The prompter's voice, pointed out one critic, could be heard all over the house.[6]

The London mob during the spring flocked to see the newest operatic spectacle, *Jack of Newbury*, but Kemble abandoned the metropolis for peaceful Dublin. The redoubtable Daly was still holding sway there by fair means or foul, and Kemble's return — his first visit in six years — had been a pleasant relief after the hugger-mugger of the season. Through Stratford and Coventry to Holyhead, the Kembles made their progress, and were welcomed to the Irish capital by Daly with a dinner party which "staid till five in the morning." Young Charles Mathews, in those days a tyro at the Dublin theatre, was thrilled at the great star's engagement, and the town shared his enthusiasm. Even *Hamlet* in "modern clothes," the season's opener on May 25, failed to dampen their ardor.

If twenty guineas had been offered for a ticket or a place in the boxes, it could not have been purchased. In all my life I never saw people more anxious to get into a theatre. . . . Kemble's reception was quite rapturous.[7]

There were unpleasantries, of course. George Frederick Cooke, that hulking, swarthy forerunner of Kean who was shortly to be the rage of London and Kemble's own nearest competitor, was drudging away for Daly, and reacting unsympathetically to the pother. at Kemble's advent. Harsh words were spoken and recriminations were tossed hither and yon, but Kemble was the lion. He was generally amiable with the underlings at the Dublin theatre — in spite of Cooke's ill will — and to the surprise of those who knew his London ways was a model of forbearance at rehearsals. "Every one was sorry when he went away." While the star was busily making the seven hundred and eighteen pounds he took back to England when he left, Dublin's society was bestirring itself mightily in his behalf. One night there was a large dinner party at Mr. Atkinson's, and "all the world" dropped in. Jephson, of course, was the model of hospitality, save that he forgot to invite Mrs. Kemble for dinner too. "I made her call for me at Jephson's about nine o'clock," records Kemble complacently, "that they might recollect I had a wife." There was a gay house party at the country place of the Earl of Milltown at Rossnorough, and back in Dublin the Earl would drop in for dinner after the play. "My Wine was very bad, and he sent me some excellent Port and Claret next Day." [8]

But the level-headed Kemble was under no illusions. He pocketed his money, bade his friends farewell, and advised the ambitious young Mathews "for God's sake get out of this place as soon as you can." He himself got out about the end

of June, after an extremely successful season, and even found
an occasion to bowl over more provincials at Glasgow, Edinburgh, and Newcastle before returning to London for the
disastrous winter season of 1795–1796.[9]

Not as single spies, but in battalions came the troubles.
The early winter passed by monotonously enough with the
old favorites for which, remarked one benevolent observer,
"the amateurs of the *Drama* are more indebted" to the Drury
Lane manager "than to half the modern dramatic writers."
Spectacle paid well, as usual: the elaborate and expensive
sets for D'Egville's ballet of the year before, *Alexander the
Great*, were very cannily utilized by Kemble for his revival
of Nat Lee's *Rival Queens* — which had long before been
rechristened with the name of the ballet. "Such an exhibition," it was generally agreed, "had never been witnessed in
this country."

Amazons and elephants — cars and bridges — battle and processions, &c. &c. — with a banquet scene, magnificently furnished —
all in the first style of *decorative* excellence.

But Wycherley's *Plain Dealer*, even though Kemble "very
attentively expunged the passages which might offend the
delicacy of a modern audience," was a failure. After all, most
pious folk made a great point of being outraged at the license
of Restoration wit. "The muse of Congreve," decided one
gentleman with crushing finality, "is an abandoned prosti-
tute." The worthy Dr. Jeremy Collier had long since stated
the case for the godly by observing that in a typical Restoration comedy (*The Double Dealer*) "there are but *Four*
ladys . . . and *Three* of the biggest of them are Whores."
The Wycherley revival, however, served at least one function:
it temporarily reconciled those inveterate enemies, Kemble
and Mrs. Jordan. The lady's "irresistible" acting even called
forth a very pretty quotation from Sterne by the hard-hearted
manager:

It may seem ridiculous enough to a torpid heart — I could have taken her into my arms and cherished her, though it was in the open street, without blushing.[10]

But tragedy stalked close behind these amiable preliminaries. George Colman had written such a resounding success in *The Mountaineers* that the powers of Drury Lane, in the amplitude of their wisdom, commissioned him to write "a play with music, with a character written expressly up to the talents of Mr. Kemble." Colman found it easy enough to woo his Muse for £1,000, and presently his version of Godwin's *Caleb Williams* was ready as a pat melodrama, replete with a gloomy recluse, a mysterious chest, a secret murder — all interspersed with snatches of song and the clowning of a couple of buffoons.[11]

Things went wrong from the start. During rehearsals, Signora Storace "barbarously" deprived Mrs. Bland of a juicy role, and the singer, feeling herself grossly wronged, withdrew from the theatre in high dudgeon. Miss Farren, displeased with her part, became a little difficult and presently threw it over completely. Poor Stephen Storace, harassed with preparing the music, was so depressed over the situation that — on the testimony of his good friend Michael Kelly — he went into a decline and before very long died. But these ill omens were but a prelude to the storm of the *première*. With a great hurly-burly the piece was finally produced on March 12, only to be pretty thoroughly damned. Critics, according to one who spoke from experience,

> Critics throng to see a New Play split,
> And thrive and prosper on the Wrecks of Wit.

The Iron Chest was denounced as "hasty, undigested"; Kemble punctuated his acting with "an incessant cough"; the evening closed in hoots and howls. The house, a large and fashionable one that paid some £460 to see the new piece, became rowdy and derisive as the evening wore on, and even though Kemble came forward to ask the audience's indulgence, poor Colman's play was "generally condemned" in an uproar of disapproval. A second performance the following week fared little better, and after two more presentations it was definitely written off as a failure.[12]

The woeful reception is hardly of interest in itself — how many ill-starred productions got an even worse one — but its repercussions were frisky enough. George Colman was not a man to suffer in silence: he was furious at the treatment his play had got, and when he addressed himself to making specific charges (in the preface to the second edition of *The Iron Chest*, published late in the spring) he poured forth the vials of his wrath on the imperturbable brow of John Kemble himself. The celebrated preface, later suppressed, is in the best vein of eighteenth-century invective. Colman was no fool, he generously admits: though his play was not "perfect," it was written with enough skill to "hold together." Then how, he wails, how "came it to fall to pieces, after four days wear? — I will explain that: — but alas! alas! my heart doth yearn, when I think on the task which circumstance has thrust upon me." The task of explanation, Colman goes on to say, involves confronting "a scowling, sullen, black Bull, right athwart my road; — a monster of ingratitude, of the Bœotian breed, perplexing me in my wanderings through the entangled labyrinth of Drury." This creature, we learn, is John Philip Kemble.[13]

Sheridan commissioned the play and agreed to pay a sum larger than any "hitherto offered on similar occasions," and Colman was grievously upset when the rehearsals of such an important piece turned out to be ludicrously inadequate. "They yclep it a rehearsal, I conjecture, because *they do* NOT *rehearse*." By the shade of Garrick, swears the embittered author, there was never a single rehearsal "wherein one, or two, or more, of the Performers, very essential to the piece, were not absent: and *all* the rehearsals which I attended, so slovenly, and irregular, that the rugged master of a theatrical Barn, might have blushed for the want of discipline." During this crucial period, both Kemble and Colman were confined to their beds by illness — Storace, the musical director, being on the point of death himself. Finally, two days before the production took place (March 12), Kemble returned to the theatre and ordered the piece to be performed "immediately." To this decree Colman, still ill, submitted with "doubt and trembling." His agitation was not lessened when Kemble sent a brief note, three hours before the curtain went up, demanding "a transposition of two of the most material scenes in the second act" — the purpose being to facilitate moving the sets. This Colman indignantly refused.

"Very ill, and very weak," the author dragged himself to the theatre to see the performance, only to find Kemble in his dressing-room "taking *Opium Pills:* and nobody who is acquainted with that gentleman will doubt me when I assert, that they are a medicine which he has long been in the habit of swallowing." * All this was bad enough, but when Kemble went out to play Sir Edward Mortimer the result made Colman writhe. By nature, build, and technique the manager was ably fitted to portray the character, but — and this is the author's chief complaint — he deliberately and malignantly ruined the piece by underplaying his role. "Never, sure, did man place the main strength of his building upon so rotten a prop!" The whole character, so rich in possibilities for even a competent performer, "could scarcely have [been] acted worse."

* Kemble was greatly afflicted with the gout, recalled Scott (*The Quarterly Review*, XXXIV [1826], 231), and took "L'eau médicinale d'Husson" to key him up for acting. The *Oracle* (January 11, 1796) reported that the manager "has got into a happy mode of treating

Seeing how things were going, Colman demanded, at the end of the first act, that Kemble apologize to the audience for his "indisposition, lest the uninformed, or malicious, might attribute the ponderosity of the performer to the heaviness of the author." Kemble angrily refused: "his indisposition, he said, was evident; he had coughed very much upon the stage, and an apology would make him '*look like a fool.*'" So the performance went on. Sir Edward Mortimer "groaned, he lag'd, he coughed, he winced, he wheezed" until the audience was thoroughly restive, and then, at Sheridan's insistence, he came forward to apologize for his condition. At first, Colman took this for an act of benevolence, but on reflection — "alas! how narrow is the soul of man! how distrustful in it's [*sic*] movements" — he was convinced that the explanation was made solely to bring discredit on the author. The evening closed in the worst possible way, and Colman reckoned his account with Kemble in this fashion:

For his illness,	Compassion,
For his conduct under it,	Censure,
For his refusing to make an apology,	A Smile!
For his making an apology,	A Sneer
For his mismanagement,	A Groan,
For his acting,	A Hiss.

At the second performance, a week later, Kemble was even worse. "He insulted the Town, and injured his Employer, and the author, sufficiently in the first instance: in the second he added to the insult and injury an hundred fold." Colman's invective is, as a technical achievement, rather interesting:

Frogs in a marsh, flies in a bottle, wind in a crevice, a preacher in a field, the drone of a bagpipe, all, all yield to the inimitable, and soporific monotony of Mr. Kemble. . . . The most

---

the *asthmatic* affection which teazes him annually — it is abstaining from *fluid* considerably."

miserable mummer, that ever disgraced the walls of a Theatre, could not have been a stronger draw-back than Mr. Kemble. He was not only dull in himself but the cause of dullness in others.

All this, of course, caused a mighty stir. Kemble, by the time Colman diverted the town with his preface, was in Ireland again, whence came unsubstantiated rumors that he was going to thrash the bumptious playwright: "some have spoke of the *horse-whip.*" Even Kemble's strongest partisans had to admit that his conduct was not of such a nature as "to exculpate him entirely from the charges urged against him," but he none the less had many supporters — among them, of course, Mrs. Inchbald. Charles Lamb, he of the unfailing good humor and forced puns, dismissed both the charge and the defense with a witticism. Some, it is true, retaliated by a counter-attack, declaring that the production, however "imperfect," could in no way detract from a play already as bad as it could possibly be. And as for Kemble's taking opium — why, "the Turks, it is said, usually took a quantity of it when they went to battle": the manager's plight was similar and his need of a stimulant as pressing, for "he had a *heart-breaking* prospect before him." After all, Kemble himself had thought nothing of the play — "very bad indeed," he confided to his journal — and he gave it no more attention than it deserved. And so the battle raged: the newspapers were filled with epigrams designed to be humorous, charges and counter-charges were hurled with the greatest abandon, and everyone had his say except Kemble himself, who as usual exhibited his Olympian detachment. Safe in Dublin, he, for one, was glad to be out of the whole mess.* [14]

* *The Iron Chest* was presently produced with great success at the Haymarket, young Robert Elliston triumphing in the role Kemble could make nothing of. The play eventually became a stock piece, and Kemble himself acted Sir Mortimer in later years — with what feelings we can imagine. As for Colman, he was, in the fullness of time, recon-

For several months before *The Iron Chest* disaster there had been calling at the house of Mr. Samuel Ireland, in Norfolk Street, a steady stream of distinguished visitors. Mr. Ireland's gifted son, William Henry, just nineteen years old, had had the singular good fortune the year before to come across an ancient chest containing, among other things, such delectable items as two plays, *Vortigern* and *Henry II*, amatory verses to "Anna Hatherewaye," early drafts of *Kynge Leare* and *Hamblette*, and devious bits of correspondence — all in the hand of William Shakespeare. The elder Ireland, a rather well-known engraver about town and a gentleman with a fine feeling for publicity, immediately took charge of things, arranging for the publication of the priceless documents and enjoying himself hugely in the furor that followed the announcement of the discovery. It must be said that the old gentleman, a literary hack and an engraver of sorts, was apparently in no way privy to the outrageous forgeries of his son. As for the facile William, he had, with some reading in the early drama and a great flair for penmanship, fabricated out of whole cloth the astonishing series of documents, and the (inaccurately) antiquated spelling, plausible imitation of Elizabethan script, and cumbersome attempt to reproduce sixteenth-century English convinced all the gullible *littérateurs* of London that here was the most miraculous find of the century. Not since *Ossian* had the town been so excited.[15]

The elder Ireland, basking in a sort of vicarious glory, had his cup running over when, on February 25, a committee including Parr, Boswell, Herbert Croft, Isaac Heard, Henry Pye (the Laureate), and sixteen other well-known men of letters called by Norfolk Street and in a solemn convocation

---

ciled to the "miserable mummer" over a bottle of wine. The virulent preface was withdrawn, and Kemble for ever after bought up and destroyed every copy of the offending second edition he could lay his hands on. Consequently, it is today a collector's item.

decided that the manuscripts were genuine. The relics, revealed "with the same guarded precaution that priests use
when they exhibit an idol," were ogled at and exclaimed over
in rapture, and Samuel Boswell was so stirred by the whole
affair that he "fell upon his knees, and in a tone of enthusiasm,
and exultation, thanked God, that he had lived to witness this
discovery, and exclaimed that he could now die in peace."
James Boaden, later to see the error of his ways,

beheld the papers with the tremor of the purest delight — touched
the invaluable relics with reverential respect, and deemed even
existence dearer, as it gave me so refined a satisfaction.

And Francis Waldron, another convert who was to turn
apostate, had "precisely" the same sensations. Only old Joseph
Ritson, that renowned vegetarian, eccentric, and scholar, was
unfooled: he, for one, "had not the slightest doubt" of the
forgeries. The general public, meanwhile, were allowed brief
glimpses of the glory through short extracts printed in the
Oracle, and the whole town was clamoring to have access to
the entire treasure. By and large, things were looking very
bright for the Irelands.[16]

Ominous clouds were appearing, however. Presently
Richard Porson, that redoubtable savant and caustic humor-
ist, hooted at the idea of subscribing for the publication of
the relics, and even refused to examine them. But Edmond
Malone's incredulity took a more violent turn. Though
"quite a gentleman in his manners, and rather of a mild disposition, except when he had to support the truth," the idea
of the public being so ignominiously duped converted the
amiable scholar into "a furious Saracen." Sheridan, more interested in the commercial than the literary aspect of the
affair, thought that *Vortigern* (which was to be made available for acting) had "some bold ideas, but they are crude and
undigested," but Kemble, strongly of Malone's persuasion,

"constantly refused" even to go by Norfolk Street to look at the "spurious" documents. Samuel Ireland, cannily playing Sheridan against Harris of Covent Garden, was holding the delectable morsel before both the great theatres, until finally Harris, in exasperation, sent an emissary "with a *carte blanche*, in order that Mr. Ireland might state his terms." But Drury Lane was favored, and Kemble, as manager, was faced with the unpleasant realization that he was to be responsible for the production of *Vortigern* — he who was convinced of its worthlessness and whose opinion throughout the negotiations had been "little regarded." Sheridan was adamant on the production going through. "You very well know," he told the disgusted actor, "that an Englishman considers himself as good a judge of Shakespeare, as of his pint of porter." [17]

For some several months before the performance of *Vortigern* took place (on the second of April), almost every Englishman appears to have been exercising that prerogative of judgment. The Ireland manuscript had been published, with much ostentation, in December, and before long there was a flood of printed matter, either favorable to the point of adulation or violently defamatory. Malone, the leader of the opposition, was busily turning out what was designed to be the crushing disproof of the documents' authenticity, but until his good stout volume was ready the gap was being filled by lesser attempts at detraction. Boaden's *Letter to George Steevens* appeared in January and was followed by Waldron's *Free Reflections* and a stream of abusive criticism by Henry Dudley in the *Morning Herald*. The gentlemen for the defense, meanwhile, were by no means sitting on their haunches. There were spirited rebuttals by James Wyatt, W. C. Oulton, and Francis Webb, and before very long all London was split in two factions, the believers and the unbelievers.[18]

At Drury Lane, however, things were going forward with the production of *Vortigern*. In November Sheridan had given Greenwood, the scene-painter, instructions to begin his preparations for the play immediately; it was to be performed, he emphasized with characteristic disregard for fact, "without Delay." Samuel Ireland, officious and bustling, was hard to keep in an equable temper. For one thing, he objected to Kemble's being in charge of the production, the scornful manager being "a lukewarm friend of the play," as he complained to Sheridan. The old gentleman refused to deliver a copy of *Vortigern* to the theatre until he was satisfied with the proposed scenery and decorations. Kemble, sorely tried, demanded the manuscript immediately; otherwise, he curtly informed Ireland, the proprietors "must suppose that you consider your Agreement with them to be at an End." But a month later, at the end of December, we find the obstinate old gentleman primly writing Kemble that "the play of Vortigern has long been ready for the Theatre & if you will inform me when you are ready to prepare the scenery, & Dresses" all would be well. Once the play was turned over to Kemble, new vexations arose:

It was much too long, and consequently many passages were expunged; and in one historical fact, thought too gross for the public ear, viz. the incestuous passion of the King towards his daughter, it underwent some further alterations.

But the weeks passed, and the date of the production came uncomfortably close.[19]

The elder Ireland became more and more apprehensive. To Sheridan he wrote querulously complaining of the way the advertising was being conducted, and hinting that "a large party is forming to damn the play unheard." In point of fact, things were becoming a little uncomfortable. Malone, almost ready with his blast, issued a handbill that promised a startling exposé, and the public at large was gradually waking up to the fact that it had been taken in. "All sensible persons," Mrs. Piozzi was told by Mrs. Siddons (who refused to act in the play), "are convinced that 'Vortigern' is a most audacious impostor." The fatal evening of the performance, poor old Ireland himself distributed a broadside at the theatre, castigating Malone's "malevolent and impotent attack upon the Shakspeare MSS." and begging the play-goers to attend the play "with that candour that has ever distinguished a British audience." [20]

All the world was out to see the climax of the great literary combat. At Drury Lane "perhaps a more crowded theatre was never seen," the house coming to the astonishing total of £725 5s. 6d. A prologue by Sir James Burgess pleaded for dispassionate judgment:

> Unbiass'd, then, pronounce your dread decree,
> Alike from prejudice or favour free.

Poor young William Henry Ireland, who had been almost crowded out of the picture by his father, watched the proceedings from behind the scenes, heavy with guilt and convinced that *Vortigern* "would not be a second time represented." His worst fears were realized. A "strong party" was out to support the performance, and for the first act or so things went calmly enough, but before long there was a turn for the worse. Dignum bellowed his lines so "as to set the whole house in a convulsive peal of laughter," and when one of the characters was killed on the stage he fell half in and half outside the curtain, so that he had to get up and walk away — an incident that brought forth "an excess of laughter." But chaos did not break out until the fifth act, when Kemble (as Vortigern) "thought the deception had gone on long enough." Throughout the house were heard muttered comparisons of certain lines to Shakespeare, but at last, when Kemble, with conduct "too obvious to the whole audience to need much comment," read with great emphasis the line,

> And when this solemn mockery is o'er,

the house broke down into ten minutes of derisive laughter. Once the audience was quiet again, however, Kemble "very politely, and in order to amuse the audience still more," repeated the line. From that point, the evening was completely wrecked; laughs were "mixed with groans," and the crowd, finding it "impossible to struggle any longer against conviction . . . , burst forth in reiterated shouts and peals of execration and laughter."[21]

The disaster, in the opinion of many persons, was an unalloyed blessing. A jubilant friend told Kemble in his dressing-room that "if the thing had been tolerated, it would be a canister tied to Shakspeare's tail to all succeeding ages, or remain a recorded monument of the dramatic taste and critical discernment of England at the close of the eighteenth century." The Irelands, of course, were furious at "the ludicrous manner in which the principal character was sustained," and Sheridan undertook to berate Kemble very roundly for "invidiously toiling to damn a production, which might have brought thousands to the treasury" — to all of which Kemble "uttered not one word in reply." The press was loudly derisive, one paper professing itself to be unable "to notice all the vulgarisms which encountered our ears" during the performance of *Vortigern*. Sheridan, the next day, split the £206 over expenses with Samuel Ireland — poor William Henry's share, through some strange arithmetic, came to only £30 — and for Drury Lane the whole unfortunate affair was a closed incident. Coming right after *The Iron Chest*, *Vortigern* was enough to weaken the prestige of any theatre.[22]

The spring season had been miserable. Such outrageous fiascos as *The Iron Chest* and *Vortigern* put Drury Lane in a ludicrous light, but their reverberations were even more annoying. Colman, of course, succeeded in airing his grievances very eloquently, but his rumblings were as nothing compared to the flood of recriminations, reprisals, and counterblasts that followed the Ireland debacle. Malone's long-awaited disproval proved to be a scholarly and brilliantly devastating examination of the papers on points of orthography, hand-writing, internal evidence, and historical accuracy; the savant's conclusion ("Life is not long enough to be wasted in the examination of such trash, when almost a single glance is sufficient to shew that it is a plain and palpable forgery") was shortly echoed by most men of discrimination. Young Ireland, seeing his game was up, bolted from his father's house and confessed everything. The audacious boy blandly admitted that the failure of *Vortigern* "did not lessen the satisfaction I felt in having at so early an age wrote a piece which was not only acted, but brought forth as the work of the greatest of men." Unhappily, poor old Samuel could find no comfort in such reflections.*

But Drury Lane had its own troubles, and left the die-hards to fight out the Ireland controversy. The season which had opened under such "auspicious" circumstances now seemed to be "going to destruction with all the celerity that could be expected." Sheridan, who, said Sam Rogers, carried the privileges of genius as far as they were ever carried, became intolerably capricious. He who once had all London at his feet by his double triumph — ladies and gallants flocking to hear his oratory against Warren Hastings and everyone else to witness *The Duenna* and *The School for Scandal* — was as brilliant as ever but far less successful. Kemble, disgusted

---

* The Ireland controversy was a long one: Malone's work was followed by William Henry Ireland's *Authentic Account*, after which the disillusioned parent joined the lists with his *Investigation of Mr. Malone's Claim*. George Chalmers was the most learned and industrious of the Ireland defenders, with his tremendous *Apology* and *Supplemental Apology*. Samuel Ireland died in 1801, and his son lived on until 1835, leading a miserable existence as a hack-writer and never again attaining the notoriety of those febrile days of 1795–1796. To the end, he bitterly reproached Kemble for his part in the *Vortigern* disaster.

with the latest abortive attempts to inject novelty into the theatre, rebelled at reading the "numberless" bad plays tendered him by aspiring authors; for his pains he was roundly rebuked by Sheridan, who spoke largely of his duties to his employers. The irony was heightened, however, when Kemble mournfully reflected that his salary was some fourteen hundred pounds in arrears: "difficulties arising from old debts" were making him very weary of Sheridan and his ways. So obvious was the "daemon of discontent" cleaving Drury Lane that even the newspapers began to take notice of it.[23]

Meanwhile, the spring was wearing itself out. Miss Lee's *Almeyda* was a new tragedy that received short shift, and Prince Hoare's *Mahmoud* was a new opera that took the town by storm. The latter piece's profits went to poor Storace's widow in memory of him whose life had been laid down for *The Iron Chest*, and Kemble, seeing in the late composer a kindred spirit, consented to take a role in the opera.

This day I followed Stephen Storace to his Grave — I shudder'd to hear the Earth and Pebbles rattle on his Coffin! — I hope never to go into Marybone Church again — I will endeavour to live better — He was only thirty-four! — One may die to-night.[24]

The string of unpleasantries came to a climax when both Kemble and Mrs. Jordan decided on *Hamlet* for their respective benefits. The expected explosion occurred. Kemble suggested in his lofty way that a comedienne should be satisfied to play Ophelia to Mrs. Siddons' Queen — a proposition which Mrs. Jordan stormily rejected. Poor Sheridan, harassed on all sides by creditors as well as temperamental actors, cut the Gordian knot by refusing the play to all concerned. This arbitration, really in favor of Mrs. Jordan since Hamlet was one of Kemble's best-loved roles, was the last straw: Kemble handed in his resignation, and Drury Lane, after thirteen years, was without the only actor who could be said to keep

CHAPTER X

The Savant

> A man that devotes his life to learning, shall he not
> be learned?
>
> THOMAS CARLYLE

B RASH YOUNG Mr. Kemble, certain of his early critics observed, was guilty of "aiming at distinction, where he has
little claim or pretension" — in the belles-lettres that formed
so important an adjunct of every true gentleman's character.
The late eighteenth century set great store by learned dilet-
tantes; indeed, even scholars, nowadays in such low repute,
were then received in the best (or almost the best) drawing
rooms. Mrs. Montagu, Mrs. Vesey, and Hannah More, estimable ladies and bluestockings as they might have been, succeeded in carving their niches as muses rather than graces.
One of the most cherished ambitions of John Kemble's life
was to be accepted in high society not merely as an actor but
as a scholar and a gentleman. For him to acquire such a status
was by no means easy: Horace Walpole had thought Garrick
as fit to write a preface to Shakespeare "as a country curate
to compose an excellent sermon from having preached one of
Tillotson's." To many persons the acting profession still
smacked of disreputable strolling, drunkenness, and ignorance. It was no slight achievement for Kemble to become the
esteemed friend of Malone and Reed, or to be spoken of as
"amongst the most judicious critics of Elizabethan literature." [1]

Such distinctions were not fortuitous. All his life, Kemble

labored as much at cultivating polite literature as he did at
making himself the first actor of his day. As a university man
— even if his university was one for refugees and thus socially
in low caste — he felt himself not only the superior of rascally
actors but the peer of professional *littérateurs.* His sporadic
excursions into literary composition were designed, one feels,
as passports into that society where one could toss off a Hora-
tian tag while discussing Shakespeare over the sherry. After
all, was not the great Fox a scholar as well as a prodigious
drinker, a man much concerned, Lady Holland points out
admiringly, with literature and "the metaphysics of grammar"? There had been those sins of Kemble's youth, *Belisarius* and *Fugitive Pieces*, which served very well as gestures
of respect for the muses in Yorkshire, but once London was
attained such sober and considered works as the essay on
Macbeth and the string of alterations of the old dramatists
proved to be ample indication that the gifted young tragedian
was of a pretty literary turn.[2]

No one proved more valuable in gaining an entrée for
Kemble into the literary society of London than Edmond
Malone — that learned and genial man who today claims perhaps more respect than any other scholar in an age of scholars.
Their friendship began soon after the youth's arrival in London. Malone was a friend of Captain Jephson; the captain had
taken a great fancy to Kemble in Dublin, and so for his
compatriot to interest himself in the young actor was natural.
Very shortly Malone saw in Kemble "a man of education and
gentlemanly manners," and enough of a scholar to worship at
the holy shrine of Shakespeare. As for the actor, he of course
was delighted to make such a friend, and although the crimes
he committed against his favorite playwright in his alterations
must have jarred poor Malone, the two soon grew very intimate. Malone was Kemble's most respected adviser on scholarly points; moreover he had that "elegance of his manners"

that marked the true gentleman. Kemble, of course, was certainly not Malone's equal in scholarship; indeed, few if any of his contemporaries were. But they got on famously. Malone liked the actor because his mind was "constitutional" and not "volatile." Lord Erskine, he told Farington, "would say more, but Kemble better things." The two were much together, dining and talking shop about the English stage, past and present. From Liverpool, in 1789, Kemble wrote familiarly enough:

Your letter found me confined to my Bed by a Pleurisy, and utterly incapable of moving; this is the eleventh Day of my Illness; but, thank God, I am on the mending Hand, and hope to be on horse-back to-morrow. . . .

I am very much obliged to you for having thought of the Manuscripts for me, and am sorry to think I should leave Town without a valedictory gripe of your Hand, but Mr. Sheridan had me in waiting from one at noon till almost one the next morning, and as I was obliged to be in my Chaise by four, prevented my making my last Compliments to all my other Friends — we did a good deal of Business at last, however, and I passed a very agreeable Day.

We should have had a very triumphant Season, but for my unfortunate Illness, which has prevented our acting our most attractive Plays — Macbeth, Othello, Hamlet, &c: — Huzza. Shakspeare for ever! —

Pray give my Compliments to Jephson, and believe me

your obliged,
and faithful Servant,
J. P. KEMBLE [3]

Malone, naturally, was on intimate terms with most of the literary set of London, and it was through him that Kemble came to know men like Reed and Dr. Farmer. When the actor set about forming his collection of old plays, Isaac Reed — whom Dr. Johnson thought "superior to all others in his knowledge of English literature" — was of especial service to him. Reed's mind was steeped in stage history, and his knowledge of dramatic bibliography was of great importance to a man who knew little of the subject. He and Kemble were soon great friends. We find them exchanging books and taking long walks together. "My cough," writes Kemble, "continues so violent, and the weather so cold, that I am oblig'd to beg to defer my Walk to Dulwich with you"; but he promises to call by the following Friday, "tho', on second Thoughts, as it is Good-friday, Saturday will be a better Day." And again, in a note asking for a book, Kemble adds that "Mrs. Kemble and I hope that your Wrist goes on as well as so dangerous an Accident can, and that we shall soon have the Pleasure of seeing you." [4]

Such friends as Malone and Reed no doubt fostered Kemble's interest in the more technical side of literary and stage history, fields in which he very soon set himself up as something of an authority. As a great manager, he was looked upon by the uninstructed as a paragon of learning, and consequently often called upon for judgments and opinions. To one correspondent he writes that he does not know precisely when the phrase "Men of Wit and Pleasure about Town" gained currency. "Shadwell in the Comedy of Epsom Wells 1673 calls three of his characters 'Men of Wit and Pleasure.' Does not 'About Town' smack of the clipp'd Cant of modern gibberish?" "My Man," he adds, "will wait for the Volume of Corneille, if you have quite done with it." And again he gives a "Scrap" of information on the Restoration theatres: the location of D'Avenant's company. Sometimes Kemble's learning is useful. For Thomas Waldron he tried to identify one Thomas Bond, an obscure Stuart actor, by a vague allusion in the prologue to the 1641 *Bussy d'Ambois*, being "almost certain that he has met with such information in some old tract, or poem; but, not having taken a memorandum, he cannot now refer to it." He assured John Taylor that he had "authority" for ascribing the dedication

He was an assiduous snapper-up of unconsidered trifles on stage history. When the litigation over the dormant patent of Drury Lane was going on, Kemble painstakingly copied out a prolix and tedious opinion handed down by Justice Hargrave — as well as many early eighteenth-century documents relating to the theatre, "faithfully transcribed, from the Copy Sent me by Mr. Isaac Reed of Staple Inn." In the Folger Library are notes and extracts by Kemble on such esoteric subjects as Siamese drama, the stage of "ces malheureux Brammes," the Roman theatre (buttressed by Latin quotations from Cicero), and the early English stage. More impressive, however, is a long list of English actors, their dates and principal roles, which he drew up. The first name is Richard Tarleton, followed by that of Richard Burbage: "he is said to be the original King Richard 3d and acted in many of Ben Jonson's plays. He died 1619." Most of the notices are equally brief. "William Cartwright performed Falstaff at Gibbon's tennis Court under Killigrew & was joint Manager with Major Mohun at the Cockpit Dr Lane." Kemble records that Mrs. Barry was "the first performer who ever had a benefit" and that Mrs. Hughes was "the first female Performer of Macbeth." There are some inaccuracies, such as Jonson's death being in 1742, and for the most part the comments are very uninteresting. He cannot help mentioning the fantastic career of Colley Cibber's scapegrace daughter, Charlotte Charke, who passed "thro various scenes of life, such as moving the Puppets at Russels Puppet Shew, keeping a public house & then falling to a Sausage Stall." Some of his more illustrious predecessors are dismissed with most perfunctory notices. "David Garrick, born at Hereford 1716 [sic] & was buried in Westminster Abbey." Working up through the eighteenth century, he merely lists his contemporaries by the dates of their London debuts. The three hundred and fifteen items in this curious document, though hardly constituting an important piece of stage history, do show Kemble's zeal for information about his profession.[7]

Another bit of antiquarianism of Kemble's is a manuscript of some hundred and thirty pages which deals with the history of the Theatre Royal in Dublin from 1730 to 1751. Consisting entirely of extracts from the Dublin *Journal*, it is made up of theatrical announcements and reviews, interspersed with occasional bits of correspondence and infrequent comments by Kemble himself. Such an item as this, of course, would catch the eye of a man who never scrupled to spend more in mounting a play than he could reasonably expect to make from it:

The Play of King Henry the 8th. which hath been so greatly admired, and hath met with so much success in London for its fine Appearance, is now in Rehearsal at the Theatre Royal in Angier-Street; and in order to encourage our Diversions, the Rt. Honble [sic] William Connoly Esqre. hath given fifty guineas to decorate it, which will make a most splendid Figure, there having been upwards of three hundred Pounds already laid out for Dresses to the said Play.

An entry for May, 1739, records that "Mr. Quin hath given such universal Satisfaction in his playing that he had 126 *l.* for his Benefit; and although the weather is so warm, yet Numbers of People flock to see that great Player." In 1749 there was an "extraordinary Demand for Shakspeare's Plays from Numbers of Persons who could not get Room in the Theatre." It may have been to meet that demand that *The Tempest*, "written by Shakspeare, and altered by Dryden," was produced on January 13, 1749, "with new Scenes, and an extraordinary Piece of Machinery Representing the rising Sun . . . Dorinda, who never saw a Man with the Song of Dear pretty Youth, by Mrs. Mozeen — Hippolito who never saw a woman by Mrs. Bland. The whole to conclude with a grand Masque of Neptune and Amphitrite." [8]

As befitted a historian of the stage, even an amateur one, Kemble kept a complete file of playbills for his theatre — both Drury Lane and later Covent Garden — on which he occasionally scribbled comments. His wife's father, Hopkins, was the prompter for Drury Lane under Garrick, and from his diary (now apparently lost, to the lasting regret of scholars) the tragedian would frequently copy notes on early performances. For example, when Mrs. King, on October 18, 1775, was billed to act Rosalind by command, Hopkins explained (and Kemble copied him) that "this Circumstance was a Contrivance of Mr. Garrick's in order to mortify Mrs. Yates, Mrs. Abington, and Miss Younge." Charles Bannister's name, observes the punctilious manager, "is spelt with one *n* in all the Bills till Saturday Decr. 12th, 1767." When Hopkins notes that Smith made his debut at Drury Lane on September 22, 1774, as Richard, Kemble politely points out that "Mr. Hopkins is mistaken, and the Play-bill is inaccurate; — for Mr. Smith acted Osmyn in the Mourning Bride at Drury Lane Theatre on Tuesday the 29th. of May 1759, — having been borrowed from Covent Garden that Evening to supply Mr. Mossop's Place, whose Father died about that Time." Of course Hopkins' enthusiastic comment on Garrick's elaborate production of *The Jubilee* (October 13, 1769) was transcribed:

It was received with Bursts of Applause — The procession of Shakspeare's characters is the most superb that ever was exhibited, or I believe ever will. — There never was an entertainment produced that gave so much Pleasure to all Degrees, Boxes, Pit, and Gallery.

Kemble's friends marveled at his diligence in collecting scraps and tags of theatrical history. His "ardent" studies, embracing "everything collateral to his art," were the wonder of his circle. In fact, John Taylor, in a fine burst of devotion trying to rationalize Kemble's consorting with Parson Este, thought that zany was cultivated because he could give "a faithful and vivid description" of the actors whom he remembered from his youth.[9]

For the most part, Kemble carried his learning (which in time became considerable) deftly and properly, as befitted a gentleman. Subscribing to a weighty thesaurus, he observed gracefully that "I think one may be allowed to wish well to the cause of learning, without having any pretension to the praise of being learned oneself." He was content to be accepted as a gifted amateur among scholars, capable of polishing off a translation of Ovid as readily as offering expert advice on matters of theatrical arcana. One of his scholarly letters, hitherto unpublished, shows very well his interests:

My dear Sir,

It would not surprize me, if you put me down for the most negligent correspondent in the world; and yet I have not for a moment forgotten the business you wrote to me on. — Having searched to no purpose after Progne in Peshall's History of Oxfordshire, whither I found myself referred on this article by that, in general very accurate book the Biographia Dramatica, I prevailed on a friend of mine of extensive english [sic] reading to try to find the information I wanted relative to this piece: — he yesterday gave me the following extract from Gutch's Edition of Wood's History and Antiquity of the University of Oxford — 4to Oxford — 1796 — vol. 2d. P. 142, or 162, I cannot well make out which: — "After the Queen had refreshed herself with a supper, she with her nobility went into Cr. Cr. Hall, where was acted before them a Latin Tragedy, called Progne, made by Dr. James Calfhill, Canon of Cr. Cr. After which was done, she gave the author thanks; but it did not take half so well as the much admired play of Palamon and Arcyte."

Progne was acted before the Queen on her Majesty's visit to Oxford in 1566. I cannot find that it was ever printed; and, as it appears not to have been very successful, perhaps the author did not venture it to the press.

I will not attempt the obligation I feel to your kind concern for my health, any more than I will to assure you how truly happy I am to learn that you are restored to the enjoyment of your charming retreat. — I suppose Mr. Eccles sometimes wanders in your groves — Let me beg to be remembered to him.

We have had, as you doubtless know, a combination among the working printers, which has thrown every publication backwards. — I shall hope, however, that Mr. Longman will use all his endeavours to expedite a work so highly interesting as yours to all lovers of polite literature, and particularly to those connected with the Drama. We had some conversation, I recollect, on the machinery of the Curtain in the ancient theatre, when I had the pleasure of being at Saint Valeri [?], and from a passage in Virgil, I remember, we were inclined to believe that it was raised and not let down as with us. I have never made any inquiry on this subject, but should imagine the question might be decided from Vitruvius.

Mr. Gifford's edition of Massinger is come out, and is very well spoken of. I hear that he has some thoughts of editing Shirley.

The generality of dissertations on the Spanish Stage are Treatises on Dramatick Poetry, the Unities, and answers to the slights thrown on their Theatre by the French. — I have not seen La Muerte de Levar by Urguijo — if, however, he is, as I suppose, the person who formerly was Secretary here to the Spanish Embassy, there may be new matter, new analogies, and new reasonings in his dissertation even on an old subject. — The oldest account I have ever met with of the Spanish Stage is by Cervantes in the preface to his plays, and the most modern I have the pleasure of reading you. —

Pray make my most respected services to your Sister, who knows me very much by remembering me, and believe, my dear Sir, that I shall always be

Yours obliged and faithful Servant,

J. P. KEMBLE [10]

The crown of Kemble's career as a dilettante of letters was his notable library. Chiefly, it has been hinted, because Garrick set about collecting dramatic curiosities, his successor emulated and far surpassed him as a bibliophile. His hobby, of course, was practiced at "prodigious expense," but he en-

joyed the sweet fruits of success in the esteem his library had
among the learned. His principal aim was to get as much
early drama as possible; of Shakespeare he bought every play
"that could be got for money." And once he was financially
established, during the 'nineties, he "steadily pursued" his
goal — of forming "a complete collection of the drama." Indeed, so avid did he become, that a rare find of his was chron-
icled (together with the price) in the press. He haunted
book-stalls and auctions, usually "close at the auctoneer's back
most busily employ'd." Leigh Hunt, an impecunious young
journalist, remembered him consorting with lords and earls
when the Duke of Roxburgh's library was sold, and Kemble
was one of the distinguished group including Lord Charlemont, the Duke of Roxburgh, and Edmond Malone which secured eight Shakespearian quartos selling "separately for
twelve pounds four shillings." Of course, book collection in
the late eighteenth century was not the millionaire's hobby it
is now. In point of fact, it was almost cheaper to buy tattered
old quartos than the shiny editions of contemporary writers.
Before the expansion of cheap literature in the nineteenth
century books were for the moneyed: Scott's cheapest book
cost twenty-one shillings, his three-decker novels brought first
a guinea and then thirty-one shillings, and Southey's *Thalaba*
sold for two guineas. One is amused to find Malone, acting as
agent for Lord Charlemont, writing apologetically that he
would need twenty guineas to buy a lot of a hundred and
twenty early quartos. "There is hardly an old play of any
rarity now to be got under four or five shillings," grumbled
Malone, "and some they even ask half a guinea for." None
the less, Kemble's really splendid collection cost him "many
thousand pounds," and he lived to see it enjoy great contemporary celebrity. No man, thought William Beloe, "knows
more, or better, whatever relates to the History of the Drama;
no man possesses more copies, or more valuable materials: no

man communicates what he knows and possesses, to his friends, with greater or more agreeable facility." [11]

As a matter of fact, Kemble's library was astonishingly good. When it was sold, after his retirement, William Spencer Cavendish, sixth Duke of Devonshire, bought the cream of it — about four thousand plays and forty volumes of playbills — for a ridiculously small sum. Kemble offered it for £2,000, to which the duke agreed, offering to pay either the full amount at once or an annuity. Kemble, feeling that his investment in Covent Garden was uncertain, chose the annuity, and he received £400 a year until his death. Unfortunately, he had the singular bibliographical bad taste to dismember all plays as he bought them, and then to have each leaf inlaid in a quarto-size mat. So mounted, they were rebound, usually about six plays to the volume, and no doubt made a very handsome appearance in his huge library * — a special room built on to his house in Bedford Square, before he moved to the elegant place in Great Russell Street. [12]

When the remainder of the library was sold at auction, following the duke's purchase of the play collection, the catalogue, of some sixty-six pages, listed no less than 1,677 titles, in addition to 181 prints and paintings. The diversity is remarkable. There is relatively little Greek, but a great mass of writings in Latin, on subjects ranging from patristic commentaries to *Martialis Epigrammata*. There are liberal selections from the Italian poets — Ariosto, Alfieri, Boccaccio; and the French section is, if anything, more complete than the English. Most of the standard authors of both languages are listed, often in several editions. The bulk of the library, of

* After this collection passed into the Duke of Devonshire's possession, he added to it considerably, until it contained more than 7,500 plays and 111 volumes of playbills. It was finally brought up for sale by Sotheby's, and was acquired by Mr. Henry Huntington in 1914. It now forms an important part of the drama section of the Huntington Library in San Marino, California.

course, is composed of theatrical works, memoirs, biographies, and pamphlets. Surprisingly enough, there is a large Spanish section, perhaps the result of Kemble's trip to Spain in 1802. It is, in short, the library of a highly cultivated and learned English gentleman. Paley's *Evidences of Christianity* rubs against Rabelais, and Shaftesbury's *Characteristics* is found side by side to the letters of Madame de Sévigné and *Senecae atque aliorum Tragoediae, Farnabii*. Some of the folios, particularly, are interesting. The 1647 Beaumont and Fletcher is listed with *Aldrete Origen y Principio de la Lengua Castellana* (1674), a fifteenth-century manuscript of Chaucer with Eusebius' *Church History*, the 1616 Jonson with Knolles' *History of the Turks*, Sandys' Ovid with Raleigh's *History of the World*, a first folio Shakespeare with Gavin Douglas' *Aeneid*. It is a remarkable collection, remarkable for its gems as for its rubbish. Even with the low price of books at that time, Kemble must have put thousands of pounds into it. By the time the collection came to be auctioned, the most valuable part of it — the now priceless Elizabethan quartos — was of course already in the possession of the Duke of Devonshire, but even so there remained enough to form an astonishingly varied and interesting library.[13]

Kemble was renowned for his generosity and assistance in opening his library to his friends. Being, as he was, on intimate terms with most of the leading men of letters of his day, he had many calls for books and manuscripts. Even William Gifford, that ogre who had taken occasion to ridicule his delivery as well as his book-collecting, was pleased to have recourse to his library when he was preparing his edition of Jonson. John Taylor brought the two together, and curiously enough they were immediately attracted to each other: "they had all the talk to themselves, and seemed to be highly gratified with each other." Before long, they were exchanging books, and Kemble would drop by to have a "look at a sheet

or two of Old Ben." Gifford sent his friend a copy of the
Jonson as soon as it was published, and in the second edition
of his essay on *Macbeth* Kemble observed that by his friend's
"learned and generous labours *Old Ben's* forgotten works and
injured character are restored to the merited admiration and
esteem of the world." Kemble appears to be one of the few of
Gifford's contemporaries who did not detest and fear him;
as an old man, who could forgive even Byron, Leigh Hunt
still remembered the savage critic as "the only man I ever
attacked, respecting whom I have felt no regret." But Kemble's relations with him were always amiable, especially since
Gifford had the grace to withdraw, in later editions of his
satires, his derogatory remarks about the actor.[14]

As a bibliophile of sorts and a man of letters Kemble cultivated the society of literary celebrities. In his own meager
writings — such as the *Macbeth* essay — he took extreme care
with his composition, weighing "every word, accent and
comma," and though unfriendly persons claimed that his
interest in literature was "minute, grammatical, and verbal,"
he seems to have had a genuine feeling for good poetry, and
certainly an encyclopedic knowledge of the drama. He was
no antiquarian; when some one gave him a manuscript of the
Canterbury Tales, he read a little of it "with difficulty" and
never finished it. But he was eager to take a prominent part
in good, orthodox literary enterprises. He placed "his whole
dramatic library" at Thomas Campbell's disposal when the
poet was preparing some lectures, and he even risked some
money in promoting the publication of Francis Twiss' *Verbal
Index* to Shakespeare, a benevolence which was heartily
acknowledged by the author in his dedication: a work on
Shakespeare could be inscribed to no more deserving person
that one "who has long been, and may long continue to be!
the boast of the British stage." A classicist on the stage,
Kemble was by way of being a classicist in literature. His

position as the leader of his profession naturally gained him a wide following among the *cognoscenti*, even though his intimacy with the scholars and literary personages of the day was not entirely a result of his acting. His elaborate and esteemed Shakespearian revivals, his interest in early English drama, his collecting, and his own casual literary productions entitled him to meet almost on equal terms professional men of letters. It was a pleasant side to his career, and one for which his contemporaries admired and respected him.[15]

CHAPTER XI

The Scene Changes

> Life is one long process of getting tired.
>
> SAMUEL BUTLER

BACK IN London by the early fall, Kemble had to endure — perhaps not reluctantly — the blandishments of Sheridan. Business was afoot, and the leisurely book-collecting and window shopping were now replaced by the incessant efforts of Sheri to regain the main prop of Drury Lane. To that end he applied all his persuasive charm. It was an office for which the personable genius was suited: he knew Kemble, and he knew the way to placate him. Once before, when Kemble had written him a very snappish letter he had jovially brushed aside the "troublesomeness" over four bottles instead of three of claret. Now, however, the nut was a little harder to crack. Kemble was well aware of his importance to the theatre, and he was determined to capitalize on it. "Surely no one has a better right to make his own proposals," decided one of the admirers of "the first actor in the kingdom." Sheri finally gave in, apparently without much of a struggle, and agreed on four guineas a night for Kemble's acting, three hundred pounds for his benefit, and some sort of settlement on back salary which he owed him.* But the managership Kemble flatly refused — he had seen too much of Sheridan and his intolerable caprices — and that uncherished office passed to

---

* At the end of 1796, we learn from Kemble's journal, Sheridan gave his manager a bond for £500 as evidence of good faith in settling his back salary, some £1367 13s. 2d.

Wroughton, one of the reliable but by no means brilliant
actors of the company. At the returning hero's first appearance, as Penruddock on September 29, the audience, remembering Colman and Ireland's harsh words, gave him "a
greeting due his merits and an ample recompense for the
dirty attack which disappointment and malignity made upon
his character *during his absence*." [1]

Although Kemble's winter was a full one, it need not detain
us long. He acted frequently and with acclaim, chiefly in
those plays by which he had made his reputation. A couple
of revivals fared badly: Thomson's *Edward and Eleonora*
proved to be "a flat and creeping business" and Jephson's new
Conspiracy was no better. But young Charles Kemble was
rising rapidly, and the divine Siddons ("that magnificent and
appalling creature," Sheri's lovely wife Elizabeth had called
her) was extravagantly admired. Kemble himself was as much
a star in society as on the stage. *Blue Beard*, the mid-winter
spectacle which he found "very heavy indeed," left many of
his evenings free, and he wined and dined with the cream of
the London intellectuals. One evening it would be with
Malone, the next with a large party at his own home, the
next with old Roger and his wife, the next with another
brilliant gathering (Luttrell, Lawrence, Boaden, the Siddons),
the next with the Marchioness of Abercorn. Rich and famous,
and unhampered by the managerial woes of running Drury
Lane, Kemble had a busy but tranquil winter. He was free
to play frequently in his beloved tragedies, and the vexation
of producing pantomimes that "would disgrace a puppet-
shew" was his no longer. [2]

At the beginning of June, the Kembles set out again for
Dublin, the city which had for the past two summers taken the
actor to its heart. A stop for visiting the Greatheeds at Guy's
Cliff (Bertie, it will be remembered, had written *The
Regent*), made the journey more pleasant. Thomas Gray had

visited the Greatheeds at Guy's Cliff forty years before, and
had been thoroughly disgusted at the artificial grotto ("with
cockle-shells and looking-glass") which had been achieved by
cutting down all the fine old trees, removing the rocks, and
laying out neat gravel paths. But the Kembles — and Mrs.
Siddons — never tired of returning to Guy's Cliff. And in
Dublin there were as many dinners and fetes as ever, some
of which Kemble refused: "one cannot eat and drink every
day." But the Earl of Charlemont was eager to show his art
treasures to the elegant London actor, and time spent with
him passed "delightfully." The Lord Chancellor, too, entertained lavishly. One of his guests, a man of very settled opinions, said decisively that "it wd. be well for Ireland if Mr.
Burke & Mr. Grattan were hang'd — and that he knew that
Mr. Burke kept a Friar in his House." Kemble, when not
being lionized (which he enjoyed thoroughly) was busy at
the theatre, acting, before July 31, nineteen times to "amazing houses." True, his benefit brought only £64, owing to
Daly's incorrigible villainy — "N.B. Mr. Daly cheated me by
not appointing my Benefit on the Night I had a right to by
the Spirit of our Agreement" — but the Dublin stay netted
Kemble £714. Limerick and Cork proved equally diverting
and remunerative, and it was after a pleasant and profitable
summer that Kemble returned to London at the end of
September.[3]

Another dull season of lugubrious tragedies seemed the
prospect for 1797–1798. Drury Lane's finances had become
so precarious that Kemble insisted on regular payments of
his salary, and until the middle of December the theatre
limped along dolorously enough. But presently Sheridan
came by one of those windfalls which periodically put old
Drury back on a sound basis. "Monk" Lewis' Castle Spectre,
though admitted on all sides to be trash, proved to be a tremendous success. Its run of forty-seven nights signified to

most thinking persons the nadir of theatrical production and
popular taste. Lady Lushington, Lewis' sister, had expur-
gated the piece with a "pure and pious mind," and the spectacle that was left was precisely suited to the taste of the
populace. Even Lady Holland, who left several dinner parties
early to see the piece, condescended to admit that it was "not
totally without merit." But such professional critics as Gifford wailed that not since the days of *Gammar Gurton* had
the stage sunk so low: "It seems as if all the blockheads in the
kingdom had started up, and exclaimed, *una voce*, Come! let
us write for the theatre." [4]

There were some, like Shelley a few years later, who held
that "in periods of decay of social life, the drama sympathizes
with that decay." The fervid excitement of the 'nineties —
political, economic, military — that was sweeping all Europe
naturally was reflected in the disorder and aimlessness of the
theatre. But the astounding success of pieces like *The Castle
Spectre* does give one pause. Oliver Goldsmith had been
disgusted with similar efforts thirty years before: "Scenes
shifting, trumpets sounding, mobs hallooing, carpets spreading, guards bustling from one door to another; gods, demons,
daggers, racks, and ratisband. But whether the king was
killed, or the queen was drowned, or the son was poisoned, I
have absolutely forgotten." By the end of the century, things
were even worse. A mournful commentator admitted that the
stage was "in the lowest possible state of degradation," and
George Frederick Cooke fervently hoped that posterity would
not believe that *The Castle Spectre* could attract crowded
houses when Shakespeare was played to empty benches. Poor
Kemble acted — one can imagine with what feelings — the
role of Earl Percy to the vast delectation of the town; he
confessed "it is a vile thing — but the Audience applauded
it very much." Happily, Sheridan was under no illusions.
When Lewis, to settle an argument with the patentee, offered

to wager all that his play had made for Drury Lane, Sheridan
·objected that he could not risk such a sum. "But," he added
quickly, "I'll tell you what I'll do, — I'll bet you all it's worth."
At which point, remarks Lady Holland, "the little author
became as mute as a fish from the rebuff." [5]

In the spring Kemble began preparing a new and important role, appearing to his friends deep in "gloomy abstrac-
tion" and even exhibiting an unusual carelessness in his dress.
The new play proved to be worth all the actor's preparation,
serving to provide him with another of those parts which
became peculiarly identified with his style of acting. *The
Stranger*, fairly insignificant in itself, gave the rising German
drama a considerable fillip and in time came to be — along
with *The Mountaineers* and *The Wheel of Fortune* — one of
the characteristic products of the era, as well as a great personal vehicle for Kemble. The actor, be it said to his credit,
was in theory opposed to such importations, but he found it
"beyond his power" to check the popular taste for German
drama. In Thompson's adroit and sympathetic translation,
Kotzebue's dreary play appealed instantaneously to the London audiences. Lady Holland decided that "the same dull
apathy of character" of both the English and the Germans
needed such extravagant emotion for stimulus, but critics like
Hazlitt stoutly decried the genre: German dramatists "do
things by contraries." In spite of the mutterings of the intellectuals, the type flourished; between 1796 and 1801 twenty
of Kotzebue's plays were produced in England. And if we
may believe Gogol, *Menschenhass und Reue* (*The Stranger*)
was a stock piece even in the remote Russian provinces.
Kemble's production found him at his gloomy best in the
title role, and Mrs. Siddons as Mrs. Haller was enormously
effective. Indeed, one lady, on seeing the actress, "sunk under
the oppression," and was not herself for three days after.
Kotzebue's "slop morality" was so popular that certain insular

critics, such as the formidable Anna Seward, noted with dis-approval that "it is the English mania to prefer the produc-tions of foreigners to those of their own country." Mean-while, the new piece flourished mightily.[6]

Kemble closed the season early, at the end of May, and once more took his well-paying art to the provinces, though not with the success he had enjoyed for the past two summers in Ireland. In Manchester he got only £178 for eight nights' acting, not receiving "the attention undoubtedly due" be-cause the local company had for six whole months before surfeited the public. Liverpool proved more profitable, how-ever, and the Earl of Derby made the actor's stay socially pleasant. At Birmingham Kemble was shown through the town's foundry — "a Favour," he notes proudly, "which has been refused to Persons of the first Rank native and foreign." The stop at Bristol Wells was saddened by the fatal illness of one of Mrs. Siddons' numerous progeny, Maria, but engage-ments at Plymouth and Exeter (whose cathedral merited a flattering comment in Kemble's journal) were filled none the less. London was regained by way of Weymouth, where Kemble acted five nights at the command of the Royal Fam-ily who were staying there, and by the first week in September, with a total profit of some £1112 for the summer's labors, the English Roscius was back prepared for another season at Drury Lane.[7]

Kemble had been fortunate of late. Relieved from the vexations of managements, he had built up his prestige enor-mously. His new roles — Penruddock, Octavian, and the Stranger — had proved thumping personal successes, suited as they were to his temperament and technique. His reputation was approaching a crest, and on all sides it was allowed that Kemble was beyond quibble the first English actor: in Shake-speare he could "nobly soar,"

And make e'en Garrick's loss be felt no more,

and his interpretations of such of the newer plays as appealed
to him were enough to make them popular as long as he cared
to act them. Rich and famous, the leader of his profession
and the intimate of peers of the realm, as the century neared
its turn, John Kemble began to assume that pontifical glory
that so well became him. He had trained the public to accept
his style of acting, he had made Shakespeare again a living
power in the theatre, and he had — not without effort — taken
his rightful place as high priest of the English stage. It had
become, admits Leigh Hunt, a "critical religion" to profess
oneself a follower of the great Kemble.[8]

But as the actor's star rose, Drury Lane's declined.
Wroughton was replaced by James Aickin — one hack by
another — but change of managers failed to check the slump.
"A bad play, badly acted, to a bad house" — so reported one
critic wearily of a typical production. Kemble played his
usual string of classics, replacing Orlando by Jaques in *As
You Like It*, perhaps as a gesture to his advancing years. For
sweet friendship's sake he appeared in Boaden's *Aurelio and
Miranda* and in Dr. Thomas Whalley's *Castle of Montval*, the
latter with some success. But although Anna Seward wrote
the author, a dignitary of Bath and a great friend of Mrs.
Siddons, that her "curiosity of perusal is extreme," the in-
exorable Kemble noted in his journal that the piece was
"very poor." A week's trip to Edinburgh in March had added
some £358 to Kemble's own exchequer, but meanwhile the
theatre itself was apparently on the brink of bankruptcy.
Once again, as with *The Castle Spectre* of the year before,
Drury Lane was saved at the last minute — this time by a
success which is still legendary. Sheridan, seeing that something drastic must be done, seized time by the forelock and
converted Kotzebue's *Spanier in Peru* into a medley of heroics,
sentiment, and spectacle that was sure to please the town.
With the unerring tact of genius he succeeded. *Pizarro* is one

of the most brilliantly and patently theatrical pieces in English drama. Although Sheri had taste enough to realize that he was writing meretricious drivel, he had the good sense to abandon himself to a production he knew could not fail. With characteristic negligence, he let poor Kemble and Mrs. Siddons have one scene as he was scribbling off the next, and Kemble tartly noted in his journal that he was forced to stay home from the theatre to receive his lines as they came in. Fanny Kemble, making an even better story, would have it that Sheri was dashing off the last scenes even as the beginning of the piece was being acted.[9]

The *première*, on the night of May 24, was not without flaws — for one thing, it lasted until nearly midnight — but by and large it was a towering success. The spectacle alone, under the master hand of Kemble, was enough to bring the pit to its feet roaring applause, while Sheridan, pleased as punch, bustled in and out of Lady Holland's box in high good spirits. The town was taken by storm. Anna Seward made bold to suggest it "was of the degenerate class," but she was as one crying in the wilderness. Most critics, like the ebullient young Crabb Robinson could only breathe ecstatic praises — "a drama absolutely without parallel." Lady Holland several times drastically curtailed her dinner in order to see the play through from the beginning, and on occasion her box was so filled with notables that no more could be squeezed in. Meanwhile Sheri was going about sprinkling his conversation with scraps from his miraculous piece. Perhaps his final triumph came when *Pizarro* itself was translated back into German.[10]

In Rolla, Kemble found another part which was to become synonymous with his name. The great Pitt thought that in the role he was "the noblest Actor that he had ever seen"; John Taylor declared that even Garrick could have made no more of it; and Sheri himself, watching from behind the

scenes, exclaimed, "Beautiful! sublime! perfection!" meanwhile clapping his hands with pleasure. *Pizarro* naturally
monopolized the rest of the season — as well as most of the
next season — and all London flocked to Drury Lane to see
Rolla snatch the baby and leap across the bridge. In spite of
the welcome profits, by July Kemble was heartily glad to forsake babies and bridges and everything connected with Rolla,
and to take to the provinces. York, Birmingham, Cheltenham
all paid well to see the great man, and when he returned in
August to supervise the house-painting in Great Russell
Street he could relax freely with his cup-fellows, Sheridan
and Steevens. "Talked much of &c." But the next morning
he was very ill — "as I deserve to be." Presently he was off
again for brief engagements at Margate and Brighthelmstone,
only to return in the middle of September with a profit of
some £1036 for his summer's acting. Old Roger's son had
come far since those days twenty-five years before when he
trudged over England sleeping in barns and acting for his
supper.[11]

Drury Lane that fall, even with *Pizarro* as a *deus ex ma-
china*, was approaching an almost incredible state of insol-
vency. These were the dark days, as Lady Blessington
afterwards told Byron, when Sheri ceased weeping at his debts
and began laughing his creditors down. It must have been
hard to laugh, though, when angry bailiffs besieged his house
in Berkeley Square and "the provisions requisite for his family were introduced over the iron railing down the area."
For Drury Lane's harassed treasurer, Peake, there would come
little *billets doux* from his master demanding twenty or thirty
pounds. Miss De Camp, later to be Fanny Kemble's mother,
recalled those

dismal Saturdays, when, after prolonged periods of non-payment
of their salaries, the poorer members of the company, and all
the unfortunate work-people, carpenters, painters, scene-shifters,

understrappers of all sorts, and plebs in general of the great dramatic concern, thronging the passages and staircases, would assail Sheridan on his way to the treasury with pitiful invocations: "For God's sake, Mr. Sheridan, pay us our salaries!" and his plausible reply of, "Certainly, certainly, my good people, you shall be attended to directly." Then he would go into the treasure, sweep it clean of the whole week's receipts (the salaries of the principal actors, whom he dared not offend, and could not dispense with, being, if not wholly, partially paid), and, going out of the building another way, leave the poor people who had cried to him for their arrears of wages baffled and cheated of the price of their labor for another week. The picture was not a pleasant one.[12]

Kemble continued a great attraction, however. It was not unusual for him to be called to the Prince of Wales' box for a cozy chat (as he proudly recorded in his journal). Large dinner parties took him into society more than ever — he was "in high vogue with the Beau Monde," if we may believe Hester Thrale Piozzi — and during the winter there were frequent meetings of a "Literary Club" (comprising Burgess, Beloe, Pye, Nares, Spencer, Sotheby, and Kemble) where much high-sounding talk went on. Presently Walter Scott and Cumberland were elected honorary members, but Sam Rogers was "black-ball'd." More black-balling occurred when Kemble read the countless new plays submitted to him: he for one was convinced that Drury Lane did not need new pieces, for "the treasures of our ancient authors were inexhaustible. Shewy after-pieces and laughable farces might be necessary; but what could be expected now in the way of the regular drama that previously had not been better done?" [13]

Those stacks of unread plays in Sheridan's study that Kemble called a "funeral pile" continued to grow, however. As George Farquhar had pointed out a century before, "*Poetry* alone, and chiefly the *Dramma*, lies open to the insults of all pretenders." Although the drama of Kemble's day has been declared to have "a mainly pathological interest," it is voluminous if unreadable. Wordsworth had written and submitted *The Borderers* and (so he said years later) "incurred no disappointment when the piece was *judiciously* returned as not calculated for the stage." But his scribbling brethren did not have such philosophic calm. A generation earlier the vitriolic Smollett had almost had apoplexy at Garrick's vacillation, and a generation later John Keats was going to think Elliston "little better than a knave" for not accepting *Otho* out of hand. When Byron, in the fullness of time, arrived at his own days of play-writing, he could not "conceive any man of irritable feeling putting himself at the mercies of an audience." Not so Coleridge and Lamb: they were both busily scribbling plays, with extraordinarily dolorous results.[14]

One chill December morning in 1799 young Lamb, timorous but resolved, deposited a manuscript called *John Woodvil* at Kemble's house in Great Russell Street. Afraid to meet the great man in person, he merely left an anonymous note, requesting an opinion, and was charmed by Kemble's condescension in offering to pass it on to the play-reading committee. But a year later nothing had been done, and the thwarted author was finally told that the play had been lost. But if he would be so good as to write out another manuscript . . . . Unable to resist "so facile and moderate demand," he did so, only to have it flatly refused. Coleridge fared little better. A great theatre-goer, he had persuaded the incorrigible Sheridan — who could never say no — to bring forward *Osorio* "with every possible advantage." But his qualms overcame his hopes, and to Thelwall he mourned: "Oh, my Tragedy! it is finished, transcribed, and to be sent off today; but I have no hope of its success, or even of its being acted." His fears were all too well founded, and presently we find him telling Cottle that all he had heard from the powers at Drury Lane was "some silly remarks of Kemble's." De Quincey would have it that *Osorio* had no chance after Sheridan, coming to the line, "Drip, drip, drip," set up a chorus of laughter among the committee by remarking, "Why, God bless me, there's nothing here but Dripping!" Coleridge decided that Sheri was "an unprincipled Rogue," and taking what comfort he could in that melancholy conclusion, he forgot about the piece for a dozen years. When it finally was produced, as *Remorse* in 1813, it had a certain measure of success.[15]

One can hardly censure the chary members of the committee. At rare intervals, when a new play was accepted, the results were almost never gratifying, either artistically or financially. Kemble thought that Henry Pye's *Adelaide* had "every claim" to his assistance because the Laureate was "a scholar and a critic," but when he acted it (on January 25), the result was no more "than a powerful struggle with intractable materials." But *Pizarro* was still making money — it had sixty-seven performances during the season — and the new spectacle, *The Egyptian Festival*, amused the town most of the spring. The principal undertaking in the way of heavy tragedy was Joanna Baillie's widely heralded *De Montfort*. Miss Baillie, a gifted bluestocking and a valued friend of Scott's, wrote her numerous "Plays on the Passions" in order to reveal what lay under "the dress and manners of men" and to lay bare the "passions" that motivated their actions. *De Montfort*, one of the first of the series, had been written "expressly" with Kemble and Mrs. Siddons in mind, and the actor was so impressed with it that he himself "altered and adapted [it] to the stage." William Capon was given a free hand with the setting, and his "unusual pile of scenery" representing a fourteenth-century church was much admired. The performance (April 29) was merely a *succès d'estime*, the intellectuals hailing it as a significant attempt. Sir Walter Scott, for instance, though Miss Baillie was "certainly the best dramatic

writer whom Britain has produced since the days of Shakespeare and Massinger." The bluestockings, of course, hastened to praise their sister. Mrs. Inchbald decided the play
marked its authoress with "the elevated character of a woman
of genius," and the redoubtable Swan of Lichfield was quite
convinced that the Plays on the Passions would put Miss
Baillie in the "first rank of those who, in this period, have
struck the Delphic lyre." But the intricately poised relation-
ships of De Montfort, Jane, and Rezenvelt were too much
for the London audiences. One critic declared it "uniformly
dull," and after only eight performances the enormously expensive production was withdrawn. With it Kemble closed
his important acting for the season.[16]

Before setting off for Ireland, Kemble had only to try to
collect his back salary, reminding Peake that his forty Guineas,
"my Salary for the week before last," as well as his twenty-five
guineas a night for *De Montfort* were still in arrears. But
once such unpleasantries were attended to, and his repertory
for Daly was settled — "I can think of no better Plays," he
wrote, than the customary string of tragedies, including
Pizarro and *The Stranger* along with Shakespeare — he left
for Dublin on May 21. Social life was as gay as ever. Refusing an invitation in Wicklow, Kemble explained, "The Truth
is, we are irrevocably engaged every Day during the Remainder of our short Stay in Ireland." The short stay netted
Kemble over £1117 for fourteen nights' acting, and before he
had returned to London by way of Glasgow, Berwick, and
Newcastle he had made about £600 more.[17]

In London again, he was bombarded by Sheridan who, in
desperation, was trying to persuade Kemble to buy a share of
the Drury Lane patent. The actor's art was an asset, but his
comfortable fortune (chiefly in Consols) would be an even
greater one. With all the easy eloquence at his command,
Sheri showed Kemble that as one of the patentees his income

would jump to four or five thousand pounds a year and that of all men he was the best equipped to assume an active interest in the great house. Kemble, he explained,

is at the head of his profession without a rival; he is attached to it, and desirous of elevating its character. He may be assured of proper respect, &c. while I have the theatre; but I do not think he could brook his situation were the property to pass into vulgar and illiberal hands — an event which he knows contingencies might produce.

Kemble was sorely tempted, notwithstanding his dear-bought knowledge of Sheri and his ways.* He wanted to be "*really* manager of a theatre," free to conduct a house devoted to classic drama, and naturally he was fond of Old Drury, where his reputation had been made. When the season began, a verbal agreement had been reached that he would, for "several thousand of pounds sterling," buy his share of the house, and the fall opened with Kemble as manager and with everyone in a roseate glow of expectancy. The actor himself was convinced he could make Drury Lane pay well. But suddenly the whole transaction fell through. The cautious Morris, Kemble's attorney, was unable to establish Sheri's clear title to the property, and in great dudgeon the prospective purchaser stopped all negotiations. Sheridan's almost comic disregard for the amenities of business drove his star actor — with his prestige and his ten thousand pounds — very shortly to Covent Garden.[18]

Meanwhile the season had to go on, and Kemble addressed himself to the management with his customary severity. Murmurings from his hard-pressed and disgruntled actors, accus-

---

* Under the proposed terms Kemble's salary was to be £500 a year as manager, he was to negotiate, through Sheridan, a loan of £10,000 for the purchase of a fourth interest, and he was to hold a private box of which "the value cannot be stated at less than £3,500" (Moore, *Sheridan*, II, 304–308).

tomed to the lax regimen of Aickin, failed to impress Kemble, and the "variety of injurious reports" which a newspaper brought against the *"rigid disciplinarian"* were brushed away as arising out of "private pique and dissatisfaction." In his main purpose he was successful: Shakespeare was put forward with conspicuous success, though with fine disregard for the condition of Old Drury treasury. *"Hundreds,* nay *thousands* of pounds have been literally thrown away, to gratify the personal vanity of the manager," complained one of his detractors, but the discriminating were pleased to see an old favorite back in harness again. Kemble, unconcerned with the management except when Shakespeare was involved, appeared in all his best roles — Hamlet ("so long the just theme of panegyric," boasted the *Times*), King John, Jaques, Lear among others. And with it all, the "business of the stage is now carried on with a punctuality unexampled since this gentleman's former management, and the most minute attention is bestowed upon *costume, etiquette,* scenery and decoration." There were still private distractions, and Kemble was as adamant as ever with his salary, whatever the cost of his elaborate productions. We find him tersely reminding Peake that unless Mrs. Siddons got her fifty pounds there would be no *King John* the following Saturday, and unless the scene painters could buy some canvas both *Cymbeline* and the Christmas pantomime would have to be put off. On occasion he adopted even stronger tactics:

It is now two days since my necessity made me send to you for sixty pounds. My request has been treated with disregard, that I am at a loss to account for.

I certainly shall go, and act my part tonight — but, unless you send me a Hundred pounds before Thursday, I will not act on Thursday and if you make me come a-begging again, it will be for Two hundred pounds before I set my foot in the theatre.[19]

These financial difficulties — nothing new in a theatre

controlled by Sheridan — were accentuated by other vexations. William Godwin, in an evil hour, had written his dolorous *Antonio* and had persuaded Sheri to produce it, and poor Kemble, as four years before with *Vortigern*, was faced with the thankless task of staging and acting in a play he had nothing but contempt for. Godwin, rather declined in fortune since his *Political Justice* had set all the young intellectuals agog seven years before, was offensively generous with his suggestions: he expected to make £500 by the venture and was not reluctant to favor Kemble with his advice as to details of the production. But the actor, sadly wise in the ways of inexperienced authors, protected none of Godwin's illusions. He sharply demanded a final version at once and told the aggrieved playwright that *Antonio* "may be acted five or six or seven nights, but that kind of success would at once be a great loss to the theatre, and I daresay a great disappointment to your expectations." Godwin, however, was not to be deterred, even when Kemble balked at playing the title role because of its "villainy." Lamb consented to write the epilogue, and was in a great pother to hear it spoken: "I must go and dress for the boxes! First night!" he wrote Manning. But on his program that night, when the evening was over, he wrote Antonio's epitaph: "Damned with Universal Consent." The one and only performance (December 13) proved an unmitigated failure. Kemble, "starched out in a ruff which no one could dispute, and in most irreproachable mustachios," was obviously not interested in the proceedings, and, as he had been known to do before to works in which he was compelled to act against his will, took no pains to make the play a success. Lamb, in fact, charged him with deliberately spoiling the accelerated action of the catastrophe:

From the beginning John had taken his stand, — had wound himself up to an even tenure of stately declamation, from which no exigence of dialogue or person could make him swerve for an instant.

The press was as bleakly unresponsive as the public — "as impotent an attempt at dramatic composition as the Stage has exhibited for many years" — and Godwin was left to sulk in failure. Lamb found him the next morning with "a kind of *blue sickness* about the eyelids." And although Kemble had the decency to write him a little note designed to be comforting ("I do assure you I thought nothing of any Trouble I took on your account"), he noted in his journal with cool complacency the single comment "Damned." Godwin the while was bitterly complaining of the way his play had been treated — and acted — to Coleridge, a friend who could give him scant consolation: he had already had cruel experience in the ways of theatrical management.[20]

Kemble straightway turned again — with relief, one imagines — to his beloved Shakespeare. Although Mrs. Piozzi thought him "out of health," the public was "in high good humour with him." *Lear* was a greatly admired production, and *Cymbeline*, though a financial failure, was a triumph of elaborate setting. Holcroft's *Deaf and Dumb* proved a gold mine for Drury Lane, although its author had to exercise all his persuasive powers to get fifty pounds for his labors. So carping a critic as Lady Holland found the piece "interesting," and Sheridan was again rescued in the nick of time: "It has at once saved the Manager from indelible disgrace, and the theatre from bankruptcy and ruin." Kemble's great triumph as the Abbé de l'Epée in Holcroft's play was not duplicated in a revival of Congreve's *Love for Love*, which even in a castrated version offended the sensibilities of the chaste audience. The last of the season was remarkable for nothing save Kemble's social activities. During a single week, for example, there occurred the Countess of Derby's assembly, Mrs. Siddons' assembly, the Marchioness of Abercorn's assembly, a large dinner party at Sheridan's, a supper at Mr. Nares', a dinner "at W. Spencer's, and go to the Opera," and a boisterous party at John Taylor's. One remembers Thackeray's formidable Countess of Kew, who thought that London after Easter

was intolerable. Pleasure becomes a business, then so offensive, that all good company is destroyed by it. Half the men are sick with the feasts which they eat day after day. The women are thinking of the half-dozen parties they have to go to in the course of the night. The young girls are thinking of their partners and their toilettes.[21]

It was presently over, however, and the theatrical season with it. Summer appearances at Worcester and Birmingham excited the local gentry but bored Kemble, and early in September began what was to be his last season with Old Drury. All London was alive with rumors and conjectures of a certain George Frederick Cooke — a fiery tragedian (an early Kean, perhaps) who for years had been a favorite in the provinces. The Harrises had brought him to Covent Garden, and for the first time since Colman and Pope had created a temporary excitement fifteen years before Kemble found his preeminence on the London stage seriously threatened. Audaciously enough, Drury Lane opened the fall with Cooke's strongest piece, *Richard III* — an action generally considered "as throwing down the gauntlet of Mr. Kemble at the feet of Mr. Cooke." The town prepared to sit back and enjoy the contest of the giants.[22]

Cooke accepted the challenge. When he made his debut as Richard, Mr. and Mrs. John Philip Kemble witnessed the performance from a front box, and the great man was "very liberal without being ostentatious in his applause." But Cooke was a formidable opponent. A superb Richard and Sir Giles Overreach, he offered the town a brand of acting it had not seen since the formal, declamatory, classically severe

Kemble had risen to dominate the whole profession. There were some, of course, like Charles Mathews, who could not conceive of Kemble's being rivaled, but many, like Crabb Robinson, flocked to see "the present *nine days' wonder*" and came away convinced his Richard surpassed Kemble's. Cooke had a roaring voice and a vigorous, impulsive style that were overwhelming to his contemporaries. Even John Taylor was afraid that the novice's success had hurt Kemble's reputation by showing the old, stylized technique to be "too systematick." Parson Este, however, when asked if he liked Cooke's acting, breathed a fervent "God forbid." Although the old favorite confined himself chiefly to his established repertory, his rival at Covent Garden was packing the theatre by playing the same pieces and — to the consternation of the faithful — was becoming the toast of the town "by the strange vicissitude of taste." People who had known Cooke in the provinces declared his best days were over and that London was seeing nothing but "the radiance of the setting sun," but he was none the less the new idol of the hour. His popularity, recalled Macready, "far excelled" Kemble's, and only eminently proper people like Canning could wonder that the vulgar, emotional ranter could even be mentioned in the same breath with Kemble.[23]

At Drury Lane, meanwhile, things were going none too well. Kemble's mother-in-law died in October, and for a week the theatre was without its star. But "*I claim no Salary,*" he pointed out in his journal. Perhaps it was because he and Sheri were on worse terms than ever. The fiasco over the title had given rise to hard feelings which this season were aggravated by intolerable financial conditions. Kemble himself was virtually without power in the actual control of the theatre: he explained to a friend that he could not even give him a pass. On all sides there were vexations. James Cobb was "really much disappointed" at not being paid for a farce he had written, and poor old Thomas King, famous when Kemble was an unknown stroller, ironically enough appealed to the disgruntled actor for money owed him by Sheridan, who seemed to think King would be "content to receive one week in four or five, and submit to leave my Acct. for years in an unsettled or disputable state." Kemble himself was penning curt little notes in a similar vein. "I wait with great Impatience for the fifty Pounds which I expected yesterday," he writes Peake. "And, pray, remember my last week's Salary." And on another occasion: "Do not put me off, for I am penniless." There were not even "Female Dresses" for the opera. But the crowning injury was the invasion of the theatre by emissaries of an angry creditor. Kemble wrote Sheridan a frantic little note wailing that "there are People in the Theatre, at Mr. Shaw's Suit, taking Inventories of the Wardrobes &c. and determined, as they assure me, to move the things away immediately. — I have said all I could to pacify them, and gain Time." Times had indeed changed at Drury Lane since Colley Cibber boasted that every week's debts were discharged before the partners took a shilling for themselves.[24]

Outraged creditors were not the only disturbances. Godwin, his head bloody but unbowed from the failure of *Antonio*, was fussily agitating for his new play, *Abbas, King of Persia*, to be brought out, but Kemble would not hear to it. "You must have the goodness not to press me further," he told Godwin sharply. The repertory, apart from Kemble's own Shakespearian vehicles, was shameful. A new opera, Mrs. Plowden's *Virginia*, was hooted off the stage, and the manager had the humiliation of coming forward and assuring the audience that since the offending piece had been "obtruded" on him he would cheerfully withdraw it. People were complaining of "shameful" faults in production: delays between plays and farces were interminable, and certain plays

(such as *The Tempest*) one critic had seen "as well performed
. . . if not better, by a provincial troop." [25]

There were rumors of an imminent clash between the
patentee and the manager, and in October the *Dramatic
Censor* announced — a little prematurely, as it happened —
that "in consequence of a violent disagreement" between
Sheridan and Kemble, the actor, "whether by *voluntary
resignation* or by *expulsion* and *discharge*," had broken off
all connections with the theatre. Open rupture was averted,
but during November Kemble did absent himself from the
infelicities of disturbing rivals and cunning creditors and
surly audiences, and undertook a short provincial tour to
Sheffield, Hull, and Liverpool. The change of scene may
have served as a restorative, for when he returned he was
determined to settle once and for all the pretensions of Mr.
George Frederick Cooke. Settling Mr. Cooke turned out to
be something of a chore. When the rivals began a duel of
playing *Richard III* night after night in competition, Cooke
was generally awarded the palm — and the town was shortly
tired of the contest. Thin audiences at both theatres gave
"evident tokens of disgust and dissatisfactions." Recalling
the days when Garrick and Barry had flaunted their respective Romeos *ad nauseam* half a century before, the theatrical
flyting served only to emphasize Cooke's superiority as Richard. Kemble's followers took what comfort they could in the
lame conclusion that however unsatisfactory their hero's
Richard, his Hamlet had not been surpassed "since the days
of Garrick." Cooke's supporters maintained that even when
drunk he equaled Kemble, and when sober —   So the mighty
contest raged. The thought of Kemble and his noble sister
acting on the same stage filled an apologist with awe: "The
Drama, justly directed, is the School of Virtue, and Heaven
has fixed its seal on the forms, the faces, the minds of these
two, its chosen disciples." It was suggested by the opposition,

however, that the chosen disciple had revived *Catharine and Petruchio* simply because he was envious of Cooke's recent success as Sir Archy MacSarcasm in *Love à la Mode*.[26]

Although the Kemble *versus* Cooke controversy rocked along most of the season, the new actor was certainly the theatrical man of the year, the most refreshing and stimulating novice the London boards had seen for a long time. After Kemble had left Old Drury and gone over to Cooke's theatre, the tempestuous tragedian's reputation declined, but he remained a valued member of the Covent Garden company for half a dozen years — in Byron's words, the most "natural" actor in the theatre. Later, broken by his excesses and wearing out his last days in America, Cooke acknowledged that Kemble was his superior, but in his heyday he was no doubt as expert in what Boaden contemptuously calls the "vulgar" style of acting as Kemble was in the "academic." [27]

Kemble, during his last six months with the house that made him famous, went with antiquarian zeal through all his famous stock pieces and revived several others. *Henry V*, an elaborately mounted production, was followed by the first *Henry IV* and *The Winter's Tale*, for which "not a single seat was disengaged." The "splendour of the dresses" and "the taste and elegance of the decorations and scenery" were mightily admired, while such discriminating critics as Southey and Mrs. Piozzi both were strongly moved by the performance: he thought the last scene "surpassed whatever I could have conceived of theatrical effect," and she could only wish Garrick could "witness the magnificence of modern Drury Lane." The close of the season was less triumphant, unfortunately. A revival of *The Double Dealer* outraged the godly: "Such a trough-full of villainy and lewdness was surely never before kneaded together! . . . Down, down with it to the lowest pit of hell." By spring it was generally understood that Kemble's days at Old Drury were numbered, and ironically

enough he who had inaugurated a brilliant career with
Hamlet twenty years before took his farewell in *Pizarro*. Two
days later, it is interesting to observe, Mrs. Powell favored the
town with her interpretation of the melancholy Dane.[28]

Kemble was tired — tired of Sheridan, tired of having to
beg for his salary, tired of running a theatre to suit somebody
else. He had made Drury Lane the best theatre in London
and the home of classical drama, but now he was going to
Covent Garden. Realizing that any possibility of buying a
partnership in his old theatre was "out of the question," he
took himself, his gifted family, and his style of acting where
he would have a fuller scope and a freer rein. When Kemble
left Drury Lane in 1802, it meant an end of the house's prestige. The theatre of Garrick "now sunk into a state of in-
feriority," and Covent Garden welcomed the greatest actor
and producer of the day.[29]

CHAPTER XII

Thou Last of All the Romans

In the truth of things, there are none utterly worth-
less, none without some drawback on their pretensions
or some alloy of imperfection.

HAZLITT

ALTHOUGH Kemble was the first actor of his generation
(and was so considered by his contemporaries), he, more
than any other first-rate figure in the annals of the English
stage, has suffered a curious loss of prestige at the hands of
posterity. For posterity always judges a bygone era by current
standards. To belittle Kemble's style — ordinarily dismissed
nowadays with the contemptuous epithet 'classical' — has become a critical habit for those who even take the trouble
to mention him at all as a brother of the glorious Siddons
who happened to gain some prominence in that arid period
between Garrick and Kean. Thus far we have tried to let his
contemporaries speak for themselves their opinion of him;
now it might be of interest to examine systematically his
impact on the theatre-goers of his day.

A characteristic modern comment on Kemble is that he
acted as if encased in armor. Such an opinion, growing in
part out of the contrast between Kemble's style and the
flexible realism and fluidity of contemporary technique, finds
support even among certain of his own associates. His "super-
cilious airs and *nonchalance*," complained one critic, "remind
one of the unaccountable abstracted air, the contracted eye-
brows and suspended chin of a man who is just going to

sneeze." And that prince of journalists, William Hazlitt, decided that Kemble was unable to express complicated emotions because of constitutional immobility. Leigh Hunt, who hardly ever had a good word to say for the English Roscius, insisted that he was too artificial, formal, and "deliberately conscious."

> Stiff, pompous, stern, each haggard feature groom'd;
> Each step predestin'd, and each look foredoom'd;
> Precise in passion, cautious ev'n in rage,
> Lo! Kemble comes, the Euclid of the stage;
> Who moves in given angles, squares a start,
> And blows his Roman beak by rules of art.[1]

Kemble's grave decorum was most painfully obvious when he tried to play a love-scene: his effort at tenderness was nothing less than a "terrible violation of his innate properties." Hunt, of course, declared roundly that he knew nothing of the passion of love, and even Mrs. Siddons confessed she did not like to play Belvidera to her brother's Jaffier: "John is too cold — too formal, and does not seem to put himself into the character; his sensibilities are not as acute as they ought to be for the part of a lover." Kemble had to admit to Lawrence that he never played opposite his sister "witht. feeling Her superiority." [2]

What, then, was it that the London audiences found to worship in Kemble? The answer is not easy to state in a word, but it is not far to seek. Kemble seemed to his public the representative of the polished, poised, and self-contained gentleman. To a generation that put great store in such things he was the *honnête homme*. He brought to the theatre the suavity and chill grace to be found in the drawing-rooms of the great. Years before, Edward Young had opined that it was virtually impossible for a common "player" to act the part of a great gentleman or tragic hero. "When persons of low education undertake characters of dignity," he told the

Duchess of Portland, "they can only guess at what it is, and so mistake." But Kemble did not guess: he appreciated propriety and decorum as much as Chesterfield or Pitt, and he made such qualities the basis of his style. His temperate, even-toned, almost dispassionate characterizations were to the histrionic art what Sir Joshua's noble and generalized portraits were to the pictorial. Indeed, Reynolds' celebrated remarks on the grand style have a curious pertinency to the formalized, stylized acting technique of John Kemble. His rectilinear, carefully paced interpretations exercised the same studied control and avoidance of the erratic as did Sir Joshua's heroic portraits. Both satisfied the eighteenth century's feeling for the clarity and outline and precision of the golden mean; both shunned the idiosyncratic and the personal; both were pitched on a higher, more idealized plane than the traffickings of everyday life. Romantic individualism was not to find its histrionic exponent until the rise of Edmund Kean in 1814, when the formal classicism of the Kemble-Siddons school was sinking into disregard. But for most of his contemporaries Kemble's carefully modulated, restrained technique was the epitome of good taste.* [3]

Not the least considerable achievement of Kemble's career was his imposition of this grand ideal of acting on his entire generation. To a set of theatre-goers accustomed to the colorful personalities of Garrick's repertory he brought an entirely different concept of histrionic art — and he saw it triumph for a quarter of a century. Even in his first years in London — years during which he was establishing himself with a certain

---

* Back in the 'forties, Sarah Fielding, a sister of the great Henry, observed that certain bluestockings made even tragedy a matter of social rank and *bon sens* — they found it infamous that vulgarians could sit dry-eyed through Cato's death but weep copiously at Barnwell's: "Oh intolerable! cry for an *odious Apprentice-Boy*, who murdered his Uncle, at the Instigation of a common Woman, and yet be unmoved, *when even Cato bled for his Country*" (*David Simple*, I, 151).

difficulty — he "never doubted for a moment that he should ultimately establish the grand and poetic, the BEAU IDEAL, as the standard of art among us." Kemble's style did become standard, though there were always those who murmured against what Henry Irving called his Crummles-like solemnity. "He is a lordly vessel," explained Sir Walter (in a paraphrase of Fuller), "goodly and magnificent, when going large before the wind, but wanting the facility to go 'ready about.' " [4]

Kemble's technique is perhaps best described by the word 'declamatory.' Probably no other actor has ever brought declamation to such a sustained pitch of high art. His scope and range were limited, but in roles — particularly those Roman parts which he staked out as his own — which were amenable to his style he was incomparable. John Taylor, who in his less pontifical moments could attack Kemble's stiffness as vigorously as anyone, had to admit that in the "heroic sphere" he was peerless. In roles suited to his technique Kemble was overpowering. Two old ladies — Joanna Baillie and Mary Russell Mitford — reliving the glories of their youth agreed that the impression he made as De Montfort "remained indelible." And Harriette Wilson, that accomplished *fille de joie*, declared she could not forget Kemble's Julius Caesar if she lived to be a hundred.[5]

Even his most fervent admirers, however, admitted that with a little more warmth and elasticity Kemble would have come nearer to the glory that was his sister's. Mrs. Inchbald, whose opinions are always worth noting, concluded that Garrick had been both an artist and an actor, Kemble merely an artist: one's scope was as wide as human nature, but the other's was confined to the "passions." Hunt, rather more blunt, decided that Kemble was "rather a teacher of elocution than an actor, and not a good teacher on that account." [6]

Declamation of high artistic merit was the goal towards which Kemble always strove. A young unknown actor in London when he first met John Taylor, he immediately undertook a defense of declamation and pointed out that it, after all, was the essence of Greek tragedy. Even so formidable a bluestocking as Anna Seward thought that such erudite rationalizing was petty. "Kemble is a scholar and a fine actor," she wrote Sir Walter, "but his sister is a finer, and knows no language but her own." Ludwig Tieck and Tate Wilkinson, each in his own way, said the same thing: "Lothario better left alone," snapped Kemble's old manager. Thomas Holcroft, whose common sense was not his worst quality in an age of much pretense, objected consistently to the theory that blank verse demands a "sing-song" recitation peculiar to itself. But Leigh Hunt was perhaps the most unregenerate of the great actor's detractors. In Kemble's acting, he thought, "there was elegance, majesty, preparation: it was Gracchus with his pitch-pipe, going to begin — but nothing came of it." [7]

Kemble's critics found a vulnerable point in his unfortunate voice, "husky and untuneable," as Macready recalled, which, because of his asthma, demanded slow and careful breathing and "obliged him for the sake of distinctness to adopt an elaborate mode of utterance, enunciating every letter in every word." No lesser man could have conquered his "habitual cough" and risen above such an enormous natural disadvantage, argued his partisans, taking a curious comfort in marveling at his pertinacity in overcoming a congenital defect. Byron, however, could overlook Kemble's "squeaking" voice because of his impressive carriage and "right conception" of character. [8]

The asthma which was one day to drive him to the south of France for relief was the principal factor in Kemble's painfully slow delivery.

His solemn voice, like death-bell heard afar,
Or death-watch clicking in an old crackt jar,
He measures out monotonous and slow,
In — one — dull — long — sing — song — to — joy — or — woe.

His *Hamlet*, judged one critic soberly, was twenty minutes longer than anyone else's — so slow, indeed, that the waggish Sheridan suggested he act with music between the pauses. Hunt thought his words came so slowly and methodically he had the appearance of computing how many lines he had learned by heart. There were many who objected to this leisurely diction. Actors complained it made them forget their cues, and theatre-goers tired of "the monotonous emphasis on every insignificant monosyllable in a sentence." [9]

Even more objectionable than Kemble's husky drawl, however, was what many critics looked upon as his wilful mispronunciations. Hunt waged a vigorous campaign against his "vicious orthoëpy," declaring some of the sounds issuing from his mouth were as intelligible as Coptic or "Hindostanee." After all, what could be done with a man who pronounced "virgin" "vargin," "hideous" "hijjus," "infirmity" "infaremity," and "beard" "bird"? By far the most celebrated of such aberrations was "aitches" for "aches." The controversy over the proper pronunciation of this word became a *cause célèbre*, with learned disputants truculently pointing out their reasons for preferring either the ancient or the modern version. Kemble, of course, imperturbably ignored the howls of the rabble. In Pope he had found authority for his pronunciation, and that was enough. One night, meeting Charles Mathews back stage as the audience was still lustily hissing one of his "aitches" he coolly took a pinch of snuff and sniffed, "Umph! how those good people think they're right." The Ettrick Shepherd told Christopher North that the actor "pronounced the word 'mewlin,' wi' a sort o' a mew like that o' a wean or a kittlin, shuin' his arms up and down as if nursin'." Such realism, he pointed out, should not stop here. "In Common consistency," Kemble ought to have carried his verisimilitude to the word "pukin'." [10]

This bulky testimony of Kemble's faults — of technique, of vocal apparatus, of mannerisms, of tempo — may be countered with an impressive array of favorable opinions. After all, for twenty-five years he was the acknowledged and virtually undisputed leader of the English stage; such pre-eminence was based on something more than grudging toleration. For the generality of the public he was a great actor and a man who, more than any of his contemporaries, could give them what they wanted from a tragedian. He was, for one thing, a strikingly handsome man. Tall, austere, and graceful, he could invest a tragic character with all the dignity and *gravitas* that belonged to a Cato or a Penruddock or a Coriolanus. His figure was so fine, thought Hazlitt, that he had "only to show himself to be admired." Crabb Robinson saw in him a resemblance to Goethe, the most "oppressively" handsome man he had ever met. With such natural endowments, Kemble brought to the stage a definite personality: whether he played Young Norval or Hamlet, he was still John Kemble, imposing himself on the role instead of being absorbed by it. His great parts suited him; he did not suit himself to them. Today we should call this tedious, and restricted in scope; to the late eighteenth century it was the style of an accomplished artist perfectly in command of his medium. Even Hazlitt, pretty generally of the Kean persuasion, admitted that in those roles "where all the passions move round a central point, and have one master key" Kemble was without a peer. Hunt, rather waspishly, put the matter differently: to him Kemble was successful in "characters that are occupied with themselves and with their own importance." And Sir Walter, a Tory in his tastes as in his politics, held his friend to be supreme, even if "sudden turns and natural bursts of passion" were not his forte. Kemble's art, narrow by our standards, was eminently satisfactory to a generation that liked its acting, like its pictures and verse, decorous and controlled.[11]

His technique was built on more reading and study than any actor's before or since his time. Kemble never forgot that his had been a university training: he cultivated letters and literature with an almost professional zeal, and to his own profession he brought his wide reading and carefully reasoned artistic tenets. That, perhaps, was why so many of his critics murmured against his coldness and intellection. His "elevation to the tragic throne," explained Hazlitt, was not by acclamation, but by careful indoctrination of the public. He was the intellectual actor *par excellence*, achieving his results by practice and method rather than by bursts of intuition and moments of genius. His, after all, was essentially an artificial art, and one which he continued to cultivate and mature throughout his long career. Boaden found him going over the role of Zanga with his wife one morning "as carefully as if it had been a new part." And when John Taylor suggested a minor change in the business of a certain scene Kemble complained that he had copied *Hamlet* forty times; now he would be obliged to copy it yet once more. Nothing was too much trouble to bring to a characterization its final polish. With a prodigious memory and a scholarly approach he was, until the very close of his career, "deepening his own conceptions and striving to improve his own performance." He was, said Hazlitt in summarizing his professional life, "the only great and truly impressive actor I remember, who rose to his stately height by the interposition of art and gradations of merit." [12]

In an era of careless production Kemble inaugurated not only a studied and decorous style but also a new conception of stage deportment. His apprenticeship in the provinces stood him in good stead: that rough and ready training made him think in terms of the theatre, and he was rarely found in a situation in which he could not, if he so desired, dominate the scene. He "will study before a glass the proper position of a finger even," scoffed one critic, and Leigh Hunt recorded with evident glee that "he never pulls out his handkerchief without a design upon the audience." This attention to stage business gave him a certain mastery over those untutored erratics like Cooke who never knew which side of the stage they would enter from. Kemble, marveled an inveterate theatre-goer, was a master of "bye-play" — "a happiness of action and play of the features, which often convey the passions of a character more forcibly than the language of the poet," beguiling "the intervals of action by an air of perpetual occupation." Every detail of the scene was looked to by the manager's careful eye, and his actors, as they complained, were "not permitted to stir or breathe but by Mr. Kemble's direction." Secondary players were expected to play their roles as they were rehearsed, and if they failed to do so, woe unto them. Kemble even paced off his movements across the stage, and any unexpected alteration would disconcert him "through the rest of the scene." [13]

A performance of Kemble's was likely to be an exercise in precision. From the single line — which he was eager to express "with the exactly appropriate accent and manner" — to the total effect of the *mise-en-scène* things were conducted with a calculation and a cool definiteness that left no room for the haphazard and the erratic. Even in his most "impetuous bursts," Mrs. Siddons complained, Kemble was "always careful to avoid any discomposure of his dress or deportment." He pleased Dr. Johnson vastly when, as a young man, he assured the Great Cham he never allowed himself to be swept away by the role he was playing. Every effect was provided for and anticipated, and his perform-

ances, architectonic in their symmetry, built up by an ordered progression to a prepared climax. The sort of emphasis
he wanted to see in a theatre, he said, was the kind "that
swells the passion of the scene, and ennobles the sentiment."
Macready, for one, could never forget Kemble's great scenes:
they involved artifice, but they attained the desired effect.
Kemble's climaxes were "worked out with wonderful skill,
on a sombre ground, which only a great master of his art
could have achieved." Such spotting of dramatic high lights
reminded Macready of the lights and shadows in a master-
piece of Rembrandt's. Kemble isolated and prepared for his
"inspired moments" (as his detractors grudgingly called
them), and therein lay his art.[14]

For better or worse, John Kemble was convinced "that the
elder dramatists alone afforded him sufficient scope, and he
was too excellent a critic not to feel the palpable deficiency
of the writers for the modern [i.e., late eighteenth-century]
stage." Throughout his career he was known pre-eminently
as the exponent of certain roles, and to such roles — Cato,
Hamlet, Macbeth, Octavian, Penruddock, Coriolanus — he
brought a power and an eloquence that made them peculiarly his own. Perhaps his most celebrated part, and the one
for which posterity chiefly remembers him, is Coriolanus.
Macready voiced the general opinion when he called the interpretation "peerless." Even in Thomson's castrated version
of the play — which to his shame Kemble almost always used
— he attained "the utmost summit of the actor's art." Bringing to the role the stature, the oppressive dignity, and the
restraint which made all his Roman characters so memorable,
Kemble as Coriolanus seemed to awe his contemporaries by
merely striding on the stage. Had he acted only in Coriolanus, thought John Galt, he would have been thought "the
very greatest male actor ever seen." Especially in his Covent
Garden days did he become identified with the role, so that

it became impossible "to think of either the character or the man, without reference to each other." [15]

Another famed characterization was that of Cato. It was in the Roman roles that the classic severity and precision of Kemble's technique were most impressive. In *Cato*, wrote one journalist as Kemble was bringing his career to its close, he was "at home. His *forte* is a regular and magnificent declamation, supported throughout with majesty, and occasionally varied with the energy of a simple passion. In this style of speaking and acting Mr. Kemble is without an equal or a rival." Most critics agreed in isolating *Cato* for unreserved praise. Boaden thought that in this play Kemble carried "the British stage to the summit of its glory"; Macready said that "imagination could not supply a grander or more noble presence"; Hazlitt was profoundly moved; young Thomas Talfourd never forgot the performance he saw; and the newspapers plied the public with superlatives. The play in which John Kemble first appeared before a London audience remained one of his and the public's favorites. Charles Lamb could think of the Prince of Denmark only in terms of Kemble, and when old Tom Davies saw the youth make his debut in the role he realized that the interpretation was a memorable one — however different from Garrick's. It was in Shakespearian roles, of course, that Kemble was most at home. Although his playing of eighteenth-century classical drama was such as to make one reputable critic call his acting the "*ne plus ultra* of the art," Kemble brought to his beloved Shakespeare the best that was in him. As Hotspur Sir Walter thought he was superb for the "irritability" of the character, while the Earl of Guilford was so impressed by his Henry V he was moved to write an essay on the subject. His Posthumous seemed to Boaden "by a thousand degrees" the best of the era, and even so cool a critic as Ludwig Tieck thought his Wolsey "verdiente Bewunderung." One is genuinely sur-

prised to find Leigh Hunt praising his Lear, a role in which
Thomas Campbell considered Kemble "unparalleled." Macbeth, of course, was a famous characterization — perhaps because, as Kemble told Taylor, "my soul and body on the
action, both!" Planché, Hazlitt, the whole world joined in
marveling at the interpretation. Lamb, who was never
ashamed of airing his emotions, confessed that when he sat
spell-bound at Kemble's Macbeth he was convinced he was
looking at a murderer.[16]

And so one could go on, almost *ad infinitum*, quoting encomia. Horace Walpole on Kemble's Benedick, Mrs. Inchbald on his Othello, even Leigh Hunt on his celebrated
Penruddock. Most of these famed roles, of course, had the
support of the peerless Siddons. There is no question that
her Volumnia, Constance, Lady Macbeth, and Gertrude were
the perfect complement for her brother's Coriolanus, King
John, Macbeth, and Hamlet. Together the two exhibited the
greatest glory of the grand style.[17]

A man who could contrive to have "no fewer than 240
persons" marching in the triumphal scene of *Coriolanus* must
have had grandiose ideas. Kemble did. He was determined
to achieve historical accuracy in costumes and sets; he was
determined to make good spectacle good drama. And though
he failed, his effort was significant. There had always been
certain pieces upon which were lavished much expensive
costuming. When D'Avenant produced *Henry VIII* the
actors, as John Downes tells in amazement, "were all new
Cloath'd in proper Habits: the King's was new, all the Lords,
the Cardinals, the Bishops, the Doctors, Proctors, Lawyers,
Tip-staves, new Scenes." But there were not many show
pieces of this sort, and during most of the eighteenth century
costuming was the most neglected department of theatrical
production. For the most part, the actor exercised complete
freedom in choosing whatever attire suited his fancy — or his

purse. "The individual taste of the actor was the only artistic law known. The expense incurred was the only managerial consideration." Generally, costumes ran to type. Comedy, until the end of the Garrick period (about 1770), was almost always decked out in the leading *current* fashions, save for such traditionally-attired characters as Falstaff (wigless, with buskins and a cape) and Shylock (with his sinister, coarse, black gaberdine). Some of the tragic characters were also costumed conventionally: breast-plates and plumed helmets for Roman heroes, or boots, baggy trousers, sash, turban, and scimitar for Zanga or Bajazet or Othello. Otherwise plays were dressed *de rigueur* in the latest fashions. Garrick's Macbeth in a British grenadier's uniform is a case in point. Even when one actor would take the trouble to secure a costume vaguely appropriate to his role, the rest of the cast would be attired in glaring contrast. "Let your own dress be ever the best, and suited to the character — never mind that of the other actors," advised one critic ironically — and the shaft is aimed directly at John Kemble. Aaron Hill, that knowing man of the theatre, had attacked this evil as early as 1724, calling attention to the "Intermixture of the Ancient, with the Modern Dresses: Where the Order of Things is so capricious revers'd, that the Courtiers of an English Monarch shall stand round him, like Beaux of Yesterday; and the Sovereign himself strut about in Trunk Breeches, and be dress'd, as *old* as a *Patriarch*." [18]

There had been occasional blasts against the carelessness of costuming. John Wilkes, in 1759, had been explicit on the subject: an actor should take care that his dress accords with "sufficient exactitude to the age, time and circumstances of his character," which propriety can come only from his antiquarian knowledge of "ancient history, and historical paintings, with the general customs and modes of dress, which then prevailed." (This is Kemble's method thirty years before

Kemble's heyday.) In the 'sixties Bonnell Thornton had concluded that accurate costuming was "absolutely necessary to keep up the general deception [of the play]." It was not, however, until old Charles Macklin had the audacity to play Macbeth in kilts, in 1773, that any sensible attempt at proper costuming was made.[19]

Even though Kemble, from the very beginning of his career, made an ostensible effort at reform, his attempts were in many instances ludicrous. For his debut as Hamlet, instead of the customary Van Dyck costume, he wore "a modern court dress of rich black velvet, with a star on the breast, the garter and pendant ribband of an order — mourning sword and buckles, with deep ruffles; the hair in powder." And five years later, as Orlando, he was decked out in "disgusting" red breeches. Sir Walter himself, in antiquarian wrath, tore from Kemble's bonnet in *Macbeth* the plume of black feathers — for all the world like "an undertaker's cushion" — and substituted the appropriate eagle quill — which emendation, the actor had the grace to remark, meant more to him than three distinct rounds of applause. One wonders why, with all his professed zeal for reform, Kemble's production of *Richard III* exhibited costumes of "the strangest medley of shabby old English and foreign habits, of shapes decorated with real lace, and made gaudy with tinsel and copper." In point of fact, improvement came slowly. Mrs. Siddons capered about as Rosalind in an attire that shockingly resembled a male's; the result, grumbled Anna Seward, because of "the scrupulous prudery of decency" looked like nothing human. The great actress, moreover, played *The Grecian Daughter* "in piles of powdered curls, with a forest of feathers on the top of them, high-heeled shoes, and a portentous hoop." But even Kemble copied Garrick's grenadier's uniform for *Othello*, and he acted Dr. Delap's *Captives* in "the genuine Scottish dress" while the rest of the cast lounged about in modern costume. Even after he went to Covent Garden such painful errors continued, so that more than one critic complained of the "scandalous neglect" of those pieces in which Kemble himself did not appear. So long as he allowed Mrs. Crouch to play one of the witches in Macbeth with a "fancy hat, powdered hair, rouge, point lace, and fine linen" he could scarcely afford to scoff at the *gaucherie* of his predecessors. He had, he sniffed, seen the costumes of an earlier day, "and very paltry and improper they were." [20]

When Kemble appeared on the London scene, opulence instead of accuracy of costuming was emphasized. Tragic queens, recalls Mrs. Bellamy, were usually dressed in black velvet, except on "extraordinary occasions" when "an embroidered or tissue petticoat" was worn — as when Mrs. Siddons' Constance amazed the pit with "a *black* body and train of satin, and a petticoat of white, disposed in certainly the most tasteful forms of that day." But Miss Farren's Imogen, suggested one critic, would have been more impressive "had the hat, jacket, and breeches been white sattin, and the cloak pink coloured, or *vice versa.*" Henderson played Sciolto in a magnificent dress of velvet, embroidered with gold and trimmed with ermine, and for Kemble's own early revival, *The Maid of Honour*, Palmer was "habited in splendid stile," Packer appearing in the fetching combination of a Roman toga and Turkish slippers with "*sable* coloured" stockings. When that memorable production of *Lover's Vows* was in progress at Mansfield Park — before Sir Thomas Bertram sternly banned the performance and burned all available copies of Mrs. Inchbald's wicked play — Mr. Rushworth boasted that as Count Cassel he was to "come in first with a blue dress, and a pink satin cloak, and afterwards . . . have another fine fancy suit by way of a shooting dress." Elegance and decoration, reasoned Kemble, were expensive, but Jaffier in a rusty cloak would be unthinkable. With enough velvet, scarlet and gold embroidery, and ermine one could make almost any costume look 'authentic.' [21]

It was one of Kemble's proudest boasts, as he remarked in his last curtain-speech, that he had always endeavored "at a union of propriety and splendor in the representation of our best plays, and particularly of those of the divine Shakspeare." Splendor there was, and to spare, but one must be chary in accepting the claim for propriety. Thomas Gilliland, admitting Kemble was "generally very judicious" in costuming his productions, objected to his short tunic and unbecoming wig ("like an old lady's worn-out *peruke*") in *The Distressed Mother,* and another critic thought his Shakespearian efforts "frequently present a motley assemblage of dresses, such as perhaps were never seen in any age or any nation." As late as 1810 the *Examiner* reported that only two years before, at Covent Garden, Benedick wore a British infantry officer's uniform, Leonato "the dress of an *English Gentleman* of the year 1750, and most of the other characters dressed in the same appropriate manner; but it must be all right, for it is under the superintendance of that man of classic lore, Mr. J. P. Kemble!!" Planché scorned Kemble's *Lear* because it was costumed "in the habits of the Elizabethan era," and he told Charles Kemble quite candidly (when the two were preparing their epoch-making 'correct' version of *King John* in 1823) that his famous brother's reforms, especially in English historical plays, may have made the productions picturesque but had little to do with propriety.[22]

So the testimony accumulates. Macready, having heard much of Kemble's "scholarly correctness," was disappointed when he saw his *Cato:* 'I expected in his costume to see a model of the *gens togata;* but the cumbrous drapery in which he was enveloped bore no resemblance, in any fold or peculiarity, to the garment that distinguished the Roman as one of the *rerum dominos.*" Leigh Hunt maintained that Kemble's celebrated productions merely gratified his taste for tinsel and finery, and even Sir Walter admitted that he carried his love of splendor "rather to the extreme." Some, like Fanny Kemble's mother, disapproved on principle. "The passions, sentiments, actions and sufferings of human beings," she argued, "were the main concern of fine drama, not the clothes they wore." And Charles Lamb, watching the "shiftings and reshiftings" of costumes during *Macbeth*, was reminded of "a Romish priest at mass." Absolute accuracy of costuming, of course, was neither feasible nor desirable. As Scott pointed out, Lear could not be "painted and tattooed" and Hamlet would not be very convincing in a bear-skin. Kemble at least inaugurated the approach that was to lead to a plausible realism. By the time he quit the stage certainly "a more accurate investigation" into the whole matter of production was observable. "Numerous absurdities still prevail," conceded Holcroft; "but they are less violent, and daily diminishing." Perhaps the most charitable view would be that expressed by a commentator on Kemble's *Lear*: "The times were Saxon, and the scenery and appendages were generally of the Saxon character. This was enough — more would have hurt the effect of the scene." [23]

Kemble's customary gravity and high seriousness led to amusing excesses in certain of his reforms. In a "spirit of Shakspearian idolatry" he had the tables resting on trestles of horn for the sylvan banqueting scene of *As You Like It*. When his role demanded a turban, he kept his dresser busy almost an hour wrapping it properly around his head. Poor Wilkinson's wardrobe-keeper was "almost frantic" trying to meet Kemble's taxing requirements on those rare occasions when he condescended to rejoin his old manager. And in his readings he was constantly on the alert for information about costumes: in Appian's *Civil Wars*, he notes, Antony wore "a square robe after the Greek fashion, with white Attick hose," and Asellio was "clad in the holy habit of cloth of gold, worn only on solemn festivals, &c." Such research bore fruit. One gentleman thought that to see Kemble's production of the triumphal scene in Coriolanus would teach a school-boy more Roman history than any text-book — this in spite of the fact that Coriolanus' own costume was accurate "even to his sword," although the other actors' dress represented a most curious conglomeration of historical epochs.[24]

Decorate the stage, Chrononhotonthologos commands,

> decorate the stage
> With all magnificence of decoration. . . .
> Songs, dances, music in its amplest order,
> Mimes, pantomimes, and all the magic motion
> Of scene descriptive and sublime.

Kemble's hankering after 'proper' costumes naturally led him on to consider settings, and in this department, too, his posthumous reputation looms larger than his achievement. Under his supervision, boasted one of his contemporaries, "the British Stage assumed a new character" — both sets and costumes became an integral factor in production. "He transported us absolutely into the days of Henry VIII. or Coriolanus." All stage historians agree that by Kemble's time a reform in stagecraft was in order. Until about 1770, theatrical sets had been chiefly side-wings and back-shutters, with an occasional box (constructed) set for special effects. Even these built sets were only flimsy canvas on frames. It was not until artists like Loutherbourg and Capon began producing elaborate, semipermanent properties that the old painted flats were replaced. Both of these men — who were only scene-designers and not producers or managers — were swept away by the wave of romantic antiquarianism that was so powerful in England during the late eighteenth century — the movement that has left such illustrious relics as Gray's excursions into Teutonic myth, Percy's *Reliques*, Chatterton's Rowley poems, Horace

Walpole's Strawberry Hill, and William Beckford's Fonthill Abbey. It was fashionable for educated persons to dabble in their national antiquity, and particularly in the visible remains of that neglected past. Even so thorough-paced a classicist as Thomas Gray could be strangely moved at "the *savage*, the *rude*, and the *tremendous*" in architecture. 'Sublime' became a stock epithet that had to be fitted (by young Edmund Burke among others) into an esthetic that provided only for the ordered and the regular. After all, "it was the architecture and not the literature of the Middle Ages that shaped men's conception of England's romantic past." More people could admire Melrose Abbey by moonlight than could read *Beowulf* in the original. As a manifestation of the current interest in old castles and ruined donjons, the efforts for a more realistic and accurately evocative stage *décor* takes on a larger significance.[25]

William Capon — Loutherbourg was chiefly occupied with burlettas and showy spectacles — and John Kemble were both eager to escape the dry formalism of earlier neo-classic settings. Their attempts at reform were characterized by both realism and romanticism, and inevitably led to a more complete theatrical illusion as well as to antiquarian research. These men, in the opinion of one eminent authority, "pioneered the way for the stage archaeologist" of the nineteenth century, and to Capon must go most of the credit. If he were contemplating a set of the Tower of London, he first of all went to study the Tower itself. And this, to the conservative element, seemed a very strange procedure indeed. Garrick, with no qualms, would have brought out an old painted flat, as much like the Tower as Elsinore or Windsor, and usable for all three. Of course, Kemble and his zealous colleague were not devastating realists. Their 'historically accurate' revivals were "faithful not to their own times but to the historical period they endeavored to recreate. They were archaeologists rather than Naturalists, realists about the past rather than the present, men who had little or no sense of the theatre but a vast devotion to history." None the less, their efforts were significant, and Boaden was right in praising his idol (even if we should temper his praise): "All the truth, all the uniformity, all the splendor and the retinue of the stage came in, but did not die, with Mr. Kemble." [26]

It was Kemble's boast that he emphasized the physical appearance of his important productions. He paid Capon (and Greenwood, another scene-painter) well — sometimes as much as two hundred pounds for a single set — and even arranged for a complete new stock of scenes after the Covent Garden fire of 1809 had destroyed most of those on hand. For mounting some of the Roman plays he had the assistance of Francis Douce, the antiquary, whose demands for accuracy were sometimes too exacting to be feasible. Of course, complete suspension of disbelief was hardly possible as long as the audience was confronted by proscenium doors with windows over them (a convention abandoned in the new Covent Garden), but for the most part the reconstructions of Rome's and England's ancient architecture were plausible enough. Even though there were lapses — as when a "carpenter's pitch kettle" had to serve for the witches' caldron in *Macbeth* — the theatre-going public was conditioned to more realistic and imaginative settings than they had been accustomed to. John Gibson Lockhart, for one, was of the opinion that "there is something very delightful in observing the progress which theatrical taste is making among us, in regard to this part of its objects at least." Even the fact that critics were beginning to notice shoddy sets is significant. During Garrick's day no one would think of complaining that "a pretty exact representation of *Hanover-square*, and some very neat *Bond-street* shops appeared two, or three times, as parts of *Rome* [in Kemble's production of *Coriolanus*]." Most people were content to marvel at the new *vraisemblance* that the great tragedian had brought to the theatre. It was difficult to believe, remarked one spectator of *Julius Caesar*, that one had not been bodily transported from Covent Garden to the Roman forum, "so complete, in all its parts, was the illusion of the scene." Majestic John Kemble, classical in his toga, rolling out his stately declamations on a stage that to his admiring contemporaries was for all the world like Augustan Rome — that is the prevailing impression one gets from reading through the theatrical documents of that bygone era. And the late eighteenth century, immensely pleased in the appearance of veracity and propriety, was undisturbed by the fact that it was not Brutus, nor was the toga the precise sort Brutus would have worn, nor would Brutus have recognized the massive piles of scenery as the forum. It was enough that a great actor had brought a new and zealous care to the staging of high tragedy.[27]

CHAPTER XIII

Pastures New

It may seem a paradox, but I cannot help being of the opinion that the plays of Shakspeare are less calculated for performance on a stage, than those of almost any other dramatist whatever.

CHARLES LAMB

DURING THOSE last tumultuous days at Drury Lane — when Sheri smiled and promised and hurried off, when the theatre was subsisting largely on faith, when Kemble raged and threatened — negotiations were already afoot. Tom Harris at Covent Garden had been approached and found eager to have Kemble and Kemble's money. But the affair was momentous, and "called for some interval of preparation." Mrs. Inchbald, serving as intermediary between Harris and her old suitor, gloried in the transaction. Meanwhile Kemble himself resolved to make a belated Grand Tour. After all, he was a celebrity, he was wealthy, and he had leisure. Garrick had, midway in his career, taken time off to descend on France with banners flying. Why not his successor? Accompanied by Robert Heathcote (his banker and a descendant of the doughty Sir Gilbert who had been privy to founding the new East India Company and the Bank of England, and had grown rich enough to be jibed by Pope and become Lord Mayor of London), the two set out early in July, 1802. Mrs. Kemble was left behind, to her sorrow, one imagines. There was a week's delay at Lord Guilford's place in Kent while Heathcote languished with a minor ailment, but finally the two fine gentlemen set forth gaily, traveling in a specially built carriage so they could "ride inside or out, as most convenient, for the purpose of seeing the country." Fair stood the wind for France.[1]

Douay was the first stop, and a disappointing one. To his brother Charles, Kemble as one alumnus to another reported only "ruin, poverty, and desolation" — the result of the closing of the university during the Revolution. "I had not the heart to go up to my old room." But at Paris all was glitter and brilliance. The French press was most flattering: Kemble's approach was heralded as a sovereign's, and the Comédie Française wined and dined its English colleague with proper ostentation. Paris, then as always, was full of notables. The Peace of Amiens had opened the Continent once again to British travelers. Young William Hazlitt was in the Louvre copying masterpieces; Lady Holland, at the other end of the social scale, was trying to rival the splendor of her London salon. Kemble danced attendance on her as well as on Lord Egremont. But there were many other places to go. At one of Benjamin West's fashionable breakfasts he charmed each and all among the intellectuals and *literati*: since he "understands and speaks perfectly well the French language," as one paper explained wonderingly, he was quite at ease. With Kemble, Thomas Poole had gone to an elegant gathering at Helen Maria Williams', the liberal political novelist; with Kemble, Michael Kelly had sat in the same theatre as Napoleon and Charles Fox. In point of fact, it was remarked on all sides how striking was the resemblance between the English actor and the conqueror of Europe: even the French, observed Kemble blandly, spoke of it. All in all, Paris was very exciting, and to Charles back home went epistles of model rhetoric about the "magnificence, filth, pleasure, poverty, gaiety, distress, virtue and vice" of the great city.[2]

The theatre, naturally, interested him most. When he had seen Voltaire, Racine, and Beaumarchais, however, he confessed to finding it all a bit cold. French classicism was too much for the English classicist. "A man should be entirely a Frenchman," he decided, "either by birth or long residence, to taste it at all." The great Talma, leader of the French stage, concerned himself valiantly with his colleague's entertainment, and the two became fast friends. Together they visited the museums, together they discussed the drama, together they even contemplated a joint production of Shakespeare (of which nothing came). But the friendship lasted: a fitful correspondence was maintained, and Talma was in London for Kemble's farewell fifteen years later. When Talma's brother came to Kemble with a letter of introduction, the Englishman did the honors nobly. And Talma's first question to a visitor from London who had seen his *Hamlet* was an eager inquiry of how he compared with Kemble.[3]

The months at Paris slipped away. Mrs. Kemble, visiting at Guy's Cliff, reported to Elizabeth Inchbald that her husband was in "perfect Health & Spirits," although she found it difficult to keep up with his movements. In October he and Mr. Ponsonby, the second son of Lord Bessborough, had set out for Spain, where Heathcote was to join them later. The journey was an execrable one: in crossing the Pyrenees, what with a broken carriage, the deep snow, and the intense cold, they thought to perish, reported Kemble. But at Bilbao "the grandeur of the country" made him forget all the inconveniences. Priscilla Kemble ecstatically relayed the information to Mrs. Inchbald: "Our Welsh Mountains are Moles to Mont Ossuna — then such Torrents — Woods — Mouldering Towers and Broken Arches of Bridges as made it delightful and amply repaid him for the risques he has run in venturing — for he says he has been often in great danger — he is in most perfect Health." There was some difficulty in getting from Bayonne to Madrid, owing to the Spanish King's having appropriated all the available mules. "He says there

is no exaggeration in the cheating tricks of Spanish land-
lords." Madrid itself was a disappointment — "a village to
any one who has lived in London," Kemble wrote Richard
Cumberland. Apart from "learning diligently" the new language and shopping for choice Spanish snuff to give to the
Prince of Wales, there was little to do. The theatre was bad,
although one of the actresses with the melodious name of
Rita Luna at least had a pleasing voice. Kemble, however,
was tiring of his travels. The affair in London was coming
to an issue, and as quickly as possible he made his way back
to Paris. At Valencia, Lord Holland insisted on his leaving
his hotel to stay with him, which both Kemble and Priscilla
considered very handsome. But the stay was a brief one:
hurrying on through Paris, Kemble reached London in
March, 1803, almost nine months after his departure.* [4]

All London was buzzing with speculations. Kemble's future
was a matter of general concern. The *Monthly Mirror*
thought there would be "very little doubt" that he and
Sheridan would come to some sort of reconciliation — but
Mrs. Inchbald had not been idle. The deal had gone through,
and in April the town was informed that its favorite tragedian
was transferring himself and his family (including Mrs. Siddons and Charles) to Covent Garden. Thomas Harris, who
has not come down to us as a man of loose emotions, declared
tenderly that he, for one, had not been so happy in many

* Roger Kemble had died while his son was in Madrid, and an
appropriately filial letter was dispatched to Charles, who was told,
among other things that "I cannot help feeling a dejected swelling at
my heart, that keeps me in a flood of tears for him in spite of all I
can do to stop 'em." In his will, a copy of which, signed January 14,
1802, is in the Folger Library, Roger left to his wife all his money ("not
out on mortgage or in the stocks") and his "household goods." Two
Drury Lane shares were willed to John, Stephen, Charles, Sarah Siddons, and Elizabeth Whitlock. As to the other children, Mrs. Twiss got
£500 and Mrs. Mason £400, while the notorious Mrs. Curtis received an
annuity of £20. Roger was well off, being worth some £1295.

years. And well he might have been: not only had he snared
the royal family of the English stage, but he had contracted
for the very substantial sum of twenty-two thousand pounds
in exchange for one-sixth interest in Covent Garden. The
Harrises, father and son, between them held seven-twelfths
of the entire stock, and the rest was sold to Kemble (one-
sixth), George White (one-eighth), and Ann Martindale (one-
eighth) in small enough parcels to prevent anyone else's
holding a majority. Kemble could put up only ten thousand
in cash (this was financed by the Heathcotes, whom he was
still paying as late as 1821, on his last trip to London); the
rest was provided for in the pious hope of accumulated profits.
As manager he was to receive £200 a year, as actor £37 16s.
for three appearances a week (and £12 8s. for each extra performance). Although the terms certainly favored the wily
Harrises — they could, at will, appoint a new manager —
Kemble at least had realized his long-cherished ambition of
being patentee of one of the great London theatres. He may,
as Boaden suggested, have envisaged a home of classical drama
to bear his own name; little could he know what lay in store
for him. Covent Garden was plainly profitable: during its
1802–1803 season it had shown a clearance of £16,199 from
its gross receipts of £68,525. And although Kemble's sixth
interest would not come to much (especially when most of it
was being applied on his principal), he at least had the satisfaction of knowing he had reached the height Garrick had
reached. He was, at forty-six, the acknowledged leader of his
profession, acting in a theatre at least partially his own.[5]

While waiting for the autumn Kemble turned whatever
honest penny he could. At Bath, in April, he caused a tremendous sensation. Within a few hours of the announcement
of his coming, the boxes had all been booked. And at Bristol
there were "prodigious crowds." "I do assure you," Priscilla
wrote Mrs. Inchbald, "I think him very, very much improved

I never saw him act so well." In London there was much bustle in preparation for the new season, and the new acting dynasty. Covent Garden itself, a dingy theatre compared to Sheridan's resplendent new house, was being renovated in white and gold, and sixteen new private boxes — to be rented to the socially prominent for £300 a season — were added to the grand tier. Kemble inaugurated his new career, of course, with *Hamlet*, just as at Drury Lane twenty years before. Although he had been welcomed to his new post with a dinner — "in England every thing is settled by a dinner" — where even Sheri was present to wish him well, things were going badly. Among the Covent Garden regulars were many jealous souls, and when Lewis, the former stage-manager, was told "in the most delicate and handsome terms" that his duties would be taken over by the interloper from Drury Lane, he organized a vigilant opposition. Ill will was rife: it was "astonishing what hatred was worked up" against the new patentee. Cooke, for instance, presented a problem. Ever since the memorable dueling over *Richard III*, he and Kemble had been avowed rivals. When Cooke learned of his old enemy's projected invasion of his own bailiwick, he was "much unsettled." Kemble — perhaps under Harris' compulsion — exhibited touching magnanimity, however. He relinquished the choice (and contested) role of Richard, contenting himself with Richmond; he surrendered to Cooke the role of Shylock; even *Douglas* was rearranged so Kemble could act the Stranger. It was good business, of course, to keep the erratic Cooke placated. After all, he retained a strong hold on a large part of the public. Kemble, to calm the troubled waters, gave a large dinner party for his new associates at Covent Garden, and all was sweetness and light. Cooke was there as large as life. "It was 'Mr. Kemble,' and 'my dear George,' and one nosegay seemed to perfume them both." But as the evening wore on and Kemble got drunker he began to complain of the newspapers' prejudice towards him, whereupon Cooke, with a look of the most "*sarcastic bitterness*," quoted the speech about ambition's ladder from *Julius Caesar*. Kemble let the matter pass and called for more brandy. During the entire season there was murmuring. Only the year before, Harris had been vexed by a serious revolt from some of his disgruntled actors; the influx of the Kemble tribe from Drury Lane did not ease the situation. Attacks that had previously been confined to the head of the family were now directed against all his connections — Charles, Mrs. Siddons, her son (Henry) and daughter-in-law. The Kembles, it was presently pointed out, "by their numerous professional branches, their numerous professional intermarriages, and their numerous professional getting and saving ways" were in a fair way to "monopolize all the theatrical emoluments." [6]

The additions to Covent Garden, in spite of the ill-natured criticism, made it the best theatrical company in England. Kemble himself, with a large staff to draw from, was determined to make his theatre the "palace of Shakespeare." He was at the height of his own powers: his style was established as the norm of what high tragedy should be, and with his long apprenticeship at Drury Lane behind him he was entering his final Olympian phase. There had been, decided a thoughtful contemporary, "four distinguishable schools" of acting since the Restoration — Betterton aped the French; Booth, Wilks, and Cibber established a typically English technique; Garrick dominated the middle of the eighteenth century; and Kemble had seen his own kind of classicism triumph in the later age. That classicism, by and large, was to continue its majestic and overpowering sway until the advent of Edmund Kean, the drunken stroller with a feverish, almost electrical romanticism. [7]

Kemble's first season with Covent Garden brought the expected Shakespearian repertory ("got up with care and cost," the journal tells us, but not entirely satisfactory to the manager) as well as such well-paying trivia as *John Bull* and *The English Fleet*. The theatre took in much money (£63,182) although it really made very little (£3,959).* For Kemble the year was an artistic success. Not only had he succeeded in persuading the parsimonious Harris to finance his expensive revivals, but he had managed, very politely and with infinite finesse, to wrest the leadership of the theatre from Cooke. By the end of the season, that gentleman, sadder and wiser, was taking what solace he could from strong drink — so much so, in fact, that he was on occasion unable to act. Those pesky private boxes Harris had built against Kemble's coming proved a source of constant vexation. Kemble, as usual, bore the brunt of the attack. He, snorted one of his detractors, "has in the plenitude of his power, and with a *modesty* peculiar to himself, violated, and without the permission of the Renters, shut them and the promiscuous and respectable public from above one third of the national Theatre." But once the boxes had been rented, and the outraged public in the top gallery had got accustomed to seeing nothing on the stage, yet another cloud loomed on Kemble's horizon.[8]

The cloud was a child whose voice had not yet changed. The 1804–1805 London season rises above the dull mediocrity of others by virtue of one of the most preposterous episodes in English theatrical history. This was the year that the Infant Roscius, Master Betty, burst into glory. Before that extraordinary event, which mercifully did not occur until December, the fall passed quietly enough. Kemble droned along with such unexciting stock-pieces as *The Mountaineers*,

* Kemble himself seems to have done very well: he drew some £2,000 from the treasury, shared the £1,260 from a private box with Harris, and was paid £315 in lieu of a benefit.

Pizarro, and *Hamlet,* all of them lavishly produced. "No expense in dresses and decorations" was spared, and the "painters and dressers" were busier than they had been in years. The public, however, was soon to be treated to a grander spectacle than Kemble's revivals — that of a thirteen-year-old child playing Hamlet. When William Henry West Betty, then eleven, saw Mrs. Siddons act in Belfast in 1802, he told his father, "with a look of such enthusiasm, and a voice so pathetic, that those who heard him will never forget the expression, '*that he should certainly die, if he must not be a player.*'" Happily, the senior Betty had no inclination to stint childish aspirations; within two years his precocious son was building up an enormous following in the provinces, and by 1804 both the great London theatres were competing for his services. The progress to the capital was a long triumph. Audiences at Sheffield were enchanted to hear the diminutive tragedian exclaim,

> As to my height, I trust on reason's plan,
> The *mind* is held — the standard *of the man.*

And when John Home saw the prodigy in *Douglas* he decided that "he is a wonderful being; his endowments great beyond conception." One spectator in Liverpool was of the opinion that the child had been sent by heaven "to preserve the theatric school from the sophistical, dull, fashionable description of passion, and restore it to its genuine and vigorous imitation." [9]

When Betty's father, after much urging, had persuaded the Belfast manager to let his son appear (in August, 1803), the regular actors were "confounded to see themselves schooled by a mere infant," but after his first performance "he was the common topic of conversation in all parts of the town." In Manchester, people who wished to see Master Betty had to apply for tickets by letter "in consequence of the great confusion that has taken place, whereby the lives of many persons have been endangered." Having received some £1,520 at Liverpool — where Prince William Frederick of Gloucester showered him with attentions — Master Betty gazed tenderly on his baby sister, sleeping in her mother's arms, and felt moved to exclaim: "Amidst the vicissitudes of life, who can tell, my dear sister, what may be thy fate? If I can help it, it shall not be *poverty*!" This pious determination was carried out when the London theatres began bidding for the boy's favor. At Leicester a letter was received from the great Kemble, expressing "the satisfaction I feel in knowing I shall soon have the happiness of welcoming" the boy to Covent Garden. Drury Lane's offer of half a clear benefit for seven nights' performances was indignantly refused, but none the less Kemble and Harris took the precaution of going to Leicester to see the fabulous Master Betty and arrange terms with him. A boy named William Macready happened to be sitting in the box near them; his report of Kemble's comment on the Infant Roscius is characteristic: "I remember John Kemble's handkerchief strongly scented of lavender, and his observation, in a very compassionate tone, 'Poor boy, he is very hoarse.'" Harris, out to get Betty at any price, finally agreed to twelve nights at fifty guineas each, plus a clear benefit — terms that Drury Lane at last met, with the result that the Infant Roscius divided his first London season between the two houses.[10]

Meanwhile, during the late fall, London was being subjected to an extensive propaganda campaign in preparation for the prodigy's coming. The boy himself was exhibited prominently — now bowling along in a carriage, now basking in a box at the theatre. John Taylor was set to work by Kemble to write an occasional prologue. The public journals, properly coaxed, announced the young genius' advent "with all imaginable consequence, and puffs in the newspapers kept

his name before the eyes of the public like a shuttle-cock."
Theatrical journalism in those days, as Leigh Hunt recalled,
"was an interchange of amenities over the dinner table; a
flattery of power on one side, and puns on the other; and
what the public took for a criticism on a play was a draft upon
the box-office, or reminiscences of last Thursday's salmon
and lobster-sauce." All the self-annointed 276,302 critics of
London that Henry Fielding ("at the last Inquisition taken
by myself") had counted were on tiptoe with expectation.[11]

December 1, 1804, finally arrived, and soldiers were sta-
tioned about Covent Garden "to protect the people against
the necessary and fatal result of the indiscriminate rush of
such an immense tide" as turned out to see Master Betty.
The house came to £638 18s. 6d., having been sold out ten
minutes after the doors opened. The boy's performance of
Achmet in *Barbarossa*, it was agreed on all sides, was nothing
short of miraculous. Kemble, who had occupied his box, was
silent, but the reticence did not extend to the rest of the
audience. London went mad over the boy, "slight, but
elegant, and extremely youthful," whose "exact height," the
public was breathlessly informed, was four feet, ten and a half
inches, his weight eighty-seven pounds. "His action is graceful, chaste, and varied, but not redundant. He appears to
possess a complete knowledge of stage business; treads the
boards with firmness and dignity; pays the most critical
attention to his brother actors; and, with the exception of
Mr. Kemble, is, perhaps, the most perfect master of attitudes
of any performer at the London theatres." At Master Betty's
second appearance, in *Douglas*, the streets around the theatre
began to fill at four o'clock and the "impatience" of those
buying tickets was "manifested by many acts of violence" —
windows were broken, a balustrade in Covent Garden gave
way under the crush, and several spectators in the pit fainted
dead away "from the excessive fatigue and crowding." And

so the triumph continued, one long ovation. The Infant
Roscius (who, after all, was only thirteen) became ill with a
"regular inflammatory fever," at which the public concern
was so great that bulletins were posted. Society flocked about
Master Betty: he was presented at Carlton House and received marked attentions from the Duke of Clarence and
Mrs. Jordan, that worthy's mistress — chiefly, thought Northcote, because they wanted to spite Kemble. Although one
paper had the temerity to report dissatisfaction with his
rendition of the role of Octavian, the great Fox thought the
boy's Hamlet was "finer than Garrick" and at Pitt's suggestion
the House of Commons adjourned to witness the performance.
"Never from my mind," declared one devotee fervently,
"will be obliterated the impressions received through the
medium of his chaste and powerful acting." The theatre
was prospering mightily. Before Betty's debut the weekly
receipts had been twelve or fifteen hundred pounds, but
immediately after his phenomenal success they almost
doubled. While Kemble was receiving £37 16s. a week, recalled Reynolds, the Infant Roscius was being paid £50 a
night. The boy's income from his first London season, "including benefits, salary, presents, &c.&c." was calculated by
one optimistic observer to be £10,000.[12]

The rage for Betty, of course, did Kemble no good. The
lad's popularity, said Scott, was "attended with feelings of
dislike as well as neglect" by the disgruntled manager. Hideously discolored broadsides illustrative of Kemble's loss of
prestige were distributed. One of them shows the tragedian
and Master Betty seated on a swiftly flying Pegasus. Kemble's
hat is falling off, and he seems to be maintaining his precarious seat behind the boy with difficulty. "Zounds," says
Kemble, "how he cuts and spurs away. If I don't take great
care, he will certainly have me off. — He has got me on to the
crupper already." Master Betty, seated serenely and comfort-

ably, is guiding Pegasus with a large whip, remarking, "Never fear Sir — we shall agree very well — but when two ride on a Horse, one must ride behind you know!" This rage for an inexperienced stripling, however gifted he might be, alarmed decent folk. "It is indecorous," protested one gentleman; "it is ungrateful; it is foolish; and tending to depress the efforts of industry and assiduity to attain to perfection." But even Horne Tooke maintained that Master Betty "was finer than John Kemble." Mrs. Piozzi, who had an opinion about everything, opined that Betty was "a fine creature" indeed.[13]

Meanwhile, the leader of the profession was deeply humiliated. For the most part, he stayed away from the theatre on the pretense of illness. During February he had a bad cough and looked "extremely ill" to Lawrence. Richard Cumberland, disgusted at the fickle public, called on Kemble and found him "sick at home," whereupon he quoted with great propriety,

> Oh! what a time have you chose out, brave Caius,
> To wear a kerchief? Would you were not sick!

Of course, there was some rationalization to be done. "I certainly had a voice in engaging the *boy* for Covent Garden," explained Kemble lamely, "as I thought the novelty might bring *grist* to the mill, wherein *I* have a share — otherwise I should have strongly opposed any such innovation — he is certainly clever — but *Hamlet* he should not have attempted." Both Kemble and Mrs. Siddons refused point-blank to act with the prodigy (though poor Cooke, because of his poverty, was compelled to). "Though they are the servants of the Public," one of their apologists pointed out, "they are not to be treated as slaves subject to the insults of every disorderly *caprice* and *whim*." Farington spoke admiringly to Mrs. Kemble about Master Betty's "great power, considering His youth," but she rather acidly replied that "it was nothing to an experienced actor." Whereupon Farington, tactician that he was, "made no further remark to Her. She had a great deal at stake & allowance was to me [*sic*] made." Kemble himself went so far as to suggest to the Infant Roscius that he was not "strong enough" to act Rolla because he could not carry the baby over the bridge. "I dare say Rolla would never have thought of it," resolutely parried the boy. "I should think he only snatch'd the child, hugg'd it close to his bosom and ran away as fast as ever he could, or the Spanish Soldiers would certainly take it from him." [14]

The fever for novelty before very long subsided, almost before the tribe of scribblers engaged on idolatrous biographies of the popular hero could bring their potboilers to the press. When Master Betty made his last round of appearances at Covent Garden in April and May, the hectic enthusiasm was already dead. And then, of course, it was left for people to wonder at themselves. The rage after the boy, decided one gentleman, originated in "the imbecility of persons of a very high rank indeed, whose minds could never soar to a higher degree of intellectual gratification than that presented by a musical farce, a farcical comedy; or the pantomimic tragi-comedy of Pizarro." Holcroft finally came to the extraordinary conclusion that the boy, though gifted, "is neither a God nor a Garrick." Young Roscius' voice — "*feminine, hollow,* and *monotonous*" — someone at last had the audacity to find fault with; and his salary, absurdly high for times of prosperous peace and outrageous for times of war, was held to be nothing less than "infamous." Sir George Beaumont, by some queer turn of thought, decided that Betty's fantastic popularity was an "imposition" on the public. Another gentleman was moved to record that "I am ashamed of, and *despise*, this silly rage of my countrymen." Kemble, now that the danger was past, could blandly agree with his colleagues in the Beefsteak Club that Young Roscius "was a recollection that should call shame to the cheek of modern London." And although the lad returned to London the following season, the engagement was pathetic; the public frenzy subsided as quickly as it rose. When Byron saw him in 1812, still touring the provinces, his report was devastating: "His figure is that of a hippopotamus, his face like the bull and mouth on the panels of a heavy coach, his arms like fins fattened out of shape, his voice like the gargling of an alderman with the quinsy." Betty finally withdrew from the stage and went to Cambridge, but he presently returned to acting and did not retire definitely until 1824. He lived until 1874, dying at the age of eighty-three.[15]

The public's return to sanity was signalized by another poster, this one of a very corpulent and chagrined John Bull being assisted from a recumbent position on the floor by Kemble and Mrs. Siddons, a benevolent winged creature — possibly an angel — hovering over their heads. John Bull is eyeing wickedly a diminutive Infant Roscius who flees away in alarm. "Ah! my good friend Mr. Kemble how do you do? Mrs. Siddons I am happy to see you," remarks John Bull. "Mercy on me what Enchantment have I been under!! Is that the Pigmy I was so attach'd to why he appears now no bigger than a pinshead!! and I declare I thought him as tall as the Monument!!" The season closed with a string of modern comedies. Mrs. Siddons made her first appearance of the year in May, in *Macbeth*, at which old Sam Rogers had to remark on her sagacity. "How wise it was," he exclaimed, "in Kemble and Mrs. Siddons quietly to withdraw from the stage during the Betty furor, and then as quietly to return to it, as if nothing unusual had occurred!" [16]

The next season, all London, heartily ashamed of itself, settled back to its regular theatrical fare. Kemble sailed majestically through the fall with his true and tried favorites, and was lauded anew on all sides. "Too much praise" cannot be given him, pointed out Holcroft, "for the correct and classical manner in which many pieces, tragedies especially, have been performed under his management." Washington Irving, on his first visit to London, frequented the theatre a great deal; though Kemble and Cooke failed to move him, Mrs. Siddons worked on his feelings until he was "a mere child." The theatre is in great glory, reported the Earl of Aberdeen in November. "Kemble and Mrs. Siddons every night — fancy after being made sick with an automate of a boy all last year, a girl 7 or 8 years old is coming out this week at Covent Garden. Ohe jam satis!" The "girl 7 or 8 years old," a Miss Mudie (poor child, even her name was unfortunate), had been widely acclaimed in the provinces, but when she made her debut she waged a losing battle from the start: the audience, chary of any more young geniuses, was restive and at last tumultuous, until "not a word could be heard from the stage, such was the marked displeasure of the house." Finally the exasperated maiden took matters in her own hands; coming forward, she told the pit roundly that "I HAVE done nothing to offend you; and as for those who are sent here to hiss me, *I will be obliged to you to turn them out.*" At this, pandemonium broke loose, and when Kemble stepped out to pacify the audience he was hissed down. "The theatre, perhaps," recorded one outraged critic, "never exhibited a scene so little to the credit of the managers; so humiliating to the actors; so painful and offensive to the audience; or so truly and irrecoverably disgraceful to the British Stage." The play (*The Country Girl*, appropriately enough) was not allowed to go on, however, until a substitute had been hurriedly summoned to replace poor Miss Mudie.[17]

There were, of course, the customary managerial woes. Kemble had to apologize abjectly for the insolence of Covent Garden's box-keepers, assuring one highly-wrought patron that the guilty man would be instantly dismissed: "I wish I knew how to inflict a more sensible punishment than by discharging him, as the box-keeper who could be capable of so shocking a piece of behaviour." Cooke, too, was troublesome, chiefly because of his drunkenness. A year later (in the fall of 1806) he turned up at the theatre for a dress rehearsal of Kelly's new *Adrian and Orilla* hardly able to walk, and Kemble had to combat everyone from Harris to the author in insisting that the piece not be postponed. If the play were changed "under the pretence of Cooke's indisposition," he declared, "he would go forward to the audience, and inform them of the true cause of their disappointment." The piece was acted, and with uncommon success — Cooke forgetting nothing "but the whole plot," recalled Kelly grimly. By the end of December, Master Betty had returned for another string of high tragedies, but without the glamor of the year before. Most of the town, like Mrs. Siddons, found him "a very clever, pretty boy, but nothing more." * 18

The spring was notable for nothing except a sumptuous revival of *Henry VIII*, a personal triumph for Kemble as Wolsey: "he here towers above all rivalry." There were the

---

* *The Romantic Lover, or Lost and Found* (January 6, 1806) though ascribed at the time to a certain Allingham very likely had the benefit of Kemble's services. J. P. Collier saw the complete copy submitted to the licenser, apparently under the title of *The Legacy*. The plot turns on the fact that Peerless, to hold his legacy, has to marry a woman with £30,000 to keep his fortune from passing into the hands of his cousin, Weston. Only a single act, the first, is extant in the Larpent Collection of the Huntington Library, and it bears little or no evidence of Kemble's authorship. A note in the manager's hand, dated January 4, 1806, declares that the comedy was to be acted at Covent Garden, and the numerous cuts and alterations in the text seem to be in the manager's writing. If the piece was Kemble's (as Collier thought), it was his last excursion into dramatic composition — and his first since his early days in Yorkshire. It is most likely that he concerned himself only with the revisions, and not at all with the writing.

usual vernal comedies, all undistinguished. Cumberland's *Hint to Husbands* seemed "wretched" to Kemble, and Dibdin's *White Plume* was "A miserable affair indeed." Leigh Hunt was very much annoyed by the flood of "farci-comedy" at Covent Garden. Why Kemble "should suffer the everlasting antics of the modern merry-andrews about him, is an enigma we never could solve; the idea of him under these circumstances is as ludicrously incongruous as it would be to see the statue of William Penn surrounded by carved dancing dogs." Poor Kemble, if the truth be known, probably had little choice in the matter. Harris, more interested in making money than in staging unremunerative revivals — however 'authentic' — was the autocrat of the theatre. When the year was finally over, Kemble came forward and made his customary thanks to the audience "after a very profitless season." [19]

The next two seasons dragged their weary lengths along quite in the usual manner. Kemble's own activities were largely confined to his revivals, and even these had been reduced in number. *Coriolanus* was the event of the autumn of 1806, a revival of "prodigious pomp and expence." It was Kemble's greatest role and was generally admitted as such. The critics could do no more than repeat their former accolades. "A glorious treat" was Crabb Robinson's opinion. "To have a gentleman of fine parts and a scholar at the head of our theatrical exhibitions," one paper observed, was an inestimable boon to an age whose other "sources of dramatic excellence are either stopped up or polluted." High classical drama received a temporary set-back one evening when, during a moving scene between Kemble and Mrs. Siddons, an apple was thrown on the stage. For once, Kemble lost his temper — or perhaps as Coriolanus he maintained a proper contempt for the *mobile vulgus*. Stalking to the front of the stage he made loud harangue:

"LADIES AND GENTLEMEN,

"I have been many years acquainted with the benevolence and liberality of a London audience; but we cannot proceed this evening with the performance unless we are protected, especially when *ladies* are thus exposed to insult,"

A person in the gallery called out — "We can't hear."

Mr. Kemble, (*with increased spirit,*) "I will *raise* my voice, and the GALLERIES shall *hear* me." (*Great tumult.*)

"This protection is what the AUDIENCE owe it to themselves to *grant* — what the PERFORMERS, for the credit of their profession, have to *demand* — and WHAT I will venture so far to *assert*, that, on the part of the PROPRIETORS, I here offer a hundred guineas to any man, who will disclose the *ruffian* who has been guilty of this act." (A murmur, only in the gallery.)

"I throw myself, Ladies and Gentlemen, upon the high sense of breeding, that distinguishes a London audience; and I hope I shall never be wanting in my duty to the public; but nothing shall induce me to suffer insult."

After which high-sounding talk the affair came tamely to an end. The apple of discord, it was revealed, had been tossed by some of the lighter ladies in the gallery, and fell on the stage only by accident. When the wounded feelings were healed on all sides, the play went on.[20]

The Tempest was an ostentatious revival in the mid-winter, and enjoyed an excellent run — perhaps because everyone was curious to hear Kemble pronounce "aches" as "aitches." The critics valiantly condemned the *pastiche* of D'Avenant and Dryden, which was, in point of fact, not much changed from his early (1789) version at Drury Lane. "As tasteless as indecent," snorted one journal, "and totally subversive of the simplicity of Shakspeare's drama." Another writer spoke scathingly of both Kemble's and Dryden's bad taste, and George Frederick Cooke (whether drunk or sober we do not know) could sit through only two acts of it. Meanwhile the public flocked to the theatre.[21]

Sometime during the year Kemble received a visit and a petition for employment from an unknown stroller named

Edmund Kean, but the great manager appeared "so cold, haughty, and repulsive" that the applicant resolved to return to the provinces where humans were kindly. One of Cooke's performances was enlivened by a bottle's being thrown from the gallery to the pit, but the culprit was seized and borne off in triumph to a Bow Street magistrate. The theatres, wailed one critic, "will short degenerate into bear gardens" if such misconduct is permitted. Also, it was tactfully suggested that orange peelings dropped from above did not add to the pleasure of decent folk in the pit below. During April Kemble was at home with "a severe rheumatism," or so the public was told. But his friends knew his intemperance was bearing fruit, even if he did not admit to having the gout. Indeed, Lawrence informed Farington, his doctor had made him quit drinking wine, and consequently he "has more strength & better spirits since He left off that habit. — He however takes medicine." The summer — or part of it, at least — was spent at Lord Guilford's hospitable country seat, Wroxton Abbey. From that pleasant retreat Kemble wrote a letter of pious condolence to Desenfans' widow in July. But he neither toured nor acted.[22]

The next winter (1807–1808) *Cymbeline*, which had been unsuccessfully revived the season before, was hopefully brought forth again, as were *Henry VIII* and *The Winter's Tale*. But nothing exciting occurred until Kemble played Iago to Cooke's Othello. Then the critics rose up against him as one man. He lacked the "perturbed spirit, or natural agitation" which the character demanded, decided one writer. Another was more blunt: "His conception of the character was erroneous; he produced no effect in it; he clearly cannot play it." The winter was a dull one. Part of the time Kemble was ill, but even when acting he looked old — or so Farington thought. Cooke was still able to bring the house to its feet, however: in *The Man of the World* he got six rounds of applause, and drew the biggest audiences since Master Betty's heyday. Kemble even failed as Lear. What was the theatre coming to? When he wanly produced *The Two Gentlemen of Verona* (for the first time since his Drury Lane days), he and everyone else seemed bored. The play, someone said maliciously, had been wakened from its long sleep on the prompter's shelf, clad "in the cast-off finery of the wardrobe," and compelled to wear itself out on the stage "for the sole purpose of making the audience fret during that period." Appropriately enough, Kemble closed a limping season by acting *Macbeth* with a "distressing lameness in his right knee." The summer he passed at Wroxton Abbey again, where he delighted the stage-struck Lord Guilford by acting Friar Lawrence in an amateur production of *Romeo*. Later, at Lord Abercorn's country place near Stanmore he and Walter Scott saw much of each other, discussing plays, their common high-born friends, and the superiority of port to sherry. Scott never failed to chuckle at the memory of John Kemble being attacked by an angry bull while they were out riding one fine morning.[23]

It was pleasant in the country, and a blessed relief from the anxieties of a London season. Something had happened. Things were no longer as they once were, when Kemble had only to stalk forth in a toga to be admired. Audiences had become fretful and ill-mannered and curiously unresponsive. The whole point of the last two disastrous seasons, of course, was simply that Kemble was aging. For almost twenty-five years he had been before the London public, and both he and the public were wearing under the strain. Although he was still the first man of the theatre, he was losing ground. No longer were his revivals social and theatrical events of the first importance. Rather they were painful duties, attended politely by the faithful and cordially damned by those younger theatre-goers who rebelled at inelastic acting. A new

generation was springing up — Leigh Hunt was already slashing at the old idol and Hazlitt was presently to begin — and
it had no place for John Kemble. True, he clung tenaciously
to his post for some years longer, but his doom was certain,
and he knew it. Not until the savagery and rancor of the
O.P. riots was he to learn what the London public really had
come to think of him. But already he could see that his
appearances were unwelcomed, his elaborate productions
unimpressive to the children of his first devotees. A deep
autumnal tone was settling on his career. And instead of
evangelizing in the provinces during the summer, he was
now content to bask in the hospitality of noble lords.

The fall brought disaster. Within a week of the new season's opening Kemble had the melancholy sight of his life's
savings going up in flames. Covent Garden, catching fire at
four in the morning, burned like tinder. The fire brigade was
as useless as John Kemble standing about and making futile
attempts to direct operations. By eight o'clock the building
was gutted. The loss, of course, was enormous. Twenty-two
persons lost their lives; a huge musical library (including
some irreplaceable scores of Händel) was destroyed; the costumes and properties were a total loss; and even the fine
cellar of the Beefsteak Club was nothing but a beautiful
memory. £100,000 would not cover the cost of the night's
work, and although the building itself was insured, Kemble's
loss was almost irreparable. The kindly Boaden, eager to be
of comfort, called the next morning to offer his condolences.
Kemble was before the mirror, making an unsuccessful attempt to shave himself; Priscilla was dissolved in tears, and
wailing that they were "totally ruined, and have the world
to begin again"; Charles Kemble and a superannuated func-
tionary of the theatre sat mutely sorrowful in the background. Even Boaden realized that the occasion did not call
for talk, and he obligingly took a place with the two silent

mourners in the corner. Presently the silence was broken. Throwing back his handsome head, Kemble unburdened his soul in a burst of Ciceronian oratory that would have been worthy of Burke: "Yes, it has perished, that magnificent theatre, which for all the purposes of exhibition or comfort was the first in Europe." But the doleful catalogue of Covent Garden's excellences we need not repeat. "Of all this vast treasure," rolled forth the peroration, "nothing now remains, but the ARMS OF ENGLAND over the entrance of the theatre — and the ROMAN EAGLE standing solitary in the market place!" [24]

This onerous burden off his conscience, Kemble set himself to the task of recouping his fortunes. Whatever the cause (never discovered) or the results of the fire, performances had to go on. Again the Haymarket was resorted to, while the harried patentees scurried about raising money. A bond issue of £50,000 was sold to subscribers who were promised a return of twenty-five pounds a year for eighty-five years, in addition to "an Annual Transferrable Free-Admission to any part of the Theatre before the Curtain." Led by the king and the Duke of York, the public very soon bought up the bonds, and their contributions, with the insurance money, was enough to finance a new theatre on the site of the old one. Robert Smirke was the architect, and his aim, as might be expected, was to build an even larger theatre than Sheridan's. The style was an unpleasantly formidable Doric. But when the corner-stone was at last laid (with impressive Masonic ceremonies which Kemble, as a Catholic, had prepared for by becoming a Mason only the night before) even the Prince of Wales himself permitted his Royal Person to lead the festivities. The Duke of Northumberland — he who had years before supplied his militia for a young actor's military scenes up in Yorkshire — established himself as the new Maecenas by presenting Kemble with £10,000 as his contribution towards a new home for national drama. Kemble, for once speechless, presently found the voice to refuse such munificence on the grounds of being unable even to keep up the interest. When the Duke announced it as a gift, however, there was dancing in the streets. Naturally, there was much bustling about necessary to keep the repertory at the Haymarket going and to supervise the building of the new house. "The disturbed state" of his affairs kept Kemble from attending even to his correspondence, although he did try to acknowledge the numerous gratuitous suggestions sent him for the construction of the new Covent Garden. It was indeed a busy winter.[25]

Acting slipped into the background, although there were occasional performances to go through. On one occasion the spectators of *Henry VIII*, watching Mrs. Siddons rise majestically from a rather small chair, were surprised and diverted to see the chair rise with her. The *Examiner*, anti-Kemble as always, kept suggesting that no time would serve so well as the present for removing him from the managership. Even the audiences grew restive at his stiffness: finally he was hissed one night, and saved himself by going into a fit of coughing "which was indeed so truly painful, that it arrested at once their ridicule and their disapprobation." But that summer it was a different story. Once again John Kemble was the conquering hero, gracious and condescending on his pinnacle. He had joined his old enemy of the Drury Lane days, Mrs. Dorothy Jordan, for a tour of Ireland, and the whole island rang with his praises. He had been popular there ever since he acted as a boy in Smock Alley, but this summer the crowds flocked to him more than ever. In two months he made fourteen hundred guineas, and "if He cd. have acted oftener might have had more." Mrs. Jordan, somewhat battered by the world since she was a heart-breaker in Dublin, did not fare so well. For one thing, she complained of being "very ill treated by the managers"; her houses did not seem to come "to her expectations"; her fellow-actors were unworthy of her, and one of them (could it have been Kemble?) came to a performance drunk. Even in society — "among the best" in Dublin — she was a disappointment. *"Entre nous,"* she wrote a friend, "I do not think I shall make as much money as I expected." The prophecy, as it happened, was all too true. Back in London, however, things were being put in readiness for opening the next season at the splendid new Covent Garden. Had Kemble known what he was coming home to, he would have spent the rest of his life acting to the adulatory Irish audiences.[26]

necessity" of raising the prices of admission, from six to seven shillings for the boxes and from three and six to four for the pit. The new house, it was glibly explained, had been built "under the enormously expensive disadvantage of circumstances singularly unfavorable"; a "sixfold rentage" had been incurred; "every article indispensable to dramatick representation" had become more expensive. It was a long and doleful catalogue, and it led the firm of Harris and Kemble to "persuade themselves that in their proposed regulation they shall be honoured with the concurrence of an enlightened and liberal Publick." [2]

The enlightened and liberal public, however, reacted with a violence no one would have predicted. There was much muttering among the young blades who made the theatre their amorous and recreational center in the evenings, and even the more solid citizens began to feel mulcted. "As illiberal as it is rapacious," thundered the *Times*. There was worse to come: when it was known that the proprietors, in "mercenary and obsequious encouragement of pride and profligacy," had provided for twenty-six private boxes by reducing the size of the popular galleries, the public's indignation was unbounded. For one thing, there was, so the righteous liked to think, a moral issue involved. The private staircase and entrances to the boxes could mean only one thing — what Thomas Holcroft years before had called "the nightly intrusion of unhappy and improper persons." Covent Garden, declared John Keats, "containeth twenty thousand punks," and there were those who thought the creatures should be kept within limits. When the manager of a great national theatre, wailed a clergyman, thus endeavors to attract the ladies of the town to his theatre "and make the place commodious for their corrupt designs, how great guilt must fall upon his head, and how dreadful must be his account hereafter." Already things were bad enough: "common pros-

titutes and kept women are so thickly scattered throughout
our theatres, that no place is free from them." England was
notorious in this respect all over Europe; decent women,
fumed Sir Walter, were actually in jeopardy when they came
to see the play. Indeed, back in the eighteenth century it had
been suggested that ladies absent themselves from the theatre
entirely: "*Musick softens*, Company naturally awakes the
Passions, the Sculpture, Imagery, and Painting of the Building, help to alarm; and when the Dress, Gestures, and Discourse of the Players, are all calculated with the same Design,
and tend to the very same point, 'tis easy to see the Consequences." At any rate, the London public of 1809 considered
that the shameful increase of private boxes "was a question
touching public morals directly." The boxes and even the
ancient calling of their occupants were taken by certain
zealous patriots as French importations. One learned dis-
putant marshaled quotations from Pliny, Tertullian, Ovid,
and Juvenal as incriminating evidence against such "convenient apartments"; the *Monthly Mirror* (which did not
object to the new prices) flatly declared that nothing could
"defend a whole tier of private boxes"; "a most intolerable
grievance," stormed one irate citizen. And so the chorus of
howls mounted.[3]

The public, already in an ugly mood and fuming over the
new prices and private boxes, yelped anew when it was announced that the celebrated soprano, Madame Catalani, had
been engaged for the new theatre at seventy-five pounds a
night. Such extravagance, one pious soul pointed out, must
be "highly displeasing in the sight of Heaven." Strong feelings against foreign singers were nothing new, of course.
Cibber, who had detested working with them, moaned that
in them was "such an innate, fantastical Pride and Caprice,
that the Government of them (here [in England] at least)
is almost impracticable." The vitriolic James Ralph, he who

wenched and argued with young Ben Franklin, became enraged at the very thought of their salaries: *"Intolerable! — so many Hundreds! — for a thing of nothing! — a Voice! — a meer ha, ha! — nasty Pusses, odious filthy Things! — Let them stay at home and starve, or sing at Reasonable Rates."* Kitty Clive hated the "Italian squalling devils who come over to England to get our bread from us" and roundly cursed them all. Even James Erskine, speaking in Parliament in support of the licensing act of 1737, deplored the fact that "Italian eunuchs and signoras" should make as much money as judges of the realm.[4]

The objection to Catalani, in point of fact, was particularly unreasoned. A superb musician, she had been a European favorite for more than a decade and since 1806 had charmed English audiences. John Bull had been chiefly interested in hearing her try the strength of her voice with orchestras: "the louder they became, the higher and more victorious she ascended." Audiences had even been known to break in the doors of the theatre to get seats for her performances. The Covent Garden patentees, foolish creatures to rely so blindly on the fickle public, had congratulated themselves in hiring such a star to inaugurate their new house, even if such ladies, as Shadwell put it long before, did come "very Deare." The public's reaction to Catalani's engagement was wholly unexpected, but violent none the less. The sybaritic managers of Covent Garden, sneered one critic, obviously engaged her for their own "gratification," and the chauvinistic Britons were in no mood to pay an extra shilling that an Italian's exorbitant fees might be met. In vain did the proprietors let it be known they would still "have felt themselves compelled to solicit" the increased prices even if Catalani hadn't been imported. "We censure the folly of hiring, at an immense expense," declared one patriot, "a woman who has already sent thousands of pounds out of the country, and to meddle in the Affair." A riot at the Smock Alley Theatre in Dublin drove the elder Sheridan from the stage in disgust. He turned from acting to elocution after the ruffians, with drawn swords, had invaded the stage, slashed the scenes, and attempted arson on the theatre. And then there was the time, in 1749, when all London undertook to exercise violent discrimination against a troop of French actors who had come "alamode de France, with servile Hypocrisy; gaudy outsides; meagre Faces; impudent Airs; empty Pockets; and d—n'd keen Stomacks to Snap the Bread out of poor Countrymen's Mouths, and cram it into their own." When the harried manager attempted recourse to law, and placed constables in the pit, the howl that went up was compelling: "Pray, what is this but Tyranny! Usurpation! and Rebellion! To wage such cruel and unequal war against their Fellow Subjects, and the King's Peace and Dignity, both in despight *of,* and contrary *to* ALL LAWS, both human and divine?" Eighteenth-century theatrical records are dotted with such occurrences. In 1722 "a set of profligate young Men of Quality" caused a riot in Lincoln's Inn Fields which kept the theatre closed more than a week; at Covent Garden, in 1762, there was a riot "without the least plea or pretense whatever" when an obstreperous hind in the gallery demanded a hornpipe ("though nothing of the sort was expressed in the bills"); "a most violent tumult" threatened the King's Theatre in 1796; Covent Garden had been in a precarious spot when it opened at the Haymarket in 1792; Kemble himself was no stranger to an angry-ugly-tempered audience yelling at him across the pit. When Drury Lane on three consecutive nights announced the popular Madame Chateauneuf, well knowing she was too ill to dance, it was playing with fire: on the first night the audience was "pretty quiet"; on the second there were a few hisses; but on the third a band of determined gentlemen first ushered out the ladies and then "went to work with the House." Certainly the English, mused Ludwig Tieck, once they are aroused are "lebhafter und ungestürmer, als irgend eine Nation in Europa." [7]

This, then, was the situation when the new Covent Garden opened its doors with a gala performance of *Macbeth* on the eighteenth of September. Though the proprietors must have known what was in the air, they hoped to ride out of the storm, and preparations for the great event went forward as if all London was in graceful, benevolent anticipation. Forgotten now was the catastrophe of a year before — when the House of Commons, against the advice of Sheridan, had repaired in a body to Westminster Bridge the better to see the flames shoot skyward. One thinks of Pepys punting down the Thames in 1666. No longer did the public remember that the fiancée of "an apprentice to a respectable butcher in Paternoster-Row" had been "disconsolate a length of time" after her young man's death in the terrifying holocaust. The imposing new theatre was built and, moreover, had a fair chance of being paid for one day. The whole town flocked to its doors on the eighteenth, and with a direful purpose. One irate gentleman, compelled to wait in line for three hours, could think of nothing but the Black Hole of Calcutta. Even after the doors had been flung open, at five o'clock, chaos ruled. Respectable burgers who had contracted for boxes found them filled with rabble, the best seats were taken by storm, and by six in the evening Covent Garden was crammed with a tumultuous, ill-tempered mob. Even after the band had struck up "God Save the King" there was continual hooting. At length the curtain was drawn to reveal a chorus which proceeded to render, as best it might, "Rule Britannia," at the conclusion of which John Kemble stepped gravely forward for what should have been the proudest moment of his life. Horace Twiss had been prevailed upon to compose a prologue for the occasion, and although it could scarcely be heard it was commonly judged as positively the worst poetry in the English language. The literary aspects of the situation, however, were reduced to insignificance by the chorus of cat-calls and whistles that made poor Kemble inaudible beyond the first few boxes. He struggled through the piece grimly, none the less, trying not to notice the insistent calls of "Old Prices," "No Catalani," and "No imposition." When a paper was handed to him from the pit, he read it hurriedly and blushingly "huddled it into his pocket." The memorable Old Price riots had begun.[8]

It was murder most foul from the beginning. Not even Mrs. Siddons could be a stately Lady Macbeth when her every line was hooted. The production, like that which had opened the new Drury Lane fifteen years before, was lavish to a degree, but in vain. A sorry sight it was, sneered one spectator, to see Kemble and his sister each carrying £500 of costumes about the stage: "it was to feed this vanity, and to pay an Italian singer, that the public was screwed." As the evening wore on the tumult became deadening. Although the pit and boxes, at the beginning, were "twenty to one" for the proprietors, the contagion from the galleries spread, and before long the entire house was in commotion. So pointed was the "indignation" of the pit against the private boxes "that almost every lady retreated," and what Thomas Lawrence, vastly disgusted, called the "respectable Majority" soon left the theatre. Respectable matrons in the boxes were subjected to such language, moaned Boaden, as never "polluted the lips of any *other* monsters, except those in a neighbouring nation." Through the whole sordid business, however, the house itself suffered no damage: the boxes were not knocked with sticks, apples were not flung from the galleries — "nothing of the usual Riot." The play, meanwhile, was limping along before an audience "rent asunder with a yah! of execration." Not a word was heard from the stage. The audience stood up with their hats on and their backs to the actors, but as soon as the miserable performers closed an act the spectators sat down again "to recruit their strength" for the next round. Kemble, sorely afflicted, went through his lines with a steely, almost hypnotic, determination. His world was tumbling down about his ears.[9]

Even after the play and the afterpiece were finished the incorrigible audience refused to leave. Then it was that a pair of Bow Street constables, summoned to the theatre by the desperate managers, had the audacity to walk forth on the stage as if to read the riot act. This was the last straw, and Kemble's most serious tactical blunder. The howl of outraged dignity that rose from the house at the sight of these minions of the law demonstrated that the public was in the ugliest and most dangerous of moods — John Bull as injured innocence. The constables presently had the discretion to withdraw, taking a few rioters with them as spoils of war, and Kemble, commanding the battlefield from his box as Napoleon did from the heights of Austerlitz, played his last trump by ordering the lights turned up. The order, unfortunately, was misunderstood, and instead of lights, water engines were brought on the stage. The last indignity to free-born Englishmen! At last, at two o'clock, the rioters joined in a final chorus of "God Save the King" and departed, happy in their knowledge that the field was theirs. Making his way home that night, Kemble, heartsick and weary, had murder in his heart. His thoughts, we may be sure, were of a different cast from De Quincey's when he boasted that "there is not in the universe such an Areopagus for fair play, and abhorrence of all crooked ways, as an English mob." [10]

"Whenever there is Danger of a Riot," noted a punctilious John Kemble in his journal in 1791, "always act an Opera; for Musick drowns the Noise of Opposition." It was on the

basis of this comfortable dictum, perhaps, that *The Beggars'*
Opera greeted the audience on the second night of Covent
Garden's new season. But it failed to work. The rioters, not
to be soothed with music, came armed with placards and
banners; a large poster demanding old prices was hoisted to
the front boxes, "a lady furnishing the pins." Meanwhile
the puppets on the stage went through their futile motions.
Out front the same uproar drowned their voices. The proprietors, aghast at the continued outrage, were determined
to hold their ground, although Lawrence heard it hinted that
they would presently "give up Catalini [*sic*]" as the Peace-
offering, and in a "Night or two all will then be quiet."
When the fruitless posturing on the stage was ended, there
was a general movement from the pit towards the front of
the house. The invaders, however, were met by a group of
fierce-looking constables and ("incredible to relate") hazard-
ous opened trap-doors. At this most recent atrocity the mob
retired to its proper place in the pit and continued its howling
with renewed zeal. An address made by a Mr. Lee was received with great approbation, even though "nineteen out
of twenty" could not hear him, and with such jocular demonstrations the evening was finally ended with several young
blades being borne off in triumph by the constabulary.[11]

By the third night things were worse than ever. Not even
Cooke, as Richard III, could distract the rioters.

> 'Twould not have matter'd much, I ween,
> Had he this night, *as usual*, been —
> That is, had he been *non se ipse*,
> Or, in plain English, had been tipsy.

The hooting continued until after the farce, when Kemble at
last took the fatal step. After deafening calls from the pit, he
came forward to parley with the mob. It must have been the
most humiliating appearance of his career. As Porson said

of Fox, he threw himself into the middle of his speech "and left it to God Almighty to get him out again." It was a fervent effort: he cited prices from the days of Queen Anne, he pointed out increased production expenses, he swore that the proprietors had not, for ten years, made even six per cent on their investment; he declared his trust in the liberality and magnanimity of a British audience; and he closed by a ringing affirmation that not for all Covent Garden was worth would he lie to his public. Even this handsome statement had no effect. Everything — recourse to law, intimidation, candor — had failed and John Kemble knew no further step to take. To the seething, howling pit he finally thundered in desperation, "Ladies and gentlemen, *I wait to know what you want.*" This was the ultimate insult — and from John Kemble, who had become a "nabob" through the good offices of his public. As if the haughty old despot did not know the cause of the rebellion. Pandemonium broke loose; broad allusions to the sordid De Camp episode were broadcast through the house; and a helpless and embittered Kemble stalked from the stage in defeat.[12]

And so the sorry business dragged along, night after night. It was open war. The managers imported not only constables but even professional fighters and "fighting Jews" to combat the rioters. The trap-doors on the stage were kept ajar to "receive any luckless adventurer, who might have attempted to make his debut without managerial sanction." A most frightening array of fire-engines adorned the stage. And in the pit all was rattles, bells, gongs, and whistles. Presently, of course, all London took sides. Kemble was censured, even by his supporters, for besetting free-born Englishmen with paid ruffians. The riots became increasingly pugilistic. One night a constable who had been thrown from the pit with considerable enthusiasm returned with a band of cohorts; in the ensuing *mêlée* one young gentleman got a nasty wound from a spike, "of three inches in length, which passed through his hand, and *sticking* there, separated from the stick, at the end of which it had been fixed." Each night the disgraceful exhibition continued; each night the placards and signs became more imaginative and abusive, the noise-makers more varied, the proprietors more obdurate. Even when Kemble had "a fair opening" to dismiss Catalani, fretted Lawrence, he delayed. "He shuts himself up too much," complained the painter, and the result was the grossly bad tactics that come from self-confidence. At length, on the sixth night, the manager proposed that a committee of unprejudiced persons examine the books of the theatre and adjudicate the new prices. Nothing could be fairer, Kemble pleaded, and the rioters agreed. While the judges * were sitting the theatre would be closed, and thus both sides could have a breathing spell. This was obviously a wise move, thought some; if the riots had continued, lives would have been lost. Sir Walter, however, made a pessimistic report to Lady Abercorn. He distrusted the truce, and looked for "the love of frolic" to revive at the slightest provocation. The committee, meanwhile, was laboring valiantly, sitting from morning to night in its perusal of the theatre's ledgers, insurance records, architect's bills, and expense accounts. When the findings were at last made public, six days later, decent folk sighed with relief: the theatre was vindicated. Covent Garden's profits, from the time of Kemble's partnership, had been six and three-eighths per cent on the investment. In the past six years the theatre had taken in £365,983, had spent £315,912, and had cleared annually £8,345. As for the new prices, they were entirely justified; without them, the proprietors stood to lose three-fourths of one per cent each year on their investment. "No liberal mind can, on a moment's

* John Sylvester, Sir Thomas Plomer, John Whitmore, J. J. Angerstein, and Sir Charles Price.

consideration, become an enemy to their necessary plan of opening the New House." [13]

If Kemble thought his troubles were over, he was mistaken. The opposition brushed aside the committee's report as one would flick a feather from his sleeve. The judgment of the committee, scoffed the *Statesman* with superb oblivion of fact, "is precisely what we expected. — We went confident that the Proprietors would *perplex* the Committee, the public — by talking about the *rate of interest*. What have the public to do with the rate of interest upon an *imaginary* capital?" The *Times* had reason to believe that the managers had lied: the 1808–1809 season had probably brought no less than £20,000 profit, and the patentees usually shared about £35,000 at the end of every "successful" season. And so the report accomplished nothing. The managers were helpless, and when they opened Covent Garden again on October 4, the rioters were out in full force. This time they had a new weapon in their battery — Kemble's enormous and illicit earnings, exaggerated reports of which were spread over a new array of placards. In vain did the manager, addressing the audience from the stage, throw himself "upon the candour of the most enlightened metropolis in the world." The rioters had scented blood, and now they would be satisfied with nothing less than total surrender. While the proprietors held grimly on, week after week, the rioting continued merrily. If the constables had let us alone, explained one insurgent, "the *fun* would have died away." But now it was a point of honor. Young Macready went to see the demonstrations and was thoroughly disgusted: an almost empty theatre through the first three acts, and then at half-price "the well-organized opposition" would rush in, dance on the benches in the pit, and drown out every sound with their jeering.[14]

Public interest in the conflict, of course, was great. Medals

were struck — one of them representing Kemble as a donkey
with John Bull riding on his back; special O.P. dances were
composed; elaborate placards and broadsides were hawked
on the streets. And as the miserable business went along, one
thing became clear: John Kemble was the symbol of oppression and the object of the mob's attacks. In him were focused
all the evils of the Covent Garden patentees, and his blood
was to be the price of peace. Probably no respectable citizen,
not in public office, was ever more violently detested than
John Kemble during the unhappy fall of 1809. "Black
Jack," as he was dubbed, became the object of every possible
sort of vilification. His past was delved into with more zeal
than good taste. His religion (and Jesuit training at Douay)
was ridiculed. Colored prints of his poverty and degradation
as a stroller were circulated. Jingles and ballads were sung of
his *hauteur*, his pride, and his hatred of the public. Hand-
bills exhorting unremitting combat appeared:

> Britons be firm! your private RIGHTS maintain,
> In spite of KEMBLE, and his Venal Train;
> Disdain submission to a Tyrant's Will,
> Nor JEWS! nor ORDERS! o'er this House shall fill;
> No Crim. Con. Boxes, SHALL our sight disgust,
> Remember, KEMBLE, that what must be, must! ! [15]

Sane persons were wondering how long such an intolerable
situation could continue when, at the end of November,
things began to come to a head. Kemble had tried to bring
the press over to his side, and the *Times* had begun to take
a more temperate attitude — perhaps, as was rumored, because it had been threatened with libel proceedings. But
when he called on Perry, of the *Morning Post*, a violent quarrel occurred and the editor "threw up his free admissions."
The *Statesman* never ceased its slashing attacks on the proprietors; it even berated those few papers that tried to report
the riots dispassionately. The press, for all its noisy commo-

tion, accomplished little in bringing about a settlement. Some of the opposition were demanding an open and abject apology from John Kemble, while he, as Sir Walter well knew, "would have died on the breach rather than yield to the authority of the public in a point where he justly conceived himself a much better judge than they." Nothing could daunt him, and the only emotion he felt was contempt. Even when defamatory O.P. songs were chanted under the windows of his fine house in Great Russell Street and mobs gathered ominously before his door, he was determined to go out and face his enemies had not the prudent Charles dissuaded him. His home was subject to frequent visits by bands of rioters (usually on their way home after the evening's frolic in the theatre) who sometimes resorted to violence. On one occasion the parlor windows were broken. Her brother, the terrified Siddons reported, was living in danger of his person; Priscilla had taken the precaution to put ladders at the garden window so they could retreat if the house were stormed. Naturally, Kemble's nerves were "much shaken." When he appealed to the authorities, little was done.[16]

Finally the slow machinery of the law was put in operation. A certain Henry Clifford, barrister, having been seized as a rioter by James Brandon, the faithful old box-keeper at Covent Garden, was forcibly carried to Bow Street, where he was dismissed. Clifford, a man of parts and something of the unofficial leader of the opposition, saw his opportunity. He immediately brought suit against Brandon for alleged assault and false imprisonment. The trial, in the Court of Common Pleas before Sir James Mansfield on December 5, was felt by all to be the deciding factor in the long combat: in it were focused the hopes of both sides, for everyone knew that when the court spoke, the war would be ended.[17]

The trial was by way of being a miniature Warren Hastings event. By eight in the morning crowds were milling about before the court and five minutes after the doors were opened every seat in the room had been fought for and finally seized. Clifford's attorney, Best, missed few tricks in his opening speech. His client, a man of family, of style, of learning, cared nothing for the paltry £100 he was seeking as damages. His was a moral cause, against oppression and tyranny. As for the financial aspects of the situation, Best continued, the patentees could realize eight per cent from the private boxes alone (let at £400 annually). Indeed, by constructing these boxes they had violated their patent, which should be instantly revoked. The boxes, after all, were not privileges for the nobility, nor were they used by those ladies "who had a life-interest in their Lords," but by those creatures who, "possessing their ascendency over them but for a season, would make that season as profitable as possible." And as for the rioting, Best went on glibly, why, there had been none. There was always noise and uproar in a theatre. "If it could be shown that a single chandelier had been broken, and that the damage of sixpence had been done to the Theatre," then a riot had occurred, and only then. Mr. Best himself, "a nervous man," had attended the alleged riot with no alarm or terror whatever, and without alarm and terror an uproar could not be called a riot. It was all very convincing and very eloquent. If Clifford had been rioting (which he had not), he should have been seized at the scene of the misdemeanor and at the moment of the disturbance, not after he had left the theatre and was walking home. Brandon had seen him leave, and had straightway ordered Taunton, a constable, to follow and apprehend him. "Why he's been doing nothing all night"; "Never mind, D—n your eyes, that's Clifford; take him." This, Mr. Best submitted, was nothing short of plain assault. The Bow Street magistrates who had released him, as well as seven character witnesses, offered proof enough of the plaintiff's innocence.

Shepherd, Brandon's attorney, did not write a new chapter in legal brilliance. He was moved, for one thing, at the thought that prejudices "had crept into the world, and had operated so powerfully upon respectable persons, as to make them disgrace themselves before the public." The sight of a person of Mr. Clifford's attainments "prostituted to the instigation of such riotous violence" by wearing an O.P. ribband in his hat was indeed grievous. True, Brandon — an "old, honest, and confidential servant of the Theatre" — had delayed seizing Clifford, but only because he realized that "serious mischief" would result if the arrest had been made on the spot. No witnesses were called.

Justice Mansfield, in his charge to the jury, upheld the prerogative of the proprietors to set whatever price they chose and to operate private boxes "at their discretion." Nothing, he pointed out, could justify the nightly scenes in Covent Garden — "scenes which were a disgrace to the country, and which tended to bring us back to a state of barbarism." Why, if question of this sort "were to be determined by multitudes of people assembling tumultuously," there would be an end to all law in the land. In spite of Best's slippery argument, the Justice continued, it was for the jury to determine whether or not there had been rioting, and the part Clifford had in instigating it. His own opinion was there *had* been rioting and that Clifford *was* instrumental in it, although his postponed arrest was justifiable under no law. The charge was a long one, and a just one: the Justice was perturbed. Persons who wantonly disturbed the peace, he warned, could not and would not be longer tolerated. And so the jury retired.

The verdict, returned after ten minutes, was bitterly disappointing to Kemble's hopes and Mansfield's wishes. Clifford was awarded damages of five pounds. While the court broke into cheers (which rapidly spread to the street without) the

voice of law and order got a last word in. Roundly berating
the jury for such a verdict, the judge warned that "shocking
mistakes will go forth, so that public outrage may be continued by a furious mob." Ahead lay nothing but revenge,
"even to the ruin of their country."

But the riots were over. The opposition had won, through
due process of law, and to Kemble was left the unwonted role
of humility. The final ignominy of surrender, however, was
made as painless as possible. The occasion, of course, was a
banquet, set in great splendor on the night of December 14
at the Crown and Anchor Tavern. Clifford, generous in his
triumph, was toastmaster to the five hundred "real friends
of the Drama, and reprobators of Managerial insolence and
brutality." There was lacking only Kemble, and he had
made known his intention of coming if he could be assured
safe conduct. Presently he made his entrance — how galling
it must have been — to "considerable applause," and everyone settled down to the business of the evening. Kemble,
lofty and superior to the end, acceded stoically to the dic-
tated terms: yes, the introduction of "hired Ruffians" into
the theatre demanded an apology; yes, the prices should be
restored to their old scale; yes, the offending Brandon should
be instantly discharged; yes, all suits against the rioters should
be dropped by the theatre. Catalani and the private boxes
were forgotten in the flush of good will that followed these
concessions, and after a number of toasts and an "excellent
Song," Kemble took his departure "amidst a good deal of
applause, mingled with some disapprobation." [18]

Meanwhile, at the theatre, a performance of *Tom Thumb*
was going on to the customary accompaniment from the pit.
When Kemble, fresh from the love feast, walked on the stage
still in his boots and great coat, it was to announce the peace
terms. But this was not enough, or at least not for the jubilant throng before him. The *instant* dismissal of Brandon
was demanded; when that unfortunate gentleman was led

out to plead his cause he was greeted with such a storm of protest, and so many oranges, that he was compelled to beat a hasty retreat. The evening closed as stormily as ever. The next night, however, Kemble himself acted *The Wheel of Fortune* to a house overflowing in every nook and corner. And although the audience was eager to see the vanquished contestant after such a long absence from the stage, it was none the less insistent on Brandon's dismissal. Not a word could be heard until Kemble, realizing that his cup was now full and running over, stepped forward and announced that Brandon, "having incurred the displeasure of the public," was no longer connected with Covent Garden. To deafening applause the old man himself came forward to deliver the formal apology that had been insisted on. From the pit was hoisted a placard, "We are satisfied." The O.P. riots were over.[19]

Horne Tooke, who was no stranger to the consequences of mob hysteria, once complained of having made two egregious blunders in his life: attributing too much virtue to people individually and too much understanding to them collectively. The observation is particularly apposite when one is trying to unravel such a complex occurrence as the O.P. riots. As one spectator put it, "there never in this world was a question publicly discussed, where so much ignorance was shewn; there never was one where so much illiberality was shewn; there never was one where the press so grossly abused its powers." The most reliable evidence points to sheer willfullness and malice on the part of the public. The proprietor's demands were not excessive; they had, moreover, been clarified and justified on a sound fiscal basis by the authorized committee. Official England spoke in the outraged protests of Justice Mansfield, private England in the scandalized comments of decent folk who shuddered to see the sacred right of property assailed. William Cobbett, one of the sanest Englishmen of his day, sympathized emotionally with some of the rioters' demands, but none the less he could but deplore the *"attempt to compel people to sell entertainment at the price pointed out by the purchaser."* [20]

To understand the riots it is necessary to go deeper into their background. Londoners were inveterate theatre-goers, and for precisely seventy-two years their theatre-going had been painfully restricted by the licensing act of 1737: only two theatres were patented to exhibit legitimate drama. The monopoly so tenaciously maintained by the two great houses had, long before 1809, become an anachronism. Walpole had engineered it originally as a gag act (chiefly against Henry Fielding), thinking it easier to keep two theatres under his thumb than twenty or thirty. Attempts at reform had been futile, but the agitation continued. Something of this unsavory restriction of commerce was undoubtedly in the minds of the few intelligent men who appear to have organized and carried to a successful conclusion the O.P. riots. It was felt, at least by some, that Covent Garden had been intolerably presumptuous in making still further demands on a public guaranteed it by act of Parliament. The opportunity for revolt came, and was seized. Just how much propaganda lay behind that frightening demonstration on September 18 will probably never be known. The press for days had been stirring up discontent, and once the agitation was under way it gained momentum at a fearful rate. It is safe to conjecture, however, that a small group of men (headed very likely by Clifford) inaugurated and directed the riots as an organized protest against monopoly infringement. Sir Walter, writing to Lady Abercorn, feared for Covent Garden with such a "disciplined" mob opposing it, and particularly "with such leaders as *Clifford*, who has just knowledge enough to keep him within the verge of law, talent enough to do mischief, and no capacity whatever to do the least good." [21]

The time was ripe, of course. England had been for twenty years sitting tightly clamped on a powder-keg: the revolution of 1789 across the Channel, the reaction and reprisals of the 'nineties, the decay and madness of the king, all lay behind; and in the future loomed some such drastic events as the Congress of Vienna, the Peterloo massacre, the tyranny of Castlereagh, and the Reform Bill of 1832. England, with "its confused prospects and baffled aspirations, with riots at home and wars abroad," was in anything but a placid mood. And then, on a more personal plane, there was John Kemble, who for several seasons had been steadily losing popularity. With a target so conspicuous and a cause so righteous, what riot could fail? Though the leaders were men like Clifford, the body of the rioters were more humble. "Clerks, apprentices, linen drapers' foremen, hair-dressers, and knife grinders," scoffed one apologist for the theatre, "have been the dignified traders of this most dignified mob; and upon *these* the name of the PUBLIC has been conferred." They were rough men, but they were ready men, and they were convinced that their rights as free-born Englishmen were being subverted. The tactics of the theatre, of course, merely fed the flames. "Hired bruisers" and trap-doors were not for a British public. The English, pointed out the *Morning Chronicle*, would have forfeited the inheritance of a thousand years if they had sub-mitted to "the gross and atrocious manner" of their persecu-tion. Although they were incidentally good fun — riots were always that — the O.P. riots were essentially the revolt of an entire community against unfair merchandizing. And even if the monopolies persisted (as they did for thirty years more), the public at least had shown that its goodwill was an absolute necessity to the theatre. The managers of proud Covent Garden were beaten to their knees. John Kemble, who had climbed so high, was in a moment cast as low as any great actor has ever been.[22]

CHAPTER XV

Dénouement

It is better to repose in the earth betimes than to sit
up late; better, than to cling pertinaciously to what
we feel crumbling under us, and to protract an inevitable fall.

WALTER SAVAGE LANDOR

DURING THAT terrible fall when the rioters demanded their
pound of flesh and all London seemed intent on de-
stroying a great career, John Kemble turned from an aging
man into an old man. When it was over, of course, he went
on again, but his day had passed, and he knew it. His faith
in his public was forever shattered. "My lord," he blurted
out to Lord Mountjoy, "CHRIST was *crucified*, DE WIT was
assassinated: so much for the world and the people." While
he paced through the rest of the season with his customary
aloofness, all over the kingdom was spreading the news of
the glorious O.P. victory in London: coachmen and postil-
lions, wearing triumphant ribbands in their hats, shouted
the good news to each other. And in London, Clifford
was the hero of the hour — a reincarnation of the "unmoved,
undaunted, fearless Hampden." At Covent Garden, however,
there was an embittered man who, though only fifty-three,
could no longer serve with his full devotion an art that had
brought him such humiliation "without the possibility of
defence or retaliation." [1]

Lear, in the spring, set the tone of the season. The old
king, in his moments of lucidity, would ask feebly after the
affairs of state and murmur pathetically that he realized his

"situation," and at the playhouse people were not fond of seeing another decayed monarch, even a theatrical one. Cooke, more incorrigible than ever, was closing his London career ingloriously. Often too drunk to act — and then the play would be hurriedly changed — he presently made his way to America, there to die a drunkard's death. But Kemble continued to act, almost in spite of himself and his public. *King John*, with its "dignity and its mixture of contempt and whining" seemed to the *Examiner* to be particularly suited to John Kemble's abilities. The summer brought ease and quiet at Lord Guilford's place, Wroxton Abbey. The long, leisurely days, the well-bred conversation, the gentility of the company all meant sweet content and golden slumbers after the hurly-burly of the rabble in the pit. Old Parson Este, who long before had done his best to make Kemble famous, was still lingering on the outskirts of preferment, seeking some niche of his own. Kemble advised him to take what he could get, however unsatisfactory it might be, "and trust to luck for a Translation. — It is always rather a good thing, in the road to preferment, to have something to give up." But the aging actor, not so confident and eager as he had been twenty years before, when Este was disgusting the town with his puffs, had the caution that comes with years. "I am but a bad, and too often an unsatisfactory, Counsellor." [2]

Even the next fall his troubles were not over. In the journal for the opening night appears the dread note, "Riots — &c." It was the old complaint: the public had made up its mind again to submit to no private boxes (a point on which it had been lenient at the peace treaty). Kemble had promised the year before to do away with them, but at his last appearance the season before he had reneged: it was only just, he pointed out in a curtain-speech, that Covent Garden be permitted as many boxes as Drury Lane. At this there rose from the pit, recalled Lawrence, "such a storm . . . as we never witness'd during the late business for overwhelming Clamour." And Clifford made it plain that "no tittle of the treaty should be violated." Great was the popular indignation, then, when it was learned that only twelve of the old boxes had been thrown open to the public. Kemble came forward with a futile attempt to explain. There had been other changes, he pointed out hopefully: "stone staircases, paving and arching of corridors, raising of lower gallery roof, etc." But a principle was at stake. The dread O.P. dance was started, a bottle was thrown upon the stage, and the evening closed in tumult. Of course the proprietors had to surrender again. The theatre was closed for a few days, the changes were made, and at last the public was satisfied that their victory was final.[3]

The new season, oddly enough, was almost like old times. Kemble acted all his best pieces — *Hamlet, Macbeth, Henry VIII, The Mountaineers* — and once more he carried all before him in triumph. The struggle and acrimony of the riots forgotten, the public took him to their hearts again. "The first tragedian of our times" acted to over-flowing houses, and Covent Garden grossed £100,000 during the winter. From America came an offer of $5,000 and all expenses for eighty performances on the Atlantic seaboard, but why should John Kemble cross the ocean when he was making that much and half again in London? He was holding high the tragic torch. Even the *Examiner* hailed his triumph. The other managers, it was pointed out, "have so little taste, with the exception of Sheridan, who cares for no taste but that of port, that were it not for Mr. Kemble's exertions, the tragedies of our glorious bard would almost be in danger of dismissal from the stage." Cooke was now gone, never to return, and his choicest roles fell to Kemble, even if his Sir Giles Overreach seemed much "too gentlemanly" after

Cooke's native "coarse violence." As usual, he was much more eager to revive Shakespeare than to experiment with new plays. Landor had just finished *Count Julian*, and Southey, who suggested spitefully that the title-role might appeal to Kemble's vanity, undertook to have it produced. As for Kemble's understanding "the power and might and majesty that the tragedy manifests," Southey added, "it is not to be expected from a man who can act in such trash as 'Cato' and the 'Revenge,' — after Shakspeare." Landor joyfully prepared his manuscript (for all the world like Lamb, ten years before), and received careful coaching from his knowing friend. Treat Kemble with "something like haughtiness," Southey warned, to make him realize that he, and not the author, is being obliged. But at the last minute Landor weakened: his play, he declared in a burst of characteristic pride, "shall never lie at the feet of Kemble." Perhaps it was just as well. Lamb could remember nothing of the characters after having read the piece, and Longmans refused to publish it even at the author's expense. Until Murray finally accepted it, a little later, Landor was implacably resolved to abandon the "tissue of humiliations" that constituted a literary life.[4]

While Landor was fuming about his play the 1811–1812 season was lurching forward with three momentous occurrences: Master Betty returned, Mrs. Siddons retired, and a live elephant made its appearance on the stage of Covent Garden. Master Betty, now a gawky youth of no charm whatever, failed to stir his audiences as he had a half dozen years before; Kemble was not again compelled to flee. As for the withdrawal of the Tragic Muse, it was generally considered the part of wisdom. The good lady, now fat and elderly, could no longer move strong men to tears. But the elephant was a different matter. Long before, Rich had been tempted to bring one of the creatures on the stage, and was deterred only when a bricklayer assured him that "if the Walls were to be open'd wide enough for its Entrance it might endanger the Fall of the House." Henry Harris, a century later, was not so easily put off. Much impressed by an elephant just brought to England he paid £900 for the animal and brought him (or her, as the case might be) forth triumphantly in *Harlequin and Padmandba*, the Christmas pantomime. Some had thought that art could go no further when, a year before, "sixteen most beautiful horses mounted by *sphais* suddenly appeared before the spectators, and were received with immense applause." Kemble had been aghast at this undertaking, but he was powerless even to stop the elephant. Critics who remembered the good old days were a little bitter: one of them had Garrick, safe in Elysium, offer some good advice:

> OTWAY begs you'll burn his plays;
> He would not have them live, in days
> When brutes and monsters are the rage.

But the creature enjoyed more popularity than most performers. Charles Greville poked sly fun at Kemble in his diary while the *Examiner* warned the public that "elephants are subject to sudden fits of rage, and have no natural forbearance in favour of theatrical amateurs." And as for Kemble, he should blush in his port for so degrading his highly-touted "classical" repertory. Poor fellow. To be held responsible for the elephant must have been the unkindest cut of all. He pegged along as best he might, combatting asthma, gout, and the depraved taste of the public. His productions still elicited gasps of admiration, even if one irate classicist pointed out that Coriolanus had no business wearing a red-bordered toga: "the *toga praetexta* was a purple border . . . which did not undergo any change, I believe, before the reign of Augustus." But a young nobleman named Byron, just back from the most exotic travels, thought Kemble made a "*glorious*" Roman.[5]

During the spring Mrs. Siddons had her last fling, acting all her great parts. Kemble, of course, ably abetted her. *Julius Caesar* was brought forth anew in a stunning production, and everyone who saw it admitted, said Charles Mayne Young, that it was "the greatest intellectual recreation" ever enjoyed. All the world was eager to get a last look at the glorious Siddons: Covent Garden's doors were besieged by "tremendous crowds," and everyone from Byron to the lowliest apprentice fought to get seats. On the twenty-ninth of June Siddons trod the boards for the last time. The play was *Macbeth*, and Kemble was so moved that he, of all men, wept. It was by way of a farewell for him too, for he was taking a long-desired vacation. His health had been wretched lately. His old enemy, asthma, was plaguing him more than ever, and gout, the fruit of long years of gargantuan excesses, had laid him low during the winter. The opium pills he had taken seemed to have no effect, but however loudly he groaned in the green-room he concealed his infirmities on the stage with "amazing" fortitude. There was some talk of financial difficulties between him and Harris: the senior partner had refused to raise his salary for acting to seventy-two guineas a week, and Kemble, if the gossip could be believed, had angrily left the theatre. His share in the patent could be had for £25,000, but since there were no candidates for the dubious honor of buying it, he contented himself merely by depriving the theatre of his acting. In a single season Covent Garden had lost its two greatest stars.[6]

Free at last of the "intolerable grievances" of managing Covent Garden, Kemble struck out for a leisurely tour — partly for acting, partly for pleasure — through England and Ireland. Liverpool, in July, welcomed its old favorite, and the month's visiting in Irish country houses was excellent

for his disposition if not for his gout. When he got to Edinburgh, in September, Scott came all the way in from Abbotsford to see him act. His Coriolanus and Cato, Lady Abercorn
was told, were "as near perfection as I can conceive theatrical
performance," but in the role of Sir Giles John Kemble was
"too handsome, too plausible, and too smooth." It was
Cooke's play still, even if Cooke had gone to America. It
was gay, back in London again, to live as a great gentleman.
The Regency was at its height, morals at their lowest. Byron,
who led the procession, mocked the society that nourished
him:

> Hoops are *no more*, and petticoats *not much*;
> Morals and minuets, virtue and her stays,
> And tell-tale powder — all have had their days.

And although the theatre was flourishing — Covent Garden
had been remodeled during the summer; now it looked like
"the fabled palace of the sun" — Kemble sullied not his hands.
Young Charles Mayne Young was filling his roles, if not well
at least in the Kemble manner; all the great man himself
had to do was draw his dividends as a patentee. In January
he contributed eighty pounds to the Actor's Fund and resigned (for the third time, as he pointed out truculently) as
one of its trustees. There were parties without number, and
when he moved on triumphantly to Bath the whole fashionable colony turned out to welcome the venerable actor. In
Edinburgh again the next winter he filled the theatre. "Almost nightly" the squire of Abbotsford was in the audience.[7]

Everything was comfortable and easy, however: the pace
was leisurely, and the provincial appearances had all the
gentility of a drawing-room call. After a year or so of such
dilettantism even the first gentlemen of the English stage
began to fret. A trip to Paris in the fall of 1813, almost twelve
years after that first breathless stay there in 1802, was disappointing. The fate of Europe was being decided on the

field at Leipsic, and Paris was not the gay capital it would
be a year later, when Napoleon would be safely put away
and the boulevards would once again blossom with high-
born English tourists and diplomats. Although Priscilla and
Mrs. Siddons came along this time to Paris, the vacation was
a short one and a dull one. Thomas Campbell, obliging as
ever, was delighted to squire the great people about to the
Louvre and the Comédie Française. Everywhere Kemble was
still welcomed as "le grand tragique" of his country. But
he was still an actor, and an actor pining for his element. By
November he was back in London again, and once more
Covent Garden saw its stately manager in his old haunts. In
point of fact, there was a splendid revival in prospect, and
John Kemble was not one to miss the occasion. *Antony and
Cleopatra* had always been one of his favorites, and only Mrs.
Siddons' refusing to play in it had deterred him from bringing
it forward long before. His sister would hate herself, she
had explained, if she let herself play Cleopatra as "it ought
to be played." This time, however, neither of the great
elders was in the cast. Kemble confined his labors chiefly to
making an acting version that would combine the "magick"
of Shakespeare with the decorum of Dryden, and to devising
sets that would impress even the jaded London audiences.*
The production, however, had only a lukewarm reception.
Young, thought one critic, was a tame Antony; he lacked that
which Kemble, for all his faults, possessed so abundantly —
"the faculty of sometimes electrifying the audience with enthusiasm." There were those who objected to the excessive
spectacle, claiming the piece was dug up only for the sake
of the "sea-fight and the funeral procession." The public

* Kemble's part in this revision, hitherto a matter of conjecture, is
proved by item 1677 in the auctioneer's catalogue of his library: "Anthony [*sic*] and Cleopatra, 2 copies, corrected for the Stage by Mr.
Kemble, and also two copies in MS."

supported nine performances of the revival, however, and for the first time in two years London had a taste of its old dramatic fare — the Kemble version of high tragedy.[8]

The conquering hero was returning, however. In January, Kemble stalked forth once more as Coriolanus, and the whole town dissolved anew in admiration. "Heartfelt approbation and silent tears," if we may believe Hazlitt, were his portion. The burst of applause that shook the house at his first performance after two years of absence was unlike anything since Garrick had got back from his Continental tour, fifty years before. The actor's art, all the newspapers agreed, could be summed up in the person of Kemble: he is the Aristotle of the theatre; "his judgment never fails him, his taste is invariably just." Only the more spiteful suggested that his return was motivated by something less than benevolence — that the crescent careers of Conway and Young had made him jealous and brought him back posthaste. But as the crowds flocked that winter to see their aging hero, he acted with all his old brilliance and control. Before long he was back in the full swing of the theatre: Shakespeare filled Covent Garden, and Kemble was blandly refusing to consider the offerings of unknown writers (even when they were sponsored by Sir Walter). He had paid Byron the compliment of requesting a play, but that erratic gentleman's "scribbling mood" was waning. Those hacks who had assailed Kemble for so many years with their unsolicited dramas were increasingly bitter; they even published an anthology of their unacted masterpieces and in the preface found occasion to remark that "men of intellects so mean and narrow" as theatre managers should have their cruel and capricious power restricted. Kemble, the butt of these attacks, went serenely on his way, imperturbable as ever. To close the season he did another round of his best roles — massive, spectacular, adorned. Indeed, the *Examiner* complained that he would never look twice at a play that could not "be converted into a pageant, but bring forward with much pretence any drama that has its proper capabilities of ostentatious spectacle." But the public was pleased, and so was John Kemble: for twenty-one performances he had drawn from the treasury the handsome sum of £1,102 10s. He was still a force in the theatre.[9]

Yes, Kemble was still a force, but one nearly spent. Hazlitt, that prince of critics, was one of the first to realize on the January evening in 1814 when Edmund Kean, as Shylock, brought his audience cheering to their feet that the Kemble school had passed away.

We wish we had never seen Mr. Kean. He has destroyed the Kemble religion; and it was the religion in which we were brought up. Never again shall we behold Mr. Kemble with the same pleasure that we did, nor see Mr. Kean with the same pleasure we have seen Mr. Kemble formerly.

Kean, of course, was a nobody — an unkempt, drunken, erratic stroller. But after that single night at Drury Lane — so much like Garrick's, long ago in Goodman's Fields — he was the new monarch of the stage. Very well it was for John Kemble to return in triumph to Covent Garden, to declaim *Coriolanus* with all his old dignity and effect, to make a thousand pounds in twenty nights. In the other house was an actor, and a kind of acting, unlike anything London had seen for almost half a century.[10]

The whole town was talking about Edmund Kean. Byron, something of a connoisseur, decided he was better than Cooke "and will run Kemble hard; his Style is quite new, or rather *renewed*, being that of Nature." Kean came at a good time: romanticism had long since triumphed in literature, but on the stage the old neo-classical tradition, chiefly because of the personal impetus of Siddons and Kemble, had enjoyed a longer vitality. Now, at last, the theatre was ripe to embrace the realistic (or so it seemed), the vigorous, and the erratic. It is significant that John Keats, about to begin a career all his own, was carried away by the new-comer (although he never troubled to express an opinion on John Kemble). Even Fanny Kemble, Charles' daughter and last of the great tribe, found Kean's Shylock "extraordinary." He was the only actor, she made bold to say, "whose performances have ever realized to me my idea of the effect tragic acting ought to produce." The critics, at long last, had a new exemplar of tragic power, and a new criterion to apply to the old school that had held the stage uncontested for twenty years.[11]

The critics, who for years had acknowledged Kemble's supremacy simply because there had been no rival, turned gleefully to the new hero. In him all of them found a power and a 'naturalness' entirely new. Kemble's Hamlet is perfect, admitted Byron, "but Hamlet is not Nature. Richard is a man; and Kean is Richard." Hunt, of course, was in ecstasy. His old enemy "faded" before Kean "like a tragedy ghost." An Edinburgh critic, a little later, had to admit that "our old and distinguished favourite" had had his day: compared to Kean's, his Sir Giles Overreach "dwindles into nothingness." Although on all sides rose paeans for the new star, Kemble remained superb in his line. Kean or no Kean, he was still the unparalleled master of the grand style. It was a style that had served him well, and he made no effort to change it. And Hazlitt, almost alone, pointed out the sober fact that Kemble was still a very great artist:

Ridiculous to set up Mr. Kean as a rival to Mr. Kemble. Whatever merits the first might have, they were of a totally different class, and could not possibly interfere with, much less injure those of his great predecessor. Mr. Kemble stood on his own ground, and stood high on it. Yet there certainly was a *reaction* in this case. Many persons saw no defect in Mr. Kemble till Mr. Kean came, and then finding themselves mistaken in the abstract idea of perfection they had indulged in, were ready to give up their opinion altogether.[12]

As Mr. Allardyce Nicoll has pointed out, Kean may hardly be said to have introduced a new realism into acting: he was as artificial in his way as Kemble in his. Where the older man had been "intellectually rhetorical," Kean was "passionately so." Kean could move his contemporaries because he sold the kind of goods they wanted: under a veneer of naturalism he was as lyrical as Shelley, but in a cheaper way. The excitement and almost physical violence of his performances appealed largely because of the contrast to Kemble's decorum and stylized severity. To one of the older persuasion Kean's acting was nothing more than "a favourable specimen of what might be expected from a provincial performer." To a public hungry for passion and extravagance it was the very essence of high art. Apart from him, declared John Keats roundly, "there is not another actor of Tragedy in all London or Europe." [13]

Kemble, of course, was quite aware of what was going on after 1814. He looked about him and saw that his life was over; his reaction was characteristically calm, rational, dispassionate. You cannot expect me to like Kean, he told Boaden, "but one thing I must say in his favour, — he is at all times terribly in *earnest*." And although the new idol had unquestionable merits, they were swallowed up in the "vices of his style." To the older theatre-goers, people who had learned to think of acting in Kemble's terms, Kean was "fit only for a burletta." There was no question of rivalry, after all: Kemble realized that his own career was safely and honorably past; he merely wondered if Kean would break and collapse under the weight of his inflated reputation. You will soon see, he prophesied to a group of mellow oldsters over their port, that the new star, like poor Cooke, would be "driven to the trick of withdrawing to America, as a frail beauty of the lobby finds it expedient to withdraw her charms from it for awhile, to reappear when her face has been long enough forgotten." After all, what could be expected from a man whose style was so "radically unsound"? [14]

Gentility, snorted Leigh Hunt. Kemble's defenders shrink from crass details of comparison, but instead talk loftily of their hero's gentility. He, for one, would forego gentility for passion, and most London theatre-goers agreed. Kean had already revived the dormant Drury Lane — poor Sheri was wearing out his last days in more poverty and dissipation than ever — and his was the name on everyone's lips. True, Kemble maintained a following, but it meant nothing, argued his enemies. The continued respect and admiration that the London audiences paid him after Kean's advent reflected "a mere prejudice, though a respectable one." The old man's sun was setting, and he realized it, but to the last he held his place: the first gentleman of the stage was not one to scurry away in terror before every young pretender. [15]

None the less, it was well to look towards the end, to put his affairs in order. For one thing, posterity would no doubt wish to know how the great Kemble had achieved his brilliant revivals. The scores of plays he had exhumed, revised, and produced would be his monument and, although the acting texts of his alterations had appeared in print (and been sold in the lobbies as librettos) throughout his career, a more substantial sepulchre was wanted. It was provided in a handsome eight-volume edition of all his alterations which had his "unwearied attention" while it was going through the press. Although the list was a sizeable one, it included only those plays in which he had found his greatest roles.* His

---

* Kemble's alterations, with the dates of their reprintings as theatre librettos, may be of interest. Jaggard (*Shakespeare Bibliography*, pp. 182 ff.) is subject to correction as to dating.

All's Well 1793, 1795, 1811
As You Like It 1794
Comedy of Errors 1811
Coriolanus 1789, 1800, 1806, 1812
Cymbeline 1800, 1810

versions of the English classics may have been sadly mangled
at times, but they were *echt* Kemble.

> He, *Mohawk* like, unfeeling cuts and lops,
> That Shakspeare's Plays appear like *modern Crops!*
> Then from the Press comes [*sic*] forth *editions* true,
> And John's *additions* meet the public view;
> No faults throughout the title page we spy,
> And J. P. Kemble strikes the wond'ring eye! ! !

Kemble made his alterations for the stage, and his editorial
labors were all in the interests of increased facility of actual

---

Hamlet 1796, 1800, 1804, 1808, 1818
Caesar 1811, 1812, 1815
I Henry IV 1803, 1804, 1811, 1815
II Henry IV 1803, 1804, 1815, 1821
Henry V 1789, 1795, 1801, 1806, 1815
Henry VIII 1804, 1815
King John 1800, 1804, 1814
King Lear 1800, 1808, 1810, 1815
Richard III 1810, 1811, 1814, 1818
Macbeth 1794, 1803, 1814
Measure for Measure 1789, 1796, 1803, 1815
Merchant of Venice 1795, 1797, 1810, 1814
Merry Wives 1797, 1804, 1815
Much Ado 1799, 1810, 1815
Othello 1804, 1808, 1814, 1818, 1823
Romeo 1800, 1811, 1831
Taming of the Shrew 1810, 1815, 1831
Tempest 1789, 1795, 1806, 1807, 1808, 1811, 1815, 1816
Timon of Athens 1788
Twelfth Night 1810, 1811, 1815
Two Gentlemen of Verona 1808, 1815
Winter's Tale 1802, 1811, 1815
Addison, *Cato* 1811
Charles Johnson, *Country Lasses*, altered as *The Farm House*, 1789
Arthur Murphy, *Grecian Daughter*, n.d.
Lodoiska 1794, 1801, 1807, 1824
Behn, *The Rover*, altered as *Love In Many Masks*, 1790
Massinger, *New Way to Pay Old Debts* 1810
Bickerstaff, *'Tis Well It's No Worse*, altered as *The Pannel* 1789
Fletcher, *Pilgrim* 1787
Young, *Revenge* 1814

performance. Textual matters were beyond both his scope and his capacities. As smoothly articulated pieces for the stage, his productions exhibit the touch of a man thoroughly familiar with the theatre. They preserve a faithful picture of actual stage representation at the close of the eighteenth century, and while reading them one can come fairly close to reproducing the venerable old favorites as they were presented to Burke and Sir Joshua and Pitt.[16]

A Select British Theatre was not Kemble's only excursion into literature in the twilight of his career. Two years after it appeared, in 1815, just as he was girding his loins for his last performances, he favored the men of taste and learning about the town with a new and greatly enlarged edition of his essay on *Macbeth* and *Richard III*. There were few enough, in all conscience, who had any recollection of the first appearance of this prim little book, and if the acrimonious George Steevens had not mauled it in his edition of Shakespeare it would no doubt have rested peacefully in its oblivion. But a rejoinder was called for, thought Kemble, and in his new treatment of the subject he parried most decorously with his learned opponent. Steevens, of course, had been dead seventeen years and more, and so Kemble's vindication (if such it was) had to be rather a posthumous one. With this essay, however, John Kemble's insignificant career as a man of letters was ended.[17]

His last two seasons had the leisure and serenity proper to age. Young was permitted to open the 1815–1816 season at Covent Garden with *Hamlet*; the old lion himself did not appear until late in October. Kean was still the rage at Drury Lane. Henry Siddons, after an unsuccessful fling at the London stage, had retired long since to Edinburgh; there he died during the winter, and Kemble engaged himself in looking after his unlamented nephew's bereaved mother. But there was little acting until spring. When the *Jubilee* commemorating Shakespeare's death was produced, he was of course on hand, and in April and May he went through his regular string of tragedies. But no longer could he act four and five nights a week, every week. In May he was seriously ill, having acted Brutus in spite of a cold that made him almost "inaudible." Farington, indeed, had news of his death, and betook himself to Great Russell Street to offer his condolences. But the windows were all open, and the servant who answered his knock reported nothing more than a severe case of gout and much "*giddiness*" which had happily passed away. On June 8 there was a gala performance of *Macbeth* for which Mrs. Siddons came out of her retirement and waddled about with little of her former majesty. Kemble himself, thought the *Times*, was nothing but "the ruin of a magnificent temple, in which the divinity still resides"; the *Examiner*, however, found the temple "unimpaired" — even though the divinity "is sometimes from home." Fifty years later, a person who had seen this very performance from the proscenium door still remembered the Kemble magic: "the sepulchral tone in which John Kemble bade Duncan not to hear the bell which summoned him to the world of shades, rings in my ears at this moment." [18]

His last appearance of the season in *Pizarro* was on the fifteenth, and immediately he set out for a summer in the provinces. When Elliston, at Birmingham, had balked at his high terms, he was informed in a chill note that "the Terms which Mr. K. formerly proposed were the same as he proposes now." If Mr. Elliston finds them too high, he "will be so good as to say so at once; as Mr. K. is keeping the Norwich Theatre in suspense." Mr. Elliston found it convenient to succumb. Dublin, too, found Kemble aged and weakened. Although his stance and peerless statuesque quality could still bring a round of applause, the performance itself was a terrible disappointment. He "literally walked through" *Othello*, and nothing, recalled Macready, relieved the tone of frigid recitation. His voice, always weak, was worse than ever — husky and labored, and utterly without feeling. Even the farewell performance had a melancholy cast. The house was small — "respectable" but certainly not the "numerous" throng that Kemble always before had attracted — and the engagement closed on a note of decayed glory. It was the same old story, of course: Kean had been in Dublin the summer before, and his memory was still green. In Liverpool, however, Kemble's farewell as Coriolanus moved both him and his audience. He first acted the play in their city, the old man told his audience in his curtain speech, and his success then had encouraged him "to persevere in my profession and determined me to pursue an industrious and methodical study of my art." Forgotten (or at least unmentioned) was the not so roseate episode of the angry Liverpoolers pelting Younger's troop from the stage, and young John Kemble with it. Once the summer's touring was over, he rested in gentlemanly ease at Lord Aberdeen's estate in the north of Scotland — a visit made "agreeably to an old promise." [19]

Then, at long last, came John Kemble's final season on the London stage. Its opening found him ill, discouraged, and ready to retire. To Talma, who was planning a visit to England, he wrote as a man whose day was past, and who remembers better things:

I do not know what may be the taste of the world with you, but our world in London are [sic] at present mad for splendid sights at the Theatre, and the most impossible extravagances are the most certainly admired. I really do not think we have any thing worth your giving yourself the trouble of a journey and a voyage to see. — If Voltaire thought our Theatre monstrous in his time, I do not know what epithets he could describe it by now. — If, however, you will not take my word for our degeneracy, come over to London, and convince yourself.

Here was no longer the ambitious and brilliant young manager who had astonished all London a quarter of a century before. The spectacle he deplored he himself had fostered, perhaps unconsciously, through his own elaborate revivals; now there was nothing left in the theatre but ostentation and Edmund Kean's ill-bred exhibitionism. His colleagues either dead or retired, his style eclipsed, his hopes of a great national theatre as a home for Shakespeare blasted by the interminable musical spectacles, John Kemble was an embittered old man.[20]

The greatest man of the theatre that the late eighteenth century produced, he had lived a curiously disappointing life. His career, outwardly brilliant, had been filled with disappointments. Sheridan's unstable policies had driven him from Drury Lane where his early efforts had been so successful. Covent Garden, which swallowed his wealth, was never at his disposal for the things he wanted to do. Harris, crass dog that he was, knew that opera and spectacle made more money than expensive Shakespearian revivals. Then the disastrous O.P. riots — surely the most harrowing attack any great English actor has ever undergone — brought distress and increased financial losses after the Covent Garden fire. The close of Kemble's career was marred, not by fire, not by riots, but by Edmund Kean. Even the old man's public had been appropriated. His health, too, was gone, and he did not even have the consolation of hoping his style would be perpetuated in the younger generation of actors. He must have thought, in those last years, what every man sometimes thinks: that his life had been a comedy of errors.

When William Hazlitt finally realized that Kemble was going, and soon would be no more a part of the London scene, he found cause for genuine lament, much as he supported Kean. "There is not one to fill his place on the stage. The mould is broken in which he was cast." That feeling was general. Kemble had been to almost two generations of theatre-goers the grand master of the English stage: there was that about him that commanded respect, however violent the opposition might be. "We feel more respect for John Kemble in a plain coat," remarked one critic, "than for the Lord Chancellor on the woolsack." Those who were of the true religion never swerved in their loyalty. Kean might come, and the heavens might fall, but who could think of Coriolanus apart from Kemble? Richard Cumberland spoke for the faithful when he boasted that in Kemble the stage had a giant "more deeply scientific, more learned and more laborious in his profession than is probably to be found in the annals of the British theatre." [21]

The man who had brought before the public twenty-five Shakespearian revivals in twenty-nine years — eight tragedies, all the histories except *Richard II* and *Henry VI*, and eleven comedies — had wrought no little niche for himself. He was the first great producer. In his determined efforts for scenic accuracy and effect he was the pioneer of the movement towards historical realism that was to culminate in Charles Kean and Beerbohm Tree. A scholar of parts and a connoisseur of letters, he had brought to his art a preparation and a care that had at first bewildered and then enchanted his audiences. Without possessing his sister's genius, he had a talent which in its own kind has never been surpassed. His was the technique of a conscious artisan. "I am only beginning thoroughly to understand my art," he lamented just as his career was closing. If his style failed to outlive him, it was because each generation must evolve its own stagecraft; Betterton would be incomprehensible to Dr. Johnson, and Garrick would appear to us extremely odd. Although Kemble's style was eclipsed by Kean's, his method of production left a permanent impression. "All the decencies and the proprieties of costumes and scenery we owe almost entirely to him," was the critical consensus at his farewell. However influential his managerial methods may have been, it was Kemble's personal tragedy that his technique was abandoned by the theatre-going public. Kean's acting, said Coleridge, was like reading Shakespeare by flashes of lightning, and against it the haughty declamation that had pleased an earlier age could not stand. Kemble passed, a fallen monarch, and was soon forgotten. He was missed by those who "had been used to him; but he was missed rather as a picture than a man." It is Leigh Hunt speaking, and we must guard against his customary bias against Kemble. In many respects, however, John Kemble was never more than a picture — a picture of the correct, the studied artist. Between the easy genius of Garrick and the frantic extravagance of Kean he ruled the London stage for a quarter of a century. He pleased his generation, and an actor may ask no more. But if Kean had appeared earlier, Kemble's fall would perhaps have been greater.[22]

CHAPTER XVI

Exeunt Omnes

My brother . . . saw death advance gradually though
fast, with the coolest tranquillity, did not even wish
to live longer, and died both with indifference and
without affectation; is that a termination to lament?

HORACE WALPOLE

KEMBLE'S last season had the melancholy cast that ordinarily
accompanies farewells. After a round of his best roles
during the fall, he passed the winter quietly, gathering his
strength for his last effort in the spring. To Edinburgh, of
course, a formal valedictory had to be made. March found
him in the northern capital, acting for the last time there
"with all the spirit of his best years." It was a changed Kemble
that Sir Walter found this time: his old friend had "made a
great reformation in his habits; given up wine, which he
used to swallow by pailfuls, — and renewed his youth like
the eagle." Of course, the gentlemen of Edinburgh undertook to bid farewell to their favorite actor in some appropriate
manner. Inevitably, a banquet was decided upon. Sir Walter
was tremendously occupied, writing down to London for a
gold snuff-box (to cost "about eighty guineas"), helping
Kemble write his farewell address, and arranging the banquet. *Macbeth*, naturally, was the only possible choice for
the last performance, and although Kemble had a cold, he
wrought valiantly. When he came forward to make his
curtain speech, the audience gave way freely to "tears and
sobs" and even the lofty Kemble's emotions were "very
conspicuous." [1]

The banquet was brilliant. Never, recalled Lockhart, had there been a gathering "in all its circumstances more impressive." The great Jeffrey (of the *Edinburgh Review*) had the chair, and all the notables of a notable era were present. Unfortunately, Jeffrey did not acquit himself very well. When he arose to make the presentation of the fabulous snuff-box, he began very promisingly, but before long he was so confused that he left his speech unfinished and gave the snuff-box to the wrong person.* But it was Kemble's fault, Jeffrey explained later: when the chairman rose, so did the guest (and "with most formidable dignity"). Naturally, Jeffrey had to address his remarks to the *honoré*, and he "found himself annihilated by the tall tragic god." Scott, characteristically, was deeply moved none the less. In Kemble, he said, we lose all that is worth losing in our drama — "a most excellent critic, an accomplished scholar, and one who graced our forlorn drama with what little it has left of good sense and gentlemanlike feeling." [2]

Returning south by way of Newcastle (where he filled an engagement), Kemble was back in London by the beginning of May. Younger men — notably Macready and Booth — had been filling his roles at Covent Garden, but they stepped aside for the triumphal farewell. And for the last time London saw Kemble stalk through those tragedies he loved so well. Although a sick man — before each performance he had to take medicine for his asthma, which was getting worse — he acted three times a week until the end of June. The town knew that the wheezy, pompous, aging actor — so quaint and eighteenth-century when compared to the ardent Mr. Kean at Drury Lane — would come again no more. Almost out of deference, it seemed, London rose to the occasion and made the farewell a success. True, it was not the

---

* Only recently Quaritch (Cat. 565 [1939]) offered the Kemble snuff-box for sale for £100.

old Kemble who used to take inspiration from his sister's fire of genius, but it was still the artful, accomplished gentleman, majestic though in ruin. Kemble could still heighten a big scene and bring the audience cheering to its feet. Macready remember his walking through *Cato* until he reached the scene in which Portius announces that something has befallen Marcus. With a burst of vigor, Kemble leaped across the stage, hurtling out his questions.

> Ha! what has he done? —
> Has he forsook his post? Has he given way?
> Did he look tamely on and let them pass?

But when he learned that his son "greatly fell," he "gasped out convulsively, as if suddenly relieved from an agony of doubt, 'I am satisfied!'" The theatre rang with applause. "This was his great effect — indeed his single effect." [3]

Some of the performances were weak. When Kemble acted *King John* (June 14) he was obviously ill, and although the interpretation was "painfully elaborate" it was empty and hollow and artificial. Hazlitt thought his Posthumous was "feeble and unimpassioned," but as the time drew near for his last performance the public became more demonstrative. When he finished what was to have been his last *Henry IV* there was such a response from the audience that it was promised for one more time. Hazlitt, ever the cynic, suspected the canny Covent Garden management of mulcting the public: "we hate all suspense: and we therefore wish Mr. Kemble would go, or let it alone." As the end approached, Kemble rose to his old heights. His *Stranger* impressed even Hazlitt as a masterpiece. "Even his defects are indirectly converted into excellences. . . . His tremulous hollow voice, labouring out its irksome way, seems to give back the echo of years of departed hope and happiness. He is like a sentiment embodied: a long habit of patient suffering, not seen but felt, appears to have subdued his mind, and moulded his whole form. We could look at Mr. Kemble in this character, and listen to him, till we could fancy that every other actor is but a harlequin, and that no tones but his have true pathos, sense, or meaning in them." Mrs. Siddons, now old and fat, was persuaded to join her brother in *Macbeth*, even though some thought the experiment unsuccessful. Lawrence was of the opinion that "It was manifest that it was time for Kemble to quit the stage. His personal powers are much weakened, & His formal, measured stiffness more expressed than when He was younger." But the lights were being dimmed for the last time.[4]

Finally the great night, the last night Kemble was ever to play before the British public, arrived. The play, of course, was *Coriolanus*, his most memorable role. For two weeks before June 23 all the boxes had been sold; several very indifferent poetasters had been brought to the point of scribbling verses on the occasion. So general was the feeling of impending fate that Mrs. Siddons was quite put out by all the attention her brother was receiving. "I hope, Mr. Rogers," she remarked tartly to old Sam, "that one day justice will be done to women." On that last night, the theatre seemed to Ludwig Tieck, who was eagerly following events, crowded to the rafters, although there was a disappointingly small "concourse" besieging the doors — no doubt because of the heat, it was explained.[5]

How many memories must have thronged back to the old man standing stiffly waiting for the curtain. Asthmatic, gouty, graying, and superseded, he must have remembered another night, thirty-four years before, when a handsome stripling from the provinces stepped for the first time on the boards of Old Drury. Then, it was all before him — those grandiose schemes for becoming the first actor in England, for presenting Shakespeare properly, for owning his own theatre, for being a great gentleman in society. Now, it was all behind. So many memories of those years when he and Siddons had been the high priest and priestess of classical drama, when Sheri promised and procrastinated, when *Vortigern* had the town agog, when he slept in fields because he was penniless, when Talma dined him in Paris, when *Coriolanus* was the boast of London, when he chatted with the Regent, when the mob cried O.P., when Covent Garden burned, when he drank till dawn. Now he was a tired old man, garbed for the last time in his Roman toga. The orchestra stopped, the buzzing from the house waned and died away, the candles flared, and for the last time John Kemble, the last of all the Romans, paced forth. His last entrance was his best one. The huge audience rose as one man, and for five minutes the cheers resounded, while he, serene and faintly condescending to the end, smiled gravely at his public.

He acted that night "with an abandonment of self-care, with a boundless energy, a loose of strength, as though he felt that he needed to husband his powers no longer." When it was all over, he came forward to speak his farewell, "tief gerührt und in Thränen aufgelost." Immediately from the pit were hoisted banners and placards — "no farewell for ever from Kemble." A scroll of white satin embossed with gold letter, lamenting a "separation so painful," was handed up from the audience. Kemble, struggling hard to check his emotions, spoke his valedictory. A great career was closed.[6]

Of course, there had to be a banquet. Nothing could more fittingly commemorate the passing of a great public figure than a gathering where men of taste ate and drank together. A committee, headed by Lord Holland, made the arrangements and offered admittance cards (at two guineas each) "in the circles of rank and talent." Kemble himself was notified, and replied, on June 1, with a most elegant little note:

You propose me an honour of which, without the slightest affectation, I think myself unworthy, and am unable to express my very deep sense.

On Friday, the 27th. instant, if that day is perfectly convenient, I will have the honour of waiting on the Meeting, where, and at what hour, they please to appoint.

Freemason's Tavern was crowded on the evening of the twenty-seventh, noble lords rubbing shoulders with commoners. Sam Rogers and Crabb Robinson went together (the place was so full, complained Rogers, that they had to sit "about halfway down the common seats"); Talma was there to represent the French stage; and Kemble's associates flocked to pay him tribute. John Taylor, of course, had to poetize on the occasion:

> Taste, Judgment, Friendship, have combin'd
> To dedicate a day,
> With emulative zeal to meet
> Genius to grace on his retreat,
> And well-earn'd honours pay.

The evening went off swimmingly. A silver medal presented to Kemble bore on one side a classically austere profile of the actor, on the other the legend, "Thou last of all the Romans fare thee well." Speeches and toasts flowed together. An ode which Thomas Campbell had written for the occasion was vastly admired (even though Jeffrey praised it as showing how the poet could "invest trivial occurrences with the mantle of solemn thought"). Talma, who praised his illustrious colleague "in a clear and powerful voice, with great boldness of utterance, and much vehemence of action," was impressed no end by the proceedings. Back home he wrote an account of the evening and of "le premier acteur du théâtre anglais, aussi justement chéri pour son noble caractère que pour ses rares talents." Kemble's farewell, everyone agreed, was a splendid one.[7]

Once the formalities of leave-taking were over, Kemble
began putting his affairs in order. He and his wife were
leaving London. His health was bad, and in the south of
France perhaps he could find relief for his old complaint,
asthma. Then too, his finances were troublesome. Covent
Garden, in spite of its tremendous receipts, was not making
money; Kemble's heavy investments were annually showing
less profits. For fifteen years most of his money had gone into
payments for his £23,000 share of the concern — and after a
lifetime's work, his savings were bringing in no return. He
had made some £1,825 by his last season's acting, and Harris
had agreed to buy his elaborate wardrobe for three hundred
guineas. On July 28 his banker was instructed to sell fifteen
hundred pounds of his stock in the five per cent Consols.
Even his library, the pride of his life, was dispersed, the
Duke of Devonshire contracting for the superb collection of
playbills and early quartos for a £400 annuity until Kemble's
death. The rest, for the time being, was kept intact. All
these transactions concluded, the Kembles were comfortable,
even without the uncertain dividends from Covent Garden.
As Kemble told Lawrence, he had raised enough money to
secure a £1,000 annuity, and he had "left His share of Covent
Garden Theatre to clear itself of the remaining expences of
the building &c of the Theatre." Poor Fanny Kemble, justly
bitter about investments in theatrical enterprises, was one
day to say that her uncle had been compelled to live abroad
to escape financial disaster. But he was spared the final catastrophe of Covent Garden, and his own last years, though not
opulent, were extremely comfortable.[8]

At last everything was arranged. The Kembles, once the
head of the house was recovered from a "bowel complaint"
brought on by drinking too much champagne one night,
first set off for the north. A stay at Lord Aberdeen's place,
Haddo Hall, was very pleasant. "It will give you pleasure to

hear," wrote Priscilla Kemble to Lawrence, "that Mr. Kemble has been in perfect Health ever since we came to this place — indeed the pure Air and perfect regularity of our lives will, I hope, lay the foundation for some comfortable years." And Kemble, in a postscript, boasted that "I have shot my Partridge, coursed my Hare, lamed my Horse, and Jockied the Gout." Presently they went on to Edinburgh, a city Kemble had always loved, and took a "good family house" on Heriot Row for five or six months. Kemble read much, borrowing books by the "armfulls" from Robert Gillies and working hard with a tutor to polish up his French.[9]

France, of course, was their ultimate goal. When winter came, the trip to the Continent was made. Paris detained them for months: there they were known and there life was pleasant. Kemble even had the chance to practice his French. In August, 1818, we find him writing to a new friend:

Je vous prie, mon très cher Monsieur de Vindé, de croire avec combien de satisfaction je reçois un billet de votre main. Si ce jour-là vous convient, j'aurai le plaisir de diner chez vous Samedi qui vient. — J'espere que Madame de Vindé aura la bonté de me permettre de lui présenter ma femme, qui est impatient d'offrir ses respects et ses remercimens à des amis, à qui son mari a tout d'obligation. — Si j'ossis croire que nous ne vous incommoderions pas, nous partirions de Paris avant midi.

From Paris the Kembles went to the south of France, where more than a year was passed in Toulouse. Although the place was tedious and unexciting after London and Paris, the climate was good for Kemble's health. Hazlitt, for one, envied him his tranquillity: "He is now quaffing health and burgundy in the south of France. He perhaps finds the air that blows from the 'vine-covered hills' wholesomer than that of a crowded house; and the lengthened murmurs of the Mediterranean shores more soothing to the soul, than the deep thunders of the pit." But by the spring of 1820, the

Kembles were on the move once more, this time to Switzerland. They had been gone from England now for three years, and both were homesick. To Lawrence, himself just back from Rome and full of new honors, Kemble wrote with a warmth and freedom he seldom permitted himself.

> After the hurry of the Exhibition, &c. pray, send me a line addressed — Monsieur Kemble.
> a la Poste Restante —
> Geneve

My dear Sir Thomas,

I cannot tell when anything gave me so much pleasure as the news of your being elected to the Presidency of the Royal Academy, and of your being placed in the Chair by the unanimous voice and conviction of the Acadamicians. May you fill and adorn it long! — What would I not give to be one of the Guests at your first dinner! — What would I not give to have poor Lysons alive at my side there, to jog me every moment, and prevent my hearing a word you said, with his eagerness to tell me what you were saying. Adieu to one of the very best men that ever were born. . . .

I expect . . . to find some traces of your pencil still in Rome, where I intend to be before the end of October. I have lingered out a very stupid year and a half and more in this place, but the climate has been of great benefit to my breast, and I pardon the Fold for the sake of the Atmosphere. After having rambled up and down in Switzerland and during the summer-months, we purpose, with the abating heats, to descend into Italy, and to pass the severest part of the winter at Naples. If another mild winter in a soft air strengthens me, sufficiently to make me able to keep the gout at bay, as I have done now for nearly a twelve-month, I shall turn homewards with a joy doubled by the prospect of a few years of tranquil enjoyment of myself, and my friends, and their prosperity.

Mrs. Kemble, in a chatty postscript, breathes the same nostalgia as her husband: "Oh how I long to see you and all my English Friends — I am truly grateful for the benefit Mr

Kemble has secured from change of Climate but as far as I have yet seen the visiting other countrys [sic] only makes me love my own the more." [10]

Poor Kemble was to return to England, and sooner than he had expected. In October, old Tom Harris died, and by the second of November Kemble was back in London, unaccompanied by his wife, to settle his financial affairs once and for all. It was a changed man who saw his old haunts after such a long absence. To John Taylor he seemed frightfully old — why, he could not even go downstairs save with difficulty. But everything was different now: the grand house on Great Russell Street was sold, and Kemble stayed with Charles and his family in Gerard Street. The children (or at least Fanny) always remembered him as he was then — white-haired, benign, and clothed with an otherworldly dignity. Such of his old friends as were left on the London scene — so animated ten short years before, so different now — seemed to consider him a creature out of the remote past. But he himself was silent and distant, although "attentive." Some of the younger men, Macready among them, were intrigued with his anecdotes of Dr. Johnson's time. [11]

Kemble had not come back for dinner parties, however. Affairs at Covent Garden were in the worst possible way. Following Harris' death, the remaining proprietors were bickering sadly, and the creditors were threatening foreclosure. The actors had taken a moratorium on their salaries. The building-debt was enormous, and each of the patentees was personally responsible for discharging it. Even though John Kemble's share was calculated by some to be worth £45,000, there was little hope of his ever realizing a profit on his investment. All the old man wanted, he made clear, was to be freed of the possibility of unpleasant litigation with the creditors. His days were nearly over, and he had had troubles enough. So to Charles, his youngest and favorite

brother, he transferred by a deed of gift his entire holdings
in the theatre. To him it was a release; to Charles, who had
no funds to tempt a creditor with, it was the chance of a lifetime. Everything was cleaned up: the great library was auctioned and brought some £2,575 (in addition to Devonshire's
annuity); even the furniture was disposed of. When it was all
over, that melancholy business, the old man drew up his will,
providing an annuity of £1,000 for Priscilla, as well as the
interest on £17,000 (£4,000 of it at her sole disposal, the remaining £13,000 to devolve at her death to Charles). Ann
Hatton, still dragging out her miserable existence in Swansea
was left £60 a year, and the mysterious Mrs. Mason, another
sister, £20. All this done, John Kemble, almost with relief,
turned his back for the last time on the city that had granted
him fame and success and fortune. By December, after only
a month in London, he was making his way back to Lausanne
and his wife. He was never again to see England.[12]

The last act of all was blessedly peaceful — a quiet, bene-
dictory close to the turbulent drama of his career. High
above Lausanne, where Lake Geneva mirrored the majestic
Alps, he and Priscilla passed their last quiet years together.
There was his garden to be looked after — which occupied
most of the mornings — and there were books to read and
friends to talk to. Every day he read his Bible, and pondered
much on it — so much so, said Talma, that he even began
to look like Isaiah. Occasionally there were visitors from
England. When Miss Berry, passing through Lausanne,
called on the Kembles she was charmed with their pretty
little house just outside the town on the road to Vevey. And
the warmth of her welcome gave her "real pleasure." Presently Mrs. Siddons — marshalling an entourage consisting
of her daughter and old Sam Rogers — paid a visit. For the
last time the two Titans were together, and then they parted.
The niece, writing back to England, reported her aunt and

uncle as "perfectly happy": "their situation is a blessed one."
The sharp-tongued Rogers, of course, had to have his *mot*.
John Kemble was as proud and haughty as ever, he thought:
he was even jealous of hearing people praise the beauty of
Mont Blanc. Mrs. Piozzi, herself an old lady now, heard
from the Kembles at rare intervals — always "well and happy"
they were. It is a pleasing picture. Mrs. Kemble found it
"impossible to describe" how highly the old actor was esteemed in his new home. If you could have seen him in the
last years of his life, she assured Sir Thomas Lawrence, "your
affection for him would have increased." Priscilla herself
sometimes languished for the bustle and splendor of London,
but she was content that her husband was content. Although
she had "lived in the best London society," she reconciled
herself to her placid surroundings. By a diligent and hideously ungrammatical correspondence she maintained her
connections, and even in Switzerland found a certain pleasure
in talking familiarly of her titled friends back home. A vain
woman to the end, concluded Fanny Kemble, she was at least
not "superficially" vulgar. Surviving her second husband
twenty-two years, until her death at ninety in charming Leam-
ington Priscilla assiduously pursued her career in society.[13]

The Kembles lived well — or as well as his health would
permit. He had a man, she a maid, and there were three
Swiss servants besides — a cook, a housemaid, and a gar-
dener. But there was not too much indiscriminate mingling
in society. The tone of the establishment was kept up. When
Macready called in 1822, he was informed that Kemble
would not be "visible" until the next day — and he did not
trouble to call back. In the fall of that year, the long-planned
trip to Italy was made. It proved to be John Kemble's last
and fatal journey. As usual, there was money and to spare:

I drop you this line, just to say that we set off for Rome the
day after to-morrow, and to beg when you write to me that you

will direct your letter for me à la Poste restante, Rome. I have written today to Messrs. Coutts [the London bankers], to tell them that I have signed a power of Attorney to Monsieur Lafitte in Paris to see out about five hundred pounds for me, to be remitted to their house, and this wise, precautionnary [*sic*] measure will put me quite at ease during my excursion. I expect to be at Rome within a Month, or five weeks at furthest.*

The trip to Rome was ill-advised from the start. Kemble was weak, far weaker than he realized, and when, in Italy, the malarial season came on, he was ordered to return to the highlands of Switzerland immediately. But the return was almost too much. In Lausanne again, the aging actor realized that at last the end was near. For Priscilla, however, he put on a great appearance of optimism. "His looks were good," she reported to Lawrence, "also his appetite; and the last week of his life he told me that he never felt better than he had done for months." As the winter wore on into February, and the snows swept down out of the Alps, he still clung to life. He worked in his garden with almost frightening intensity — "more like a labourer than a gentleman, from an opinion that it did him good. On Wednesday, February 19, in excellent spirits, he dined with a friend down in the town; on Thursday, some guests came in for tea and a game of rubber (to which he was "very partial"); on Sunday, a bright, clear day, he walked for two hours in the sunny garden. But on Monday the blow struck.[14]

At nine o'clock Kemble was still in his room, "well and in more than common spirits." Priscilla stepped out for a moment, but had scarcely left when he called her back. Very quietly and calmly he told her that he had just suffered

---

* This letter, dated Lausanne, September 7, 1822, and addressed to Alexander Murray, Symonds Inn, Chancery Lane, London, was pointed out to me through the good offices of Mr. Robert F. Metzdorf, Curator of the Adams Collection of the Rush Rhees Library of the University of Rochester. The original is in the Adams Collection.

a stroke. And as his lady became more terrified, Kemble put on for the last time his cloak of dignified indifference. Almost superciliously he dressed himself and walked "across three Rooms without assistance," apparently unchanged save for a peculiar alteration of his mouth. Presently the "Medical Men" arrived, and they, like the patient, knew the case was grave. After they had bled him in both arms they asked the frightened Priscilla to leave the room "whilst they laid him in his Bed." When his wife came back she too knew that he would never rise again.[15]

He prepared for death as soberly and carefully as he would for a new role in a play. First of all, there was an alteration to be made in his will, but once that chore was past he addressed himself with all his accustomed suavity to the decorous art of conversation. His passing was to be as poised and stately as his art had been. George, his old man servant, burst into tears, only to be mildly rebuked. "George, if you love me, either cease crying, or leave the room; reserve your tears till I am not sensible of them." And when the faithful valet seized his hand and kissed it, even Kemble was moved. "Poor fellow, I know not whether I have been a good master to him or not; — at all events, I have taken care he shall have no occasion for another." He did not suffer, Priscilla gratefully assured Sir Thomas, "although he struggled eight and forty Hours." At last he knew that his time had come: ordering his weeping wife to be led from the room, he settled in his pillows, closed his eyes, and died. It was February 26, 1823, just sixty-six years since a poor stroller's wife had, on a wintry day in Lancashire, borne her first son.

In death, as in life, Kemble maintained his invulnerable dignity. "In his Coffin," said his lady, "his Face was as calm as if he had been in a sweet sleep, and not the least Feature altered." When the funeral occurred, on the first of March, the Dean of Raphoe read the service at the little villa, and

Mr. Cheesebrough, Kemble's own clergyman, officiated at the cemetery. Of course, all the English colony attended, and one lady of fashion, with tender propriety, even postponed a great rout. Priscilla Kemble had her husband buried in the foreign cemetery, just outside the town. No monuments were allowed, but she arranged for a vault of black marble. And George, who could not be made to leave his master for an instant during his last illness, planted a row of cypress around the slab. Fanny Kemble, years later, visited the spot on the hill where the Alpine flowers were running wild. She wondered that the dead could be content to lie so still, such was the glorious beauty of the place. There John Kemble lies to this day.

Notes

ABBREVIATIONS

The following abbreviations have been used:

Bernard — *Retrospections of the Stage.* 2 vols., London, 1830.

Boaden — *Memoirs of the Life of John Philip Kemble, Esq.* 2 vols., London, 1825.

Fitzgerald — *The Kembles.* 2 vols., London, [1871].

Genest — *Some Account of the English Stage.* 10 vols., Bath, 1832.

Journal — The manuscript journal of John Philip Kemble, British Museum Ad. MSS 31,972–31,975.

Life — *The Life of John Philip Kemble, Esquire.* London, [1809].

Oulton — *The History of the Theatres of London.* 2 vols., London, 1796.

Wilkinson — *The Wandering Patentee.* 4 vols., York, 1795.

Williams — *Memoirs of John Philip Kemble, Esq.* London, 1817.

NOTES

Prologue

1. *Collections of the New York Historical Society for the Year 1884,* II, xii; Campbell, *Mrs. Siddons,* p. 3; Britton, *Topographical Sketches,* III, 50–51; Matthews, *Hundred of Wormelow,* pp. 9, 138; *Miscellanea II* (Catholic Record Society), p. 265; *London Sessions Records 1615–1685* (C.R.S.), pp. 36, 378.

2. Webb, *Memorials of the Civil War,* II, 116; Cam, *Forgotten Shrines,* p. 334; *Douay College Diaries* (C.R.S.), p. 236; *Domestick Intelligence,* Aug. 26, 1769; Collier, *Old Man's Diary . . . for the First Six Months of 1832,* p. 43; Matthews, *Hundred of Wormelow,* pp. 128–129. Further material on Venerable John Kemble may be found in Challoner, *Memories of Missionary Priests;* Phillot, *Hereford,* pp. 230–231; Gillow, *English Catholics;* Webb, *Memorials,* II, 428; Raikes-Bromage, *Father John Kemble; The Eccentricities of John Edwin,* II, 156 ff. Sir John Hawkins in his fourth edition of Walton's *Complete* [*sic*] *Angler* (1784), pt. II, p. 18, n., starts on its long course the persistent story of Father Kemble's farewell smoke; cf. Duncumb, *Collections,* I, 373.

3. Campbell, *Mrs. Siddons,* p. 4; *Quarterly Review,* XXXIV (1826), 205; Clement Parsons, *The Incomparable Siddons,* p. 4.

4. Atkyns, *Gloucestershire,* p. 391; Dyde, *Tewkesbury,* pp. 90–91; *New History of Gloucestershire,* p. 747; *History of the Town of Cirencester,* p. 283. Cf. *Miscellanea VI* (C.R.S.), p. 82; *Miscellanea* (C.R.S.), p. 113, n. and p. 229; *Obituaries* (C.R.S.), p. 82.

5. *General Magazine and Impartial Review,* Dec., 1790, pp. 551–552; *Theatre,* XXIV (1894), 236; Colby, *Holcroft,* I, 144; Henderson, *Adolphus,* p. 89; *Eccentricities of John Edwin,* II, 158; Lewes, *Memoirs,* I, 86. On Roger Kemble's brothers and sisters see Hannam-Clark, *Drama in Gloucestershire,* pp. 71–72; *Gentleman's Magazine,* LXV (1795), 351; Fitzgerald, *The Kembles,* II, 68–69; *Eccentricities of John Edwin,* II, 157; Samuel Richardson, *Letters,* p. 60.

6. Lewes, *Memoirs,* I, 86–93.

7. Lewes, *Memoirs,* I, 86–93; *Theatric Tourist* (1805), p. 57.

8. *Monthly Mirror,* N.S. III (1808), 8; Hannam-Clark, p. 71.

9. Genest, III, 121–124; Nicoll, *History of Early Eighteenth Century Drama,* p. 323; Fielding, *Joseph Andrews,* bk. III, ch. X; *Weekly Miscellany,* No. 58, July 28, 1790; Boaden, I, 444; Hitchcock, *Irish Stage,* I, 53–56, 94; Campbell, *Mrs. Siddons,* p. 8.

10. Boaden, I, 4; Spielmann, "Shakespeare's Portraiture," *Studies in*

the First Folio, pp. 23 ff.; *Cabinet*, III (1808), 201; *Secret History of the Green Room*, II, 3.

11. Boaden, I, 6; *Notes and Queries*, 3d Series, VIII (1865), 205; Ryan, *Dramatic Table Talk*, II, 19.

12. Campbell, *Mrs. Siddons*, p. 8.

13. Boaden, I, 5; Campbell, *Mrs. Siddons*, pp. 1–2; Countess of Strafford (ed.), *Leaves from the Diary of Henry Greville*, 4th Series, pp. 345–346; Dunlap, *Cooke*, I, 32.

14. Ralph, *Taste of the Town* (1731), p. 223; Colby, *Holcroft*, I, 153–156; Kirkman, *Macklin*, II, 35; Chetwood, *General History of the Stage*, pp. 87–90; Alwin Thaler, "Strolling Players and Provincial Drama after Shakspere," *PMLA*, XXXVII (1922), 243–280; Weston, *Memoirs*, p. 12; *Memoirs of an Unfortunate Son of Thespis*, p. 84; Wilkinson, *Memoirs*, I, 142; Holman, *Lamb's "Barbara S——"*, p. 20; Colby, *PMLA*, XXXIX (1924), 642–654; Bernard, *Retrospections*, I, 94; Templeton, *The Strolling Players*, I, 60; S. Rosenfeld, *Strolling Players and Drama in the Provinces, 1660–1765* (1939), *passim*; T. S. Graves, "Some Facts about Anthony Aston," *JEGP*, XX (1921), 391–396.

15. Parker, *View of Society*, p. 49; Dunlap, *Cooke*, I, 12; Bernard, I, 11; Dibdin, *Reminiscences*, I, 74, 148. Oppobrious references to strollers are legion; a few typical instances are Nicoll, *Development of the Theatre*, p. 61; Cobbin, *Stage Playing*; Simpson, *Discourse on Stage Entertainments*; Hill, *Aphoristic Observations*; *London Magazine*, XLII (1793), 458; Lamb, *Works*, pp. 315–316; Oldmixon, *Apollo Turn'd Stroller*.

16. *Memoirs of Sylvester Daggerwood*, I, 103–104; Gayton, *Pleasant Notes upon Don Quixote* (1654), p. 271; Edwin, *Life and Adventures*, p. 9; Goldsmith, "Adventures of a Strolling Player," *Works*, I, 295 ff.; Colby, *Holcroft*, I, 163.

17. Colby, *Holcroft*, I, 149; *Notes and Queries*, 3d Series, I (1862), 268; Bennett, *History of Tewkesbury*, p. 205, n.

18. Campbell, *Mrs. Siddons*, p. 271.

19. Campbell, *Mrs. Siddons*, p. 89; *General Magazine and Impartial Review*, Dec., 1790, p. 553; Fanny Kemble, *Records of a Girlhood*, pp. 1–2; Gilliland, *Dramatic Mirror*, II, 800; Genest, VI, 511; *Monthly Mirror*, N.S. III (1808), 6; Colby, *Holcroft*, II, 182; Parsons, *The Incomparable Siddons*, p. 133; Whalley, *Journals and Correspondence*, II, 228; *Theatre*, XXIV (1894), 237–238.

Chapter I

1. MS memoirs of Ann Hatton, Folger Library.

2. Journal, Feb. 1, 1799; *Farington Diary*, VII, 85; Campbell, *Mrs. Siddons*, p. 8.

3. Campbell, p. 3; Fitzgerald, *The Kembles*, I, 21; Boaden, I, 8.

4. *Authentic Narrative of Mr. Kemble's Retirement*, p. 72; Cuthbert Bede in *The Titan*, XXV (1857), 178–179; MS journal of Roger Kemble, Harvard Theatre Collection; *Theatre*, N.S. VIII (1886), 117–127.

5. Harvard playbills.

6. Boaden, I, 8; MS memoirs of Ann Hatton, Folger Library; Fitzgerald, I, 25; Richardson, *Letters*, pp. 60–61.

7. Petre, *Notices of English Colleges and Convents*, p. 3.

8. *Monthly Mirror*, III (1797), 68; *Cabinet*, III (1808), 289; Boaden, I, 7–10; British Museum Ad. MS 18,204; *Gentleman's Magazine*, LIII (1783), 309; *European Magazine*, IV (1783), 334. See William H. McCabe, "Notes on St. Omers [*sic*] College Theatre, 1592–1762," *PQ*, XVII (1938), 225–239; "The Play-List of the English College of St. Omers," *Revue de Littérature Comparée*, XVII (1937), 355–375.

9. Kelly, *Reminiscences*, I, 345; *European Magazine*, IV (1783), 334; clipping in *Kembleiana*, vol. I, Harvard Theatre Collection; *Morning Post*, Mar. 7, 1783.

10. Williams, *Kemble*, p. 7; Constable and Gillies, *Personal Reminiscences*, p. 300.

11. Lewes, *Memoirs*, I, 95; *Life of John Philip Kemble*, pp. 3–4; Fitzgerald, I, 39.

12. *Secret History of the Green Room*, 1790, p. 5; Ryley, *The Itinerant*, I, 263; ffrench, *Mrs. Siddons*, p. 29; Lewes, *Memoirs*, I, 95–97; Baker, *Our Old Actors*, p. 283.

13. Goldsmith, *Vicar*, chap. XIX; cf. Mozeen, *Young Scarron*, p. 63; *European Magazine*, XXII (1792), 230–231; Boaden, I, 15.

14. Gilliland, *Dramatic Mirror*, II, 801; *Life of John Philip Kemble*, p. 4; *Oxberry's Dramatic Biography*, I, 163; Dunlap, *Cooke*, I, 116; Williams, p. 8.

15. *Secret History*, p. 282; Williams, p. 809; *Life*, p. 6; Boaden, I, 15; prints and caricatures, Harvard Theatre Collection.

16. Mozeen, *Young Scarron*, pp. 146–147; Taylor, *Records*, p. 188; Goldsmith, *Works*, I, 295; *Memoirs of the Present Countess of Derby (Late Miss Farren)*, p. 6, n.

17. Williams, p. 9; cf. *Six North Country Diaries*, Pub. Surtees Society, ed. John Crawford Hodgson, CXVIII (1910), 294.

18. *Authentic Memoirs of the Green-Room*, I, 109; *Cabinet*, III (1808), 290–291; Taylor, *Records*, pp. 82–83.

19. *Thespian Dictionary*, pp. 212–213; Hannam-Clark, *Drama in Gloucestershire*, p. 73; Williams, pp. 8–10; Kelly, II, 107–108; Bennett, *History of Tewkesbury*, p. 205, n. On Watson's later career see Humphries-Willoughby, *At Cheltenham Spa*, p. 36. *Thespian Dictionary*, sig. 2I2; Kelly, II, 106; *Secret History of the Green Room*, p. 284; Gilliland, *Elbow Room*, p. 8, n.

20. Dunlap, *Cooke*, I, 116–118.

21. *Life*, p. 8; *Memoirs of the Present Countess of Derby*, pp. 11–12; Williams, p. 12.

22. ffrench, *Mrs. Siddons*, pp. 49–50; Genest, V, 625 ff.; Broadbent, *Annals of the Liverpool Stage*, p. 70.

23. Boaden, *Mrs. Inchbald*, I, 74–83.

24. Boaden, *Mrs. Inchbald*, I, 81–82; ffrench, pp. 51, 52; Fitzgerald, I, 70; Boswell, *Johnson* (Oxford ed.), I, 24.

25. *Theatric Tourist*, p. 53; Broadbent, *Annals*, p. 71; Boaden, *Mrs. Inchbald*, I, 91 ff.; Molloy, *Kean*, I, 163–164; MS letter, Kemble to Mrs. *Inchbald*, Forster MS 322, South Kensington Museum.

26. ffrench, *Mrs. Siddons*, p. 53; Broadbent, *Annals*, p. 72.

27. MS memoirs of Ann Hatton, Folger Library; *Belisarius*, MS 13.L, Larpent Collection, Huntington Library; MS letter, Kemble to Wilkinson, Folger Library.

CHAPTER II

1. Bernard, *Retrospections*, I, 112–113, 151; Sheppard, *Evolution of the Drama in Hull*, p. 38; Everard, *Memoirs*, p. 85; *Monthly Mirror*, VI (1798), 248.

2. Wilkinson, *Wandering Patentee*, I, 307–308; II, 5, 6–7; Genest, VI, 294; Harvard Theatre Collection playbills.

3. Harvard Theatre Collection playbills.

4. Burke, *Works*, V, 441; *Belisarius*, MS 13.L, Larpent Collection, Huntington Library, *passim*.

5. *Belisarius*, *passim*; Wilkinson, II, 9, 15; Reynolds, *The Dramatist*, act I; Gilliland, *Dramatic Synopsis*, p. 90.

6. Cottle, *Reminiscences*, p. 19, n.; *European Magazine*, IV (1783), 335; *Gentleman's Magazine*, LIII (1783), 309; *Oxberry's Dramatic Biography*, I, 166; Gilliland, *Dramatic Mirror*, II, 802; Taylor, *Records*, p. 291.

7. Wilkinson, II, 11, 14; Boaden, I, 243; Bernard, *Retrospections*, I, 176–177; *Narrative of the Life of Mrs. Charlotte Charke*, p. 189; Fielding, *Tom Jones*, bk. XVI, chap. v; Goldsmith, *She Stoops to Conquer* (Dolby's British Theatre, unpaged biographical sketch of Kemble).

8. Wilkinson, II, 14, 105, 106; ffrench, *Mrs. Siddons*, p. 51; Hitchcock, *Irish Stage*, I, 89–90; Boaden, *Mrs. Jordan*, I, 37–38; *European Magazine*, IV (1783), 335; Fitzgerald, I, 81; *Quarterly Magazine*, XXXIV (1826), 241; *Biographia Dramatica*, I, 423; MS letter, Kemble to Mrs. Inchbald, Forster MS 322, South Kensington Museum; *The Female Officer*, MS 14.S, Larpent Collection, Huntington Library; *New Monthly Magazine and Literary Journal*, XXXIV (1832), 179; Boaden, I, 24; Taylor, *Records*, p. 291; Galt, *Lives of the Players*, II, 252; *The Project*, Harvard Theatre Collection MS.

9. Boaden, I, 33; *Biographia Dramatica*, I, 422; *New Monthly Magazine*, XXXIV (1832), 175; Wilkinson, II, 32.

10. Wilkinson, II, 19–27; Kelly, *Reminiscences*, I, 309–310.

11. Wilkinson, II, 50, 51, 55, 56.

12. Boaden, I, 34; MS note in Kemble's hand on Drury Lane playbill for *The Mourning Bride*, Oct. 8, 1770, photostat in Harvard Theatre Collection; *European Magazine*, XIII (1792), 5–6; Boaden, *Mrs. Inchbald*, I, 96–98; *Biographia Dramatica*, I, 387; Kemble, *Fugitive Pieces*, p. 34.

13. Wilkinson, II, 57, 62, 64; *Oxberry's Dramatic Biography*, I, 169; Boaden, *Mrs. Inchbald*, I, 94, 99.

14. Boaden, *Mrs. Inchbald*, I, 101, 104; MS letter, Kemble to Mrs. Inchbald, Forster MS 322, South Kensington Museum; Wilkinson, II, 81, 88.

15. Boaden, *Mrs. Inchbald*, I, 106–107.

16. Walpole, *Letters*, V, 283; Chancellor, *Pleasure Haunts*, pp. 258 ff.; *Morning Chronicle*, May 22, 1782; Harvard Theatre Collection scrapbook *Kembleiana*, Vol. I, clippings from unnamed London papers.

17. Weston, *Memoirs*, p. 4; Hunt, *Autobiography*, I, 164; Boaden, *Mrs. Jordan*, I, 382; Everard, *Memoirs*, p. 78; *Theatric Tourist*, p. 41; Holbrook, *Dramatist*, pp. 52, 55 ff.; Ryley, *Itinerant*, I (1808), 69; *Thespian Oracle*, pp. 17–18; *Eccentricities of John Edwin*, I, 5–9; Templeton, *Strolling Player*, I, 48; Holcroft, *Alwyn*, I, 129 ff.; Wilkinson, II, 94.

18. *Fugitive Pieces*, pp. vi, i, 7, 9, 24; Boaden, I, 32; *Life*, p. 19; *Crosby's Pocket Companion*, p. 3; Hazlitt, *Works* (ed. Howe), XII, 301; Congreve, *Way of the World*, I, i.

19. Boaden, *Mrs. Inchbald*, I, 114; MS letter, Kemble to Mrs. Inchbald, Forster MS 322, South Kensington Museum.

20. Fitzgerald, I, 80; *Fugitive Pieces*, pp. 10, 15, 28, 37; *Authentic Memoirs of the Green-Room*, p. 149; Boaden, I, 33; MS letter, Kemble to unnamed correspondent, Treasure Room, Widener Library; Dyce, *Dyce Collection*, I, 452; MS letter, Kemble to Mrs. Inchbald, Forster MS 322, South Kensington Museum.

21. Wilkinson, II, 104, 105, 116, 117; Dibdin, *Annals of the Edinburgh Stage*, p. 180; MS letter, Kemble to Mrs. Inchbald, Harvard Theatre Collection.

22. Wilkinson, II, 113, 117, 118.

23. Wilkinson, II, 92, 118.

24. Bernard, *Retrospections*, I, 223; Gordan, *Personal Memoirs*, I, 341–342; Barrington, *Personal Sketches*, II, 40.

25. Bernard, I, 275; *Public Advertiser*, Jan. 31, 1783; Prior, *Malone*, pp. 145–147; Molloy, *Romance of the Irish Stage*, II, 213.

26. Boaden, I, 38–39; Gilbert, *History of the City of Dublin*, II, 107; Herbert, *Irish Varieties*, p. 270.

27. Lewis, *Selection of the Letters of Horace Walpole*, pp. 230, 353; Prior, *Malone*, p. 80; Herbert, *Irish Varieties*, p. 23; MS letter,

Kemble to Jephson, Folger Library; Boaden, *Mrs. Siddons*, I, 257; *Gentleman's Magazine*, LIII (1783), 310; *European Magazine*, IV (1783), 334.

28. W. J. Lawrence in *Notes and Queries*, 9th Series, VII (1901), 221–222; *Gentleman's Magazine*, LIII (1783), 310.

29. *European Magazine*, IV (1783), 336; *Crosby's Pocket Companion*, p. 3; *Gentleman's Magazine*, LIII (1783), 310.

30. Williams, p. 14; Barrington, *Personal Sketches*, I, 281, 283; Boaden, *Mrs. Jordan*, I, 11; *European Magazine*, IV (1783), 336; Taylor, *Records*, p. 86; Harvard Theatre Collection scrapbook *Kembleiana*.

31. *Life*, pp. 10–11; *Elephantasmagoria*, p. 21, n.

32. Bernard, I, 237, 258–261.

33. Bernard, I, 235–236.

34. Young, *Memoirs of Mrs. Crouch*, I, 175; Bernard, I, 228–251.

35. Bernard, I, 250–254; Kelly, *Reminiscences*, II, 166.

36. Bernard, I, 254; Young, *Mrs. Crouch*, I, 182–183, 189; Taylor, *Records*, p. 82; *Secret History of the Green Room*, II, 92, 94.

37. Boaden, *Mrs. Inchbald*, I, 168, 169, 171.

38. Bernard, I, 275; Boaden, *Mrs. Inchbald*, I, 171.

39. ffrench, *Mrs. Siddons*, p. 97; Boaden, *Mrs. Inchbald*, I, 168; Campbell, *Mrs. Siddons*, pp. 30–32.

CHAPTER III

1. Williams, p. 16; MS letter, Kemble to Mrs. Inchbald, Forster MS 322, South Kensington Museum; Boaden, *Mrs. Inchbald*, I, 181.

2. *Gentleman's Magazine*, LIII (1783), 309; *Life*, p. 13; *Crosby's Pocket Companion*, pp. 1–2; *Secret History of the Green Room*, I, 309; *Monthly Mirror*, I (1795), 45; Williams, *Pin Basket*, pp. 17–18; Hunt, *Dramatic Essays*, pp. 124–127; Johnson, *Idler*, no. 60; Dowden, *Southey*, p. 156; *Theatre; or the Letters of Candidus*, p. x.

3. Heywood, *Apology for Actors* (1612), sig. F3ʳ; *Narrative of the Life of Mrs. Charlotte Charke*, p. 103; F. C. Green, *Minuet*, p. 32. See P. J. Crean, "The Stage Licensing Act of 1737," *MP*, XXXV (1938), 239–255.

4. Seward, *Letters*, I, 142; Southey, *Letters*, II, 217; Lamb, *Works*, p. 292; Rymer, *Monsieur Rapin's Reflections* (1694), sig. A5ᵛ; Flecknoe, "A Short Discourse of the English Stage" attached to *Loves Kingdom* (1664), sig. G5ᵛ; Mathias, *Pursuits of Literature*, p. 73; Lewis, *Selection of the Letters of Horace Walpole*, p. 342; *Anti-Jacobin*, no. XXXVI; Digeon, *Novels of Fielding*, p. 62, n. 2. See Boswell's *Letters* (ed. Tinker), I, 192.

5. Nicoll, *History of Late Eighteenth Century Drama*, p. 39; Watson, *Sheridan to Robertson*, p. 147; Shaw, *Plays: Pleasant and Un-

pleasant, p. xiii; Cross, *Development of the English Novel,* pp. 61–63;
Elton, *Survey of English Literature 1738–1780,* I, 311.

6. Campbell, *Mrs. Siddons,* p. 203; Taylor, *Records,* p. 81; Davies,
Dramatic Miscellanies, III, 150–151; *Morning Chronicle,* Oct. 1, 1783;
European Magazine, IV (1783), 456; *Morning Herald,* Oct. 14, 1783;
Genest, VI, 293; Boaden, I, 116; Gray, *Theatrical Criticism,* p. 262;
Critical Observations on Mr. Kemble's Performance . . . at Liverpool,
p. 6; Leslie, *Memoirs of . . . John Constable,* p. 21; *Remarks on Mr.
John Kemble's Performance,* pp. 6–7; Twining, *Papers of the Twining
Family,* p. 110.

7. *European Magazine,* IV (1783), 309; *Morning Herald,* Oct. 1,
1783; Oulton, *History,* I, 126; *London Chronicle,* Sept. 30–Oct. 2, 1783;
Henderson, *Adolphus,* p. 93; Parsons, *The Incomparable Siddons,* p.
134; Boaden, II, 5; Macready, *Reminiscences,* p. 52; Kelly, *Reminiscences,* I, 45; *London Magazine,* I (1783), 456; Davies, *Dramatic Miscellanies,* III, 151; Taylor, *Records,* p. 82; Hawkins, *Kean,* II, 23; *Crosby's
Pocket Companion,* p. 4.

8. Rogers, *Table-Talk,* p. 70; Boaden, I, 301; *Genuine Narrative of
the Life . . . of Mr. John Henderson,* p. 53; Cumberland, *Memoirs,*
p. 302.

9. Adolphus, *Bannister,* I, 102; *Morning Herald,* Oct. 16, 1783;
Henderson, *Adolphus,* p. 93; *New Spectator,* Feb. 10, 1784; Williams,
Children of Thespis, p. 63; Boaden, I, 119; Pearson, *Swan of Lichfield,*
p. 68.

10. *Morning Herald,* Oct. 21, 1783; *Morning Chronicle,* Oct. 21,
1783.

11. *Morning Chronicle,* Nov. 11, 1783; *European Magazine,* IV
(1783), 336.

12. Boaden, *Mrs. Siddons,* II, 53; *Morning Chronicle,* Nov. 24, 1783;
European Magazine, IV (1783), 388; Davies, *Dramatic Miscellanies,* III,
148.

13. *Secret History of the Green Room,* p. 13; Fitzgerald, II, 98–99;
Morning Herald, Nov. 22, 1783; *European Magazine,* IV (1783), 336;
Ann Hatton memorandum, Folger Library MS; Curtis, *Poems,* p. 18.

14. MS letter, Curtis to Collier, Folger Library; MS letter, Kemble to
Curtis, Harvard Theatre Collection; MS copy of Roger Kemble's will,
Folger Library.

15. *Morning Herald,* Oct. 21, 1783; Gilliland, *Elbow Room,* p. 28;
MS letter, Kemble to unnamed correspondent, Harvard Theatre Collection; MS letter, Kemble to Mrs. Inchbald, Forster MS 322, South
Kensington Museum; *Monthly Mirror,* III (1797), 70; Boaden, I, 133;
Morning Chronicle, Jan. 23, 1784; Nicoll, *History of Late Eighteenth
Century Drama,* p. 85; *New Spectator,* Apr. 20, 1784; Adolphus, *Bannister,* I, 109.

16. *Testimony of Truth to Exalted Merit,* pp. 4–5; *Morning Chronicle,* Dec. 8, 1783.

17. *Theatrical Inquisitor,* I (1812), 100–101; Fitzgerald, *The Kembles,* I, 178–179.

CHAPTER IV

1. Pearson, *Swan of Lichfield,* p. 93, n. 2; Maria Edgeworth, *Life and Letters* (ed. Hare), II, 448; Campbell, *Mrs. Siddons,* p. 203; Henderson, *Adolphus,* p. 94; Dunlap, *Cooke,* I, 119; Boaden, I, 281; Taylor, *Records,* p. 83.

2. *Morning Chronicle,* Sept. 22, 1784; *Morning Herald,* Sept. 22, 1784; Fielding, *A Journey from this World to the Next,* chap. X; *The New Rosciad,* p. 13.

3. Oulton, *History of the Theatres of London,* I, 134; Genest, VI, 329; *Morning Chronicle,* Oct. 6, 1784; *Morning Herald,* Oct. 6, 1784.

4. *Morning Chronicle,* Oct. 26, 1784; Lily B. Campbell, "The Rise of a Theory of Stage Presentation in England during the Eighteenth Century," *PMLA,* XXXI (1917), 163; Fitzgerald, I, 237–238; *Parker's General Advertiser,* Sept. 30, 1784; Cumberland, *Memoirs,* II, 219–220; *Morning Herald,* Dec. 3, 1784.

5. Boaden, *Mrs. Siddons,* II, 124; *Morning Chronicle,* Oct. 30, 1784, Jan. 28, Feb. 7, 1785; Lounsbury, *Shakespeare as a Dramatic Artist,* p. 73; Ward, *History of English Dramatic Literature,* II, 275–276; Collier, *History of English Dramatic Poetry,* II, 92; *European Magazine,* VII (1785), 142; *Morning Post,* Jan. 28, 1785; *London Magazine,* IV (1785), 138; Boaden, I, 238, 261; Campbell, *Mrs. Siddons,* pp. 136–137; De Quincey, *Selected Writings* (ed. Stern), p. 528, n. 1; Colby, *Holcroft,* II, 157; "Peter Pindar," *Works,* I (1797), 356.

6. Kemble, *Macbeth Reconsidered,* p. 10; *Morning Chronicle,* Nov. 23, Apr. 1, 1785; *Times,* Oct. 25, 1788; *Morning Post,* Sept. 7, 1785.

7. *Morning Post,* Sept. 7, 1785.

8. Bernard, *Retrospections,* I, 24; Williams, p. 18; *Morning Chronicle,* Oct. 1, Oct. 10, 1785; clipping, *Kembleiana,* vol. I, Harvard Theatre Collection; Taylor, *Records,* p. 159; Williams, *Children of Thespis,* pp. 51–52.

9. *Morning Chronicle,* Oct. 7, 10, 1785; *Morning Post,* Oct. 9, 1785.

10. *Morning Chronicle,* Oct. 17, 22, 28, 29, Nov. 23, Dec. 29, 1785; *Morning Post,* Nov. 21, 1785; Genest, VI, 377; Winter, *Shakespeare on the Stage; Third Series,* pp. 80–82; Boaden, I, 322; Isaac Reed, *Notitia Dramatica,* British Museum Ad. MS 25,392; Williams, p. 19; Boaden, *Mrs. Siddons,* II, 204–205; Prior, *Malone,* p. 126; *Morning Post,* Mar. 27, 1786.

11. Whatley, *Remarks on Some of the Characters of Shakespeare,* pp. 2, 9, 10; Robinson, *English Shakesperian Criticism in the Eighteenth*

Century, pp. 180–181; Raysor, *Modern Language Notes*, XLII (1927), 498; Babcock, *Genesis of the Shakespeare Idolatry, 1766–1799*, pp. 47, 134, 144–145, 168–169; *Eighteenth Century Essays on Shakespeare* (ed. Nichol Smith), p. xxxvii.

12. Kemble, *Macbeth Reconsidered*, pp. 4, 36; Whatley, p. 29.

13. *Monthly Review*, LXXX (1789), 553; Hazlitt, *Works*, VII, 301; *Morning Post*, Sept. 20, 1786.

14. *Morning Post*, Sept. 20, Oct. 6, 1786; Cibber, *Apology*, I, 94; *Poetical Miscellany* (ed. Richard Steele), pp. 44–45; Vanbrugh, *Provoked Wife*, III, ii; Pope, *Dunciad*, IV, 45; Warren, *Pope as Critic and Humanist*, pp. 182–183; Allardyce Nicoll, "Italian Opera in England, 1705–1710," *Anglia*, XLVI (1922), 257–281; *Spectator*, no. 18 (for Addison's untiring attacks on Italian opera see nos. 5, 13, 22, 28, 29, 31, 39); Lewis, *Selection of the Letters of Horace Walpole*, pp. 3, 343, n. 1; M. G. Lewis, *Life*, II, 63; Thackeray, *The Newcomes*, chap. I.

15. Carey, *Chrononhotologos*, scene i; Kelly, *Reminiscences*, I, 290; Boaden, I, 336; Oulton, I, 161; Dent, *Foundations of English Opera*, p. 1; Genest, VI, 425; *New Spectator*, no. 6, March 9, 1784; Goldsmith, *The Citizen of the World*, chap. LXXIX; *The Devil; Containing a Review and Investigation of all Public Subjects Whatever*, no. V (1786), p. 74; *Morning Post*, Oct. 26, 1786; Fanny Kemble, *Records of a Girlhood*, p. 60; Boaden, *Mrs. Jordan*, I, 96. See Franz Montgomery, "Early Criticism of Italian Opera in England," *Musical Quarterly*, XV (1929), 415–425.

16. *Morning Post*, Nov. 23, 1786; *European Magazine*, X (1786), 433; Boaden, I, 347.

17. Vulliamy, *Mrs. Thrale of Streatham*, p. 278; Prior, *Malone*, p. 134; Boaden, I, 348–349; Oulton, I, 156; Boaden, *Mrs. Siddons*, II, 226; Pearson, *Swan of Lichfield*, p. 126.

18. Boaden, I, 348; *A Short Criticism on the Performance of Hamlet by Mr. Kemble*, pp. 1–2; *Talma: Correspondance avec Madame de Staël*, p. 56.

19. Boaden, I, 374; Williams, pp. 19–21; *Annual Biography and Obituary*, VIII (1824), 24; *Crosby's Pocket Companion*, p. 4.

20. Clipping dated Dec. 3, 1787, *Kembleiana*, vol. I, Harvard Theatre Collection; Adolphus, *Bannister*, I, 193–194; Fitzgerald, I, 272–273; *Authentic Memoirs of the Green-Room*, I, 113–115; *Life of John Philip Kemble*, pp. 21–22.

21. Boaden, I, 374; *Farington Diary*, III, 28; Wheatley, *London Past and Present*, I, 334; Fanny Kemble, *Records of a Girlhood*, p. 105.

22. *Monthly Mirror*, II (1796), 43; Adolphus, *Bannister*, I, 195–196.

23. Fielding, *The Historical Register*, III, i; Lewis, *Selection of the Letters of Horace Walpole*, p. 191; *Monthly Mirror*, N.S. III (1808), 33; Boaden, *Mrs. Siddons*, II, 250; *Cibber's Two Dissertations on the*

Theatre, p. 35; Boswell, *Johnson* (Oxford ed.), I, 132, 393; Henry Morley, *Journal of a London Playgoer*, p. 22; James Love, *Poems on Several Occasions*, p. 25; William Combe, *Doctor Syntax's Three Tours*, part I, canto xxiv.

24. Vanbrugh, *Works* (ed. Dobrée and Webb), II, 89; Oliphant, *Plays of Beaumont and Fletcher*, p. 145; Sprague, *Beaumont and Fletcher on the Restoration Stage*, pp. 90–91, 245; Collier, *Short View of the Immorality and Profaneness of the English Stage* (1698), p. 57; Boaden, I, 373; Boaden, *Mrs. Jordan*, I, 116.

25. Fletcher, *The Pilgrim . . . now very much Alter'd, with several Additions* (1700), I, i.

26. *The Pilgrim* (altered by J. P. Kemble), II, i; V, iii.

27. Boaden, I, 451–452; *New Monthly Magazine and Literary Journal*, XXXIV (1832), 174.

28. Boaden, *Mrs. Siddons*, II, 234; Boaden, I, 378–379.

29. Boaden, I, 383; MS annotation on a Drury Lane playbill, Jan. 31, 1788, photostat in Harvard Theatre Collection.

30. Seward, *Letters*, II, 128; Boaden, I, 388; Boaden, *Mrs. Siddons*, II, 240; Gifford, *The Baeviad and the Maeviad* (1797), p. 75; Whalley, *Journals and Correspondence*, II, 19–20.

31. MS note by Kemble on Drury Lane playbill, May 5, 1788, photostat in Harvard Theatre Collection.

32. Prior, *Malone*, pp. 145–147; clipping dated Aug. 17, 1788, *Kembleiana*, vol. I, Harvard Theatre Collection; Fitzgerald, I, 264.

Chapter V

1. *Morning Post*, Oct. 8, 1788.

2. *Morning Post*, Sept. 24, Oct. 2, Oct. 11, 1788; *Journal*, Sept. 25, 1788.

3. *Authentic Narrative of Mr. Kemble's Retirement*, p. viii; *Quarterly Review*, XXXIV (1826), 224; Boaden, *Mrs. Jordan*, I, 137; *Authentic Memoirs of the Green-Room*, I, 107; Hunt, *Autobiography*, II, 18.

4. Boaden, II, 321, n.; *Morning Post*, Oct. 16, 1788; Taylor, *Records*, pp. 84–85; Kelly, *Reminiscences*, I, 333; *Quarterly Review*, XXXIV (1826), 231; Nicoll, *Late Eighteenth Century Drama*, p. 41; *Secret History of the Green Room*, p. 290; Macready, *Reminiscences*, p. 113; *Authentic Memoirs of the Green-Room*, pp. 59–60; Oulton, II, 213–214; Fitzgerald, *New History of the English Stage*, II, 342; Genest, VII, 57–58.

5. *Present State of the Stage in Great Britain and Ireland*, pp. 15–16; Boaden, *Mrs. Jordan*, I, 136; Boaden, II, 100; Sergeant, *Mrs. Jordan*, pp. 119–120; *Morning Chronicle*, Dec. 16, 1788; *World*, Oct. 15, Dec. 28, 1788; *Morning Herald*, Sept. 26, 1788; *Morning Post*, Oct. 15, 1788.

6. *World*, Oct. 17, 1788; *Short Criticism of the Performance of Ham-*

let by *Mr. Kemble*, p. vii; Taylor, *Records*, p. 396; Colby, *Holcroft*, II, 131; Gray, *Theatrical Criticism in London to 1795*, p. 257, n. 8, 259–260; *Morning Post*, Oct. 29, 1788; clipping, dated Dec. 2, 1788, *Kembleiana*, vol. I, Harvard Theatre Collection.

7. *General Advertiser*, Nov. 3, 1788; *World*, Nov. 3, 10, 1788; *Morning Herald*, Nov. 3, 1788; *Morning Post*, Oct. 21, 29, 1788; *Times*, Oct. 29, 1788; *Evening Advertiser*, Oct. 29, 1788; *Journal*, Nov. 17, 1788; Gray, *Theatrical Criticism*, p. 262.

8. *World*, Oct. 21, Dec. 1, 22, 1788; Sir Henry Wotton, *Life and Letters* (ed. Smith), II, 32; *Quarterly Review*, XXXIV (1826), 228; Boaden, I, 407; Odell, *Shakespeare from Betterton to Irving*, II, 50; *Journal*, Nov. 25, 1788; Williams, p. 22; *Morning Post*, Nov. 26, 1788; *Morning Herald*, Dec. 8, 1788; *Times*, Jan. 5, 1789.

9. *Morning Post*, Nov. 12, 17, 20, 26, 1788.

10. *Morning Post*, Dec. 1, 1788; Henry Irving *Shakespeare*, IV, 354.

11. Jerrold, *Story of Dorothy Jordan*, p. 124; *The Great Illegitimates!!*, p. 46; *Morning Post*, Nov. 8, 1788; Jan. 11, Mar. 10, 1789; *Narrative of the Life of Mrs. Charlotte Charke*, p. 62.

12. *Times*, Oct. 27, 1788; *Public and Private Life of that Celebrated Actress . . . Mrs. Jordan*, p. 22; Wilkinson, *Memoirs*, I, 145–146; *Journal*, memoranda at the beginning of the 1791–1792 season; Genest, VII, 610.

13. *Morning Chronicle*, Jan. 2, 1789; *Theatric Tourist*, p. 53; Gilliland, *Dramatic Mirror*, I, 223–224; *Star*, Jan. 3, 1789; Boaden, I, 451; *Monthly Mirror*, VI (1798), 48.

14. Nicoll, *Late Eighteenth Century Drama*, pp. 123, 178; *Journal*, Nov. 28, 1788; Oulton, II, 30; *Morning Post*, Dec. 10, 24, 1788; Boaden, I, 425; Taylor, *Records*, p. 86.

15. *Public Advertiser*, Oct. 30, 1788; *Biographia Dramatica*, I, 423; Boaden, I, 412; *Journal*, memorandum at the end of the 1788–1789 season.

CHAPTER VI

1. Williams, *Kemble*, p. 22; *Boswell's Johnson* (ed. Hill), II, 463 (cf. I, 194; II, 199; III, 209; V, 42); Murphy, *Garrick*, p. 376; Lewis, *Selection of the Letters of Horace Walpole*, p. 85; Sterne, *Letters* (Shakespeare Head ed.), p. 304.

2. Chapman, *Complete History of Theatrical Entertainments*, p. 35; Lady Morgan, *Book of the Boudoir* (1829), I, 115; MS letter, Mrs. Piozzi to Samuel Lysons, Nov. 28, 1789, Harvard Theatre Collection; *Quarterly Review*, XXXIV (1826), 214; Princess Liechtenstein, *Holland House*, II, 181; Fanny Kemble, *Records of a Girlhood*, p. 267.

3. Hazlitt, *Works*, VI, 342; *Remarks on Mr. Kemble's Performance of Hamlet and Richard the Third*, p. 10; Boaden, I, 2; Hunt, *Auto-*

biography, I, 153; *Boswell's Johnson* (ed. Hill), II, 269; *Boswell's Life of Johnson* (ed. Croker), p. 741.

4. Taylor, *Records*, p. 83; Sichel, *Sheridan*, I, 170, n. 4; II, 408; Journal, Dec. 15, 1799; Constable and Gillies, *Personal Reminiscences*, p. 299; Hunt, *Autobiography*, I, 152; Huish, *George the Fourth*, I, 484–485; Coleridge, *Table Talk*, I, 4–5; Boaden, II, 535; *Mirror*, I (1823), 235–236.

5. Boaden, I, v; *Georgian Era*, IV, 401; Constable and Gillies, p. 301; Hazlitt, *Works*, VI, 397; *Some General Advice to Theatrical Managers*, p. 22; Beattie, *Campbell*, I, 362; Roberts, *Rogers*, p. 110; *Farington Diary*, IV, 181–182; Clayden, *Rogers*, p. 353–354; Mathews, *Memoirs of Charles Mathews*, II, 219-220; Taylor, *Records*, p. 309; Coleridge, *Table Talk*, I, 3–4.

6. Taylor, *Records*, p. 235; *Reminiscences and Recollections of Captain Gronow*, II, 258; Hazlitt, *Works*, XI, 28; XII, 41; Boaden, II, 283; Kelly, *Reminiscences*, I, 345; *Farington Diary*, V, 18; Sichel, *Sheridan*, I, 142.

7. Taylor, *Records*, p. 83; *Farington Diary*, I, 86; V, 78; VIII, 239.

8. Lockhart, *Scott*, II, 95; Scott, *Familiar Letters*, I, 156; Scott, *Post-Bag* (ed. Partington), p. 364; *Quarterly Review*, XXXIV (1826), 213.

9. Douglas, *Diaries* (ed. Bickley), I, 245, 407; *Quarterly Review*, XXXIV (1826), 214; Taylor, *Records*, p. 79; *Farington Diary*, VIII, 113; Kelly, *Reminiscences*, II, 294–295; Nicoll, *Late Eighteenth Century Drama*, pp. 19–20; *Number I, of the Lives and Traits of the Bon Ton Theatricals*, June 14, 1790. Further material on the private theatricals may be found in Lord David Cecil, *Young Melbourne*, p. 52; Samuel Foote, *Table-Talk* (ed. Cooke), p. 14; Disraeli, *Vivian Grey*, chap. IV; Johnson, *Hayley*, I, 283, 311; Barham, *Edward Theodore Hook*, I, 27–30; M. G. Lewis, *Life and Correspondence*, I, 196; Doran, *In and About Drury Lane*, I, 108–135; *Notes and Queries*, 12th Series, XII (1923), 112–113.

10. Lawrence, *Letter-Bag* (ed. Layard), p. 10; Taylor, *Records*, pp. 448–449; Fanny Kemble, *Records of a Girlhood*, pp. 207–208; Fitzgerald, *The Garrick Club*, pp. 194–195; Robinson, *Diary*, I, 242; Lawrence, p. 174.

11. Taylor, *Records*, p. 83; MS letter, Kemble to Flaxman, Harvard Theatre Collection; *Farington Diary*, II, 188; IV, 171; VI, 228, 235; Colby, *Holcroft*, II, 188; Hazlitt, *Works*, VI, 343.

12. Trelawney, *Recollections*, p. 42; Cecil, *Young Melbourne*, chap. I, *passim*; Sichel, *Sheridan*, I, 136–144; Cibber, *Apology*, I, 261; Lady Morgan, *Book of the Boudoir*, I, 114–115; Rogers, *Reminiscences and Table Talk*, p. 147; Boaden, *Mrs. Jordan*, II, 78.

13. Henderson, *Adolphus*, pp. 88–91; *Quarterly Review*, XXXIV (1826), 241; Rogers, *Reminiscences and Table Talk*, p. 147; Reynolds, *Life and Times*, II, 94–95.

14. Kelly, *Reminiscences*, II, 159–161; Taylor, *Records*, pp. 85, 128, 189; Lady Holland, *Journal*, I, 191; Dunnicliffe, *Outpourings*, p. 12.

15. Lady Morgan, *Book of the Boudoir*, I, 110; Williams, *Pin Basket*, p. 23; Reynolds, *Life and Times*, II, 93–94; Taylor, *Records*, pp. 373–374.

16. Taylor, *Records*, pp. 188–189.

17. R. J. Allen, *Clubs of Augustan London*, p. 137; Chetwood, *General History of the Stage*, p. 143; *Spectator*, no. 358; Escott, *Club Makers and Club Members*, pp. 95 ff.; Timbs, *Clubs and Club Life in London*, pp. 113, 126; Arnold, *Life and Death of the Sublime Society of Beef Steaks*, p. xxi; Boaden, II, 456.

18. Reynolds, *Life and Times*, II, 89–90; Gordon, *Personal Memoirs*, II, 323; Page, *George Colman the Elder*, p. 187; *The London Clubs, Their Anecdotes and History*, pp. 17–18; Marsh, *Clubs of London*, pp. 116–117.

19. Taylor, *Records*, p. 128; MS letter, Kemble to Mrs. Inchbald, Forster MS 322, South Kensington Museum; Lockhart, *Scott*, II, 95; Collier, *An Old Man's Diary . . . for the Last Six Months of 1832*, pp. 63–64.

20. Gordon, *Personal Memoirs*, I, 320–322.

21. Reynolds, *Life and Times*, II, 354; *Life of John Philip Kemble*, pp. 33–37; Taylor, *Records*, pp. 189, 291; *Farington Diary*, VI, 277.

CHAPTER VII

1. *Journal*, Dec. 23, 1788, Jan. 10, Feb. 25, 1789; MS letter, Sheridan to Peake, *Kembleiana*, vol. I, Harvard Theatre Collection; Gray, *Theatrical Criticism in London to 1795*, p. 294.

2. Boaden, I, 278–279; Vincke, "Shakespeare auf der englischen Bühne siet Garrick," *Jahrbuch der Deutschen Shakespeare Gesellschaft*, XXII (1887), 4; *Some General Advice to Theatrical Managers*, p. 19; Wheatley, *London Past and Present*, III, 193; MS letter, Kemble to Prince Hoare, Harvard Theatre Collection.

3. Manley, *Secret Memoirs and Manners of Several Persons of Quality* (1709), I, 209; *Theatrical Inquisitor*, II (1813), 29; Wycherley, *The Country Wife*, III, ii.

4. *Journal*, Jan. 26, Feb. 7, Mar. 23, April 20, Sept. 27, 1789.

5. Campbell, *Mrs. Siddons*, p. 252; Boaden, II, 2; Henry Irving *Shakespeare*, IV, 4; Fielding, *The Historical Register*, III, i; Hazlitt, *Works*, XVIII, 191; *Monthly Mirror*, N.S. III (1808), 51; Kemble, *Macbeth, and King Richard the Third*, 1817, p. 127; Tieck, *Dramaturgische Blätter*, II, 141.

6. Child, *Shakespearian Productions of John Philip Kemble*, pp. 8, 18; *Biographia Dramatica*, I, 424; A. O. Lovejoy, " 'Nature' as Aesthetic Norm," *MLN*, XLII (1927), 446–447; C. C. Green, *The Neo-Classic Concept of Tragedy*, pp. 11–13, 16; Sheridan, *The Critic*, I, i.

7. *Companion to Shakespeare Studies* (ed. Granville-Barker and Harrison), p. 339; Kemble, *Macbeth, and King Richard the Third*, pp. 52–53; Marsh, *Clubs of London*, II, 101–102; *Remarks on Mr. Kemble's Performance of Hamlet and Richard the Third*, p. 6.

8. *Remarks on Mr. Kemble's Performance*, p. 39; *Select British Theatre* (ed. Kemble), I, vi.

9. Fitzgerald, *Letters . . . to Fanny Kemble* (ed. Wright), p. 212; Shaw, *Unpleasant Plays*, p. xix; Odell, *Shakespeare from Betterton to Irving*, II, 85; Baker, *Shakespeare as a Dramatic Artist*, p. 173.

10. Boaden, II, 8; Gray, *Theatrical Criticism*, p. 264; *Attic Miscellany*, I (1789), 120. See R. W. Babcock, "The Attack in the Late Eighteenth Century upon Alteration in Shakespeare's Plays," *MLN*, XLV (1930), 446–451.

11. Downes, *Roscius Anglicanus* (ed. Summers), pp. 34–35; Spencer, *Shakespeare Improved*, p. 203; *Shakespeare Adaptations* (ed. Summers), p. lvi; *The Tempest* (altered by J. P. Kemble), *passim*; Odell, *Shakespeare from Betterton to Irving*, II, 58–59.

12. Genest, VI, 577; *Journal*, Oct. 13, 1789; Young, *Memoirs of Mrs. Crouch*, I, 73–74.

13. Johnson, *Hayley*, I, 398–400; Lady Holland, *Journal*, II, 106; *Attic Miscellany*, I (1789), 120; Adolphus, *Bannister*, I, 228; Genest, VI, 579–580; *Journal*, Oct. 24, 28, 1789; Lewis, *Selection of the Letters of Horace Walpole*, p. 359; Lucas, *Seneca and Elizabethan Tragedy*, p. 104.

14. *Journal*, Nov. 7, 1789; Jan. 15, 1790; Oulton, II, 55; *Attic Miscellany*, I (1789), 200.

15. *Journal*, Jan. 19, 1790; Boaden, II, 48; *Morning Post*, Jan. 22, 1790.

16. *Public Advertiser*, Feb. 8, 1790; Sergeant, *Mrs. Jordan*, pp. 138–139; *The Great Illegitimates!!*, pp. 27–28; Jerrold, *Story of Dorothy Jordan*, p. 114; *Notes and Queries*, 10th Series, VII (1907), 131, 191.

17. Boaden, II, 14; Aphra Behn, *Works* (ed. Summers), I, xxxviii; *Spectator*, no. 51; Sackville-West, *Aphra Behn*, p. 80.

18. Genest, VI, 590; *Attic Miscellany*, I (1789), 317; Boaden, II, 14.

19. Boaden, II, 14; *Journal*, May 4, 1791; Howe, *Hazlitt*, p. 12.

Chapter VIII

1. *General Magazine and Impartial Review*, Sept., 1790, p. 421; *Journal*, Sept. 14, 18, 20, 21, 22, Nov. 1, 7, 1790.

2. Sterne, *Letters*, p. 52; *Journal*, memorandum at the beginning of the 1791 season.

3. *Journal*, memorandum at the beginning of the 1791 season.

4. Williams, *Kemble*, p. 14; *Cabinet*, I (1807), 274; Williams, *Children of Thespis*, p. 48; Taylor, *Records*, p. 84; *Oxberry's Dramatic*

Biography, I, 187; *Journal*, Nov. 10, 1790; J. P. Collier, *An Old Man's Diary . . . for the Last Six Months of 1832*, pp. 3–4; Boaden, II, 30; *Theatrical Guardian*, no. 5, Apr. 2, 1791; Reynolds, *Life and Times*, II, 356–357; Galt, *Lives of the Players*, II, 266.

5. *Journal*, Dec. 7, 1790, Jan. 1, 24–30, Feb. 27, Apr. 29, May 4, 1791; Piozzi, *Letters* (ed. Knapp), p. 30; *Attic Miscellany*, II (1791), 232; Boaden, II, 32; Walpole, *Letters*, IX, 302; *Theatrical Guardian*, no. 4, Mar. 26, 1791. See Boswell's *Letters* (ed. Tinker), II, 431.

6. Boaden, *Mrs. Jordan*, I, 192–197.

7. Fitzgerald, I, 264–265; Sergeant, *Mrs. Jordan*, pp. 155–157; Boaden, *Mrs. Jordan*, I, 197.

8. Piozzi, *Letters*, p. 48; Moore, *Sheridan*, II, 179; *Public Advertiser*, Sept. 19, 1791; Oulton, II, 100; *Journal*, Sept. 21, 1791.

9. Kelly, *Reminiscences*, II, 17; Oulton, II, 100; *Morning Post*, Sept. 23, 1791; *Public Advertiser*, Sept. 23, 1791.

10. *London Chronicle*, Sept. 24, 1791; *Journal*, Sept. 24, 1791; *New Theatrical Dictionary*, 1792, p. 400; Oulton, II, 103–106; Kemble's note on Drury Lane playbill, Nov. 26, 1791, Dec. 10, 1791, photostat in Harvard Theatre Collection; *Morning Post*, Dec. 12, 1791; undated clipping in a theatrical scrapbook of the Rare Book Room of the Boston Public Library.

11. *Cymon* (1769), p. vi; Dibdin, *Reminiscences*, I, 197–198, 201; Genest, VII, 47; H. N. Hillebrand, *Kean*, p. 13.

12. *Journal*, Jan. 10, 18, 1792; Genest, VII, 47–49; Boaden, II, 58, 60; *Morning Post*, Mar. 5, 1792; Boaden, *Mrs. Jordan*, II, 125; Taylor, *Records*, p. 86; *European Magazine*, XXI (1792), 236; Bernard, *Retrospections*, II, 204–205; *Quarterly Review*, XXXIV (1826), 241; Fitzgerald, *New History of the English Stage*, II, 343.

13. *Journal*, Mar. 25, 28, Apr. 29, May 5, 1792; Dibdin, *Reminiscences*, I, 201.

14. John Jackson, *History of the Scottish Stage* (1793), p. 94; Paul, *Godwin*, I, 41–42, 45; *Thespian Magazine and Literary Repository*, I (1793), 78.

15. *Journal*, Sept. 19, 1792; memorandum at the beginning of the 1791–1792 season.

16. *Thespian Magazine*, II (1793), 115; *Journal*, Sept. 10, 1792; memorandum at the beginning of the 1792–1793 season; Walter Nicholson, *Struggle for a Free Stage*, pp. 142–143; *Morning Chronicle*, Apr. 13, 1793.

17. Boaden, II, 75; Boaden, *Mrs. Jordan*, I, 260.

18. *Thespian Magazine*, I (1793), sig. Ff; "Peter Pindar," "Ode XV," *Works* (1797), I, 81–82; *Journal*, Jan. 24, 1793; Kelly, *Reminiscences*, II, 37; Adolphus, *Bannister*, I, 300.

19. Sergeant, *Mrs. Jordan*, p. 188; Boaden, *Mrs. Jordan*, I, 222–223;

Public and Private Life of . . . Mrs. Jordan, p. 30; *Morning Chronicle*, Feb. 26, 1793; *Thespian Magazine*, I (1793), 250–251.

20. *Morning Chronicle*, Mar. 19, 1793; Journal, June 16, 1792; memorandum at the end of the 1792–1793 season.

21. Southey, *Espriella Letters*, I, 190–191; *Morning Post*, Apr. 22, 1794; *Thespian Magazine*, III (1794), 89–90; Watson, *Sheridan to Robertson*, pp. 58–59; Boaden, II, 123; Gilliland, *Dramatic Mirror*, I, 135–137; Nicoll, *Late Eighteenth Century Drama*, p. 23.

22. Cibber, *Apology*, I, 321; Boaden, *Mrs. Jordan*, I, 254; Southey, *Espriella Letters*, I, 189; Nicholson, *Struggle for a Free Stage*, p. 186, n. 1.

23. Kemble, *Macbeth, and King Richard the Third*, p. 171; Kelly, *Reminiscences*, II, 63–64.

24. Spencer, *Shakespeare Improved*, p. 152.

25. Boaden, II, 101; *Oracle*, Apr. 22, 1794.

26. Boaden, *Mrs. Jordan*, I, 254; Kelly, *German Visitors to English Theatres in the Eighteenth Century* (1936), p. 134; Oulton, II, 139; Spencer, *Shakespeare Improved*, p. 162; Henry Irving *Shakespeare*, V, 347; *Morning Post*, Apr. 22, 1794.

27. Fitzgerald, I, 311; *Farington Diary*, VII, 59; *Quarterly Review*, XXXIV (1826), 228; Campbell, *Mrs. Siddons*, p. 263; *Times*, Sept. 19, 1811; Journal, memorandum at the beginning of the 1791–1792 season; Molloy, *Kean*, I, 13; Hillebrand, *Kean*, p. 14; Hawkins, *Kean*, I, 9–10; *Thespian Magazine*, III (1794), 222; *Oracle*, Apr. 22, 1794.

28. Journal, July 2, 1794; Boaden, *Mrs. Jordan*, I, 266–267; Samuel Johnson, *Lives* (1854), II, 184; *More Kotzebue* (1799), p. 15, n.; Edward Green, *Observations on the Drama* (n.d.), p. 38.

29. Steele, *Conscious Lovers*, II, ii; Taylor, *Records*, p. 189; Dryden, *Dramatic Works* (ed. Summers), V, 344.

30. *Lodoiska. An Opera; by J. P. Kemble* (1824), act III, *passim*; Kelly, *Reminiscences*, II, 67.

31. Dryden, *Essays* (ed. Ker), II, 7; *Georgian Era*, IV, 300; *Morning Post*, June 10, 1794; *Oracle*, June 10, 1794.

Chapter IX

1. Howe, *Hazlitt*, p. 97, n. 1; *Oracle*, June 10, 1794; Boaden, *Mrs. Jordan*, I, 266; Journal, July 1, 1794; *Gentleman's Magazine*, XX (1750), 422.

2. *Morning Post*, Oct. 4 and 27, 1794; Journal, Oct. 28, 1794; Boaden, *Mrs. Jordan*, I, 275; Journal, Dec. 30, 1794; Boaden, I, 90; *Thespian Magazine*, II (1793), 215, 225–226, 269–270; Boaden, II, 140; Journal, Feb. 12, 1795; *Oracle*, Feb. 13, 1795. Kemble wrote a scenario for *Alexander the Great*; a copy of the extremely rare pamphlet is in the British Museum.

3. Boaden, I, xxiii; Fanny Kemble, *Records of a Girlhood*, p. 6; Hunt, *Autobiography*, I, 135; Newton, *Amenities of Book-Collecting*, p. 160; Williams, pp. 24-25; *Authentic Memoirs of the Green-Room* (*for 1799*), pp. 31–32; Piozzi, *Letters*, p. 120.

4. *Crosby's Pocket Companion*, p. 56; *Farington Diary*, I, 89; Dutton, *Dramatic Censor*, IV, 19–20.

5. Kelly, *Reminiscences*, II, 84; *Critical Observations on Mr. Kemble's Performances at the Theatre Royal, Liverpool*, p. 32; Cumberland, *Memoirs*, p. 344; Fitzgerald, *Memoirs of an Author*, I, 224.

6. Boaden, *Mrs. Jordan*, I, 285; Madame D'Arblay, *Diary and Letters* (ed. Dobson), V, 250–251; *Journal*, March 22, 1795; *Evening Mail*, March 23, 1795; *Oracle*, March 23, 1795; *Morning Advertiser*, March 23, 1795. In the Burney Collection of the British Museum there are numerous contemporary criticisms of the play.

7. *Journal*, May 15–23, 1795; Anne Mathews, *Memoirs of Charles Mathews*, I, 144, 150–151.

8. Williams, pp. 31–32; Mathews, *Memoirs of Charles Mathews*, I, 152; *Journal*, June 1, 2, 27, 1795.

9. Mathews, *Memoirs of Charles Mathews*, I, 152.

10. *Morning Herald*, March 9, 1796; Boaden, II, 149; *Monthly Mirror*, I (1795), 121, 179 ff., 233 ff., 308; Mason, *Literary Miscellanies*, II, lxii; *Gazetteer, and New Daily Advertiser*, Feb. 29, 1796; Collier, *Short View*, p. 12; Boaden, *Mrs. Jordan*, I, 291–292; Boaden, II, 154. On Kemble's disquieting pronunciation see Henry Cecil Wyld, *A Short History of English* (1937), pp. 223, 254, n. 1, 283.

11. Lawrence, *Old Theatre Days and Ways*, pp. 59–60.

12. *Gazetteer, and New Daily Advertiser*, March 3 and 21, 1796; Williams, p. 29; Kelly, *Reminiscences*, II, 87; Congreve, *Mourning Bride*, "Epilogue"; *Gazetteer*, March 14, 1796; *Monthly Mirror*, I (1795), 309; Taylor, *Records*, p. 444; *Journal*, March 12, 1796.

13. Colman, *Iron Chest* (2d ed.), "Preface," *passim*.

14. *Monthly Mirror*, II (1796), 251–252; cf. p. 304; Williams, p. 26; *Gazetteer*, March 14, 1796; Lamb, *Dramatic Essays* (ed. Matthews), p. 133; *Monthly Mirror*, II (1796), 235, 311, 312; *Remarks on Mr. Colman's Preface*, pp. 7, 10; *Journal*, March 12, 1796; *Quarterly Review*, XXXIV (1826), 232; *Pin Basket*, p. 26; Dunlap, *Cooke*, I, 81; Raymond, *Elliston* (1846), I, 87; *Iron Chest* (2d ed.), "Postscript," *passim*; Williams, p. 30, n.; Taylor, *Records*, p. 444; *Drama, or, Theatrical Pocket Magazine*, IV (1823), 266.

15. Zoltan Haraszti, "Ireland's Shakespeare Forgeries," *More Books: The Bulletin of the Boston Public Library*, IX (1934), 333–350; Bodde, *Shakspere and the Ireland Forgeries* (1930), *passim*; Babcock, *The Genesis of the Shakespeare Idolatry*, pp. 26, 89; Payn, *The Talk of the Town* (2d ed., 1885), *passim* (this is an amusing fictional account

of the entire imbroglio); Inglesby, *The Shakspeare Fabrications*, pp. 99–102; Mair, *The Fourth Forger* (1938), *passim*.

16. *Mr. Ireland's Vindication*, p. 20; Bodde, pp. 17–18; *Quarterly Review*, XXXIV (1826), 233; Boaden, *A Letter to George Steevens*, p. 2; Ritson, *Letters*, II, 92; Waldron, *Free Reflections*, p. 6; *Oracle*, Oct. 9, 1795.

17. Ward, *History of English Dramatic Literature*, I, 564; Taylor, *Records*, p. 324; Boaden, II, 167; W. H. Ireland, *Confessions*, p. 139; Marsh, *Clubs of London*, pp. 107–108; *Quarterly Review*, XXXIV (1826), 233; British Museum Ad. MS 30,348.

18. *Miscellaneous Papers and Legal Instruments . . . in the Possession of Samuel Ireland, of Norfolk Street, passim.*

19. British Museum Ad. MS 30,348; *Vortigern* (1799), p. vi.

20. British Museum Ad. MS 30,348; *Fraser's Magazine*, LXII (1860), 173; Campbell, *Mrs. Siddons*, p. 270; Prior, *Malone*, p. 225, n.

21. Taylor, *Records*, p. 142; Journal, April 3, 1796; British Museum Ad. MS 30,348; *Vortigern* (1832 ed.) for Pye's and Burgess' prologues; W. H. Ireland, *Confessions*, pp. 150, 152–154, 158; Marsh, *Clubs of London*, p. 110; *Farington Diary*, I, 145; *Notes and Queries*, 2d Series, III (1857), 442, 493; *Monthly Mirror*, I (1795), 371; *Contemporary Review*, XLIV (1883), 244–247; *Fraser's Magazine*, LXII (1860), 167–178.

22. Marsh, *Clubs of London*, pp. 109–110; *Vortigern* (1832 ed.), p. iv; Sichel, *Sheridan*, II, 276; *Gazetteer*, April 4, 1796; Ireland, *Confessions*, pp. 140, 160.

23. *Morning Post*, Sept. 23, 1795; Boaden, *Mrs. Jordan*, I, 300–301; Rogers, *Reminiscences and Table Talk*, p. 41; *Morning Chronicle*, Jan. 22, 1796; Ireland, *Confessions*, p. 159; Gilliland, *Dramatic Synopsis*, pp. 86–87; Journal, *passim*; Boaden, II, 185; *Monthly Mirror*, II (1796), 41.

24. Journal, March 21, 1796.

25. *Gazetteer*, April 18, 1796; Boaden, *Mrs. Jordan*, pp. 199–200; Jerrold, *Story of Dorothy Jordan*, pp. 207–208; *Morning Herald*, May 3, 1796; *Monthly Mirror*, II (1796), 42; Boaden, II, 187. Mrs. Kemble retired from the stage on May 23; see Oulton, *History of the Theatres of London*, I, 10–11; Journal, *passim*.

CHAPTER X

1. *Literary Magazine, and British Review*, June, 1790, p. 434; Lewis, *Selection of the Letters of Horace Walpole*, p. 251; John Mitford, *A Letter to J. P. Kemble, Esq.*, p. 4.

2. Lady Holland, *Journal*, I, 149.

3. Prior, *Malone*, p. 125; Boaden, II, 544–555; *Farington Diary*, III, 242; numerous references to Malone in the journal, *passim*; MS letter,

Malone to Isaac Reed, Harvard Theatre Collection; MS letter, Kemble to Malone from Liverpool, July 7, 1789, Folger Library.

4. Colby, *Holcroft*, II, 158; Boaden, II, 433; Nichols, *Literary Anecdotes of the Eighteenth Century*, II, 672; MS letter, Kemble to Reed, Mar. 18, 1788, Harvard Theatre Collection.

5. MS letter, Kemble to unnamed correspondent, Jan. 14, 1798, Harvard Theatre Collection; MS letter, undated, Kemble to unnamed correspondent, Harvard Theatre Collection; F. G. Waldron, *Shakspearian Miscellany*, pp. 25–26; Taylor, *Records*, p. 152; Walpole, *Letters*, IX, 215.

6. Henry Irving *Shakespeare*, V, 252; Bakeless, *Marlowe*, p. 240; Marsh, *Clubs of London*, pp. 103–104; Boaden, II, 100; Taylor, *Records*, p. 85; Campbell, *Mrs. Siddons*, p. 162. For Dryden's high reputation in the late eighteenth century see Sichel, *Sheridan*, I, 7; Rogers, *Reminiscences and Table Talk*, p. 30; Kelly, *Reminiscences*, II, 312; Hunt, *Autobiography*, II, 24.

7. British Museum Ad. MS 12,201; MS notes on the drama by Kemble, Folger Library scrapbook; MS list of English actors (not in Kemble's hand, but bearing a note, "copied from a MS of J. P. Kemble 1821"), Harvard Theatre Collection.

8. MS notes on Dublin theatres, dated Aug. 10, 1797, Harvard Theatre Collection.

9. Photostatic copies of Kemble's annotated playbills, Harvard Theatre Collection; Boaden, I, 157; Taylor, *Records*, p. 402.

10. MS letter, Kemble to unnamed correspondent, Feb. 13, 1812, Harvard Theatre Collection; Taylor, *Records*, p. 85; MS letter, Kemble to unnamed correspondent, June 24, 1805, Harvard Theatre Collection.

11. Boaden, *Mrs. Jordan*, II, 145; *Biographia Dramatica*, I, 425; Boaden, II, 103; Merriam, *Moxon*, p. 19; Scott, *Private Letter-Books* (ed. Partington), p. 23; Hunt, *Autobiography*, I, 153; *Monthly Mirror*, III (1797), 124; W. W. Greg, "Editors at Work and Play," *Review of English Studies*, II (1926), 173; Beloe, *Anecdotes of Literature and Scarce Books*, I, xii.

12. Collier, *An Old Man's Diary . . . for the First Six Months of 1832*, p. 21.

13. *Catalogue of the Valuable and Extensive Miscellaneous Library . . . of John Philip Kemble, Esq.* (1821), *passim*; Beloe, *Anecdotes of Literature*, I, 364 ff.

14. Gifford, *The Baeviad and the Maeviad*, ll. 358, 32, respectively; Taylor, *Records*, p. 442; MS letter, Kemble to Gifford, June 22, 1812, Harvard Theatre Collection; Kemble, *Macbeth, and King Richard the Third*, p. 164, n.

15. Constable and Gillies, *Personal Reminiscences*, p. 301; Douglas, *Diaries* (ed. Bickley), II, 216; Boaden, *Mrs. Jordan*, II, 145; Beattie,

Campbell, II, 322; Taylor, *Records*, p. 83; Francis Twiss, *Complete Verbal Index to the Plays of Shakspeare*, I, vi–vii; British Museum Ad. MS 33,964, letter from Kemble to Gilliland, Nov. 8, 1808, in thanks for a presentation copy of one of Gilliland's books.

CHAPTER XI

1. Moore, *Sheridan*, II, 308–309; *Monthly Mirror*, II (1796), 301, 376; Oulton, I, 16.

2. Boaden, II, 190; Foss, *Sheridan*, p. 263; Journal, Jan. 17–24, 1797; *Monthly Mirror*, III (1797), 35.

3. Journal, summer of 1797, *passim*; Gray, *Works*, II, 257–258.

4. Gifford, *The Baeviad and the Maeviad*, p. 68; Lewis, *Life*, I, 211–212; Lady Holland, *Journal*, I, 167, 184.

5. Shelley, *Essays*, I, 23; Goldsmith, *Works*, III, 81; *Ecce Homo*, p. 4, n.; Thaler, *Shakspere to Sheridan*, p. 19; *Biographia Dramatica*, I, 87; Genest, VII, 333; Lady Holland, *Journal*, I, 184; Journal, Dec. 15, 1797.

6. Lady Holland, *Journal*, I, 211–212; Boaden, II, 209–210; Hazlitt, *Characters of Shakspeare's Plays*, p. 111; Hereford, *Age of Wordsworth*, pp. 138–139; Hawkins, *Memoirs*, I, 137; Gogol, *Dead Souls*, bk. I, chap. I; White, *Remains*, II, 219; *Theatre*, pp. 69–73; Elton, *Survey of English Literature 1780–1830*, II, 309; Pearson, *Swan of Lichfield*, pp. 236–237; Sellier, *Kotzebue in England*, pp. 9–16; Thompson, *Kotzebue*, pp. 55–108; Moore, *Sheridan*, II, 275.

7. *Monthly Mirror*, VI (1798), 48; Journal, summer of 1798, *passim*.

8. *Farington Diary*, I, 245; *Druriad*, p. 9; Hunt, *Autobiography*, I, 173.

9. *Monthly Mirror*, VI (1798), 303; Kelly, *Reminiscences*, II, 157–158; Boaden, II, 228; Journal, Mar. 12–23, Apr. 23, May 22, 1799; Seward, *Letters*, V, 239; Fanny Kemble, *Records of a Girlhood*, p. 174.

10. Seward, *Letters*, V, 240; Robinson, *Diary*, I, 38; Wraxall, *Posthumous Memoirs*, I, 52; Lady Holland, *Journal*, I, 251, 255, 256, 278.

11. Boaden, II, 239, 242; Taylor, *Records*, p. 270; Taylor, *Poems*, II, 70; Boaden, *Mrs. Jordan*, II, 17; *Critical Observations*, p. 37; Journal, summer of 1799, *passim*.

12. Countess of Blessington, *Conversations with Lord Byron*, p. 240; Wraxall, I, 49; Fanny Kemble, *Records*, p. 174.

13. Piozzi, *Letters*, p. 193; Journal, Sept. 24, Nov. 7, 1799; Feb. 20, 1800; Boaden, II, 100.

14. Sichel, *Sheridan*, I, 33; Farquhar, "Discourse on Comedy," *Critical Essays of the Eighteenth Century* (ed. Durham), p. 258; Hereford, *Age of Wordsworth*, p. 135; Wordsworth, *Works*, I, 100–101; Smollett, *Roderick Random*, chaps. LXII–LXIII; Keats, *Letters*, II, 483; Byron, *Works*, p. 399; Smollett, *Letters*, pp. 156 ff.

15. Lamb, *Letters*, I, 162–163, 221, 235; II, 211, 212; Manning, *Let-*

ters to Charles Lamb, p. 43; Coleridge, *Unpublished Letters*, I, 72; Coleridge, *Letters*, I, 231; Cottle, p. 120; De Quincey, *Selected Writings*, p. 361.

16. Boaden, II, 252, 257; *Bell's Weekly Messenger*, Jan. 26, May 4, 1800; Baillie, *Series of Plays*, I, 3; Scott, *Familiar Letters*, I, 99; *De Montfort* (ed. Inchbald), Preface; Seward, *Letters*, V, 324; Carhart, *Baillie*, p. 110; MS letter, Kemble to unnamed correspondent, Apr., 1799, Folger Library; Campbell, *Mrs. Siddons*, p. 302; Oulton, I, 60; Dutton, *Dramatic Censor*, II (1800), 127, 159–160; Genest, VII, 467.

17. MS letter, Kemble to Peake, Harvard Theatre Collection; MS letter, Kemble to Daly, May 12, 1800, Folger Library; MS letter, Kemble to unnamed correspondent, Folger Library; Journal, summer of 1800, *passim*.

18. Journal, Jan., 1801, *passim*; Moore, *Sheridan*, II, 303, 304–309; Boaden, *Mrs. Jordan*, II, 39; Sichel, *Sheridan*, II, 274; *Quarterly Review*, XXXIV (1826), 231; *Dramatic Censor*, IV (1800), 241; Boaden, II, 272; Oulton, I, 70; Fitzgerald, *New History*, II, 358–359.

19. Boaden, II, 272, 290; *Dramatic Censor*, III (1800), 3, 191, 215–236; *Authentic Memoirs of the Green-Room*, I, 117; Boaden, *Mrs. Jordan*, II, 65; *Bell's Weekly Messenger*, Sept. 21, Oct. 5, 1800; *Morning Post and Gazetteer*, Oct. 21, 1800; *Times*, Oct. 21, 1800.

20. Paul, *Godwin*, II, 41–43, 46; Lamb, *Letters*, I, 228; II, 230–231; Lamb, *Dramatic Essays*, pp. 135, 138; *Morning Post*, Dec. 15, 1800; *Times*, Dec. 15, 1800; *Bell's Weekly Messenger*, Dec. 14, 1800; Ritson, *Letters*, II, 201; Newton, *Amenities of Book Collecting*, p. 236; Coleridge, *Biographia Epistolaris*, I, 208.

21. Lady Holland, *Journal*, II, 136; Thackeray, *The Newcomes*, chap. I; Boaden, II, 289; *Monthly Mirror*, XI (1801), 97; Odell, *Shakespeare from Betterton to Irving*, II, 95; Boaden, *Mrs. Jordan*, II, 81–82; Kelly, *Reminiscences*, II, 179; *Annual Biography*, VIII (1824), 49; Journal, *passim*. See *Notes and Queries*, CLXXIII (1937), 402–405.

22. *Theatrical Repertory*, Sept. 19, 1801.

23. Taylor, *Records*, pp. 312, 400; Mathews, *Memoirs*, I, 140; Robinson, *Diary*, I, 53; *Farington Diary*, I, 342; V, 208; *Theatrical Repertory*, Jan. 11, 1802; Bernard, *Retrospections*, I, 19; Macready, *Reminiscences*, p. 51.

24. Journal, Oct. 21, 1801; MS letter, Kemble to unnamed correspondent, Oct. 11, 1801, Harvard Theatre Collection; British Museum Ad. MS 25,915; MS letter, King to Kemble, Apr. 23, 1801, Harvard Theatre Collection; MS letter, Kemble to Peake, Dec. 2, 1801, Harvard Theatre Collection; Cibber, *Apology*, II, 112–113.

25. Paul, *Godwin*, II, 65–70; Boaden, *Mrs. Jordan*, II, 63–64; Boaden, II, 278–279; *Theatrical Repertory*, Nov. 7, 1801, Feb. 8, 1802.

26. *Dramatic Censor*, IV (1801), 136; Harvard Theatre Collection

scrapbook *Kembleiana*, vol. I, clipping, Nov. 10, 1801; *Theatrical Repertory*, Nov. 21, Dec. 7, 1801; Thaler, *Shakspere to Sheridan*, p. 149; *Life*, pp. 15–16; *Remarks on Mr. John Kemble's Performance*, p. 2; *Theatrical Recorder*, Nov. 30, 1801.

27. Byron, *Letters*, V, 437; Dunlap, *Diary*, II, 428; Bernard, *Retrospections of America*, p. 371; Boaden, II, 289.

28. *Theatrical Repertory*, Dec. 21, 28, 1801; Mar. 1, 29, 1802; *Journal*, Mar. 25, 1802; *Monthly Mirror*, XIII (1802), 281–282; Boaden, II, 314.

29. Genest, VII, 565.

CHAPTER XII

1. White, *Algunos Intérpretes Ingleses de Hamlet*, p. 22; Raven, *'Hamlet' Bibliography*, p. 255; *Examiner*, Dec. 15, 1816; Hazlitt, *Works*, XVIII, 198; Hunt, *Autobiography*, I, 147; *Thespiad*, pp. 15–16; Douglas, *Diaries*, II, 216; *Candid and Impartial Strictures*, p. 2; Hunt, *Dramatic Essays*, p. 7; Fitzgerald, I, 61.

2. *Eccentricities of John Edwin*, II, 339; Hunt, *Dramatic Essays*, p. 4; Collier, *Old Man's Diary . . . for the First Six Months of 1833*, p. 4; *Farington Diary*, VIII, 107.

3. Edward Young, *Letters*, pp. 57–58; Sarah Fielding, *David Simple*, I, 151.

4. Boaden, *Mrs. Siddons*, II, 252; *Fortnightly Review*, XXXVI (1906), 327; Parsons, *The Incomparable Siddons*, p. 137.

5. Wilson, *Memoirs*, I, 61; Taylor, *Poems*, I, 35; II, 15; M. R. Mitford, *Recollections*, p. 153.

6. "Remarks" prefixed to Cumberland's *Wheel of Fortune* in *The British Theatre*, vol. VII; Hunt, *Autobiography*, I, 175.

7. Taylor, *Records*, p. 82; Pearson, *Swan of Lichfield*, p. 300; Tieck, *Dramaturgische Blätter*, II, 170; Wilkinson, *Wandering Patentee*, II, 5; Holcroft, *Theatrical Record*, I (1805), 274; Hunt, *Dramatic Essays*, p. 224.

8. Macready, *Reminiscences*, p. 112; Gilliland, *Dramatic Mirror*, II, 807; Savits, *Shakespeare und die Bühne des Dramas*, p. 17; *British Public Characters of 1798*, I, 370; Boaden, I, 257; *Monthly Mirror*, III (1797), 118; Hunt, *Dramatic Essays*, p. 8; Tieck, *Dramaturgische Blätter*, II, 138.

9. *Thespiad*, p. 16; *Children of Thespis*, p. 48; *Theatric Tourist*, p. 60; *Quarterly Review*, XXXIV (1826), 223; Kelly, *Reminiscences*, II, 250; Hunt, *Dramatic Essays*, p. 7; Reynolds, *Life and Times*, I, 151; *Johnson's England* (ed. Turberville), II, 182; *Theatrical Repertory*, Sept. 26, 1801; Bernard, *Retrospections*, II, 203; Davies, *Dramatic Miscellanies*, III, 150; *Theatrical Inquisitor*, II (1813), 103.

10. Hunt, *Dramatic Essays*, p. 11; *Dramatic Censor*, 1811, 429–434;

Mathews, *Memoirs*, II, 221; Taylor, *Records*, p. 241; *Boswell's Life of Johnson* (ed. Croker), p. 560, n. 3; Hunt, *Autobiography*, I, 179; Wilson, *Noctes Ambrosianae*, III, 304–305.

11. Hazlitt, *Works*, XVIII, 166; Hunt, *Autobiography*, II, 141; Robinson, *Diary*, I, 71–72; Sichel, *Sheridan*, I, 605; Wilkinson, *Wandering Patentee*, II, 28–29; Hunt, *Dramatic Essays*, p. 5; Scott, *Familiar Letters*, I, 278; Lockhart, *Scott*, II, 262–263; Mantzius, *History of Theatrical Art*, VI, 31.

12. Hazlitt, *Works*, XX, 315; Boaden, I, 295; Taylor, *Records*, p. 270; Kelly, *Reminiscences*, II, 64; Gillies and Constable, *Personal Reminiscences*, p. 300; Hazlitt, *Works*, XII, 305.

13. *Festival of Wit*, I, 122; Hunt, *Dramatic Essays*, p. 8; Gilliland, *Dramatic Mirror*, II, 808; Moore, *Memoirs*, V, 13; Ryan, *Dramatic Table Talk*, II, 18; *Theatric Tourist*, pp. 51–52.

14. *Quarterly Review*, XXXIV (1826), 215; Macready, *Reminiscences*, p. 112; *Boswell's Life of Johnson* (ed. Croker), p. 742; Boaden, II, 523; *Theatrical Recorder*, I (1805), 274.

15. Boaden, I, 279; Macready, *Reminiscences*, p. 110; *Variorum . . . Coriolanus* (ed. Furness), p. 730; Kilbourne, *Alterations and Adaptations of Shakespeare*, pp. 125–126; "Remarks" prefixed to *Coriolanus, British Theatre* (ed. Inchbald), vol. VI; Galt, *Lives of the Players*, II, 273; Tieck, *Dramaturgische Blätter*, II, 164; *Quarterly Review*, XXXIV (1826), 224.

16. *Bell's Weekly Messenger*, May 10, 1817; Boaden, II, 527; Macready, *Reminiscences*, p. 101; Hazlitt, *Works*, VI, 356; Talfourd, *Dramatic Works*, p. 6.

17. Lamb, *Works*, p. 291; *Remarks on Mr. Kemble's Performance*, pp. 2–3; Davies, *Dramatic Miscellanies*, III, 150; Cumberland in *The Theatrical Inquisitor*, II (1813), 102; *A Short Criticism . . . of Hamlet*, passim; Galt, *Lives*, II, 255–256; Gilliland, *Dramatic Synopsis*, pp. 117–124; Gilliland, *Dramatic Mirror*, II, 811; *Quarterly Review*, XXXIV (1826), 219; *Theatrical Repertory*, Jan. 25, 1802; Boaden, I, 344; II, 307; Tieck, II, 153; Bernard, *Retrospections*, I, 227; Kelly, *Reminiscences*, I, 345; *Cabinet*, I (1807), 204–205; "Remarks" prefixed to *King John, The British Theatre*, vol. VIII; Hunt, *Dramatic Essays*, p. 225; Campbell, *Mrs. Siddons*, p. 229; *Monthly Mirror*, N.S. III (1808), 461; Taylor, *Records*, p. 249; Planché, *Recollections*, I, 23; Lamb, *Works*, 298; Hazlitt, *Works*, XVIII, 341; *Farington Diary*, I, 202; Lockhart, *Scott*, V, 228.

18. Walpole, *Letters*, IX, 215; *Farington Diary*, I, 202; "Remarks" prefixed to *Othello, The British Theatre*, vol. V; Hunt, *Dramatic Essays*, p. 5; Harrison, *Payne*, p. 46; *Remarks on Mr. John Kemble's . . . Hamlet and Richard the Third*, pp. 10, 19; Young, *Memoir of Charles Mayne Young*, I, 62; Downes, *Roscius Anglicanus*, p. 24; Camp-

bell in *University of Wisconsin Studies in Language and Literature,* II (1918), 194; MacMillan, *Drury Lane Calendar,* pp. xxviii–xxxiii; Nicoll, *Development of the Theatre,* pp. 177 ff.; *Some General Advice to Theatrical Managers,* p. 24.

19. British Museum Ad. MS 38,621, R. J. Smith's notes on the drama, f. 187; *Connoisseur* (1803), I, 209; Nicoll, *Late Eighteenth Century Drama,* p. 36.

20. Boaden, I, 104; Genest, VIII, 616–617; *Critical Observations on Mr. Kemble's Performances at the Theatre Royal, Liverpool,* p. 8; *Morning Post,* Oct. 8, 1788; *Quarterly Review,* XXXIV (1826), 226; Scott, *Familiar Letters,* I, 198–199; *Morning Chronicle,* Nov. 7, 1783; Seward, *Letters,* I, 165; Fanny Kemble, *Records of a Girlhood,* p. 190; Boaden, I, 256, 326; *Monthly Mirror,* N.S., III (1808), 329; *New Spectator,* No. 2, Feb. 10, 1784; Genest, VIII, 618; Kemble's annotation of a playbill for *Macbeth,* Nov. 25, 1776, quoted from Harvard Theatre Collection photostat of the Huntington Library original; Nicoll, *English Theatre,* p. 151.

21. Bellamy, *Apology,* I, 130; Boaden, *Mrs. Siddons,* II, 62; *Morning Chronicle,* Jan. 5, Oct. 19, Dec. 4, 1784; *London Magazine,* IV (1785), 138; Austen, *Mansfield Park,* chap. XIV; *Morning Post,* Oct. 24, 1785; *World,* Oct. 15, 1788.

22. *Authentic Narrative of Mr. Kemble's Retirement,* p. 6; *Dramatic Synopsis,* p. 131; *Drama, or, Theatrical Pocket Magazine,* IV (1823), 21; *Examiner,* Jan. 21, 1810; Planché, *Recollections,* I, 53; *The Theatre; or the Letters of Candidus,* p. 64; Nicoll, *Development of the Theatre,* p. 193.

23. Macready, *Reminiscences,* p. 101; Hunt, *Dramatic Essays,* p. 128; *Quarterly Review,* XXXIV (1826), 227; Douglas, *Diaries,* II, 217; Fanny Kemble, *Records of a Girlhood,* p. 190; Lamb, *Works,* p. 302; Tieck, II, 142; *Theatrical Recorder,* I (1805), 430; *Bell's Weekly Messenger,* Dec. 24, 1803.

24. Taylor, *Records,* p. 317; *Monthly Mirror,* N.S., II (1807), 359; Mathews, *Charles Mathews,* I, 259; Kemble's reading notes, Folger Library; *Theatrical Review,* p. 48; Nicoll, *Late Eighteenth Century Drama,* p. 35; *Oracle,* Oct. 22, 1795.

25. Carey, *Chrononhontonthologos,* sc. i; Watson, *Sheridan to Robertson,* p. 165; *Select British Theatre,* I, vii; Lawrence in *The Magazine of Art,* XVIII (1895), 172 ff., 289 ff.; Sprague Allen, *Tides in English Taste,* II, 86; Gray, *Works,* II, 280; cf. Addison, *The Drummer,* Act I.

26. Nicoll, *Late Eighteenth Century Drama,* pp. 29–30; J. M. Brown, *Modern Theatre in Revolt,* p. 29; Boaden, I, xx–xxi.

27. Foote, *Companion to the Theatres,* p. 120; Planché, *Recollections,* I, 54; Forster, *Dramatic Essays,* p. 55; *Bell's Weekly Messenger,* Nov. 3, 1805; Lockhart, *Peter's Letters to his Kinsfolk,* p. 179; Gilliland,

Dramatic Synopsis, p. 23; Nicoll, *Late Eighteenth Century Drama*, p. 35; Young, *Memoir of Charles Mayne Young*, I, 60.

CHAPTER XIII

1. Boaden, II, 355-356; *Quarterly Review*, XXXIV (1826), 231; *Oxberry's Dramatic Biography*, I, 173; Harvard Theatre Collection *Kembleiana*, vol. I.

2. Boaden, II, 357; Howe, *Hazlitt*, p. 63; Lady Holland, *Journal*, II, 161; *Biographie Universelle (Michaud)*, XXI, 509-510; *Annual Biography*, VIII (1824), 26; *Farington Diary*, II, 34; *Monthly Mirror*, XIX (1802), 132; Sandford, *Poole*, II, 85-86; Kelly, *Reminiscences*, II, 194.

3. *Monthly Mirror*, XV (1803), 188; XIV (1802), 132-133; MS letter, Kemble to Talma, May 14, 1816, Folger Library; Hémon, *Cours de Littérature à l'image des Divers Examen*, VI (1893), 67; *New Monthly Magazine and Literary Journal*, XXVIII (1830), 460.

4. MS letter, Priscilla Kemble to Mrs. Inchbald, Forster MS 322, South Kensington Museum; Harvard Theatre Collection *Kembleiana*, vol. I; Boaden, II, 360, 362, n.; *Farington Diary*, III, 254; *Monthly Mirror*, XV (1803), 57; *Drama, or, Theatrical Pocket Magazine*, IV (1823), 267; Roger Kemble's will, Folger Library.

5. *Monthly Mirror*, XV (1803), 198; MS letter, Priscilla Kemble to Mrs. Inchbald, Forster MS 322, South Kensington Museum; Fitzgerald, *New History*, II, 236; *Farington Diary*, II, 186; Wyndham, *Annals of Covent Garden Theatre*, I, 296; Boaden, II, 375-376; Covent Garden ledgers, British Museum Egerton MS 2305; Bunn, *The Stage*, I, 64; Boaden, *Mrs. Jordan*, II, 137; Covent Garden account book, British Museum Ad. MS 29,953.

6. Genest, XII, 597; Penley, *Bath Stage*, p. 89; Genest, VII, 596-598; MS letter, Priscilla Kemble to Mrs. Inchbald, Forster MS 322, South Kensington Museum; Boaden, II, 376, 381; Boaden, *Mrs. Jordan*, II, 124, 143; Gower, *Private Correspondence* (ed. Countess Granville), I, 481; Gilliland, *Dramatic Synopsis*, p. 28; *Quarterly Review*, XXXIV (1826), 232; *Kembliana* (1804), p. 7; Eaton, *Actor's Heritage*, p. 288; *Life of John Philip Kemble*, pp. 30-31; Dibdin, *Reminiscences*, I, 400-401; Gilliland, *Dramatic Mirror*, II, 814; Hunt, *Dramatic Essays*, p. 104; *Thespiad*, p. 19, n.; Dunlap, *Cooke*, I, 225.

7. Hunt, *Dramatic Essays*, p. xviii; Taylor, *Records*, p. 317; Boaden, II, 374; Harral, *Infant Roscius*, p. 41; Bernard, *Retrospections*, I, 226.

8. Boaden, *Mrs. Jordan*, II, 75-78; Covent Garden ledger, British Museum Egerton MS 2302; British Museum Ad. MS 29,954; Gilliland, *Elbow Room*, p. 6; *Kembliana*, p. 18.

9. Odell, *Shakespeare from Betterton to Irving*, II, 96; *Monthly Mirror*, XVII (1804), 132; Harral, *Infant Roscius*, p. 13; Bisset,

Critical Essays . . . of the Young Roscius, p. 46; Jackson, *Strictures upon the Merits of Young Roscius,* pp. 41–42; *Authentic Sketch of the Life of William Henry West Betty,* p. 27.

10. Merrit, *Memoirs of the Life of Wm. Henry West Betty,* p. 28; *Memoirs of Mr. W. H. W. Betty,* p. 9; *Wonderful Theatrical Progress of W. Hen. West Betty,* pp. 32, 70; Harral, p. 21; Harley, *Authentic Biographical Sketch of . . . Betty,* p. 33; Macready, *Reminiscences,* p. 12.

11. Taylor, *Poems,* I, 82; *Young Roscius Dissected,* p. 8; Hunt, *Autobiography,* I, 172; Fielding, *Covent Garden Journal* (ed. Jensen), no. 3.

12. *Life of Wm. Henry West Betty,* p. 22; *Journal,* Dec. 1, 1804; Harral, p. 22; *Farington Diary,* III, 27; *Roscius in London,* pp. 47–48, 56, 60; *Memoirs of Mr. W. H. W. Betty,* p. 12; *Bell's Weekly Messenger,* Feb. 3, 1804; Rogers, *Reminiscences and Table Talk,* p. 54; *Tribute to the Genius of the Young Roscius,* p. 3; Reynolds, *Life and Times,* II, 364; *Young Rosciad,* p. 19, n.; *Quarterly Review,* XXXIV (1826), 234; Dunlap, *Cooke,* I, 280; Fitzgerald, II, 140.

13. Watson, *Sheridan to Robertson,* p. 62; Russell, *Prose Rosciad,* p. 8; Piozzi, *Marginalia* (ed. Merritt), p. 110; Hazlitt, *Works,* XL, 49; *Farington Diary,* V, 17.

14. *Farington Diary,* III, 27–28, 60, 61; Reynolds, *Life and Times,* II, 362; Cumberland, *Memoirs,* p. 316; *Young Rosciad,* p. 15, n.; Genest, VII, 663–664; *Prose Rosciad,* p. 7, n.; Gower, *Private Correspondence,* II, 13.

15. *Young Roscius Dissected,* p. 19; *Theatrical Recorder,* II (1808), 53; *Prose Rosciad,* pp. 12, 14; *Farington Diary,* V, 142; Marsh, *Clubs of London,* p. 111; *Young Rosciad,* p. 12; Byron, *Correspondence* (ed. Murray), I, 73.

16. Master Betty posters, Harvard Theatre Collection; Rogers, *Reminiscences and Table Talk,* p. 55.

17. *Theatrical Recorder,* II (1805), 347; Stanley Williams, *Washington Irving,* I, 71–72; *Two Duchesses* (ed. Vere Foster), p. 250; Hillebrand, *Kean,* p. 28; *Journal,* Nov. 23, 1805; Williams, p. 39; *Monthly Mirror,* XX (1805), 341; Russell, *Representative Actors,* p. 363; Byron, *Correspondence,* II, 159.

18. Kelly, *Reminiscences,* II, 236–239; Campbell, *Mrs. Siddons,* p. 329.

19. *Bell's Weekly Messenger,* Oct. 5, 1806; *Journal,* March 8, Apr. 10, 1806; Hunt, *Dramatic Essays,* p. 139; *Monthly Mirror,* XXI (1806), 412; British Museum Egerton MS 2304, Ad. MS 29,956.

20. *Monthly Mirror,* XXII (1806), 346; Robinson, *Diary,* I, 147; *Bell's Weekly Messenger,* Nov. 9, 1806; *Cabinet,* II (1807), 119 ff.; Boaden, II, 428–429.

21. Marsh, *Clubs of London*, p. 105; Genest, VIII, 47; *Cabinet*, I (1807), 69; *Monthly Mirror*, XXII (1806), 766; Dunlap, *Cooke*, I, 327; Hawkins, *Kean*, I, 62.

22. *Theatrical Review*, p. 138; Dunlap, *Cooke*, I, 332; British Museum Egerton MS 2305, Ad. MS 29,957; *Farington Diary*, IV, 161; V, 208; Boaden, II, 435.

23. *Cabinet*, III (1808), 136; *Farington Diary*, IV, 161; *Examiner*, Jan. 21, 1808; Boaden, II, 448; *Monthly Mirror*, N.S. III (1808), 51, 129, 130, 268, 337-338; Genest, VIII, 91 ff.; Gilliland, *Elbow Room*, p. 8, n.; Dibdin, *Annals of the Edinburgh Stage*, pp. 242-243; Lockhart, *Scott*, II, 95.

24. *Monthly Mirror*, N.S. IV (1808), 386; Stockdale, *Covent Garden Journal*, I, 41; Smeeton's *Authentic Statement of the Dreadful Conflagration of Covent Garden Theatre*, pp. 8, 11-14; Boaden, II, 458-459, 468.

25. *Journal*, Sept. 20, 1808; Dunlap, *Cooke*, II, 452; MS letter, Kemble to Dr. Burney, Dec. 26, 1808, Folger Library; *Monthly Mirror*, N.S. V (1809), 123; Taylor, *Records*, p. 290; *Cabinet*, IV (1808), 357; MS letter, Kemble to Charles Sharp, Harvard Theatre Collection; MS letter, Kemble to William Earle, Harvard Theatre Collection.

26. Genest, VIII, 127; *Examiner*, Sept. 25, Dec. 11, 1808; British Museum Egerton MS 2307; Ad. MS 29,631; Jerrold, *Story of Dorothy Jordan*, p. 290; *Farington Diary*, V, 208; Barrington, *Personal Sketches*, II, 45; Sergeant, *Mrs. Jordan*, p. 244.

Chapter XIV

1. Howard, *Thoughts on the Present Condition of the Stage*, pp. 5-6; *Morning Chronicle*, Nov. 4, 1809; Galt, *Lives of the Players*, II, 276; Foote, *Companion to the Theatres*, pp. 45-50; Stockdale, *Covent Garden Journal*, I, 46-62; Boaden, II, 376-377; Lewis, *Selection of the Letters of Horace Walpole*, p. 140; MacMillan, *Drury Lane Calendar*, pp. xvi-xx.

2. *Statesman*, Nov. 6, 1809; *Reason versus Passion*, p. 37; Williams, *Kemble*, p. 48; Thaler, *Shakspere to Sheridan*, p. 37; Fitzgerald, *New History*, I, 222-223.

3. Boaden, II, 493; *Times*, Sept. 13, 1809; *Examiner*, Nov. 19, 1809; Keats, "The Castle Builder," l. 17; Plumptre, *Inquiry into the Lawfulness of the Stage*, p. 25; *Monthly Mirror*, N.S., III (1808), 117; Puckler-Muskau, *Tour in England, Ireland, and France*, p. 43; *Quarterly Review*, XXXIV (1826), 237; *"What-Do-You-Want?" Explained in a Poetical Epistle*, p. 17; *Address to the Ladies on the Indecency of Appearing at Immodest Plays* (1756), p. 14; Nicholson, *Struggle for a Free Stage*, p. 177; *Four Letters on the Theatre*, pp. 2-3;

The Rebellion, p. 6; *Covent Garden Journal,* I, 155; *Letter to John Kemble,* pp. 8–9, 13–14; Watson, *Sheridan to Robertson,* p. 14; Smollet, *Roderick Random,* chap. XLV, Southey, *Espriella Letters,* I, 192; Irving, *John Gay's London,* p. 339; Macaulay, *History,* chap. III; Pierce Egan, *Life in London,* chap. IX; Richardson, *Clarissa Harlowe,* letter XL; *Poems on Affairs of State,* II, 374.

4. *Old Prices,* p. 16; *Few Strictures on the Engagement of Mad. Catalini,* p. 8; Cibber, *Apology,* II, 88–89; Ralph, *Taste of the Town,* p. 13; Abraham Hill, *Familiar Letters,* pp. 16–17; Wilkinson, *Memoirs,* II, 29; Nicholson, *Struggle,* p. 57; Byron, *Don Juan,* IV, xxxiii–xc.

5. Hunt, *Autobiography,* I, 137; Kelly, *Reminiscences,* II, 187; *Short Address to the Public,* p. 6; *Four Letters on the Theatre,* p. 11; *Rebellion,* p. 7; Boaden, II, 494; *Dramatic Scorpion,* p. 56; *Few Strictures,* p. 7.

6. Puckler-Muskau, *Tour,* p. 43; Gray, *Works,* III, 156–157; *Stage Condemn'd,* p. 114; Nicoll, *Development of the Theatre,* p. 170; Lord Brougham, *Life,* I, 91; Sarah Fielding, *David Simple,* I, 119–120.

7. Victor, *History of the Theatres of London and Dublin,* I, 44–46; MacMillan, *Drury Lane Calendar,* p. xiii; Hitchcock, *Historical View of the Irish Stage,* I, 248; *Some Considerations On the Establishment of the French Strollers* (1749), pp. 3–4, 19; Green, *Minuet,* pp. 18–19; Thaler, *Shakspere to Sheridan,* p. 145; *Monthly Mirror,* I (1796), 245; *Rejected Addresses* (ed. Boyle), p. 150; *Theatrical Recorder,* I (1805), 359–360; Kelly, *Reminiscences,* II, 230–233; Tieck, *Dramaturgische Blätter,* II, 169.

8. Williams, p. 44; *Examiner,* Sept. 24, 1809; *Rebellion,* p. 2; *Reason versus Passion,* p. 12; *Covent Garden Journal,* I, 149–150; Clayden, *Rogers,* I, 63–64; Roberts, *Rogers,* p. 286; Dunlap, *Cooke,* II, 88–90.

9. *Reason versus Passion,* p. 20; *Rejected Addresses,* p. 54; *La Belle Assemblee,* VII (1809), 124; *Statesman,* Nov. 6, 1809; Lawrence, *Letter-Bag,* pp. 63–64; Boaden, II, 498; *Examiner,* Sept. 24, 1809; *Covent Garden Journal,* I, 150; *Rebellion,* p. 4; Tegg, *Rise, Progress, and Termination of the O.P. War,* p. 3.

10. Williams, p. 50; *Rebellion,* p. 5; Boaden, II, 495; Tegg, p. 6; Lawrence, *Letter-Bag,* p. 64; De Quincey, *Selected Writings,* p. 154.

11. Kemble's journal, memorandum at beginning of 1791–1792 season; *Covent Garden Journal,* I, 153, 154, 155; *Rebellion,* p. 7; Lawrence, *Letter-Bag,* p. 64.

12. *Covent Garden Journal,* I, 155–157; Tegg, pp. 12–13; Dunlap, *Cooke,* II, 101; Rogers, *Reminiscences and Table Talk,* p. 48; Boaden, II, 496; *Life,* p. 49.

13. Williams, p. 51; *A Letter to John Kemble,* p. 7; *Statesman,* Oct.

13. Keats, *Letters*, II, 409; Nicoll, *English Theatre*, p. 170; Taylor, *Records*, p. 314; Robinson, *Diary*, I, 274.

14. Hawkins, *Kean*, I, 242, 358; Stirling, *Old Drury Lane*, II, 148–149; Irving, *English Actors*, p. 58; Boaden, II, 555; Young, *Memoir*, I, 65; Marsh, *Clubs of London*, pp. 114–115; Hunt, *Dramatic Essays*, p. 223.

15. Hunt, *Dramatic Essays*, p. 223; Hazlitt, *Works*, XVIII, 298.

16. *Select British Theatre* (ed. Kemble), I, viii; Woodward, *Familiar Verses*, p. 9.

17. *Plays of William Shakspeare* (ed. Johnson and Stevens), XI, 266–269; Kemble, *Macbeth, and King Richard the Third*, 1817, p. 8.

18. Campbell, *Mrs. Siddons*, p. 358; *New Monthly Magazine*, V (1816), 453; *Farington Diary*, VIII, 1; *Examiner*, June 17, 1816; undated clipping, Harvard Theatre Collection.

19. MS letters, Kemble to Elliston, Harvard Theatre Collection; Macready, *Reminiscences*, pp. 87–88; Broadbent, *Annals of the Liverpool Stage*, p. 129; MS letter, Kemble to the Ipswich manager, July 8, 1816, Folger Library; *Farington Diary*, VIII, 7–8.

20. MS letter, Kemble to Talma, May 14, 1816, Folger Library.

21. Watson, *Sheridan to Robertson*, pp. 166–167; Hazlitt, *Works*, XVIII, 225; Boaden, II, 257; *Theatrical Inquisitor*, II (1813), 102; Mudford, *Cumberland*, p. 466.

22. Child, *Shakespearian Productions of John Philip Kemble*, p. 4; Cheney, *The Theatre*, p. 395; Cole, *Kean*, I, 37; *Bell's Weekly Messenger*, May 10, 1817; Hunt, *Dramatic Essays*, pp. 215–216; Harrison, *John Howard Payne*, p. 54.

CHAPTER XVI

1. Lockhart, *Scott*, III, 106; Scott, *Some Unpublished Letters*, p. 93; Scott, *Familiar Letters*, I, 429; Constable and Gillies, *Personal Reminiscences*, p. 302; *The Sale-Room*, Apr. 5, 1817.

2. Lockhart, *Scott*, III, 107–108; Ryan, *Dramatic Table Talk*, I, 246–248; Cockburn, *Jeffrey*, I, 254; Forster, *Dramatic Essays*, pp. ix–x.

3. MS letter, Kemble to unnamed correspondent, Apr. 4, 1817, Harvard Theatre Collection; *Farington Diary*, VIII, 96; *Examiner*, Oct. 28, 1816; Macready, *Reminiscences*, pp. 101–102.

4. *Morning Post*, June 16, 1817; *Examiner*, Dec. 9, 1816; Hazlitt, *Works*, XVIII, 225, 231, 233–234; *New Monthly Magazine*, VII (1817), 452; *Farington Diary*, VIII, 131; Macready, *Reminiscences*, p. 111; *Le Telescope Dramatique*, June 1, 1817; Ryan, *Dramatic Table Talk*, I, 231.

5. Taylor, *Poems*, II, 15–18; MS letter, Kemble to unnamed correspondent, Apr. 25, 1817, Harvard Theatre Collection; Roberts, *Rogers and his Circle*, p. 110; Tieck, II, 163; Fitzgerald, *Letters . . . to Fanny*

Kemble, p. 176; *Nineteenth Century*, VII (1880), 276–296; *British Stage and Literary Cabinet*, I (1817), 154; Harrison, *Payne*, p. 48.

6. *Annual Biography*, VIII (1824), 37; Tieck, II, 166; *New Monthly Magazine*, VIII (1817), 62; *British Stage and Literary Cabinet*, I (1817), 155.

7. *Oxberry's Dramatic Biography*, I, 176; MS letter, Kemble to the banquet committee, June 1, 1817, Harvard Theatre Collection; Clayden, *Rogers*, I, 246–267; Roberts, *Rogers*, p. 110; Taylor, *Poems*, II, 17; Jeffrey, *Contributions to the Edinburgh Review*, II, 457; Beattie, *Campbell*, II, 331; Hawkins, *Kean*, II, 15–16; *Talma: Correspondance avec Madame de Staël*, p. 203; *Authentic Narrative of Mr. Kemble's Retirement, passim*.

8. The Covent Garden ledger, British Museum Ad. MS 29,637; deed of sale, Kemble to Harris, Folger Library; MS letter, Kemble to his banker, July 28, 1817, Folger Library; *Farington Diary*, VIII, 140; Fanny Kemble, *Records of a Girlhood*, p. 35.

9. *Farington Diary*, VIII, 140; Lawrence, *Letter-Bag*, pp. 119–120; Constable and Gillies, *Personal Reminiscences*, pp. 299, 302–303.

10. MS letter, Kemble to M. Vindé, Aug. 3, 1818, Harvard Theatre Collection; Hazlitt, *Works*, XVIII, 355; MS letter, Kemble to Lawrence, Apr. 15, 1820, Harvard Theatre Collection.

11. *Drama, or, Theatrical Pocket Magazine*, IV (1823), 375–376; Taylor, *Records*, p. 291; Wheatley, *London Past and Present*, III, 193; Fanny Kemble, *Records of a Girlhood*, p. 35; Armstrong, *Fanny Kemble*, p. 29; Macready, *Reminiscences*, p. 170.

12. Macready, *Reminiscences*, p. 170; MS indenture, Kemble to Gilbert Heathcote and Gilbert Heathcote, Jr., Jan. 1, 1821, Harvard Theatre Collection; Dunlap, *Diary*, III, 621; *Catalogue of the Excellent Household Furniture . . . of J. P. Kemble, passim*; MS of auctioneer's receipts for the Kemble sale, Harvard Theatre Collection; Robinson, *Diary*, I, 456; *Drama, or, Theatrical Pocket Magazine*, IV (1823), 373; Donaldson, *Recollections of an Actor*, pp. 358–359.

13. *New Monthly Magazine*, IX (1823), 186; *Biographie Universelle (Michaud)*, XXI, 510; Berry, *Journals*, III, 320; Campbell, *Mrs. Siddons*, p. 363; Piozzi, *Letters*, p. 537; Rogers, *Reminiscences and Table Talk*, p. 148; Clayden, *Rogers*, I, 311; Lawrence, *Letter-Bag*, pp. 174–175; Fanny Kemble, *Records of a Girlhood*, p. 105.

14. Macready, *Reminiscences*, p. 182; MS memorandum of Priscilla Kemble's concerning the Lausanne household, Feb. 24, 1823, Harvard Theatre Collection; MS letter, Kemble to Murray, Sept. 7, 1822, Rush Rhees Library, University of Rochester; *Annual Biography*, VIII (1824), 52; Lawrence, *Letter-Bag*, p. 175; *Lodoiska . . . With Prefatory Remarks . . . by W. Oxberry*, p. vii.

15. Lawrence, *Letter-Bag*, p. 175.

16. *Lodoiska*, p. viii; Lawrence, *Letter-Bag*, p. 175.

17. *Lodoiska*, p. viii; Lawrence, *Letter-Bag*, p. 175; *Annual Biography*, VIII (1824), 53–54. Fanny Kemble, *Records of a Girlhood*, p. 36. On the statue of Kemble, executed by Flaxman, that formerly stood in the north transept of Westminster Abbey (until it was removed, with Fanny Kemble's permission), see Stanley, *Westminster Abbey*, p. 337; *Records of a Girlhood*, p. 65; Lawrence, *Letter-Bag*, p. 176; Macready, *Reminiscences*, p. 316; Pratt, *Westminster Abbey*, II, 646; *Literary Gazette, and Journal of Belles Lettres*, Mar. 15, 27, 1823.

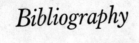

Bibliography

BIBLIOGRAPHY

There follows a list of the books most frequently referred to in the notes. The several hundred not given here have adequate reference when they occur in the notes.

Adolphus, John, *Memoirs of John Bannister, Comedian.* 2 vols., London, 1839.

Authentic Memoirs of the Green-Room (for 1799). London, [1799].

Authentic Memoirs of the Green-Room; Involving Sketches, Biographical, Critical, and Characteristic, of the Performers of the Theatres-Royal. 2 vols., London, n.d.

The Autobiography of Leigh Hunt, with Reminiscences of Friends and Contemporaries. 2 vols., New York, 1850.

Baker, David Erskine; Reed, Isaac; and Jones, Stephen (edd.). *Biographia Dramatica; or, A Companion to the Playhouse.* 3 vols., London, 1812.

Beattie, William, *Life and Letters of Thomas Campbell.* 3 vols., London, 1849.

Bernard, John. *Retrospections of the Stage.* 2 vols., London, 1830.

Boaden, James. *The Life of Mrs. Jordan.* 2 vols., London, 1831. *Memoirs of Mrs. Inchbald.* 2 vols., London, 1833. *Memoirs of the Life of John Philip Kemble, Esq.* 2 vols., London, 1825. *Memoirs of Mrs. Siddons.* 2 vols., London, 1827.

Campbell, Thomas. *Life of Mrs. Siddons.* London, 1839.

Castalia Countess Granville (ed.), *Private Correspondence 1781 to 1821* (of Lord Granville Levenson Gower). 2 vols., London, 1916.

Clayden, P. W. *Rogers and his Contemporaries.* 2 vols., London, 1889.

Colby, Elbridge. *The Life of Thomas Holcroft Written by Himself.* 2 vols., London, 1925.

Coleridge, Ernest Hartley (ed.). *Letters of Samuel Taylor Coleridge.* 2 vols., London, 1895.

The Complete Works and Letters of Charles Lamb. Modern Library Giant, New York, 1935.

Countess of Strafford (ed.). *Leaves from the Diary of Henry Greville.* 4th Series, London, 1905.

Cunningham, Peter (ed.). *The Letters of Horace Walpole Earl of Orford,* 9 vols., London, 1866.

Dunlap, William. *Memoirs of the Life of George Frederick Cooke.* 2 vols., London, 1813.

Familiar Letters of Sir Walter Scott. 2 vols., Boston, 1894.

Fitzgerald, Percy. *The Kembles.* 2 vols., London, [1871].

Genest, John. *Some Account of the English Stage.* 10 vols., Bath, 1832.

Gibbs, J. W. M. (ed.). *The Works of Oliver Goldsmith.* 3 vols., London, 1884.

Gilliland, *The Dramatic Mirror.* 2 vols., London, 1808. *A Dramatic Synopsis.* London, 1804.

Gray, Charles Harold. *Theatrical Criticism in London to 1795.* Columbia University Press, 1931.

Grieg, James (ed.). *The Farington Diary by Joseph Farington, R.A.* 8 vols., London, 1923–1928.

Griggs, Earl Leslie (ed.). *Unpublished Letters of Samuel Taylor Coleridge.* 2 vols., London, 1932.

[Haslewood, Joseph.] *The Secret History of the Green Room.* 2 vols., London, 1790.

Henderson, Emily (Adolphus). *Recollections of . . . John Adolphus.* London, 1871.

Hill, George Birkbeck (ed.). *Boswell's Life of Johnson.* 6 vols., New York, 1891.

Howe, P. P. (ed.). *The Complete Works of William Hazlitt.* 21 vols., London and Toronto, 1933–1934.

Hunt, Leigh. *Dramatic Essays* (ed. William Archer and Robert W. Lowe), London, 1894.

Ilchester, the Earl of (ed.). *The Journal of Elisabeth Lady Holland.* 2 vols., London, 1908.

Irving, Henry and Marshall, Frank A. (edd.). *The Works of William Shakespeare.* 8 vols., London, 1888 ff.

Kemble, Frances Ann. *Records of a Girlhood.* New York, 1879.

Layard, George Somes. *Sir Thomas Lawrence's Letter-Bag.* London, 1906.

Letters of Anna Seward. 6 vols., Edinburgh, 1811.

[Lewes, Charles Lee.] *Memoirs of Charles Lee Lewes.* 4 vols., London, 1805.

Lewis, W. S. (ed.). *A Selection of the Letters of Horace Walpole.* New York and London, 1926.

The Life and Times of Frederick Reynolds. Written by Himself. 2 vols., London, 1826.

The Life of John Philip Kemble, Esquire. London, [1809].

Lockhart, John Gibson. *Memoirs of Sir Walter Scott.* 5 vols., London, 1900.

Lowe, Robert W. (ed.). *An Apology for the Life of Mr. Colley Cibber Written by Himself.* 2 vols., London, 1889.

Lucas, E. V. (ed.). *The Letters of Charles Lamb.* 3 vols., [London], 1935.

MacMillan, Dougald. *Drury Lane Calendar 1747–1776.* Oxford University Press, 1938.

[Marsh, Charles.] *The Clubs of London.* 2 vols., London, 1828.

Mathews, Anne. *Memoirs of Charles Mathews, Comedian.* 4 vols., London, 1838.

Matthews, Brander (ed.). *The Dramatic Essays of Charles Lamb.* New York, 1891.

Memoirs of Richard Cumberland. Written by Himself. New York, 1806.

Moore, Thomas. *Memoirs of the Life of the Right Honourable Richard Brinsley Sheridan.* 2d ed., 2 vols., London, 1825.

Murray, John (ed.). *Lord Byron's Correspondence.* 2 vols., London, 1922.

A Narrative of the Life of Mrs. Charlotte Charke . . . Written by Herself. London, 1755.

Nicoll, Allardyce. *A History of Late Eighteenth Century Drama, 1750–1800.* Cambridge University Press, 1927.

Odell, George C. D. *Shakespeare from Betterton to Irving.* 2 vols., New York, 1920.

[Oulton, Walley Chamberlain.] *The History of the Theatres of London.* 2 vols., London, 1796.

Oxberry's Dramatic Biography and Histrionic Anecdotes. 2 vols., London, 1826.

Partington, Wilfred (ed.). *The Private Letter-Books of Sir Walter Scott.* New York, 1930.

Paul, C. Kegan. *William Godwin: His Friends and Contemporaries.* 2 vols., London, 1876.

Pearson, Hesketh (ed.). *The Swan of Lichfield.* London, 1936.

Pollack, Sir Edward (ed.). *Macready's Reminiscences.* New York, 1875.

Powell, G. H. (ed.). *Reminiscences and Table Talk of Samuel Rogers.* London, 1903.

Prior, Sir James. *Life of Edmond Malone.* London, 1860.

Prothero, Rowland (ed.). *The Works of Lord Byron . . . Letters and Journals.* 6 vols., London, 1922–1924.

Reminiscences of Michael Kelly, 2d ed., 2 vols., London, 1826.

Roberts, R. Ellis. *Samuel Rogers and his Circle.* London, 1910.

Sadler, Thomas (ed.). *Diary, Reminiscences and Correspondence of Henry Crabb Robinson.* 2 vols., Boston, 1869.

[Scott, Sir Walter.] Revue of Boaden's *Memoirs of the Life of John Philip Kemble, Quarterly Review,* XXXIV (1826), 196–242.

Sichel, Walter. *Sheridan.* 2 vols., Boston and New York, 1909.

Specimens of the Table Talk of the Late Samuel Taylor Coleridge. 2 vols., London, 1835.

Stoddard, Richard H. (ed.). *Personal Reminiscences by Constable and Gillies.* New York, 1876.

Taylor, John. *Poems on Various Subjects.* 2 vols., London, 1827. *Records of my Life.* New York, 1833.

Thaler, Alwin. *Shakspere to Sheridan.* Harvard University Press, 1932.

The Thespian Dictionary. 2d ed., London, 1805.

Tieck, Ludwig. *Dramaturgische Blätter.* 2 vols., Breslau, 1826.

Watson, Ernest Bradlee. *Sheridan to Robertson.* Harvard University Press, 1926.

Wilkinson, Tate. *Memoirs of his own Life.* 4 vols., York, 1790. *The Wandering Patentee.* 4 vols., York, 1795.

[Williams, John Ambrose.] *The Children of Thespis*. 13th ed., London, 1792. *Memoirs of John Philip Kemble, Esq.* London, 1817. *The Pin Basket*. London, 1796.

Young, Julian Charles. *A Memoir of Charles Mayne Young, Tragedian*. 2 vols., London and New York, 1871.

Most of the newspapers cited are from the incomparable Burney Collection of the British Museum.

Some sixteen letters, various notes and memoranda of Kemble's, Roger Kemble's will, and Ann Hatton's very useful memoir of her family are from the manuscript collection of the Folger Shakespeare Library in Washington, D. C.

The Harvard Theatre Collection has supplied a great store of data: numerous playbills, posters, and theatrical prints; Roger Kemble's professional journal; John Philip Kemble's list of English actors and MS records of the Dublin stage; the manuscript of *The Female Officer*; thirty-three MS letters; notes and memoranda of Priscilla Kemble and others.

From the Larpent Collection of the Huntington Library in San Marino, California, I have used ten MSS of plays which Kemble either wrote or altered: *The Maid of Honour; Oh! 'Tis Impossible; The Female Officer; Belisarius; The Roman Actor; Celadon and Florimel; Love in Many Masks; The School for Scandal Scandalized; The Projects; The Legacy*.

The British Museum has supplied me some thirty-two extremely useful MSS: John Philip Kemble's journal; many letters; the Covent Garden ledgers and account books.

From the Forster Collection of The South Kensington Museum I have used the interesting letters from John and Priscilla Kemble to Elizabeth Inchbald.

Index

INDEX

Where possible, plays are listed both by title and author; unimportant proper names are noted if their context demands. The Notes are not included. The following abbreviations have been used throughout: CG for Covent Garden Theatre; DL for Drury Lane Theatre; JPK for John Philip Kemble.

Abbas, King of Persia, 245
Abercorn, Lord (James Hamilton), as JPK's friend, 141, 143, 290
Aberdeen, Lord (George Hamilton), and JPK, 332, 342
"Academicus," defends JPK, 24
Actor's Fund, and JPK, 322
Actors, English, listed by JPK, 216–217
Addison, Joseph, on opera, 105; *Cato*, 16, 20, 23, 93, 97, 104, 338
Adelaide, 237
Adolphus, John, on JPK's London debut, 84
Adrian and Orilla, 286
Agamunda (Huniades), 177
Aickin, Francis, as JPK's partner at Liverpool, 133–134; duels with JPK, 177–178
Aickin, James, DL manager, 232, 240
Alexander the Great (Lee's *Rival Queens*), 65, 196
Alexander the Great (ballet), 191, 196
All for Love, 27, 71, 119
All in the Wrong, 183
All's Well, 191
Almack's, 57
Almeyda, 209
Alterations, vogue for, 113–114; JPK's published, 328–330. *See also* Kemble, John Philip; Revivals
Amphytryon, 93
Andreozzi, Gaetano, and music for *Lodoiska*, 189
Andrews, Charles, entertains JPK, 172
Anna, 182
Anti-Jacobin, The, quoted, 81
Antonio, 241–242

Antony and Cleopatra, 323
Arne, Thomas, and music for *The Tempest*, 161; *Artaxerxes*, 176
Artaxerxes, 176
As You Like It, 167, 232, 240, 265
Aurelio and Miranda, 232
Austen, Jane, quoted, 263

Baddeley, Robert, roles, 83, 115, 168
Baillie, Joanna, *De Montfort*, 237–238, on JPK, 252
Baker, Mrs. (provincial manager), renown, 14
Ballantyne, John, and JPK, 143
Bampfylde, Charles, and JPK, 148
Bannister, Charles, and JPK, 140
Bannister, John, and JPK's wedding, 111–112; JPK's friend, 142, 144
Barbarossa, 280
Barington, Jonah, duels with Daly, 70
Barry, Spranger, and Garrick, 246
Bath, 16–17, 54, 172, 274–275
Bayonne, 272
Beaumarchais, Pierre Auguste Caron de, JPK's opinion of, 271–272
Beaumont, George, on Betty, 284
Beaux' Stratagem, The, 40, 135
Beckford, William, 267
Beefsteak Club, history of, 150–151, 291; JPK at, 159, 283
Beggars' Opera, The, 16, 191, 304
Behn, Aphra, *Lucky Changes*, 108; *The Rover*, 164–165
Belfast, 278
Belisarius, 33, 35–36, 38, 41–46, 212
Bellamy, Mrs. Anne, on costuming, 263
Belle's Stratagem, The, 65, 69

Below, William, on JPK, 221–222; and the Literary Club, 235

Bernard, John, on strollers' properties, 13; at Smock Alley, 64; touring with JPK, 72–73

Berwick, 238

Betterton, Thomas, style, 276

Betty, William Henry West, popularity, 277–284; return, 319

Bickerstaff, Isaac, *Love in a Village*, 14

Bilbao, 272

Birmingham, 2–8, 32, 34, 231, 234, 243, 331

Blagdon, William, as JPK's friend, 168

Bland, Dorothy, *see* Jordan, Dorothy

Bland, Maria Theresa, and Signora Storace, 197

Blessington, Lady (*née* Marguerite Power), on Sheridan, 239

Blue Beard, 227

Bluestockings, renown, 211; and Fanny Burney, 193; and Joanna Baillie, 238

Boaden, James, on Roger Kemble, 11; and spouting club, 57; on Thelwall and Cobbett, 57; on *Richard Coeur de Lion*, 106–107; on JPK's Lear, 117; on JPK as DL manager, 123; on JPK's revivals, 129; on JPK's fame, 139, 155; on JPK's manner, 146; on the new DL, 184; on the Ireland forgeries, 203, 204; advised by JPK, 215; *Aurelio and Miranda*, 232; on JPK's style, 256; on JPK's Posthumous, 259; on JPK's Cato, 259; on CG fire, 291–292; on O. P. riots, 302

Bond, Thomas, mentioned by JPK, 214

Books, price of, 221

Booth, Barton, 276

Borderers, The, 236

Boswell, James, on Savage's parentage, 34; on intoxication, 146; and the Ireland forgeries, 202–203

Bourgeois, Francis, 99; and JPK, 145–146

Boxes, private, *see* Covent Garden Theatre; O. P. riots

Braganza, 66, 101

Braham, John, fame, 105

Brand, Hannah, *Agamunda*, 177

Brandon, James, and O. P. riots, 309–313

Brecknock, 15, 19–20, 24

Brereton, William, 111

Brereton, Mrs. William, *see* Kemble, Mrs. John Philip

Brighthelmstone (Brighton), 234

Bristol, 24

Bristol Wells, 231

Bromsgrove, 16

Brown, John, *Barbarossa*, 280

Burdett, Francis, and JPK, 148

Burgess, James, prologue to *Vortigern*, 206

Burgoyne, John, *Richard Coeur de Lion*, 104, 105–107; epilogue to *The Tempest*, 162; *The Heiress*, 168

Burke, Edmund, on plays, 42; political career, 82; as orator, 83; and the sublime, 267

Burney, Charles, as JPK's friend, 149, 168, 194

Burney, Fanny (Mme D'Arblay), quoted, 154; *Edwy and Elgiva*, 193–194

Bussy d'Ambois, 214

Butler, Frances Kemble, *see* Kemble, Fanny

Butler, Samuel, quoted, 226

Butterfelt, 72

Byron, Lord (George Gordon), and DL, 124; and Lady Blessington, 234; on playwrighting, 236; on Cooke, 247; on JPK's style, 253, 321; on Betty, 284; on the Regency, 322; solicited by JPK, 324; on Kean, 325, 326

Caleb Williams, 197

Camden, William, 3

Campbell, Thomas, and JPK, 140–141, 224; on JPK's Lear, 260; in Paris with JPK, 323; at JPK banquet, 341

Canning, George, on JPK and Cooke, 244

Canterbury, 7, 34

Capon, William, sets for *Macbeth*, 185; sets for *De Montfort*, 237; technique, 266–268

Captives, The, 101

Careless Husband, The, 134, 154

Carey, Henry, quoted, 106, 266

Carlisle, Earl of (Frederick Howard), on large theatres, 295

Carlisle House, history of, 56–57

Carlyle, Thomas, quoted, 211

Carmelite, The, 97, 99

Carroll, Lewis (Charles L. Dodgson), quoted, 295

Castle of Montval, The, 232

Castle Spectre, The, 228–230

Catalani, Angelica (Mme Valabrègue), furor over, 297–299

Catharine and Petruchio, 119, 247

Cato, 16, 20, 23, 93, 97, 104, 338

Chalmers, George, on the Ireland forgeries, 208 n.

Chamberlain and Crump (provincial managers), Crump with Roger Kemble, 15; hire JPK, 25; hire Henry Siddons, 25; reputation, 25, 39

Charke, Charlotte (née Charlotte Cibber), on strollers, 13; JPK on, 216

Charles the First, 20

Chatterton, Thomas, 206

Cheltenham, 26 n., 29, 30, 77, 234

Cherubine, Maria L. C. Z. S., music for *Lodoiska*, 189

Chesterfield, Lord (Philip Dormer Stánhope), quoted, 79; and licensing act, 80

Chetwood, William, 150

Child, Harold, on JPK's alterations, 158–159

Churchill, Charles, quoted, 3

Cibber, Colley, Wilkinson's opinion of, 45; on opera, 104; on drunkenness, 146–147; *Richard III*, 158, 160; *Apology*, 215; Style, 276; on foreign singers, 297

Cibber, Theophilus, on alterations, 114; at Beefsteak Club, 150

Cirencester, 5–6

Clandestine Marriage, The, 29

Clarence, Duke of (William IV), and Mrs. Jordan, 64, 138; at Beefsteak Club, 150

Cleone, 107

Clifford, Henry, and O. P. riots, 309–315, 316, 318

Clive, Kitty, on foreign singers, 298

Clonmel, 9

Cobb, James, *The Haunted Tower*, 163, 166, 167, 175, 181; unpaid by Sheridan, 244–245

Cobbett, William, on O. P. riots, 313–314

Coleridge, Samuel Taylor, on Kean, 69; on JPK, 141; *Osorio*, 236–237; and Godwin's *Antonio*, 242

Collier, Jeremy, on Beaumont and Fletcher, 114–115; on Restoration comedies, 196

Collier, John Payne, and Ann Hatton, 8 n.; on JPK's plays, 48 n., 50, 286 n.

Colman, George (the elder), *The Clandestine Marriage*, 29

Colman, George (the younger), drinks with JPK, 142; at Beefsteak Club, 150; epilogue to *Macbeth*, 185; *The Mountaineers*, 191; *The Iron Chest* episode, 197–201, 207–208, 227; *Blue Beard*, 227; *John Bull*, 277

Comédie Française, praised by JPK, 125; entertains JPK, 271

Comedy, eighteenth-century, 81

Comedy of Errors, The, 50

Congreve, William, *The Mourning Bride*, 16; quoted, 60; *Love for Love*, 108, 242; obscenity in, 196; *The Double Dealer*, 196, 247

Conspiracy, 227

Conway, Henry Seymour, 66; *False Appearances*, 156

Conway, William A., at CG, 324

Cooke, George Frederick, as a stroller, 12–13; in Ireland, 195; on *The*

Castle Spectre, 229; challenges JPK in *Richard*, 243–244, 246–247; in *Love à la Mode*, 247; with JPK at CG, 275–276, 277, 289–290; and Betty, 282; drunkenness, 286, 304, 317; and *The Tempest*, 288

Cooper, Thomas, rebuffed by JPK, 178–179

Coriolanus, 45, 126, 129, 156, 287, 339–340

Cork, 9, 72, 75, 228

Cork, Lady (Mary Monckton Boyle), 149

Corneille, Pierre, admired by JPK, 214, 215

Cornelys, Theresa, manager of Carlisle House, 56–57

Costuming, in *A New Way*, 62–63; in *Maid of Honour*, 98; in *The Captives*, 101–102; at DL under JPK's management, 126, 128; in *The Tempest*, 162; in spectacle, 176–177; in *Macbeth*, 185, 187; cost, 240; in *The Winter's Tale*, 247; JPK's reforms in, 260–262; at new CG, 302

Cottle, J., and Coleridge, 236

Count Julian, 319

Count of Narbonne, The, 66–68, 70, 119

Countess of Salisbury, The, 93

Country Girl, The, 285

Country Lasses, The (*The Farm House*), 134

Covent Garden Theatre, finances, 274, 277, chap. XIV *passim*, 342, 345–346; private boxes, 277, 296–297, 317–318; fire, 291–292; new theatre, 292–293, 295; new prices, 295–296. *See also* Harris, Thomas; Kemble, John Philip

Coventry, 7–8, 16, 194

Cowley, Hannah, *The Belle's Stratagem*, 65, 69; *A School for Graybeards*, 108; *The Fate of Sparta*, 118; and the *World*, 127

Critique de l'Ecole des Femmes, 50

Cross, Wilbur, on the novel, 82–83

Crouch, Anna Maria Phillips, courted by JPK, 72–75; and Michael Kelly,

75; in *Richard Coeur de Lion*, 106; difficulties over salary, 131; in *The Tempest*, 162; in *Cymon*, 177; in *Lodoiska*, 189; in *Macbeth*, 263

Culberson, Miss, *Anna*, 182

Cumberland, Richard, as a playwright, 81; on Henderson, 86; *The Carmelite*, 97, 99; *The Impostors*, 156; *The Wheel of Fortune*, 193; and the Literary Club, 235; as JPK's correspondent, 273; and Betty, 282; *A Hint to Husbands*, 287; on JPK's style, 334

Cummins (Yorkshire actor), rivalry with JPK, 46, 47, 52–53; acting ability, 47; as Wilkinson's lieutenant, 55–56

Cymbeline, 45, 101, 240, 242, 289

Cymon, 176, 177, 181–182

Daly, Richard, and Miss Frances, 65; as JPK's manager, 65–77, 194, 228, 238; altercation with JPK, 69–70; as a duellist, 70

D'Avenant, William, *The Tempest*, 21; *Macbeth*, 185; mentioned by JPK, 214; production of *Henry VIII*, 260

Davies, Thomas, on JPK's London debut, 83, 89, 259

Deaf and Dumb, 242

Declamation, basis of JPK's style, 253

Dejaure, Jean-Elie Bedenc, *Lodoiska*, 187

Delap, John, *The Captives*, 101–102, 262

Della Cruscans, patronized by JPK, 118–119; connection with Parson Este, 127; and the *World*, 127

De Montfort, 237–238

Dent, Edward, on English opera, 106

De Quincey, Thomas, and Coleridge's *Osorio*, 236–237; on English mobs, 303

Derby, Lord (Edward Stanley), as JPK's friend, 142

Desenfans, Noel Joseph, and JPK, 146, 289

Devil to Pay, The, 16

Devonshire, Duke of (William Spencer Cavendish), buys JPK's library, 222, 342; entertains, 243

Dibdin, Thomas, *The English Fleet,* 277; *The White Plume,* 287

Dignum, Charles, in *Vortigern,* 206

Distressed Mother, The, 46, 54, 264

Dobson, Susanna, befriends JPK, 46

Dodsley, Robert, *Cleone,* 107

Doncaster, 40, 45, 55

Douay, refuge for the Kembles, 4, 22; JPK at, 22–24; Charles Kemble at, 163–164; revisited by JPK, 271

Double Dealer, The, 196, 247

Douce, Francis, and JPK's revivals, 268

Douglas, 190, 280

Downes, John, on Shadwell, 161; on D'Avenant, 260

Drama, English, at close of 18th century, 80–83. *See also* Alterations; German drama; Spectacle; and entries for individual authors

Dramatic Censor, The, 246

Droitwych, 16

Drury Lane Theatre, Mrs. Siddons' success, 17, 75; hires JPK, 78; decadence, 79–80, 122; JPK's debut at, 83–84; artifices to gain patronage, 79, 154, 162–163; fire, 108; personnel, 124; new DL, 180, 181, 183–187; rehearsals, 198–199; negotiations for patent, 239; and Betty, 279; and Kean, 325–335. *See also* Kemble, John Philip; Sheridan, Richard Brinsley

Dryden, John, *The Tempest,* 21; *Amphytryon,* 93; *The Secular Masque,* 114; *All for Love,* 119; quoted, 121, 189; and opera, 188; JPK's admiration for, 215

Dublin, *see* Kemble, John Philip, for various engagements; Smock Alley Theatre

Dublin theatre, investigated by JPK, 217

Dudley, Henry, on Ireland forgeries, 204

Dudley, Lord (John William Ward), and JPK, 172

Duenna, The, 49, 208

Dunn, William, drinks with JPK, 152

Edinburgh, 40, 55, 58, 62, 63, 94, 143, 178, 196, 232, 322

Edinburgh Review, The, 337

Edward and Eleanora, 227

Edward the Black Prince, 87

Edwy and Elgiva, 193–194

Egremont, Lord (George O'Brien Wyndham), in Paris, 271

Egyptian Festival, The, 237

Elliston, Robert, and *The Iron Chest,* 201 n.; and Keats, 236

Elrington, Thomas, employs John Ward, 9

Emilia Galotti, 191

English College, *see* Douay

English Fleet, The, 277

Erskine, James, on foreign singers, 298

Erskine, Lord Thomas, Malone's opinion of, 213

Estcourt, Richard, and Beefsteak Club, 150

Este, Parson, originates Bishop Warburton anecdote, 28 n.; friendship with JPK, 127–128, 317; and the *World,* 127; on JPK's *Henry VIII,* 128, 129, 218–219; on Cooke, 244

Etherege, George, quoted, 42

European Magazine, The, 82, 89, 90

Examiner, The, 264, 293, 317, 318, 320, 331

Exeter, 231

Fair Penitent, The, 26, 52, 183

False Appearances, 156

False Friend, The, 162

Farington, Joseph, *Diary* quoted, 143, 213, 282–283, 289, 331

Farm House, The (The Country Lasses), 134

Farmer, Richard, and JPK, 213

Farquhar, George, *The Recruiting Officer,* 7; *The Beaux' Stratagem,*

40, 135; on dramatic composition, 235

Farren, Elizabeth (Countess of Derby), and Younger, 31, 34; quarrels with JPK, 132, 154, 168–169; as JPK's guest, 142; in *The Tempest*, 162; in *The False Friend*, 162; as Lady Teazle, 171; as hostess, 172; costumes, 263

Fate of Sparta, The, 118

Feltham, Owen, quoted, 39

Female Officer, The (The Project), 48–50, 101

Fenton, Elijah, 9

Fielding, Henry, on biography, 3; on Fenton, 9; on acting, 47; on academic disputes, 96; on alterations, 113, 157; on critics, 280

Fielding, Sarah, on acting, 251 n.

Fitzgerald, Edward, on JPK's alterations, 160

Fitzpatrick, Richard, prologue for *Macbeth*, 184

Flaxman, John, and JPK, 145

Fletcher, John, *The Maid's Tragedy* (with Francis Beaumont), 98; *Rule a Wife and Have a Wife*, 108; *The Pilgrim*, 113–117

Folger Shakespeare Library, Ann Hatton MS, 18 n.

Foote, Samuel, 39, 80; *The Mayor of Garratt*, 144

Ford, Richard, and Mrs. Jordan, 164

Fox, Charles James, politics, 82; scholarship, 212; on Betty, 281

Francis, Dorothy (née Bland), see Jordan, Dorothy

Fugitive Pieces, 58–61, 212

Furnivall, Fanny, and Roger Kemble, 7–8

Galt, John, on JPK's Coriolanus, 258; on new CG, 295

Gamester, The, 89, 97, 128

Garrick, David, and Wilkinson, 39; *Isabella* (based on Southerne's *Fatal Marriage*), 75, 190; debut, 75; acting tradition, 79; supplanted by new style, 83, 109; style, 84–85; social

status, 137–138; *Jubilee*, 156, 218, 330–331; versatility, 171; *Cymon*, 176, 177, 181–182; and *Macbeth*, 185; quoted, 190; JPK on, 216; and Smollett, 236; and Barry, 246; and costuming, 261; and sets, 267, 268; *The Country Girl* (based on Wycherley's *Country Wife*), 285

Gay, John, *The Beggars' Opera*, 16, 191, 304

Genest, John, on *Lodoiska*, 189

Gentleman's Magazine, The, 68 n., 79

George Barnwell, 16, 251 n.

George III, effect on English life, 81–82; and *Lear*, 117, 316–317; on JPK, 144; on Shakespeare, 157

German drama, 230. See also Kotzebue, August

Gifford, William, on *The Regent*, 118–119; and JPK, 220, 223–224; on *The Castle Spectre*, 229; edits Massinger, 220, 223–224

Gillies, Robert, 343

Gilliland, Thomas, on JPK's plays, 45; on costuming, 264

Glasgow, 196, 238

Glenbervie, Lord (Sylvester Douglas), 144

Glorious First of June, The, 197

Gloucester, 8, 24, 30

Godwin, William, as JPK's guest, 142; and Tom Cooper, 178; *Caleb Williams*, 197; *Antonio*, 241–242; *Abbas, King of Persia* refused by JPK, 245

Goethe, Johann Wolfgang von, quoted, 95; compared to JPK, 255

Gogol, Nikolay V., and German drama, 230

Goldsmith, Oliver, quoted, 26, 28, 137; on bad plays, 229

Goodall, Mrs., altercations with JPK, 129–131

Gordon, Pryse, 152

Gosse, Edmund, quoted, 58

Gray, Thomas, on Guy's Cliff, 227–228; and the antique, 266, 267; on riots, 299

Greatheed, Bertie, *The Regent*, 118; and JPK, 168, 227
Grecian Daughter, The, 74 n., 262
Greenwood (scene painter), 205, 268
Grétry, André E. M., music for *Richard Coeur de Lion*, 106
Greville, Charles, 320
Guilford, Earl of (Francis North), as JPK's friend, 141, 144, 270; Wroxton Abbey, 144, 289, 290, 317; on JPK's *Henry V*, 259
Guy's Cliff, 227, 272

Händel, George Frederick, scores burned, 150, 291
Hamblette, 202
Hamlet, 31–32, 52, 53, 55, 83–85, 86, 96, 101, 194–195, 209–210, 240, 249, 275, 278, 318
Harlequin and Padmandba, 320
Harris, Thomas, rejects Belisarius, 35–36; attempts to hire JPK, 78; as manager, 79; produces *Marcella*, 163; and DL patent, 181; and Ireland forgeries, 204; negotiates with JPK, 270, 273–274; illness, 295; and the CG elephant, 319–320; differs with JPK, 321; death, 345
Hartson, Hall, *The Countess of Salisbury*, 93
Harvard Theatre Collection, bills for Roger Kemble, 15; Roger Kemble's journal, 15–17; MS of *The Female Officer*, 48 n., JPK's letter to Miss De Camp, 192
Hatton, Ann Kemble, on John Ward, 8–9; on her parents, 9–11; and her family, 89–91; lectures, 90; poems, 90; marital career, 90–91; last years, 91–92; and JPK, 91; and her father, 91–92; Roger Kemble's legacy to, 273 n.; JPK's legacy to, 346
Haunted Tower, The, 163, 167, 175, 181
Havard, William, *Charles the First*, 20
Hayley, William, Macaulay's opinion of, 82; *Marcella*, 162–163
Haymarket, riots, 174; Cibber on, 184; CG at, 292

Hazlitt, William, on JPK and Mrs. Inchbald, 59–60; as a critic, 79; on the drama, 83; on JPK's essay, 104; on alterations, 157, 160; sees JPK for first time, 166; on German drama, 230; quoted, 249; on JPK's style, 250, 255, 333–334; on JPK's appearance, 255; on JPK's reputation, 256; on JPK's Macbeth, 260; in Paris, 271; on JPK's return, 324; on Kean and JPK, 325 ff.; on JPK's farewell, 338; on JPK in France, 343
Heathcote, Robert, 270
Heiress, The, 168
Henderson, John, style, 79; as JPK's rival, 85, 95; reputation and early death, 86, 100; as Sir Giles, 62, 89
Henry II, 202
Henry IV, 247, 338
Henry V, 157, 160–161, 166, 167, 190
Henry VI, projected revival, 215
Henry VIII, 128–129, 157, 159, 286, 289, 293, 318
Hereford, 3–5, 6, 8
Heywood, Thomas, 80
Hill, Aaron, 261
Hint to Husbands, A, 287
Hitchcock, Robert, leaves Wilkinson, 62, 63; hires JPK for Daly, 64
Hoare, Prince, submits a play to JPK, 155; *Mahmoud*, 209
Hogarth, William, 150
Hogg, James ("The Ettrick Shepherd"), 254
Holcroft, Thomas, on strollers, 12; duties as a stroller, 13; *Seduction*, 108; and Bourgeois, 146; *Deaf and Dumb*, 242; on JPK's style, 253, 284–285; on costuming, 265; and Betty, 283; on prostitutes in theatres, 296
Holland, Lady (Elizabeth Vassall Fox), and the theatre, 138; and drunkenness, 147; and scholarship, 212; and *The Castle Spectre*, 229; on German drama, 230; and *Pizarro*, 233–234; on *Deaf and Dumb*, 242; in Paris, 271

Holland, Lord (Henry Richard Vassall Fox), with JPK in Valencia, 273; at JPK's banquet, 340
Holyhead, 194
Home, John, *Douglas*, 190, 280; on Betty, 278
Hopkins, W., Garrick's prompter, 111; commentaries, 218
Hopkins, Mrs. W., in *Hamlet*, 83; and JPK's marriage, 111; death, 244
Hull, 40, 55, 61, 62, 246
Huniades (*Agamunda*), 177
Hunt, Leigh, and spouting club, 57; as a critic, 79; on JPK in society, 139; on Miss De Camp, 191; on JPK's book-buying, 221; on JPK's reputation, 232; opposes JPK's style, 250, 252, 253, 255, 259, 260; on JPK's pronunciation, 254; on JPK's costuming, 264–265; on criticism, 280; on "farci-comedy," 287; on Kean and JPK, 326 ff.
Huntington Library, Larpent Collection, 43 n.; Kemble playbills, 222 n.

Impostors, The, 156
Inchbald, Elizabeth, attachment to JPK, 32–34; at Russel Moor, 32–33; with Wilkinson, 42 ff.; in *Belisarius*, 44–45; loses husband, 53–54; *A Simple Story*, 55; courted by Suett, 56; courted by JPK, 54–55, 59–60; in Ireland with Daly, 75–76; assists JPK, 78; *The Jealous Wife*, 122; as JPK's guest, 142; and *The Iron Chest*, 201; on Joanna Baillie, 238; on JPK and Garrick, 252; *Lover's Vows*, 263; as JPK's agent, 270, 273
Inchbald, Joseph, and JPK, 32–33; with Wilkinson, 53; death, 53–54; JPK's opinion of, 54
Incledon, Charles, 147
Ireland forgeries, initial success, 202; defended by Wyatt, Oulton, Webb, 204; controversy, 201–207, 208 n.
Ireland, Samuel, 201–207
Ireland, William Henry, and the *Vortigern* fiasco, 201–207

Irving, Henry, knighted, 138; on JPK, 252
Irving, Washington, 285
Isabella, 75, 190

Jack of Newbury, 194
Jane Shore, 16, 41, 118
Jealous Wife, The, 122
Jeffrey, Francis, at JPK's banquet in Edinburgh, 337; on Campbell, 341
Jephson, Robert, tutors JPK, 66–67, 68, 212; theatrical career, 66; and Mrs. Siddons, 76; as playwright, 81; *Braganza*, 101; *Julia*, 108–109; in London, 168; in Ireland, 195; *Conspiracy*, 227
John Bull, 277
John Woodvil, 236
Johnson, Charles, *The Country Lasses*, 134
Johnson, Samuel, on biography, 3, 58; quoted, 19; on critics, 79; on *Cleone*, 107; on actors, 137, 139; on JPK, 139, 257; at Beefsteak Club, 150; and Fanny Burney, 193
Jordan, Dorothy (*née* Bland), at Cork, 64; and Duke of Clarence, 64, 138; and Daly, 65; in *Richard Coeur de Lion*, 106; as Miss Prue, 108; in *The Pilgrim*, 115; difficulties with JPK, 131–133, 164, 168–170, 182, 209–210; perfidy, 173–174; angers the public, 175; moves JPK, 196–197; and Betty, 281; in Ireland, 293–294
Journalistic criticism, venality of, 79, 280; resented by JPK, 93–94. *See also* O. P. riots
Jubilee, The, 156, 218, 330–331
Julia, 108
Julius Caesar, 23, 48, 126, 321

Kean, Charles, 334
Kean, Edmund, style, 69, 251, 276; ruins JPK's *Macbeth*, 187; solicits JPK, 288–289; as JPK's rival, 325–335
Keats, John, and Elliston, 236; on

prostitutes in CG, 296; on Kean, 326, 327

Kelly, Fanny, 12

Kelly, Michael, on JPK and Miss Phillips, 74; in *Richard Coeur de Lion*, 107; coached by JPK, 124; as JPK's friend, 141, 142; in *The Tempest*, 162; in *Lodoiska*, 189; in *Cymon*, 177; and *The Wheel of Fortune*, 193;. with JPK in Paris, 271; on Cooke, 286; *Adrian and Orilla*, 286

Kemble, Captain George, 5

Kemble, Charles, at Douay, 163–164; letter to, 171; marriage, 193; popularity, 227; and Planché, 264; as JPK's correspondent, 270, 273 n.; to CG, 273; and O. P. riots, 309; as CG patentee, 345–346

Kemble, Mrs. Charles (*née* Marie Thérèse De Camp), in *Richard Coeur de Lion*, 106; attacked by JPK, 191–193; on Sheridan's finances, 234–235; on costuming, 265

Kemble, Daniel, 5

Kemble, Elizabeth, at DL, 86–87. *See also* Whitlock, Elizabeth

Kemble, Fanny (Frances Ann Butler), on Mrs. Roger Kemble, 17; daughter's marriage, 18 n.; on JPK's singing, 107; on JPK's house, 138; on Kean, 326; on JPK's finances, 342; on Priscilla Hopkins Kemble, 347; on JPK's grave, 350

Kemble, Fanny (daughter of Roger), at Wolverhampton, 14

Kemble, George (of Wiltshire), 3

Kemble, George, 4

Kemble, John Philip, birth and early years, 20; at Worcester, 20, 21; debut, 20–21; at school in Staffordshire, 21–22; at Douay, 22–24; studies at Douay, 22–23; acting at Douay, 23; leaves Douay, 23–24; angers father, 24, 25; with Chamberlain and Crump, 25–28; stroller's debut in *Theodosius*, 26; drunkenness in youth, 26; financial difficulties, 26–28; early wanderings, 28–30; escapades with Watson, 29–30; in

debtor's prison, 30–31; with Younger at Liverpool, 31–38; and Mrs. Inchbald, 32–34; at Russel, 32–33; Liverpool riot, 34–35; *Belisarius*, 33, 35–36, 38, 41–46; application to Wilkinson, 36–38; early repertory, 36–38; debut with Wilkinson, 40; at Hull, 40–41; rivalry with Cummins, 47 ff.; public readings, 48, 53; alteration of *Caesar* and *The Roman Actor*, 48, 113; *The Female Officer*, 48–50; alteration of *The Comedy of Errors*, 50; *The School for Scandal Scandalized*, 50; rioting at York, 50–52; epitaph for Joseph Inchbald, 54; summer touring in Yorkshire, 54–55; courting Mrs. Inchbald, 54–55, 59–60; expedition to London, 56–58; *Fugitive Pieces*, 58–61, 212; last months with Wilkinson, 61–62; 63–64; inquiries about Henderson's Sir Giles, 62–63; with Daly in Ireland, 75–77; debut in Dublin, 65; and Robert Jephson, 66–67; *The Count of Narbonne*, 67–68; popularity in Dublin, 68–69; roles at Smock Alley, 68 n.; troubles with Daly, 69–71; touring in Ireland, 71–73; and Bernard, 72–73; and Miss Phillips, 73–75; last months in Ireland, 75–77; social success, 76–77; comes to London, 78; debut at DL, 83–84; success, 83–84; innovations in *Hamlet*, 84, 96; and Henderson, 85–86; *Edward the Black Prince*, 87–88; *Richard* III, 88; eclectic style, 88; *A New Way*, 88–89; *The Gamester*, 89; and Ann Hatton, 89–91; scholarship, 92–93; impatience with criticism, 93–94; back to Liverpool, 94; efforts to gain a following, 94–95; animosity of the critics, 95–98; defends Mrs. Siddons, 96–97; rivalry of Pope and Holman, 97, 100, 243; *The Carmelite*, 97, 99; *The Maid of Honour*, 98; *Othello*, 98; reads for Royal Family, 98–99; in Ireland again, 99; rising fortunes, 100; *Braganza*, 101; Shakespearian

Kemble, John Philip, *cont.*
repertory, 101; *The Project*, 101;
The Captives, 101–102; essay on
Macbeth, 102–104; successful new
season (1886–87), 104; *Richard
Coeur de Lion*, 104, 105–107; as a
singer, 106–107; *Cleone*, 107; attempts at comedy, 107–108; *Julia*,
108–109; marriage, 110–112; and
Lord North, 110; *The Pilgrim*, 113–
117; method in alterations, 116–117,
157–161, 165–166; *Lear*, 117–118;
Della Cruscans, 118–119; *Much Ado*,
119; in Ireland and York, 119–120;
DL manager, 122; begins journal,
122 n.; managerial technique, 123–
125; relations with Sheridan, 123–
124, 181, 208–209, 226–227, 238–239,
240–241, 244–245, 247–248 (*see*
Sheridan, Richard Brinsley); reputation as a purist, 124–125; classical repertory, 125; and Parson Este,
127–128; as Romeo, 128; *Henry
VIII*, 128–129; meets opposition,
129–133, 177, 240 (*see* Farren,
Elizabeth; Goodall, Mrs.; Jordan,
Dorothy); leases Liverpool theatre,
133–134; performances of 1788–89,
134–135; estimate of managerial
success, 135–136; place in society,
137–140, 227; dignity, 140–141; close
friends, 141–145; and painters, 145–
146; intemperance, 146–153, 175–
176, 289; experience as manager,
154; attitude towards new plays,
155–157, 235–238; difficulties of
management (1789–90), 157–158;
Henry V, 157, 160–161;

on Shakespearian chronicle plays,
159; *The Tempest*, 161–162; *Marcella*, 162–163; *Two Gentlemen*,
163; to Douay for Charles, 163–164;
The Rover (*Love in Many Masks*),
165–166; high society, 167–168; re-
calcitrant actors, 168–170; as Charles
Surface, 170–171; financial success,
172–173; with Wilkinson again,
173–174; at the Haymarket, 174,
175; in court, 175–176; opera and

spectacle, 176–177, 181–182, 183,
185–186, 186, 191, 319–320; duels
with Aickin, 177–178; touring
again, 178–179; memoranda, 179–
180; construction of new DL, 180–
181; trouble with Sheridan, 181;
new DL, 183–187; costuming, 186;
innovations in *Macbeth*, 186–187;
Lodoiska, 187–189; the new theatre, 190–191; the De Camp episode,
191–193; Dublin, 194–196; *The Iron
Chest* episode, 197–201; physical
complaints, 199; the Ireland forgeries, 201–207; troubles with Sheridan, 208–209; resigns as manager,
209–210; literary ambitions, 211–
213; as *littérateur*, 214–215; as
scholar, 216–220; library, 220–225;
negotiations with Sheridan, 226–
227; Ireland again, 227–228; *The
Castle Spectre*, 228–230; *The Stranger*, 230–231; the summer's touring,
231; decline of DL, 232; *Pizarro*,
232–234; new plays, 235–237; *De
Montfort*, 237–238; Ireland, 238; almost a patentee, 238–239; salary
unpaid, 240–241, 244–245; social
activities, 242–243; rivalry with
Cooke, 243–247; farewell to DL,
247–248; modern reputation, 249–
250; decorum of style, 250–252;
declamation, 253; voice, 253–254;
pronunciation, 254–255; appearance, 255–256; care of preparation,
256; stage-management, 256–258; as
Coriolanus, 258; as Cato, 259; as
Hamlet, 259; other roles, 259–260;
costuming, 260–265; authenticity, 265–266; pageantry, 266–269;
abroad, 270–273; to CG, 273–274;
rivalry at CG, 275–276; CG repertory, 276–277; CG finances, 277 n.;
and Master Betty, 277–284; return
to the theatre, 284–285; as CG
manager, 285–290; as Iago, 289–290;
an aging actor, 290–291; CG fire,
291–292; new theatre, 292–293; Ireland, 293–294; size of new CG, 295;
new prices, 295–296; Catalani, 297–

299; O. P. riots, 301–315; repercussion of O. P. riots, 316–318; prosperity, 318–319; and Landor, 319; withdraws from CG, 321; leisure, 321–324; return to CG, 324–325; and Kean, 325–335; literary remains, 328–330; touring, 331–332; retrospect of career, 332–335; farewell to Edinburgh, 336–337; last London season, 337–340; banquet, 340–341; cleaning up, 342; Edinburgh and leisure, 323; France, 343–344; letter to Lawrence, 344; London again, 345–346; peace in Lausanne, 346 ff.; last illness 348–349; death and burial, 349–350; will, 346, 349

Kemble, Mrs. John Philip (née Hopkins), at DL, 93; marriage to Brereton, 111; marriage to JPK, 111–112; as a wife, 112; as an actress, 112–113; retirement, 113; on Lawrence, 145; reforms JPK, 153; at Guy's Cliff, 272; on JPK's trip abroad, 272–273; on JPK at Bath, 274–275; on Betty, 282–283; on CG fire, 291; in Paris, 322; to Lawrence, 342–343, 344–345, 347, 348, 349; character, 347

Kemble, Roger (the elder), 6

Kemble, Roger (the younger), birth and education, 6–7; becomes a stroller, 7; and Fanny Furnivall, 7–8; and John Ward, 8; marriage, 8; appearance and ability, 11; as manager, 14–15; at Brecknock, 15, 24; at Worcester, 15, 16, 20–21; produces The Tempest, 21; ledger and journal, 15–17; at Coventry, 16; repertory, 14, 16–17; at Droitwych, 16; at Bromsgrove, 16; at Bath, 16–17; troubles with actors, 16–17; affluence, 16–17; retirement, 17–18; only London performance, 18; old age and death, 18; painted by Lawrence, 18; opinion of actors, 21; plans for JPK, 22; will, 273 n.

Kemble, Mrs. Roger (née Sarah Ward), elopes with Roger Kemble, 8; early life, 9–10; children, 11; as an actress, 8, 11; death, 18

Kemble, Stephen, with Daly and Wilkinson, 64; touring in Ireland, 72; at Liverpool, 92; manager at Newcastle, 173; legacy, 273 n.

Kemble, Mrs. Stephen, 18

Kemble, Thomas, Anne, and William, early recusants, 5–6

Kemble, the Venerable John, career and martyrdom, 4–5

Kemble, William, Walter, and Jane, early recusants, 4

Kentish Town, 18

King, Thomas, as JPK's rival, 85; surrenders Macbeth to JPK, 99; DL manager, 109, 121; resigns managership, 121–122; exonerates JPK, 123; returns to DL, 167; in The School for Scandal, 171; unpaid by Sheridan, 245

King John, 93, 101, 159, 240, 264, 317, 338

King Lear, 44, 45, 117–118, 160, 240, 242, 316

Kotzebue, August, Menschenhass und Reue (The Stranger), 230–231; Spanier in Peru (Pizarro), 232–234

Kreutzer, Rodolphe, music for Lodoiska, 189

Kynge Leare, 202

Lamb, Charles, on JPK's style, 85; on opera, 105; on The Iron Chest, 201; submits MS to JPK, 236–237; and Godwin's Antonio, 241–242; on JPK's Hamlet, 259; on JPK's Macbeth, 260; on costuming, 265; quoted, 270; and Count Julian, 319

Lamb, Mary, 111

Landor, Walter Savage, quoted, 316; Count Julian, 319

Larpent Collection, 43 n.

Lausanne, 346 ff.

Lawrence, Thomas, paints Roger Kemble, 18, 145; on Priscilla Kemble, 112; and JPK, 145, 250; and Mrs. Siddons, 145; and Betty, 282; on JPK's reformation, 289; on O. P. riots, 304, 306, 318; on JPK's farewell, 339

Lee, Nathaniel, *Theodosius*, 26; *The Rival Queens (Alexander the Great)*, 65, 196

Lee, Sophia, *Almeyda*, 209

Leeds, 40, 52, 58, 61, 63, 120

Leeds, Duke of (Francis Osborne), 172

Legacy, The (The Romantic Lovers), 286 n.

Leicester, 279

Leith, 178

Leominster, 10

Lewes, Lee, on Roger Kemble, 7 ff.

Lewis, Matthew Gregory ("Monk"), *Timour the Tartar*, 105; *The Castle Spectre*, 228-230, 232

Lewis, William Thomas ("Gentleman"), resents JPK at CG, 275

Licensing act, consequences of, 80, 314-315

Lillo, George, *George Barnwell*, 16, 251 n.

Limerick, 71, 72, 75, 228

Linley, Thomas, 48 n.; arranges music for *Romeo*, 128; in *The Tempest*, 161; with JPK at Bath, 172

Literary Club, the, 235

Liverpool, 19, 31, 34-36, 78, 92, 94, 116, 213, 231, 246, 278, 321, 332

Locke, Matthew, music for *Macbeth*, 99

Lockhart, John Gibson, 268

Lodoiska, 187-189, 190

Lounsbury, Thomas, on alterations, 160

Loutherbourg, de (scene-painter), 266, 267

Louvet de Couvrai, Jean-Baptiste, 187

Love à la Mode, 247

Love for Love, 108, 126, 242

Love in a Village, 14

Love in Many Masks (The Rover), 164-166

Love Makes a Man, 93

Lover's Vows, 263

Lucky Changes (A School for Graybeards), 108

Lushington, Lady Maria Lewis, expurgates *The Castle Spectre*, 229

Luttrell, Henry, 227

Lyly, John, quoted, 45

Macbeth, 40, 66, 68, 99, 101, 183-187, 190, 284, 290, 301, 318, 321, 331, 336, 339

Macbeth Reconsidered, 102-104, 330

Macklin, Charles, on John Ward, 9; on strollers, 12; as Shylock, 93; *Love à la Mode*, 247; and costuming, 262; *The Man of the World*, 289

Macready, William, on Cooke, 244; on JPK's style, 253, 258, 338; on JPK's *Coriolanus*, 258; on JPK's *Cato*, 259; on JPK's costuming, 264; and Betty, 229; on O. P. riots, 307; at CG, 337; on JPK's old age, 345, 347

Madrid, 272-273

Mahmoud, 209

Maid of Honour, The, 98, 99, 263

Maid's Tragedy, The, 98

Malone, Edmond, correspondence with JPK, 1-2, 119-120; as JPK's friend, 103, 141, 168, 212-214; aids Jephson, 108-109; on Ireland forgeries, 203, 204, 205, 208; book-buying, 221

Manchester, 31, 33, 231, 278

Man of the World, The, 289

Mann, Horace, 56

Mansfield, James, and Clifford trial, 209-213

Marcella, 162-163

Margate, 234

Marlowe, Christopher, JPK on, 215

Martindale, Ann, CG patentee, 274

Mary Queen of Scots, 134, 156

Mason, Mrs. (daughter of Roger Kemble), 91, 273 n., 346

Mason, Mrs. (Yorkshire actress), 50-51, 52

Massinger, Philip, *The Roman Actor*, 48, 113; *A New Way*, 50, 62-63, 88-89, 97, 112-113; *The Maid of Honour*, 98, 99, 263; admired by JPK, 215; Gifford's edition of, 220, 223-224

Mathews, Charles, with JPK in Dub-

lin, 194–196; admires JPK, 244; on
JPK's pronunciation, 254
Mayor of Garratt, The, 144
Measure for Measure, 191
Meres, Francis, 215
Merry, Robert, 127
Metzdorf, Robert F., 348 n.
Miller of Mansfield, The, 18
Miriamne, 9
Mitford, Mary Russell, on JPK, 252
Molière (Jean Baptiste Poquelin), 50
Montagu, Elizabeth Robinson, and the
witches in *Macbeth,* 186; as a blue-
stocking, 211; praised by JPK, 215
Montagu, George, 114
Monthly Mirror, The, 273, 297
Moody, John, in *The Tempest,* 162
Moore, Edward, *The Gamester,* 89, 97,
128
Moore, Thomas, on JPK and Sher-
idan, 239 n.
More, Hannah, and Southey, 46;
Percy, 52; as a bluestocking, 211
Morgan, Lady (*née* Sydney Owen-
son), on JPK in society, 138; on
JPK's drunkenness, 149
Morgann, Maurice, 102
Morning Chronicle, The, 83–84, 88,
93–94, 100, 101, 315
Morning Herald, The, 86, 87–88, 204
Morning Post, The, 24, 100–101, 123,
127, 129, 130, 132, 174
Mountaineers, The, 191, 197, 230, 277,
318
Mourning Bride, The, 16
Much Ado about Nothing, 119
Mudie, Miss, 285
Mulock, Dinah Maria, 30 n.
Murphy, Arthur, *Zenobia,* 51; pro-
logue for *Braganza,* 66; *The Gre-
cian Daughter,* 74 n.; and JPK, 168;
All in the Wrong, 183
Mysterious Mother, The, 114

Napoleon, compared to JPK, 271
Nares, Robert, and JPK, 235, 243
New Spectator, The, 87
New Way to Pay Old Debts, A, 50,
62–63, 88–89, 97, 112–113

Newcastle, 63, 173, 179, 196, 238, 337
Newport Pagnell, 15
Nicoll, Allardyce, on Kean's style,
327
Norfolk, Duke of (Charles Howard),
drunkenness, 148, 151
North, Lord Frederick, reactionary
policies, 82; and JPK's marriage,
110–111
Northcote, James, and JPK, 140, 146
Northumberland, Duke of (Hugh
Percy), befriends JPK, 45–46, 292–
293

Odell, G. C. D., on JPK's alterations,
160
O'Keefe, John, 81
O. P. riots, chap. XIV *passim,* 317–
318
Opera, English, 104–107, 187–189. *See
also* Spectacle
Oracle, The, 185, 187, 199 n., 203
Oroonoko, 13, 36
Orphan, The, 16
Osorio (Remorse), 236–237
Ossian furor, 202
Othello, 9, 33, 34, 98, 157–158, 173,
331–332
Otho, 236
Otway, Thomas, *The Orphan,* 16;
Venice Preserved, 141, 164
Oulton, W. C., 204

Palmer, John, 167
Pantheon, 57
Paris, 271–272, 322–323
Parsons, William, epigram on Han-
nah Cowley, 118
Peake, Richard, drinks with JPK, 152;
and Sheridan's debts, 234–235;
dunned by JPK, 238, 240, 245
Pembridge Castle, 5
Pepys, Samuel, 301
Percy, 52
Percy, Thomas, 266
Perry, James, drinks with JPK, 149;
and O. P. riots, 308
Philips, Ambrose, *The Distressed
Mother,* 46, 54, 264

Phillips, Anna Maria, *see* Crouch, Anna Maria Phillips
Phillips, Peregrine, with JPK in Ireland, 73; at JPK's DL debut, 83
Pilgrim, The, 113–117, 157
Piozzi, Hester Thrale, returns to London, 108; epilogue to *The Regent*, 118; and the Kembles, 138, 168, 172, 235; on JPK's disgrace, 192; on Haymarket riots, 175; on Ireland forgeries, 205; on JPK's health, 242; on *The Winter's Tale*, 247; on Betty, 282; on JPK in Switzerland, 347
Pitt, William (the younger), early brilliance, 82; on JPK as Rolla, 233; and Betty, 181
Pizarro, 232–234, 237, 238, 248, 278, 331
Plain Dealer, The, 126, 196
Planché, J. R., on JPK's *Macbeth*, 260; on JPK's costuming, 264
Playbills, annotated by JPK, 218–219
Plowden, Mrs. F., *Virginia*, 245
Plymouth, 231
Politics, English, 81–82
Ponsonby, Frederic C., with JPK in Spain, 272
Pontefract, 40, 55
Poole, Thomas, 271
Poor Old Drury, 175
Pope, Alexander, on opera, 104; on styles in acting, 109; on Mrs. Behn, 165; as JPK's authority in pronunciation, 254
Pope and Holman, as JPK's rivals, 97, 100, 243
Porson, Richard, 103; on Ireland forgeries, 203; on Fox, 304–305
Powell, Mrs. (also known as Mrs. Farmer, Mrs. Renaud), in *Hamlet*, 248
Prescot, 19
Prince of Wales (George IV), and Mrs. Fitzherbert, 82; and the theatre, 138; and JPK, 139, 140, 178, 235, 273; at Beefsteak Club, 150; and new CG, 292
Project, The, see *The Female Officer*

Provoked Husband, The, 13
Public Advertiser, The, 127, 174
Purcell, Henry, 161
Pye, Henry, 202; *Adelaide*, 237

Racine, Jean Baptiste, not liked by JPK, 215, 271–272
Ralph, James, on foreign singers, 297–298
Ranelagh Gardens, 56
Recruiting Officer, The, 7, 40
Reed, Isaac, and Bishop Warburton anecdote, 28 n.; and JPK, 211, 214, 216; reputation, 213–214
Regent, The, 118
Remorse (Osorio), 236–237
Revivals, JPK's procedure for, 128–129. See also Alterations
Reynolds, Frederick, 81; at Beefsteak Club, 151; and Betty, 281
Reynolds, Joshua, and the Grand Style, 85, 251; as host, 168, 178
Rich, John, and Beefsteak Club, 150; on elephants, 319–320
Richard Coeur de Lion, 104, 105–107
Richard II, discussed by JPK, 215
Richard III, 71, 88, 126, 158, 159, 160, 167, 243 ff., 262
Richardson, Samuel, on actors, 7, 22
Richardson, William, 102
Riots, theatrical, 34–36, 50–52, 174, 299–301, chap. XIV *passim*
Ritson, Joseph, 203
Rival Queens, The (Alexander the Great), 65, 196
Rivals, The, 168
Robertson, Tom, 129
Robinson and Thornton, managers at Tewkesbury, 14
Robinson, Henry Crabb, on *Pizarro*, 233; admires Cooke, 244; on JPK and Goethe, 255; on JPK's costuming, 287; at JPK banquet, 341
Rogers, Samuel, on Henderson, 86; on JPK, 141, 147; on Sheridan, 208; and the Literary Club, 235; on Betty, 284; at JPK banquet, 341; in Switzerland, 246–247
Roman Actor, The, 48, 50, 113

Romantic Lovers, The (*The Legacy*),
    286 n.
Rome, 347–348
Romeo and Juliet, 126, 128
Romp, The, 101
Rover, The (*Love in Many Masks*),
    164–166
Rowe, Nicholas, *The Fair Penitent*,
    26, 52, 183; *Jane Shore*, 16, 41,
    118
Roxburgh, Duke of (John Ker), li-
    brary sold, 221
Rule a Wife and Have a Wife, 108
Rymer, Thomas, 81

St. James Chronicle, The, 128
St. John, John, quarrels with JPK,
    134; *Mary Queen of Scots*, 134, 156
Saintsbury, George, quoted, 60–61
Scholarship, status in England in
    JPK's day, 103. *See also* chap. X,
    passim
School for Gray-beards, A, 108
School for Scandal, The, 41, 46, 170–
    171, 208
School for Scandal Scandalized, The,
    50, 55
Scott, Walter, on JPK at DL, 123; as
    JPK's friend, 143, 290; on JPK's
    intemperance, 147, 290; and the
    Literary Club, 235; on Joanna
    Baillie, 237–238; on JPK's style,
    255–256, 259, 322; and costuming,
    262, 265; and Betty, 281; on pros-
    titutes in theatres, 297; on O. P.
    riots, 306, 308, 314; and JPK's Edin-
    burgh banquet, 336–337
Scudamore, Captain, 4
Secular Masque, The, 114
Sedaine, Michel-Jean, 104, 106
Sedgeley Park, 21–22
Seduction, 108
Select British Theatre, A, 328–330
"Senex," attacks JPK, 135
Sets, for *De Montfort*, 237; style in,
    266–268
Seward, Anna, on comedy, 80; on Mrs.
    Siddons, 87, 95; on Jephson's *Julia*,
    109; on German drama, 231; on

Pizarro, 233; on Joanna Baillie, 238;
    on JPK, 253; on costuming, 262
Shadwell, Thomas, *The Tempest*,
    161–162; quoted, 167; cited by JPK,
    214; on foreign singers, 298
Shakespeare, William, quoted, 190.
    See also entries for individual plays;
    Alterations; Kemble, John Philip
Shatford, Thomas, travels with JPK,
    25–26
Shaw, George Bernard, quoted, 82; on
    alterations, 160
Sheffield, 62, 63, 246, 278
Shelley, Percy Bysshe, on the decay of
    drama, 229
Sheridan, Richard Brinsley, *The
    School for Scandal*, 50, 170–171; DL
    patentee, 79–80, 109, 208–209; as
    playwright, 80; as orator, 83; con-
    flicts with JPK, 133, 142, 226, 246;
    and new DL, 167, 180–181; and Mrs.
    Jordan, 168–170; as host, 178; and
    singers, 181; and *The Iron Chest*,
    189; and the Ireland forgeries, 203–
    204, 204–205; and Lewis, 229–230;
    Pizarro, 232–234; last days, 328
Sheridan, Mrs. Richard Brinsley (*née*
    Elizabeth Linley), on Mrs. Siddons,
    227
Sheridan, Thomas, and public read-
    ings, 48; coaches JPK, 93; and riots,
    300
Sichel, Walter, quoted, 146
Siddons, Henry (the elder), with
    Roger Kemble, 14–15; with Cham-
    berlain and Crump, 25; with
    Younger, 32 ff.; on *The Regent*,
    119
Siddons, Henry (the younger), at CG,
    276; death, 330
Siddons, Maria, and Lawrence, 145;
    death, 231
Siddons, Sarah Kemble, birth, 15, 19–
    20; success at DL, 17–75; aids JPK,
    31; with Younger, 31–32; at Russel
    Moor, 32–33; with Wilkinson, 33;
    and the Liverpool riots, 35; at
    Dublin, 76; helps JPK in London,
    78–79; celebrity, 87, 95; in *The*

Gamester, 89; angers the public, 96–97; ruins an epilogue, 98; and the Royal Family, 98–99; and Brereton, 111; as Queen Katharine, 129; withdraws from DL, 157, 161; on the Ireland forgeries, 205–206; as Mrs. Haller, 230; loses daughter, 231; on JPK's composure, 250, 257; as JPK's partner, 260; to CG, 273; on Betty, 286; legacy, 273 n.; and O. P. riots, 302; retires, 319, 321; in Paris, 323; on Cleopatra, 323; on JPK's farewell, 339; in Switzerland, 246

Siddons, Sarah (daughter of Sarah Kemble Siddons), and Lawrence, 145

Siege of Belgrade, The, 172, 181

Smirke, Robert, and new CG, 292

Smith, Thomas, popularity, 75; and *The Gamester*, 89; as JPK's rival, 95, 101; retires, 126

Smock Alley Theatre (Dublin), status in 1781, 64–65; personnel, 64; JPK's opinion of, 65. *See also* Daly, Richard

Smollett, Tobias, on Garrick, 236

Southerne, Thomas, *Oroonoko*, 13, 36

Southey, Robert, on Gifford, 79; on drama, 80; and new DL, 183; *Thalaba*, 221; on *The Winter's Tale*, 297; and Landor, 319

Spanier in Peru, 232

Spectacle, 176–177, 181–182, 183, 185–186

Spouting clubs, 57

Statesman, The, 307, 308

Steele, Richard, on foreign singers, 105; on Estcourt, 150; on Mrs. Behn, 165

Steevens, George, 103; and JPK, 234, 330

Sterne, Lawrence, on Garrick, 138, 171

Storace, Stephen, and *The Iron Chest*, 197, 199; benefit for widow, 209; burial, 209

Stranger, The, 230–231, 238, 338

Stratford, 9, 194

Strawberry Hill, 56, 266–267

Strollers, social status, 11–12; poverty, 12, 13; method of traveling, 12–13; audiences, 13; duties, 13; costuming, 28. *See also* Prologue and chaps. I and II, *passim*

Suett, Richard, and Mrs. Inchbald, 56; as JPK's friend, 142

Summers, Montague, on Mrs. Behn, 164–165

Swan, Cornelius, befriends JPK, 47–48

Talfourd, Thomas Noon, on JPK's *Cato*, 259

Talma, François-Joseph, and JPK in Paris, 272; as JPK's correspondent, 332; and JPK banquet, 341; on JPK in retirement, 346

Tancred and Sigismunda, 93, 97

Tate, Nahum, *Lear*, 117

Taylor, John, on JPK and Daly, 70; on JPK's DL debut, 84, 85; on JPK's management, 124; on JPK's personality, 140, 143; as JPK's intimate, 142–143, 243, 253; *The Stage*, 143; on JPK and Lawrence, 145; on JPK's drunkenness, 149–150, 153; on Charles Surface, 170; and JPK in regard to Cibber, 214–215; advised by JPK, 215; on Parson Este, 218–219; on JPK's Rolla, 233; on JPK's style, 252, 256; prologue for Betty, 279; at JPK banquet, 341; on JPK's old age, 345

Taylor, Jeremy, quoted, 167

Tempest, The, 21, 161, 167, 217, 246, 288. *See also* D'Avenant, William; Shadwell, Thomas

Tewkesbury, 5, 29

Thackeray, William Makepeace, quoted, 105, 243

Theatre, prostitutes in, 296–297; size of, and new DL, 184; and new CG, 295. *See also* Spectacle

Thelwall, John, Boaden on, 57; and Coleridge, 236

Theodosius, 16, 26

Thompson, Benjamin, *Emilia Galotti*, 191; *The Stranger*, 230–231. *See also* German drama

Thomson, James, *Tancred and Sigismunda*, 93, 97; *Edward and Eleanora*, 227
Thornton, Bonnell, on costuming, 262
Thrale, Cecilia, 168
Thrale, Hester Lynch, *see* Piozzi, Hester Thrale
Tickell, Mary, and JPK, 139
Tieck, Ludwig, on alterations, 158; on JPK's style, 253; on JPK's Wolsey, 259; on JPK's farewell, 339, 340
Times, The, 129, 240, 296, 307, 308, 331
Timour the Tartar, 105
Tobacco Road, 129
Tom Thumb, 312
Tooke, Horne, and JPK, 168; on human nature, 313
Topham, Edward, 127
Touchstone of Truth, The, 53
Toulouse, 343–344
Toy Shop, The, 52
Tree, Beerbohm, 334
Troilus and Cressida, projected revival, 215
Turnham Green, 148
Twining, Richard, on JPK's DL debut, 84
Twiss, Francis, and JPK, 138, 224
Twiss, Horace, prologue for new CG, 301–302
Twiss, Mrs. Horace (*née* Kemble), 273 n.
Two Gentlemen of Verona, The, 163, 290

Valencia, 273
Vanbrugh, John, *The Provoked Husband*, 13; quoted, 104; *The Pilgrim*, 113–117; *The False Friend*, 162
Vauxhall, 56
Venice Preserved, 41, 64
Vesey, Elizabeth, 211
Vestris, Gaetano A. B., Walpole on, 105
Vevey, 346
Virginia, 245
Voltaire (François Marie Arouet),

JPK's opinion of, 271–272; on England, 332
Vortigern, 202–207, 241

Wakefield, 40, 54, 58, 170
Waldron, Francis G., 204
Waldron, Thomas, 214
Walpole, Horace, on Carlisle House, 56–57; on *The Count of Narbonne*, 66; epilogue for *Braganza*, 66; on comedy, 81; on opera, 105; *The Mysterious Mother*, 114; on Garrick, 114, 137–138, 211; and JPK, 172, 215; on JPK's Benedick, 260; quoted, 336
Walpole, Robert, and Fielding, 314
Warburton, William, befriends JPK, 28
Ward, John, and Roger Kemble, 7; origins, 8–9; marriage, 9; as stroller, 9–10; children, 9; and Shakespeare restoration, 9; retirement and death, 10
Warwick, 34
Waterford, 64
Watson, John Boles, escapades with JPK, 29–30; manager at Cheltenham, 30
Webb, Francis, 204
West, Benjamin, 271
Weston, Thomas, 57
Whalley, Thomas, with JPK at Bath, 172; *The Castle of Montval*, 232
Whatley, Thomas, 102–103
Wheel of Fortune, The, 193, 227, 230, 313
White, George, CG patentee, 274
White Plume, The, 287
Whitlock, Elizabeth Kemble, 273 n.
Wilberforce, William, 82
Wilkes, John, final security, 82; at Beefsteak Club, 150
Wilkinson, Tate, renown, 14, 33, 39; early career, 39; as manager, 39 ff.; opinion of JPK, 40–41, 253; produces *Belisarius*, 41–46; encourages JPK to write, 48–50; troubles with actors, 53; with JPK again, 120, 173–174, 265

Wilks, Robert, 276
Williams, Helen Maria, in Paris, 271
Williams, John Ambrose ("Anthony Pasquin"), on the Kemble family, 87; vilifies JPK, 100, 170
Wilson, Harriette, 252
Wilson, John ("Christopher North"), 254–255
Winter's Tale, The, 104, 247, 289
Woffington, Peg, in Ireland, 9; and Wilkinson, 39
Wollstonecraft, Mary, 142
Wolverhampton, 25–26, 34
Wonder, The, 132
Woodfall, William, attacked by JPK, 94
Worcester, 16, 20–21, 30–31, 243
Wordsworth, William, and The Borderers, 236

World, The, 126–128, 131
Wroughton, Richard, 122; DL manager, 226–227
Wyatt, James, 204
Wycherley, William, The Plain Dealer, 196. See also Collier, Jeremy

York, 40, 46, 55, 61, 63, 120, 173–174, 224
York Annual Register, The, 48
Young, Charles Mayne, on Mrs. Roger Kemble, 11; on Caesar, 321; at CG, 322, 323, 324, 330
Young, Edward, on acting, 250–251
Younger, Joseph, hires JPK, 31, 39; as JPK's manager, 31–38; riot at Liverpool, 34–35; and Belisarius, 39, 41

Zenobia, 51

Feliciter Explicit